At home with the poor

Manchester University Press

To buy or to find out more about the books currently available in this series, please go to: https://manchesteruniversitypress.co.uk/series/studies-in-design-and-material-culture/

general editors
Sally-Anne Huxtable
Elizabeth Currie
Livia Lazzaro Rezende
Wessie Ling

founding editor
Paul Greenhalgh

At home with the poor

Consumer behaviour and material
culture in England, c.1650–1850

Joseph Harley

Manchester University Press

Copyright © Joseph Harley 2024

The right of Joseph Harley to be identified as the author of this work has been asserted in accordance with the Copyright, Designs and Patents Act 1988.

Published by Manchester University Press
Oxford Road, Manchester, M13 9PL
www.manchesteruniversitypress.co.uk

British Library Cataloguing-in-Publication Data
A catalogue record for this book is available from the British Library

ISBN   978 1 5261 6084 3   hardback

First published 2024

The publisher has no responsibility for the persistence or accuracy of URLs for any external or third-party internet websites referred to in this book, and does not guarantee that any content on such websites is, or will remain, accurate or appropriate.

Typeset by Newgen Publishing UK

Contents

List of figures	*page* vi
List of tables	viii
Acknowledgements	xi
List of abbreviations	xiii
	Introduction	1
1	Accommodating the poor	31
2	Material wealth and material poverty	55
3	Building blocks of the home	84
4	Comforts of the hearth	117
5	Eating and drinking	143
6	Non-essential goods	180
7	Contrasting genders and locations	206
	Conclusion	220
	Select bibliography	224
	Index	246

Figures

0.1	Rowntree's Life-Cycle of Poverty	*page* 8
0.2	Chronological distribution of the pauper inventories, 1670–1835	16
1.1	Green's Farm, the former home of Benjamin Bobby (b.1804, d.1857) and Susannah Bobby (b.1805–06, d.1858), painted by Richard Cobbold, 1860	44
1.2	Madget's Cottage, the home of Richard Harbour (b.1786, d.1864) and Susan Harbour (b.1791, d.1873), painted by Richard Cobbold, 1860	45
1.3	Buck's Cottage, painted by Richard Cobbold, 1860	46
1.4	Gardener's Cottage, the home of James Flatman, painted by Richard Cobbold, 1860	47
1.5	The cottages of Mary Cox (b.1811, d.1877) and John Bush (b.1789, d.1870), painted by Richard Cobbold, 1860	47
1.6	Browne's Cottages (right), painted by Richard Cobbold, 1860	48
1.7	John Clare Cottage, today	48
1.8	The cottage of Moll King (b.1760s/70s, d.1862), Billy Rose (b.1792, d.1863) and John Mayhew (b.1797, d.?), painted by Richard Cobbold, 1860	49
1.9	Harbour's Hut, the home of James Harbour (b.1791, d.1863) and Ann Harbour (b.1791, d.1877), painted by Richard Cobbold, 1860	50
1.10	Minter's Cottage, the home of William Minter (b.1799–1801, d.1869) and Maria Minter (b.1805–07, d.1886), painted by Richard Cobbold, 1860	50
2.1	Pauper inventories of Widow Todd's goods, Redenhall with Harleston and Wortwell, Norfolk, 1731 and 1738	75

2.2	Pauper inventories of Elizabeth Trew's goods, Redenhall with Harleston and Wortwell, Norfolk, 1731 and 1745	76
2.3	Inventories of Daniel Drake's goods, Little Waltham, Essex, 1805 and 1816	76
2.4	Inventories of Rhoda Cook's goods, Tolleshunt D'Arcy, Essex, 1808 and 1809	77
2.5	Workhouse storage inventories of John and Ann Clare's goods, Beaminster, Dorset, 1822 and 1828	78
3.1	Bed of Judy and James Fuller, painted by Richard Cobbold, c.1851–54	87
3.2	Portrait of Dinah Garrod, painted by Richard Cobbold, c.1848–49	92
3.3	Portraits of Mary Burrows (top left), Isaac Fake (top right), Anne Taylor (bottom), painted by Richard Cobbold, c.1840–60s	94
3.4	Warming pan (top) and ceramic bedwarmer (bottom), c. nineteenth century	96
3.5	George Morland, *The Happy Cottagers (The Cottage Door)*, 1790	104
3.6	Long oak table, c. eighteenth century	107
3.7	George Walker, *Woman Making Oat Cakes*, 1814	109
4.1	George Cruikshank, *A Distressed Father*, 1824	126
4.2	Thomas Vivares, *A Family at Home*, 1800	128
4.3	Portraits of Barbara Batley (left) and Poll Parker (right), painted by Richard Cobbold, c.1848–52 and c.1852	130
4.4	*Family Argument*, c.1810	131
4.5	*Story of a Smoky Chimney*, 1857	133
4.6	Randle Holme, picture of a fire shovel, two pairs of tongs and a pair of bellows, 1688	135
4.7	John June, *Miseries of a Garreteer Poet*, 1751	136
4.8	Randle Holme, picture of lantern, 1688	138
5.1	Randle Holme, picture of a brass pot (left), adjustable pot-hook (centre) and posnet (right), 1688	147
5.2	Skillet, c.1700–1900	147
5.3	Randle Holme, pictures of trivets, 1688	148
5.4	Randle Holme, picture of a gridiron, 1688	150
5.5	Portrait of James Jolly and his horse, painted by Richard Cobbold, c.1840s–1862	156
5.6	William Redmore Bigg, *Poor Old Woman's Comfort*, 1793	169
6.1	Portraits of Bet Mattock (left) and Sarah Scott (right), painted by Richard Cobbold, c.1862 and c.1849–55	188
6.2	Portrait of Ann Harbour (left) and Mary Ann Goddard (right), painted by Richard Cobbold, c.1863–65 and 1855–63	193
6.3	Thomas Heaphy, *Inattention*, 1808	199

Tables

0.1	Inventories found among parish and miscellaneous archival collections, c.1622–1841	*page* 13
1.1	Average number of rooms in pauper homes, over time, 1670–1835	32
1.2	Average number of rooms in pauper homes, by county, 1670–1835	33
1.3	Total number and percentage of pauper inventories which note particular rooms, 1670–1835 (extract)	35
1.4	Functions of chambers in pauper homes, 1670–1835	36
1.5	Functions of halls in pauper homes, 1670–1759	37
1.6	Functions of kitchens in pauper homes, 1670–1835	38
1.7	Functions of parlours in pauper homes, 1670–1835	40
1.8	Functions of pantries and butteries in pauper homes, 1670–1835	40
1.9	Types of rooms with various goods in them, 1670–1835	42
1.10	Functions of rooms with various goods in them, 1670–1835	42
2.1	Average total value of goods owned by paupers, 1670–1835	57
2.2	Average total value of goods in probate inventories, 1675–1800	58
2.3	Average and median number of items owned by paupers, 1670–1835	59
2.4	Percentage of pauper inventories which use particular adjectives to describe items, 1670–1835	61
2.5	Ratio of items in pauper inventories described as 'old', 1670–1835	62
2.6	Percentage of indoor and outdoor paupers who owned various items, 1770–1835	74

3.1	Percentage of paupers who owned mattresses, 1670–1835	86
3.2	Percentage of paupers who owned feather mattresses, 1670–1835	88
3.3	Percentage of paupers who owned bed hangings, 1670–1835	90
3.4	Percentage of paupers who owned window curtains, 1670–1835	91
3.5	Pauper ownership of bedding and pillows/bolsters, 1670–1835	93
3.6	Percentage of paupers who owned warming pans, 1670–1835	96
3.7	Pauper ownership of storage units, 1670–1835	98
3.8	Percentage of paupers who owned boxes and chests of drawers, over time, 1670–1835	99
3.9	Pauper ownership of seating, 1670–1835	103
3.10	Pauper ownership of seating, over time, 1670–1835	104
3.11	Pauper ownership of tables, over time, 1670–1835	108
3.12	Pauper ownership of tables, 1670–1835	111
4.1	Average number of hearths in pauper homes, 1670–1835	119
4.2	Location of hearths in pauper homes, 1670–1835	119
4.3	Functions of pauper rooms with hearths in them, 1670–1835	120
4.4	Percentage of paupers who owned hearth items related to coal and wood use, 1670–1835	121
4.5	Types of fuel used by paupers, c.1650s–1830s	122
4.6	Pauper ownership of hearth items related to coal and wood use in Essex and Norfolk, 1670–1835	124
4.7	Percentage of paupers who owned tubs and washing-/laundry-related items, 1670–1835	125
4.8	Percentage of paupers who owned various fire irons, 1670–1835	134
4.9	Pauper ownership of lighting goods, 1670–1835	137
4.10	Functions of pauper rooms with lighting in them, 1670–1835	138
5.1	Percentage of paupers who owned various boiling and stewing goods, 1670–1835	145
5.2	Percentage of paupers who owned various boiling and stewing goods, by county, 1670–1835	146
5.3	Percentage of paupers who owned various cooking items, 1670–1835	149
5.4	Percentage of paupers who owned various cooking items, by county, 1670–1835	151
5.5	Percentage of paupers who owned various food and drink processing goods, 1670–1835	154

5.6	Percentage of paupers who owned various food and drink processing goods, by county, 1670–1835	158
5.7	Pauper ownership of various dinnerware, 1670–1835	160
5.8	Pauper ownership of various dinnerware, by county, 1770–1835	161
5.9	Percentage of paupers who owned knives, forks and spoons, 1670–1835	163
5.10	Percentage of paupers who owned tea items, 1670–1835	165
5.11	Percentage of paupers who owned tea items, by county, 1770–1835	165
5.12	Percentage of paupers who owned tea paraphernalia, over time, 1670–1835	167
5.13	Pauper ownership of tea paraphernalia, by county, 1770–1835	167
5.14	Percentage of paupers who owned coffee items, 1670–1835	171
6.1	Percentage of paupers who owned books, 1670–1835	182
6.2	Percentage of paupers who owned pictures or prints, 1670–1835	187
6.3	Percentage of paupers who owned looking glasses, over time, 1670–1835	189
6.4	Percentage of paupers who owned looking glasses, by county, 1770–1835	189
6.5	Percentage of paupers who owned timepieces, over time, 1670–1835	191
6.6	Percentage of paupers who owned timepieces, by county, 1790–1835	191
7.1	Average number of items owned by male and female paupers, 1670–1835	209
7.2	Percentage of paupers who owned tea items, by gender, 1770–1835	210
7.3	Percentage of paupers who owned non-necessities, by gender, 1670–1835	212
7.4	Average number of items owned by paupers, by urban–rural location, 1708–1835	214
7.5	Percentage of paupers who owned furniture and items related to eating, drinking and cooking, by urban–rural location, 1708–1835	215
7.6	Percentage of paupers who owned non-necessities, by urban–rural location, 1708–1835	216

Acknowledgements

Parts of this book were conceived as early as 2009 when I was an undergraduate student at the University of Leicester. In a third-year module led by Steve King, I was introduced to the study of poverty, the voices of the poor and, in one week, their material lives. Thanks go to Steve for being able to spark my fascination in a way that no other topic had quite prior to this. From here, I went on to write a master's dissertation at the University of Warwick on consumer behaviour in Essex and later a PhD at the University of Leicester on the material lives of the poor. Thereafter, two postdoctoral fellowships, two research posts and teaching positions at many more institutions followed while writing and research on this topic continued.

From this long gestation, I owe a number of people thanks for helping me in lots of ways, such as giving advice, the lending of resources, offering me a job(!), reading through drafts and being a friend to talk to. These include Tom Almeroth-Williams, Aaron Andrews, Julie Attard, Jennie Brosnan, Fiona Cosson, Paul Elliott, Freya Gowrley, Simon Gunn, Tim Hitchcock, Vicky Holmes, Mark Knights, Erin Lafford, Ruth Larsen, Paul Maddrell, Helen Rogers, Katy Roscoe, Keith Snell, Thomas Sokoll, Jon Stobart, Alannah Tomkins, Deborah Toner, Will Tullett, Emily Whewell, Paul Whickman, Nic Wilson, my ARU colleagues (too many to name) and the numerous people who commented on my many presentations on this research. Thanks also go to the reviewers, and I am especially grateful to Alison Backhouse who kindly gave me her database which records the pledges received by the pawnbroker George Fettes of York. My PhD supervisors, Peter King and Roey Sweet, were brilliant in helping me to shape the early stages of this research. Roey continues to be a supportive friend and mentor who I can always go to for advice.

I spent months in dozens of archives over the course of this research looking at thousands of records for sources. In most cases, the process would go as follows: collect numerous sources from the reading desk, flick through them quickly until I found something (most of the time I found nothing), photograph the pages, return them to the desk, and move on to the next ones. I must have made everybody's lives much more difficult with my continuous requests and speedy searches through records. However, staff were always friendly and went out of their way to help me. These long trips would not have been possible without the kind financial support of organisations including the AHRC, the Economic History Society and the Power and Postan fund, and internal funding from the University of Derby and Anglia Ruskin. Thanks also go to the organisations who have kindly allowed me to reproduce their pictorial materials here and bring the homes of the poor further to life.

I end by thanking the most important people in my life: my family, including Barrie and Vicky Bishop and Rob and Sue Harley. My wife, Claire, has been a continual supporter of my work, as well as a sounding board for ideas (and moans). She even responded with humour when I would continuously say 'I have pauper inventories for there' whenever an obscure place appeared on a road sign or was mentioned on TV. My son, James, was born while this book was being written. Seeing him grow up and the ways he sees and uses things around the home has helped me to understand the domestic sphere in so many more ways than any book ever has.

Abbreviations

CCAL   Canterbury Cathedral Archives and Library, Canterbury
DHC   Dorset History Centre, Dorchester
ERO   Essex Record Office, Chelmsford
KHLC   Kent History Library Centre, Maidstone
LRO   Lancashire Record Office, Preston
NRO   Norfolk Record Office, Norwich
ODNB   Oxford Dictionary of National Biography
ROLLR   Record Office for Leicestershire, Leicester and Rutland, Wigston
SA   Suffolk Archives, Ipswich
WAS   Wigan Archives Service, Leigh
YALH   York Archives and Local History, York

Introduction

In the winter of 1699–70, Daniel Potter found three men standing at his door. The visitors, John Kingsbury, William Tadpock and Arthur Nolson, were the churchwardens and overseers of the poor for the small village of Tolleshunt D'Arcy in Essex. They had come to look around Potter's two-roomed home and take an inventory of his possessions, as he was receiving poor relief from the men. According to the source, Potter's hall and parlour contained approximately 34 items. His possessions consisted largely of essential goods that would have been in regular use, such as a cooking pot and furniture including two beds, two cupboards, a box, and chairs and tables. There was little under Potter's roof that did not have a specific purpose and which was unnecessary to his immediate daily needs.[1] Over one hundred years later in the same village, Widow Playle found herself in a similar predicament in May 1803. The widow had recently started to receive poor relief from authorities, following the death of her husband Joseph a few weeks earlier. In exchange for 6s. a week, the parish decided to list her goods in an inventory.[2] Although both people needed assistance and came from the same village, the two documents are very different. The home of Widow Playle had two more rooms than Potter's dwelling and it contained a range of consumer goods which were well beyond his reach. Most of Widow Playle's furniture was made from decorative woods such as ash, elm and mahogany, and she owned a bureau and chest of drawers, which offered her a fashionable and convenient way to store her possessions. She had clearly developed a taste for tea, as she possessed a range of goods connected to its consumption, such as a mahogany tea board and tea chest. She slept on a feather mattress surrounded by green curtains and her home was adorned with a clock, a looking glass and even a mahogany model of a cat.[3]

Around 12 miles to the south-west of Colchester, the village of Tolleshunt D'Arcy is largely unremarkable. Agriculture remained its main industry, and its population grew slowly over the course of the industrial revolution. Yet, here we see just one example of a considerable transformation that happened in the homes of the poor across the country. This book traces these changes in the consumer behaviour and material culture of the poor over the long eighteenth century (c.1650–1850). It shows how a greater range of items found their way into humble abodes, particularly from the latter decades of the eighteenth century. The goods had a vast effect on the daily and domestic lives of the poor. Items from furniture to fire irons to tableware to so-called 'luxury' goods meant that greater numbers of the poor lived in spaces which were more comfortable, private, respectable, convenient and decorative. With each generation, more and more people from labouring backgrounds owned greater numbers of possessions which their grandparents would have thought it impossible or highly unlikely to own. In following these developments, the volume advances our understanding of poverty by focusing on the home, where the poor slept, ate, drank, worked and rested. More specifically, the book makes a number of innovative arguments and is important for five reasons.

First, the history of consumption and material culture is now a cornerstone of British, European and world history from the early modern period to the present. We have a detailed understanding of the domestic spheres and consumer behaviours of the middling sort and the elite, and the meanings, motivations and emotions that underpinned people's decisions to acquire various items.[4] But besides the odd case study on select groups such as paupers, lodgers and labourers and research on clothing, the poor have been almost wholly forgotten in this literature.[5] This is a considerable omission, given that the poor in their broadest sense made up well over half of contemporary populations between the seventeenth and nineteenth centuries.[6] *At home with the poor* takes a crucial and long overdue step to address this conspicuous gap in the literature. The book shows that while the middling sort increasingly acquired a greater range of belongings between the late seventeenth and mid-eighteenth centuries,[7] it was not until the late eighteenth century that many of the same goods entered the homes of the poor in significant numbers. Although up to one hundred years separates the two groups, I argue that these changes in indigent consumption and domestic life were highly important and had a transformative effect on their lives. Even if an individual owned only a few extra chairs than his or her ancestors had, this still signified an important move which enhanced the domestic sphere.

Second, by focusing on the domestic sphere and belongings, the book gets to the very heart of what it meant to be 'poor'. There are a number of ways in which poverty can be defined, and people took their identity from a range of sources, but one of the most significant is the possessions that they owned. Goods were a visual reminder of one's place in society and signalled position, wealth and status to others.[8] Through their belongings, we can see how the poor felt about themselves and how their priorities and desires shifted over the long eighteenth century. It is shown that the home was an important site for impoverished men and women. Even with their meagre resources, people invested a lot of time and effort in improving the domestic space through new goods, which brought them enjoyment and made their homes more private, more respectable and ultimately more comfortable. These cultural and social aspects that underpinned the poor's growing commercial sensibilities have often been ignored in favour of economic factors such as supply and income.

Third, it is now well established that the consumer behaviour and material culture of the middling sort and the elite was often highly dependent on location. For instance, research has found that those who lived in London or the home counties tended to own a much greater range of possessions than those who resided in remote and rural areas, such as Cornwall and Cumbria.[9] Numerous studies have also considered how consumption and the use of goods could differ between men and women.[10] Once again, the poor have been neglected in this literature. We simply do not know the extent to which gender affected consumer behaviour, whether the homes of the rural poor differed from those in urban spaces, or whether factors such as proximity to London and the nature of the local economy affected consumption patterns. This book addresses these problems and in so doing builds a more comprehensive picture of national and regional changes in consumption. In sum, it is found that although women were more likely to engage in tea drinking, there were far more similarities in consumption between the two genders than differences. With regard to location, however, various goods tended to be acquired by greater numbers of poor men and women who lived in the home counties and in towns and cities, while fewer numbers owned these items in more rural, remote and less commercial areas such as Dorset, Leicestershire and Rutland.

Fourth, this book is notable as it uses the largest and most diverse sample of sources ever assembled to study the homes of the poor. Thus far, most historians have used case studies which focus on particular groups or have analysed only one or two types of source to research the topic. Without comparing their findings with those of other regions, different groups or alternative records, it is unclear how representative and accurate the results are. For instance, research on probate inventories taken of labourers' goods – which record the belongings that people owned at death for the purposes of inheritance and debt – has shown that the material lives of labouring people was improving over the seventeenth and eighteenth centuries.[11] However, it has commonly been argued that these sources largely capture the goods of atypical labourers, who often had access to land and were more similar to the middling sort.[12] When compared with the inventories of paupers such as Daniel Potter and Widow Playle above, the conclusion that the probate inventories are broadly representative appears somewhat optimistic.[13] We also have case studies which have shown that paupers in Norfolk and Essex owned various consumer goods over the eighteenth and nineteenth centuries.[14] Yet without comparisons with other regions, it is unknown how representative the findings are for paupers who lived elsewhere.[15] Through the use of sources 'from above' and 'from below' for a range of regions in England, this book offers the most comprehensive and holistic study of the material lives of the poor to date. It catalogues both national and regional changes in consumer behaviour and shows how material improvements could vary according to familial status, age, location and myriad other demographic, geographic, social and cultural factors.

Finally, this research is important as it sits at the intersection of numerous historiographical debates, such as the agency of the poor, the construction of the 'self' and the role of demand during the industrial revolution. It shows how impoverished people could have considerable control over their lives despite their limited resources, and that they took significant steps to enhance their homes. Some of their material gains were restricted to certain points in the life-cycle, such as when they were healthy and had regular employment, and many of these improvements were limited when people lived in rural and remote areas. Yet, despite these obstacles, the poor continued to show a propensity to consume goods and personalise their homes. This could be done through purchasing sought-after items such as clocks, or achieved inexpensively by painting a piece of furniture, putting a penny print on the wall, or adding a colourful blanket to a worn-out bed. These historiographical debates and many more will be returned to at intermittent times in the volume. The remaining sections of this introduction discuss sources, methodologies and the conceptual issues that underpin this research. But first, we must define who the poor were.

Defining the poor

The poor were a large, complicated and constantly changing section of the population who were perceived by people very differently across time and area. To many early modern commentators, the poor were a natural part of civilisation that benefited society through their labours. They were often viewed as deserving objects of charity and nearest to heaven, while the rich faced hell if they became covetous or took too much pride in their wealth. By the turn of the nineteenth century, the poor were increasingly treated with distrust and seen as so numerous that they threatened society by stripping it of food and resources through poor relief. Poverty was viewed in pejorative terms at this time and it was felt that legislators needed to make drastic changes to stop the group from spiralling out of control. Vagrants, beggars, single mothers, the idle and drunkards were continually singled out as immoral and undeserving of sympathy.[16]

This book moves away from these homogeneous and subjective ideas of poverty. It focuses on those who were in receipt of poor relief or charity of some sort, and the 'labouring sort' who worked for hourly/daily wages, such as agricultural labourers, weavers, servants, miners, soldiers, artisans, blacksmiths, porters, builders, wheelwrights and various industrial workers.[17] In quantitative terms, the poor defined in this way made up well over half of the English population across the seventeenth, eighteenth and nineteenth centuries.[18] Agricultural labourers and workers in manufacturing and their families alone comprised around 37.5 per cent of society at the turn of the nineteenth century.[19] Around one in ten of the population was collecting poor relief of some sort at any time,[20] while around two-fifths to half of the inhabitants of the south of England were helped by local poor law authorities at some point in their lifetimes.[21] It is much more difficult to estimate how many people received voluntary charity, as the breadth and depth of this form of assistance differed across England. However, based on local and regional studies most historians have found that charity rarely matched what poor relief provided and that it supported fewer people. Nonetheless, where present it gave families an important lifeline, especially when they found that parish relief was not forthcoming or was insufficient for their needs.[22]

Defining the poor by their occupation or being in receipt of assistance of some sort is challenging, as there were considerable differences in experiences depending upon location, wages, family circumstances, age and various other factors. For example, the numbers of people who received poor relief could vary even across neighbouring parishes, and not everybody who was destitute was given aid.[23] It has also been argued that welfare was much less generous in the north than in the south, meaning that paupers there could not rely on poor relief and had to make ends meet through other informal economies.[24] Industrial workers generally earned more money than their counterparts in agriculture.[25] Families would pass between periods of relative prosperity and impoverishment over short spaces of time as a result of deaths in the family, periods of sickness and old age (see Chapter 2). Poverty was usually something that people were born into and would experience at frequent intervals throughout their lives.[26] Yet there were some individuals who started off poor but worked their way up to become financially successful.[27] Others fell from the upper echelons of society to destitution as a result of a sudden disaster such as a house fire or bankruptcy.[28] To circumvent these myriad issues, each source used in this study has been cross-referenced to confirm that the individuals were not of the middling sort or atypically wealthy compared with their peers. The findings have been sub-divided in numerous ways to track and uncover nuances in material wealth. Regional variations are considered throughout the book, and differences between genders and between urban and rural areas are particularly addressed in Chapter 7. By considering how people acquired and sold things at different periods in their lives, the volume also considers how poverty varied over the life-course and how it could differ between individuals. Through these various forms of analysis, this research gets closer to what poverty was actually like for representative groups of the poor, and how it changed over the long eighteenth century.

Economics of poverty and income

By focusing on data such as wages and prices rather than actual lived experiences, many economic historians have argued that the labouring sort had only a limited ability to consume provisions such as food, clothing and household goods. Others have underplayed the importance of the myriad informal ways in which the deprived made thrift, such as the second-hand trade and neighbourly help, since these facets cannot be easily quantified. This book consciously moves away from the methodologies and theories employed by economic historians to consider consumption and material life. At its very core, this study is a social and cultural history of the home. In turn, it paints a much more positive picture of the domestic sphere.

The infamous 'standard of living debate' – which seeks to answer whether people became better off during the industrial revolution – has been raging for decades, and opinion is now largely in the pessimistic camp. Recent studies such as those of Emma Griffin, Jason Long and others have attempted to erode these gloomy perspectives and outline some of the more positive aspects of industrialisation.[29] Yet with regard to consumption, studies have tended to argue that wages were too low and that provisions cost too much for the labouring poor to ever significantly benefit from industrialisation.[30] The wage was undoubtedly the central source of income for most people, and cost was an important consideration, but it is imperative to examine wider factors when studying consumption. People were very creative and used a wide variety of methods to make do, such as credit, theft, inheritance, gifts, charity, common rights, the second-hand market and welfare.[31] These strategies tend not to be considered in economic histories, but they were widely used by the poor to acquire items. Further to this, studies which analyse changes in consumables are often based on estimates which surmise that everybody acquired the same type and quantity of certain items as one another. However, these assumptions can be misleading. For instance, candles are often noted in cost-of-living indexes, yet expenditure on candles was very low among some rural populations who continued to use homemade rushlights well into the nineteenth century.[32]

Introduction 7

It is well established that poverty among labouring populations varied considerably depending upon age, marital status, health and gender,[33] yet most economic studies have not taken these factors into sufficient consideration. Rather, many have used snapshots of prices, trade statistics and other related data to make blanket assumptions about the working classes' ability to purchase various goods.[34] As the broad ideas of B. Seebohm Rowntree show, this is a highly problematic supposition to make, since most people went through periods of being relatively well off and destitute over the 'life-cycle of poverty' (Figure 0.1). The model in Figure 0.1 shows how impoverishment was more probable during childhood or when people had their own children, as the young were unable to contribute to household earnings and there were more bodies to support. When children started to work and became old enough to move out, parents would often enjoy a few years of relative prosperity. This was interrupted when the couple became old, as they struggled to work, their health declined and their earnings dwindled.[35] By using sources which record individual experiences of how people would go through periods of material wealth and material poverty, this book presents a much more balanced, dynamic and ultimately optimistic perspective on changes in consumer behaviour.

People's relationship to their goods was often fundamentally different to the logic of economics. Even when it did not make financial sense to do so, families might stretch themselves and accumulate debt to purchase new possessions. Demand and individual desire for items has long been dismissed by economic historians,[36] who instead generally choose to emphasise supply-side changes such as cost and technology as the leading cause of changes in consumer behaviour.[37] Jan de Vries's ideas on how households became more 'industrious' to earn greater sums of money and acquire new 'wants' have helped to change the tide,[38] but old ideas have been found to die hard. In a 2014 leading textbook on economic history, for instance, Sara Horrell argued that supply-side factors such as technology, prices and trade 'appear at the forefront of change' and 'underpinned these changing consumption choices rather than tastes'.[39] I do not claim here that economic considerations are unimportant and should be neglected – wages, price and supply probably had a greater impact on the poor's ability to consume than on that of any other social group – but I argue that one must look further afield and consider other facets too. Only through consideration of lived experiences from a social and cultural perspective can we get closer to the lives of the poor and to the heart of changes in consumption.

Cultural and social contexts of consumption

Scholars working in anthropology, sociology, social history and other similar disciplines once principally used ideas of emulation, conspicuous

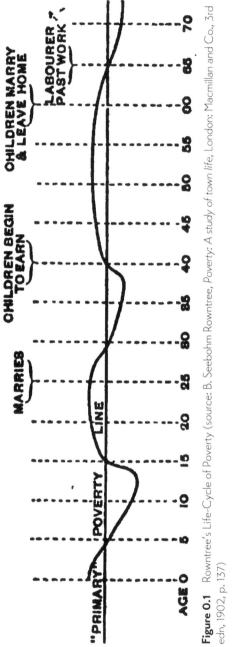

Figure 0.1 Rowntree's Life-Cycle of Poverty (source: B. Seebohm Rowntree, *Poverty: A study of town life*, London: Macmillan and Co., 3rd edn, 1902, p. 137)

consumption, class distinction and 'trickle-down' theory to account for changes in consumption. In a nutshell, such concepts categorise the wealthy as leaders of consumption who want to show off and protect their wealth and status through prominent displays of prosperity, while the poor continually try to catch up and imitate their social superiors.[40] These theories have their uses with particular items,[41] but for long periods of time they were used incorrectly by historians to look at goods where their application is more difficult to comprehend.[42] People had individual choices and personal preferences which are not reliably taken into account in these models. Most of the poorer classes would have had only limited contact with the elite and simply would not have known how they furnished their abodes.[43] Indigent populations could also be 'involuntary' consumers and have little choice in what they owned. Servants, for example, were given uniforms and sometimes cast-off clothing by their masters. Paupers and almshouse residents were at times granted clothing, food, fuel and household goods by authorities in charge.[44] As these concepts are unsuitable for explaining all types of consumption and material life among the poor, this book turns to many of the same social and cultural ideas that underpinned middling consumption, such as the desire for respectability, comfort and privacy.

Acquiring goods was a deeply personal thing to do and inherently tied to identity. Books, for example, could be procured for interests and hobbies, as well as to appear as knowledgeable and well read to guests perusing one's shelves. Identity could be, as Dror Wahrman argues, tied to 'two contradictory impulses: identity as the unique individuality of a person ... or identity as a common denominator that places an individual within a group'.[45] Comprehending which was most important to the poor is difficult, as they were often at the mercy of poor law authorities and so they may have suppressed personal identities so as to appear more deserving. In turn, this may have meant that some kept only items that were seen as adequate to their levels of hardship or refrained from acquiring goods that might have been perceived as superfluous or showy.[46] In spite of these caveats, many people acquired similar items to one another and obtained belongings which were deeply personal, varying according to preferences in material, colour, design and numerous other characteristics, especially from the latter decades of the eighteenth century. A primary aim of this book is to examine collective changes in consumption over the long eighteenth century and to consider the shared motivations and common identities that came from owning particular goods, while also acknowledging that people were individuals with discrete tastes and preferences.[47]

Studying consumption and material culture through the lens of emotions and the senses has proven to be a useful and versatile way to consider domestic life. Objects have the power to shape emotions and emotions have the power to shape objects, according to a host of biological, anthropological, cultural and social factors. The same paradigm can also be applied to particular spaces, such as the home. Until recently, the emotional connection between people, objects and spaces was treated tacitly and implicitly by researchers, as emotional investment in items or spaces could be involuntary and subconscious, as well as personal and restricted to very specific circumstances. But there has been something of a sustained effort in recent years to theorise, define and study emotion more centrally through the changing use of words, spaces and objects.[48] Closely allied to this, we also have sensory experience – that of smell, taste, touch, sound and sight – which, although often transitory, ephemeral and culturally malleable, could also evoke emotional responses in people and influence how they used objects and spaces.[49] Taken together, these factors had the power to shape domestic life and use of goods. Fire irons, for instance, were used to produce and hold fire in place in a hearth. Close to the embers, people might feel joy, relief and contentment while resting after a hard day's labour, helped by the heat, light, smells and sounds of crackling embers. The same space could also evoke feelings of stress, anger and annoyance, such as in the mother who found herself soaked in sweat with aching limbs and burning lungs from turning a spit for several hours. These sensory and emotional experiences are often hidden in sources such as inventories and account books, as they tend to note goods in a detached and impassive manner. However, through careful deduction and close reading of first-hand sources and visual representations of the poor, this book gets closer to the poor's sensory and emotional experience of domestic life. Often this is only a partial, brief and obscure glimpse, but the study does take one step closer to understanding how the poor felt about their homes and particular goods.

One of the most important motivations for new consumer practices was the growing desire for comfort. From the eighteenth century, the term 'comfort' was linked to physical wellbeing and emotional and psychological satisfaction with material surroundings.[50] Sleep, for instance, generally requires the physical comfort of a bed, in addition to the psychological comfort of feeling safe and content in a familiar space.[51] By the late eighteenth and early nineteenth centuries, these ideas of comfort were essential to the poor as well as the middling sort and the elite. In pauper letters written by William James to the overseer of Chelmsford, he stated that he 'only [had] our Bed, & a few things' and asked the overseer for help paying the rent 'to stop the threatining proceedings of my Landlady, to take away the *Comfort*, of our few goods from us'.[52] Likewise, in a letter written by John Hicks in 1805, he asked for weekly relief from the overseer of Upminster, Essex to make 'me *tollerable* comfortable'.[53] These examples indicate that even if people owned very few goods or were in difficult situations, they still wanted to be comfortable and felt that they had an inherent right to be. Thus, ideas of physical and psychological comfort were very important to people and can implicitly and explicitly be linked to a considerable range of goods that are studied here, such as beds, seats, curtains and fire irons.

The desire to feel and to be seen as respectable was important among large numbers of the indigent population, especially by the late eighteenth century.[54] In essence, 'respectability' equated to being of good moral character and social standing, but it is a slippery notion and has been interpreted and appropriated by both contemporaries and researchers differently. Geoffrey Crossick and Robert Gray have argued that the 'respectable' poor included only those who were skilled and never needed charity, poor relief, credit or pawnbroking to make ends meet.[55] Others, such as F. M. L. Thompson, Jennifer Davis and Lynn MacKay, have persuasively shown that the notion of respectability crossed class boundaries and that there was no hard-and-fast distinction among different groups of the poor.[56] Many people even hung on to or aspired to the notion of respectability when they were homeless or entered relief lists.[57] Elizabeth Goodman, for instance, writing from London in 1833 to the overseer of Rayleigh, Essex, asked for 'common necessaries amongst them a decent Stuff Gown' for work, as 'I must go respectable or not at all'.[58] As this example shows, possessions were used to signal, maintain and defend people's respectability. Respectability gave meaning to consumption; it could underpin how people used goods and how they wanted their use of items to be perceived by others.[59] Woodruff Smith has traced the connection between consumption and respectability among the middling sort, arguing that it was 'probably the primary factor defining consumption in Western economies' by the nineteenth century.[60] The poor have largely been missed from this debate, and the connection between respectability and consumption for those with meagre resources remains opaque.[61] Here, it is argued that respectability is crucial to understanding the poor's acquisition and use of a range of household goods from the late eighteenth century.

Quite often the poor would acquire one item over another for its perceived convenience. The meaning of the term 'convenience' has gone through several changes. In the words of John Crowley, it had 'strong connotations of harmony and conformity to a given order, as in "congruity of form, quality or nature"', in the fifteenth and sixteenth centuries,[62] whereas today it is heavily linked to time and efficiency, such as in the notion of convenience food. During the long eighteenth century, the term was generally associated with suitability, ease and how well adapted something was to satisfying requirements.[63] To this end, chests of drawers were convenient for storing and retrieving clothing as they were made up of drawers, whereas boxes were less convenient as people would need to rummage through various goods in a deep container to find what they wanted.

It has been claimed by leading historians that privacy – the act of being alone or free from unwanted attention or intrusion – 'mattered little' among the early modern poor.[64] Others, such as Lynn MacKay and Amanda Vickery, have conversely argued that privacy was desirable among indigent populations but was very difficult to obtain.[65] It is similarly argued here that privacy was important in the homes of the poor, even if many people found it challenging to achieve and needed to compromise in some form. Privacy is essentially a choice, and people did, indeed, increasingly choose to seclude themselves from the outside world and members of their own households. Privacy became crucial for nurturing intimate relations, managing bodily functions and conducting inner discourse away from outside pressures.[66] Evidence for its importance can be found in the writings of social commentators and the poor alike, especially from the late eighteenth century. For example, upon coming to Norwich to look for work in 1804, Richard Gooch stayed in an inn for one night and was pleased when he eventually 'acquired a *private*, and more comfortable abode'.[67] A number of autobiographies note the value of 'private' prayer and bible reading in secluded spaces. John MacDonald said that he commonly 'kneeled down to pray to God' in 'a private part of the garden'.[68] As a 21-year-old shoemaking apprentice in Taunton, Somerset, James Lackington remarked that he 'often privately took the Bible to bed with me, and in the long summer mornings read for hours together in bed'.[69] Material goods such as bed hangings, locks and window curtains were acquired by people to cultivate privacy in domestic spheres. Total privacy for bathing, sleep, relieving oneself and being intimate with partners was, however, not always possible. Most rooms in poor abodes were multifunctional spaces used for a variety of purposes, and objects such as bed hangings offered only limited seclusion from outside influences.

As well as acquiring goods for their inherent properties, people would procure items for their lasting financial value. Coinage was scarce and banks were not used by most, so the poor would buy possessions during periods of relative prosperity as a form of saving, with the idea of selling them later if they needed to realise cash to pay bills and acquire basics such as food. This was beneficial as it allowed people with modest resources to enjoy the benefits of capitalism, while having the security of knowing that their items could be sold or pawned if they needed money.[70] Chapter 2 considers how people would offload their possessions during times of sickness and downturns in the life-cycle of poverty. These periods of difficulty could also be brought on by financial mismanagement, such as the drinking away of household finances, or be the consequence of broader economic problems. This widespread selling of goods during tough intervals meant that there was always choice and a considerable stocks of items on the second-hand market for the poor. The bulk of literature on this process has examined how people would pledge and trade clothing.[71] However, as this book shows, household goods such as watches, clocks, silver items and tea paraphernalia were also acquired during more affluent periods and then traded when bills started to mount.

Sources and methodology

Numerous historians have commented on the lack of research on the material lives of the poor,[72] but little has been done to address this problem. It is not uncommon for scholars to claim that there are not enough sources to study indigent populations,[73] to suggest that the poor are too difficult to study,[74] or to state that there is little point in researching them since they could not afford anything more than food and a few basic household necessities.[75] This research breaks down these incorrect assumptions through the analysis of a multitude of under-utilised sources which record the experiences of thousands of impoverished individuals. These records include inventories, writings of the poor, contemporary pictures, surviving artefacts, poor law minute and account books, pawnbroking records, newspapers, trade directories, and the wills of paupers and people in workhouses and almshouses. The sources have been subjected to both quantitative and qualitative analysis to track the poor's consumption and use of various household items such as furniture, fire irons, tableware and non-necessities. This section will now focus on the book's use of inventories, ego documents, pictures and extant objects, which can be particularly tricky to use.

This book utilises 2,400 inventories such as pauper and workhouse-related inventories made between 1622 and 1841 (Table 0.1). The inventories

Table 0.1 Inventories found among parish and miscellaneous archival collections, c.1622–1841

	Dorset	Essex	Kent	Lancs	Leics/Ruts	Norfolk	Total
Pauper inventories	60	228	61	11	72	230	662
Unknown	23	104	77	26	45	118	393
Poorhouse/ workhouse contents	11	142	105	8	45	31	342
Goods-given	5	56	55	70	18	51	255
Other	1	152	33	1	8	23	218
Debt-related	13	45	58	37	8	34	195
Goods taken	10	59	47	28	13	28	185
Poorhouse/ workhouse admittance-related	40	40	25	1	3	7	116
Almshouse-related	0	0	3	0	0	13	16
Family abandonment	0	0	4	7	0	3	14
Bastardy-related	1	1	0	1	0	1	4
Total	164	827	468	190	212	539	2,400

have been located from 505 English parishes in seven counties: Dorset, Essex, Kent, Lancashire, Leicestershire, Norfolk and Rutland. These counties make up a mix of areas which have been widely researched by welfare historians (especially Essex) and ones which have received less attention (such as Dorset and Kent). The inventories are used here principally to chronicle material changes over time and area. These sources are notoriously challenging to find and use, as the majority of them are uncatalogued in archive search engines and have rarely been subject to systematic research by historians. Most were found through the laborious task of searching through thousands of overseers' accounts, vestry minutes and miscellaneous bills and receipts.[76] In order to ensure that the results are accurate and consistent over time, each of the inventories has been cross-referenced with poor relief sources as well as birth, marriage and death records, to identify which of them are records of paupers' goods. Those which record the belongings of people who were not on relief have been omitted, leaving a sample of 1,766 inventories. This was a necessary step to take: as noted above, levels of poverty could vary considerably among people and for systematic analysis it is important to focus on only one group. Without knowing whether somebody was receiving relief, it is very difficult to know how poor the people in the inventories actually were, since information on work and status is rarely forthcoming in the sources. Some of the inventories are clearly dubious and not of paupers' goods, as they record hundreds of pounds' worth of stock and goods, while others appear to have been made of people who were impoverished but did not receive poor relief.

A diverse range of inventories survives among parish and miscellaneous archival records. Nearly 400 of the inventories have been classed as 'unknown', as relevant background information could not be found to classify them and determine whose goods they were appraising. Goods-given inventories list the items given to people by the parish. They are especially useful for looking at the informal ways in which the poor acquired items and what parishes deemed as necessary to own. The contents of poorhouses and workhouses are catalogued in inventories of poorhouse/workhouse contents. Among these records, there are also inventories of inmates' belongings which were taken in the period immediately before they entered a parish institution (poorhouse/workhouse admittance-related inventories). Debt was a common part of life for many, and when it got out of control people's possessions could be distrained to recover the money owed. Just under half of these debt-related inventories list the goods of paupers (45 per cent). Goods-taken inventories document the belongings that parishes took from paupers. When husbands or wives deserted their families and left them chargeable to the parish, the goods that they left behind were often subject to appraisal in a family abandonment inventory. Similarly, bastardy-related inventories chronicle the distraint and sale of the belongings of putative mothers or fathers of a child born out of wedlock. The inventories noted in this paragraph are used primarily to provide qualitative examples and to facilitate understanding of the functions, appearances, conditions, constructions and meanings of various items belonging to paupers. This is because some of these inventories record only a fraction of the goods that paupers owned rather than their wider material wealth. Goods-taken inventories, for instance, sometimes record only the goods that were taken to pay the funeral expenses of a spouse or child. When making an inventory to reclaim money from a debtor, creditors were legally allowed to inventory only enough possessions to pay the debt rather than somebody's entire worldly goods.[77]

The most important set of sources from this sample are pauper inventories, which were made by parochial officials under the old poor law to record the possessions that somebody on poor relief owned.[78] The paupers would then generally continue to use their belongings after the inventory was taken, and at a later date, usually when they died, the goods would revert to the parish, where they would be sold, given to other paupers or used to furnish the parish poorhouse/workhouse. They should be viewed as a representation of the home, as there is no guarantee that they are complete, yet on the whole they record a range of cheap, mundane and valuable items in situ. This makes them highly valuable and unique sources which can be used to systematically measure changes in pauper material wealth over time and area. Hundreds of different types of items from the pauper inventories were selected for analysis and most of the goods were broken down into sub-sections, such as material, size and condition, to gain a holistic view of the entire household and trace the poor's ownership of goods from basic items to non-necessities.[79] Six hundred and sixty-two inventories have been located for 1670 to 1835. Of these, six have been omitted as they mainly list clothing or are heavily damaged, leaving a sample of 656.

Pauper inventories tended to be made of older parishioners who were on poor relief as a result of sickness and life-cycle-related problems such as the death of their partner. This was because these types of parishioner were expensive to maintain and were expected to be on relief until they died, so their goods acted as a way in which the parish could recoup some funds. Just under four-fifths of these paupers received a pension from their parishes, at an average of 2s. 4d. per week, but most also received intermittent cash payments and various items from officials. The remaining one-fifth were on casual relief, which was generally made up of irregular cash allowances, rent payments and goods in kind. Around four-fifths of the inventories were made in rural parishes. The inventories are fairly evenly split between female- and male-headed households, meaning that the results do not significantly over-represent one gender. These gendered and urban–rural differences are analysed further in Chapter 7 to determine the extent to which they shaped and influenced consumer practices.

Officials did not prioritise appraising the goods of paupers who were materially richer than most or the middling sort who had fallen on hard times. Rather, parishes appraised the possessions of a wide spectrum of paupers with varying levels of material wealth. For example, where valuations are noted in the pauper inventories, the sources record estates worth a total average of only £4 3s. 2d. between 1681 and 1825. Compared with the probate inventories of labourers and the middling sort, this sum is very small.[80] While a handful of pauper inventories record hundreds of objects, more than half of them (55 per cent) list no more than 40 items. These counts of goods are, of course, imperfect, yet one would expect these figures to be much higher if affluent people were a priority of authorities. The two most common current or former occupations of the paupers in the inventories were agricultural labourer and weaver. This further indicates that the parishioners in the sample were from the labouring sort and typical of most other people who received poor relief.[81]

As well as studying language and other linguistic subtleties, the pauper inventories have been subjected to quantitative analysis to uncover material experiences and consumption over the long eighteenth century. Quantitative analysis of the inventories is particularly tricky, as their survival is patchy for some areas and decades (Figure 0.2). Regionally, the majority of sources were made in Essex and Norfolk, meaning that the data is heavily skewed towards the east of England. For Dorset, Kent and Leicestershire/Rutland, the numbers of inventories are relatively low, but there are enough exist to identify broad trends in consumer behaviour. Only 11 pauper inventories have been located from Lancashire.[82] Systematic analysis of the county is therefore not possible and unless otherwise specified, all the data in this book is constructed using the pauper

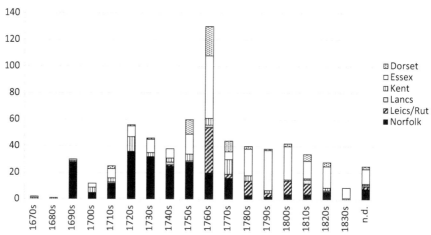

Figure 0.2 Chronological distribution of the pauper inventories, 1670–1835

inventories from Dorset, Essex, Kent, Leicestershire/Rutland and Norfolk. Chronologically, most of the pauper inventories were created between the 1720s and 1800s. Fairly minimal numbers survive for the late seventeenth century, and most of these were made in Norfolk. The practice of making pauper inventories appears to have been declining by the early nineteenth century, and over half of the sources found for this period came from Essex. There are no pauper inventories dated prior to the 1760s for Leicestershire and Rutland, so the measurement of trends over time is difficult for these counties. Dorset and Kent have relatively even distributions of inventories across the eighteenth and nineteenth centuries, yet their sample sizes are small, which means that data from these counties can be questioned. With these issues in mind, it is important to note that the statistical results for some regions and periods are arguably tentative and problematic. Yet, through careful methodical analysis, these issues are curtailed and revealing trends are found.

To recreate individual life experiences, over 2,100 narratives of the poor have been surveyed, such as autobiographies, diaries, biographies of the poor written by third parties, and pauper letters addressed to parochial officials to request relief.[83] Material wealth and use of goods tend to be mentioned only occasionally and anecdotally in these sources, but when noted they offer unique insights into domestic life and identity formation. Such sources have primarily been used by historians to study aspects such as class formation, literacy and marriage: they have not been used on any scale to study changes in consumption and domestic life other than that which relates to books and other reading materials.[84] While only inventories of people on poor relief have been used, these personal accounts capture the experiences of a broader group of 'poor' people who came from labouring backgrounds. On occasion, the narratives record stories of rags to riches, but it is evidence only from their poverty-stricken and labouring years that is used here. Through these sources, the book considers how consumer behaviour changed over the life-cycle, and how people transitioned from periods of material wealth to material poverty as they went from being self-sufficient to being reliant on poor relief. These first-hand records also sometimes detail people's emotional and sensory connections to their possessions, as well as how items were used and acquired.

Personal narratives are highly valuable sources, but they should be read with caution. Most significantly under-record people's material lives and needs. Numerous writers, for instance, recount experiences of insolvency, life-cycle-related problems and unemployment, but not the extent to which they went without food, clothing and other items as a result of these difficulties. Some chose to mention only their most pressing and expensive priorities, such as rent and medicine, while others vaguely noted how they needed the 'common necessaries of life', indicating that they had a range of needs. In addition, the types of people who wrote these testimonies and the intentions of the authors are not uniform across the sample. Most autobiographies were published during or shortly after the writer's lifetime, while the bulk of pauper letters and third-party accounts were never expected to be read by anyone other than the authors and recipients. Depending on the intended audience, the writings may contain certain elements of false or misremembered information, exaggeration, silences and rhetorical ploys, as the writers sought to portray themselves in a better and more compelling light to readers. Only a small number of first-hand accounts have been found for the seventeenth century and the first three-quarters of the eighteenth century. With the exception of pauper letters, very few of the testimonies were composed by women.[85] No source offers the historian absolute truth, yet these narratives appear to be surprisingly honest on the whole, especially since the veracity of the writers was often subject to checks by publishers, poor law authorities and neighbours.[86]

In recent years, the analysis of physical objects has become a popular approach taken by historians. In a method first developed by archaeologists and social anthropologists, researchers use an item or a series of objects to interpret the meanings, uses and importance of those things to people. Objects from the ephemeral to the grandiose are seen to have agency and thus the ability to inform our understanding of past societies and of various themes, such as identity, fashion, gender, the senses, emotions and manufacture.[87] Owing to the fact that mostly only objects of value, adornment and beauty have survived to the present day, the material culture of poverty has been particularly difficult to study and has not been subjected to such sustained research as has that of the elite and the middling sort.[88] By using surviving examples of artefacts and pictorial representations which best match the items referred to in the inventories, this book gets around this problem. It goes beyond the ostentatious objects that tend to be found in museum collections and considers relatively cheap articles, such as those sold by auction houses and private sellers, to get closer to the more 'ordinary' goods that the poor probably used.[89] As Deborah Cohen argues, 'the ugly and the ephemeral' often tell us more than 'the beautiful and the transcendent'.[90]

In a similar manner to extant objects, contemporary prints and paintings of poor abodes are used only when their content resembles the findings of the inventories and writings of the poor. This is because it can be very difficult to tell whether pictures are accurate representations, or whether they offer fictionalised and exaggerated portrayals of people and locations to satisfy the consumers who bought them.[91] George Morland, for example, is one of the most famous eighteenth-century painters of the labouring sort, but the accuracy of his artwork has been subject to debate.[92] Other sets of pictures are less controversial and offer the historian a truer representation of the poor. Most notably, the clergyman Richard Cobbold

(1797–1877) left behind a unique archive of paintings which depict the people and buildings in his village of Wortham, Suffolk. His paintings closely match the descriptions of individuals and their abodes in his writings, and there is no reason to think that he falsified the portraits, since he did not do them to satisfy a paying client.[93] The pursuit was simply a hobby of the parson. Cobbold said that the pictures 'are genuine specimens of the features they record' as he 'intimately' knew everyone in his village and remarked that there was only one building in Wortham which he had never entered.[94] He was adamant in wanting to portray the poor in his village accurately, saying that history is full of 'Lords', 'ancestry' and 'the wealthy', while there was 'no record' of the poor who 'toil for us'.[95] Each painter or engraver, nevertheless, clearly had their own objectives and we are still seeing the world through their depictions of it, so each picture is treated with caution.

Regional dimensions

The book uses sources from nearly every English county, as well as parts of Scotland, Wales and Ireland. However, owing to the use of inventories from local and county archives, Dorset, Essex, Kent, Leicestershire/ Rutland and Norfolk are a particular focus of this study. Before briefly looking at the regional attributes of these counties, it is important to acknowledge that the poor *everywhere* experienced difficult circumstances over the eighteenth and nineteenth centuries. This was the result of myriad changes, such as the demise of customary access to commons for foraging and grazing animals through enclosure. Considerable population growth and the economic impact of the Napoleonic wars also resulted in widespread unemployment and under-employment.[96] The poor in Essex and Norfolk particularly suffered, as the bulk of their textile industries moved to the north during the industrial revolution.[97]

Notwithstanding these enduring hardships, the counties act as interesting regions to study. The areas were chosen as their diverse socioeconomic and geographical characteristics allow one to consider how consumer behaviour and domestic life varied across England. London was at the centre of fashion, trades and industries and was well connected to Essex and Kent through road and water networks. The home counties also had some of the highest densities of retail outlets in the country, and labourers generally received higher wages there compared with elsewhere.[98] In contrast, the poor of Dorset, Leicestershire, Norfolk and Rutland were located far enough away from the capital for its influence to be less pronounced, and they experienced some unique difficulties. While there were local and regional nuances, greater proportions of the populations of these counties lived in sparsely occupied agrarian areas. Wages were notoriously low for agricultural labourers in Dorset and Norfolk,[99]

20   At home with the poor

while Leicestershire and Rutland possessed the lowest number of markets in the sample.[100] It is argued throughout the book that the material lives of the poor in Essex and Kent improved at a faster rate than those of their counterparts elsewhere. This was largely the result of the position and economies of Essex and Kent, which meant that people there had greater access to goods and were more open and receptive to fashions from London. Thus, economic factors were important, but so too were social and cultural facets.

Structure

The book is arranged thematically and most of the chapters take the reader around the home one set of items or one method of analysis at a time. Using pauper inventories, the next chapter sets the scene by considering the size of pauper homes, how their rooms were used and where they displayed sought-after items such as clocks and pictures. It is revealed that most pauper homes were smaller than those of the middling sort and their rooms were generally multifunctional. This suggests that homes might have been fairly cramped, as people had only a limited number of rooms in which to cook, eat, rest, sleep and work. Meanwhile, items of display tended to be placed not in 'frontstage' rooms used primarily for entertaining guests, but where they were most useful. Despite this, poor homes were not inflexible and people still took pride in their abodes. Chambers, for instance, were the most common rooms in pauper homes and were used on a fairly consistent basis for sleeping. Kitchens too became more common as archaic spaces such as halls were seen as less useful.

Chapter 2 considers how people went through periods of material wealth and material poverty over their lifetimes. It starts by outlining some of the key aggregate changes in the consumer behaviour of the poor between 1650 and 1850, including the average and median number of items that indigent populations owned and how the value of their possessions changed over the period. The adjectives that appraisers used to describe people's belongings, such as 'new' and 'old', are also assessed. Through this, it is argued that the poor owned more and better belongings as the long eighteenth century progressed. The remainder of the chapter considers some of the limits of these advances using first-hand sources and inventories which record people's goods at different points in the life-cycle. The sources indicate that during relatively prosperous years when poor people were healthy, family sizes were small and they had decent employment, they consumed a wide range of goods, including various foodstuffs, fuel, clothing and household possessions. However, during difficult periods such as old age and sickness, people often went cold and hungry and their belongings were pawned or sold to make ends meet. Family priorities shifted at these points and people redirected their resources to acquiring the most basic items, such as bread and medicine for their loved ones. Similarly, this chapter shows how households could descend into material poverty as a result of unemployment, desertion, poor budgeting, imprisonment or a sudden disaster such as a house fire, burglary or flood. These findings are important as they help to explain the paradox of how some labouring people faced extreme hardship while others were active consumers.

From here, Chapters 3–6 explore which goods increasingly entered the abodes of the poor, what the items looked like, how they were used and the multitude of effects that they had on everyday life. Where possible, the chapters consider regional differences and how use of possessions differed between contrasting groups, such as the old and young and the healthy and sick. Chapter 3 analyses furniture and furnishings. It argues that the homes of impoverished people became more comfortable, private and convenient as a result of their rising ownership of feather beds, chests of drawers, bed hangings and other items. The following chapter moves on to the hearth. It illustrates how the fireplace was a focal point of the home, where people would do chores, work and relax in the evenings with their nearest and dearest. Items connected to the hearth, such as lighting and fire irons, are also scrutinised to show how dwellings became safer and more practical over the period. Significant regional differences in energy use are identified. In Lancashire, Leicestershire and Rutland coal was the main form of fuel used by the poor, but in Dorset, Essex, Kent and Norfolk most indigent people used peat, faggots or firewood well into the nineteenth century. This is an important finding, as fuel had a direct impact on how those with limited resources prepared food and how well they kept themselves warm.

Chapter 5 considers cooking and dining patterns. While cooking practices are likely to have remained rudimentary and changed little in pauper homes, there were some important changes in how food and drink was consumed. Growing numbers of people acquired more decorative eating and drinking vessels over more archaic materials including pewter and wood. Ownership of knives and forks grew by the late eighteenth century, showing that there was a considerable transformation in people's eating and dining habits, as they moved away from eating with their hands and began to use personal cutlery. Tea drinking went from being a rare luxury to a ubiquitous necessity in the homes of paupers and the labouring sort over the eighteenth century. Chapter 6 traces the poor's ownership and use of 'non-essential' items such as timepieces, looking glasses, books and pictures. In general, these items became more common from the late eighteenth century and the poor in London and the home counties acquired them before those who lived in more rural and remote areas of the country. These items transformed people's way of life. Looking glasses, for instance, were not just opulent items reserved for vanity: they also helped to enhance and brighten the domestic sphere, make tasks such as shaving easier, and create a sense of comfort. As well as having obvious practical advantages, clocks and watches were hugely important to working people for the pride, prestige and symbolic power that they brought to individuals.

The final chapter breaks down the findings further by reviewing the influence that gender and urban–rural differences had on consumer behaviour. This is important to do as neither topic has been subject to serious study regarding the poor. Most of the research on gendered consumption, for example, has focused on more obvious items such as male and female attire rather than their household possessions. The results indicate that gender had a minimal impact on people's levels of ownership, while those in urban spaces tended to own more goods overall and more non-necessities than their peers in rural spaces.

Using multifaceted and extensive numbers of sources, *At home with the poor* opens the doors to the homes of the forgotten and brings to the fore thousands of narratives of everyday domestic life. The book gets to the very core of what poverty physically looked like before, during and after the industrial revolution. It chronicles the untold ways in which the poor improved their domestic sphere over three centuries. This could come from purchasing various items or organising their houses better. Even those who could afford little found ways to enhance their living conditions, such as by painting furniture, lining their walls with ephemeral prints or adding a cloth to a worn-out table. Just because somebody was poor, it did not mean that they were happy living in squalor. For too long historians have ignored the material face of poverty and the site where people lived out their years and experienced both joy and sadness: the home.

Notes

1 ERO D/P 105/18/5.
2 ERO D/P 105/12/2.
3 ERO D/P 105/8/1.
4 Some of the key texts include: Neil McKendrick, John Brewer and J. H. Plumb, *The Birth of a Consumer Society: The commercialization of eighteenth-century England* (London: Hutchinson, 1982); Carole Shammas, *The Pre-Industrial Consumer in England and America* (Oxford: Oxford University Press, 1990); John Brewer and Roy Porter (eds), *Consumption and the World of Goods* (London: Routledge, 1993); Lorna Weatherill, *Consumer Behaviour and Material Culture in Britain 1660–1760* (London: Routledge, 2nd edn, 1996); Amanda Vickery, *The Gentleman's Daughter: Women's lives in Georgian England* (New Haven: Yale University Press, 1998); Mark Overton, Jane Whittle, Darron Dean and Andrew Hann, *Production and Consumption in English Households, 1600–1750* (London: Routledge, 2004); Deborah Cohen, *Household Gods: The British and their possessions* (New Haven: Yale University Press, 2006); Jane Hamlett, *Material Relations: Domestic interiors and middle-class families* (Manchester: Manchester University Press, 2010); Tara Hamling and Catherine Richardson (eds), *Everyday Objects: Medieval and early modern material culture and its meanings* (London: Routledge, 2010); Frank Trentmann (ed.),

The Oxford Handbook of the History of Consumption (Oxford: Oxford University Press, 2012); Paula Findlen, Early Modern Things: Objects and their histories, 1500–1800 (London: Routledge, 2013); Jon Stobart and Mark Rothery, Consumption and the Country House (Oxford: Oxford University Press, 2016); Tara Hamling and Catherine Richardson, A Day at Home in Early Modern England: Material culture and domestic life, 1500–1700 (New Haven: Yale University Press, 2017); Catherine Richardson, Tara Hamling and David Gaimster (eds), The Routledge Handbook of Material Culture in Early Modern Europe (London: Routledge, 2017); Joanne Sear and Ken Sneath, The Origins of the Consumer Revolution in England: From brass pots to clocks (London: Routledge, 2020).

5 On the clothing of the poor, see, among others: Beverly Lemire, Fashion's Favourite: The cotton trade and the consumer in Britain, 1660–1800 (Oxford: Oxford University Press, 1991); Beverly Lemire, Dress, Culture and Commerce: The English clothing trade before the factory, 1660–1800 (Basingstoke: Palgrave, 1997); John Styles, The Dress of the People: Everyday fashion in eighteenth-century England (New Haven: Yale University Press, 2007). On the case study approach and for examples of this, see below.

6 Peter H. Lindert and Jeffrey G. Williamson, 'Revising England's Social Tables, 1688–1812', Explorations in Economic History, 19 (1982), pp. 385–408; Robert C. Allen, 'Class Structure and Inequality during the Industrial Revolution: Lessons from England's social tables, 1688–1867', Economic History Review, 72:1 (2019), pp. 88–125.

7 See note 4.

8 Alexandra Shepard, Accounting for Oneself: Worth, status, and the social order (Oxford: Oxford University Press, 2015).

9 Weatherill, Consumer Behaviour, esp. pp. 43–69; Overton et al., Production and Consumption; Carl B. Estabrook, Urbane and Rustic England: Cultural ties and social spheres in the provinces 1660–1780 (Manchester: Manchester University Press, 1998), pp. 128–63; Sear and Sneath, Consumer Revolution, pp. 204–29; Henry French, The Middle Sort of People in Provincial England 1600–1750 (Oxford: Oxford University Press, 2007), pp. 141–200.

10 Lorna Weatherill, 'A Possession of One's Own: Women and consumer behaviour in England, 1660–1740', Journal of British Studies, 25:2 (1986), pp. 131–56; Maxine Berg, 'Women's Consumption and the Industrial Classes of Eighteenth-Century England', Journal of Social History, 30:2 (1996), pp. 415–34; Margot Finn, 'Women, Consumption and Coverture in England, c.1760–1860', Historical Journal, 39:3 (1996), pp. 703–22; Margot Finn, 'Men's Things: Masculine possession in the consumer revolution', Social History, 25:2 (2000), pp. 133–55; Vickery, Gentleman's Daughter; Amanda Vickery, Behind Closed Doors: At home in Georgian England (New Haven: Yale University Press, 2009); Karen Harvey, The Little Republic: Masculinity and domestic authority in eighteenth-century Britain (Oxford: Oxford University Press, 2012), esp. pp. 82–6, 99–133; Jane Whittle and Elizabeth Griffiths, Consumption and Gender in the Early Seventeenth-Century Household: The world of Alice Le Strange (Oxford: Oxford University Press, 2012).

11 Craig Muldrew, Food, Energy and the Creation of Industriousness: Work and material culture in agrarian England, 1550–1780 (Cambridge: Cambridge University Press, 2011), pp. 163–207; Ken Sneath, 'Consumption, Wealth, Indebtedness and Social Structure in Early Modern England', PhD thesis (University of Cambridge, 2008), pp. 231–328; Sear and Sneath, Consumer Revolution, pp. 273–98.

12 For example, Weatherill, Consumer Behaviour, pp. 191–4; Barry Coward, The Stuart Age: England, 1603–1714 (Harlow: Longman, 3rd edn, 2003), p. 55; Peter King, 'Pauper Inventories and the Material Lives of the Poor in the Eighteenth and Early Nineteenth Centuries', in Tim Hitchcock, Peter King and Pamela Sharpe (eds), Chronicling Poverty: The voices and strategies of the English poor, 1640–1840 (Basingstoke: Palgrave, 1997), pp. 156, 176.

13 Joseph Harley, 'Consumption and Poverty in the Homes of the English Poor, c.1670–1834', *Social History*, 43:1 (2018), pp. 81–104.

14 King, 'Pauper Inventories', pp. 155–91; Adrian Green, 'Heartless and Unhomely? Dwellings of the poor in East Anglia and north-east England', in Joanne McEwan and Pamela Sharpe (eds), *Accommodating Poverty: The housing and living arrangements of the English poor, c.1600–1850* (Basingstoke: Palgrave, 2011), pp. 69–101; Barbara Cornford, 'Inventories of the Poor', *Norfolk Archaeology*, 35 (1970–73), pp. 118–25.

15 We also have case studies on groups such as workhouse and almshouse residents, lodgers, criminals and sailors. While these studies are important and help to chip away at the topic, they largely stand in isolation and it is unclear just how representative they are for wider impoverished populations. For instance, see: Joanne McEwan and Pamela Sharpe (eds), *Accommodating Poverty: The housing and living arrangements of the English poor, c.1600–1850* (Basingstoke: Palgrave, 2011); Joseph Harley, 'Material Lives of the Poor and their Strategic Use of the Workhouse during the Final Decades of the English Old Poor Law', *Continuity and Change*, 30:1 (2015), pp. 71–103; Angela Nicholls, *Almshouses in Early Modern England: Charitable housing in the mixed economy of welfare 1550–1725* (Woodbridge: Boydell Press, 2017), pp. 138–87; John Styles, 'Lodging at the Old Bailey: Lodgings and their furnishings in eighteenth-century London', in John Styles and Amanda Vickery (eds), *Gender, Taste, and Material Culture in Britain and North America 1700–1830* (New Haven: Yale University Press, 2006), pp. 61–80; Sara Horrell, Jane Humphries and Ken Sneath, 'Consumption Conundrums Unravelled', *Economic History Review*, 68:3 (2015), pp. 830–57; Anne Helmreich, Tim Hitchcock and William J. Turkel, 'Rethinking Inventories in the Digital Age: The case of the Old Bailey', *Journal of Art Historiography*, 11 (2014), pp. 1–25; Beverly Lemire, '"Men of the World": British mariners, consumer practice, and material culture in an era of global trade, c.1660–1800', *Journal of British Studies*, 54:2 (2015), pp. 288–319.

16 Paul Slack, *Poverty and Policy in Tudor and Stuart England* (London: Longman, 1988); J. R. Poynter, *Society and Pauperism: English ideas on poor relief, 1795–1834* (London: Routledge and Kegan Paul, 1969); Karel Williams, *From Pauperism to Poverty* (London: Routledge and Kegan Paul, 1981); Gertrude Himmelfarb, *The Idea of Poverty: England in the early industrial age* (London: Faber & Faber, 1984).

17 This list is not exhaustive. For further context, see: Frederic Morton Eden, *The State of the Poor*, Vols. 1–3 (London: J. Davis, 1797); David Davies, *The Case of Labourers in Husbandry* (London: G. G. and J. Robinson, 1795); E. P. Thompson, *The Making of the English Working Class* (London: Penguin, reprint of 1963 edn, 1991); John Rule, *The Labouring Classes in Early Industrial England 1750–1850* (London: Longman, 1986); Emma Griffin, *Liberty's Dawn: A people's history of the industrial revolution* (New Haven: Yale University Press, 2013).

18 Lindert and Williamson, 'Revising', pp. 385–408; Allen, 'Class Structure', pp. 88–125.

19 Calculated from Allen, 'Class Structure', p. 120.

20 Williams, *Pauperism to Poverty*, pp. 149–50.

21 Tim Wales, 'Poverty, Poor Relief and Life-Cycle: Some evidence from seventeenth century Norfolk', in Richard M. Smith (ed.), *Land, Kinship and Life-Cycle* (Cambridge: Cambridge University Press, 1984), pp. 351–404; Steven King, *Poverty and Welfare in England 1700–1850: A regional perspective* (Manchester: Manchester University Press, 2000), p. 80; Henry French, 'How Dependent were the "Dependent Poor"? Poor relief and the life-course in Terling, Essex, 1752–1834', *Continuity and Change*, 30:2 (2015), p. 201; Richard Dyson, 'Who were the Poor of Oxford in the Late Eighteenth and Early Nineteenth Centuries?', in Andreas Gestrich, Steven King and Lutz Raphael (eds), *Being Poor in Modern Europe: Historical perspectives 1800–1940* (Bern: Peter Lang, 2006), pp. 54–6.

22 For instance, see: Samantha Williams, *Poverty, Gender and Life-Cycle under the English Poor Law 1760–1834* (Woodbridge: Boydell and Brewer, 2011), pp. 149–54; Richard Dyson, 'Welfare Provision in Oxford during the Latter Stages of the Old Poor Law, 1800–1834', *Historical Journal*, 52:4 (2009), pp. 943–62; Alannah Tomkins, *The*

Experience of Urban Poverty, 1723–82 (Manchester: Manchester University Press, 2006), pp. 79–119.

23 Samantha Shave, *Pauper Policies: Poor law practice in England, 1780–1850* (Manchester: Manchester University Press, 2017), pp. 150–96; Steve Hindle, *On the Parish? The micro-politics of poor relief in rural England c.1550–1750* (Oxford: Clarendon Press, 2004), pp. 361–449.

24 King, *Poverty and Welfare*.

25 This may mean that people in industrial areas could afford more consumer goods. Yet, on the other hand, Emma Griffin has argued that families in industrial districts were often worse off than agricultural labourers despite earning higher wages, since they tended to spend large proportions of their incomes on alcohol and other unnecessary things. Emma Griffin, *Bread Winner: An intimate history of the Victorian economy* (New Haven: Yale University Press, 2020).

26 Barry Stapleton, 'Inherited Poverty and Life-Cycle Poverty: Odiham, Hampshire, 1650–1850', *Social History*, 18:3 (1993), pp. 339–55.

27 For example, see the autobiographies of John Brown, *Sixty Years' Gleanings from Life's Harvests: A Genuine Autobiography* (Cambridge: J. Palmer, 1858); James Lackington, *Memoirs of the First Forty-Five Years of the Life of James Lackington* (London: self-published, 1792); David Whitehead, *The Autobiography of David Whitehead of Rawtenstall (1790–1865): Cotton spinner and merchant*, ed. Stanley Chapman (Helmshore: Helmshore Local History Society, 2001).

28 Tawny Paul, *The Poverty of Disaster: Debt and insecurity in eighteenth-century Britain* (Cambridge: Cambridge University Press, 2019).

29 Griffin, *Liberty's Dawn*; Jason Long, 'The Surprising Social Mobility of Victorian Britain', *European Review of Economic History*, 17:1 (2013), pp. 1–23.

30 Sara Horrell and Jane Humphries, 'Old Questions, New Data, and Alternative Perspectives: Families' living standards in the industrial revolution', *Journal of Economic History*, 52:4 (1992), pp. 849–80; Sara Horrell, 'Home Demand and British Industrialization', *Journal of Economic History*, 56:3 (1996), pp. 561–604; Charles H. Feinstein, 'Pessimism Perpetuated: Real wages and the standard of living in Britain during and after the industrial revolution', *Journal of Economic History*, 58:3 (1998), pp. 625–58.

31 Steven King and Alannah Tomkins, *The Poor in England 1700–1850: An economy of makeshifts* (Manchester: Manchester University Press, 2003).

32 Gertrude Jekyll, *Old West Surrey: Some notes and memories* (London: Longmans, Green and Co., 1904), pp. 101–7; William Cobbett, *Cottage Economy* (London: self-published, 3rd edn, 1826), pp. 193–7.

33 For example, Tim Wales, 'Poverty, Poor Relief', pp. 351–404; Williams, *Poverty, Gender*, pp. 101–30; Steven King, *Writing the Lives of the English Poor, 1750s–1830s* (London: McGill-Queen's University Press, 2019), pp. 282–308.

34 Of course, there are exceptions. For example, studies on household budgets have considered how household incomes and outgoings differed according to gender, family size and other factors. Horrell and Humphries, 'Old Questions', pp. 849–80; Horrell, 'Home Demand', pp. 561–604; Sara Horrell, Jane Humphries and Jacob Weisdorf, 'Beyond the Male Breadwinner: Life-cycle living standards of intact and disrupted English working families, 1260–1850', *Economic History Review*, 75:2 (2022), pp. 530–60.

35 B. Seebohm Rowntree, *Poverty: A study of town life* (London: Macmillan and Co., 3rd edn, 1902).

36 Exceptions to this are rare. Three of the most notable are: Elizabeth W. Gilboy, 'Demand as a Factor in the Industrial Revolution' (originally published in 1932), in R. M. Hartwell (ed.), *The Causes of the Industrial Revolution* (London: Routledge, 1967), pp. 121–38; D. E. C. Eversley, 'The Home Market and Economic Growth in England, 1750–1780', in E. L. Jones and G. E. Mingay (eds), *Land, Labour and Population in the Industrial Revolution: Essays presented to J. D. Chambers* (London: Edward Arnold, 1967), pp. 206–59; E. L. Jones, 'The Fashion Manipulators: Consumer

tastes and British industries, 1660–1800', in L. P. Cain and P. J. Uselding (eds), *Business Enterprise and Economic Change: Essays in honour of Harold F. Williamson* (Kent: Kent State University Press, 1973), pp. 198–226.

37 Joel Mokyr, 'Demand vs. Supply in the Industrial Revolution', *Journal of Economic History*, 37 (1977), pp. 981–1008.

38 Jan de Vries, *The Industrious Revolution: Consumer behaviour and the household economy 1650 to present* (Cambridge: Cambridge University Press, 2008). De Vries's 'industrious revolution' theory will not be used here to conceptualise the poor's consumer behaviour. This is because a central part of his theory revolves around changes to people's working patterns, which is not a central component of this book. I have also argued elsewhere that aspects of the concept do not hold up to empirical evidence. See: Joseph Harley, 'Domestic Production and Consumption in English Pauper Households, 1670–1840', *Agricultural History Review*, 69:1 (2021), pp. 25–49.

39 Sara Horrell, 'Consumption, 1700–1870', in Roderick Floud, Jane Humphries and Paul Johnson (eds), *The Cambridge Economic History of Modern Britain*, Vol. 1: *1700–1870* (Cambridge: Cambridge University Press, 2nd edn, 2014), p. 247.

40 Thorstein Veblen, *The Theory of the Leisure Class: An economic study of institutions* (New York: Macmillan, 1899); Georg Simmel, 'Fashion', *The International Quarterly*, 10 (1904), pp. 130–55; Pierre Bourdieu, *Distinction: A social critique of the judgement of taste* (London: Routledge, 1979).

41 For more nuanced studies which use these ideas, see: French, *Middle Sort*, pp. 147–53; Stena Nenadic, 'Middle-Rank Consumers and Domestic Culture in Edinburgh and Glasgow', *Past and Present*, 145 (1994), pp. 122–56; Jon Stobart, *Sugar and Spice: Grocers and groceries in provincial England, 1650–1830* (Oxford: Oxford University Press, 2013).

42 Most notably, see: Neil McKendrick, 'The Consumer Revolution of Eighteenth-Century England', in McKendrick, Brewer and Plumb, *Birth of a Consumer Society*, pp. 9–33.

43 Peter N. Stearns, *Consumerism in World History: The global transformation of desire* (London: Routledge, 2nd edn, 2001), p. 30.

44 Styles, *Dress*, pp. 247–302; Nicholls, *Almshouses*, pp. 138–87.

45 Dror Wahrman, *The Making of the Modern Self: Identity and culture in eighteenth century England* (New Haven: Yale University Press, 2004), p. xii.

46 Ian Woodward, *Understanding Material Culture* (London: Sage, 2007), p. 137.

47 Some, such as Cohen, *Household Gods*, esp. pp. 122–44, have argued that self-expression and the personalisation of homes was not a feature of domestic life until the late Victorian period (at least among the middle classes). In contrast, this book argues that even the poorest had some agency in what they acquired and how they furnished their abodes, particularly from the closing decades of the eighteenth century.

48 Rob Boddice, *The History of Emotions* (Manchester: Manchester University Press, 2018); Rob Boddice, *A History of Feelings* (London: Reaktion Books, 2019); Jan Plamper, *The History of Emotions: An introduction*, trans. Keith Tribe (Oxford: Oxford University Press, 2015). On emotion, objects and spaces, see: Gerhard Jaritz (ed.), *Emotions and Material Culture* (Vienna: Verlag der Österreichischen Akademie der Wissenschaften, 2003); John Styles, *Threads of Feeling: The London foundling hospital's textile tokens, 1740–1770* (London: The Foundling Museum, 2010); Sarah Tarlow, 'The Archaeology of Emotion and Affect', *Annual Review of Anthropology*, 41 (2012), pp. 169–85; Anna Moran and Sorcha O'Brien (eds), *Love Objects: Emotion, design and material culture* (London: Bloomsbury, 2014); Susan Broomhall (ed.), *Emotions in the Household, 1200–1900* (Basingstoke: Palgrave, 2008); Susan Broomhall (ed.), *Spaces for Feeling: Emotions and sociabilities in Britain, 1650–1850* (London: Routledge, 2015); Stephanie Downes, Sally Holloway and Sarah Randles

(eds), *Feeling Things: Objects and emotions through history* (Oxford: Oxford University Press, 2018); Sally Holloway, *The Game of Love in Georgian England: Courtship, emotions and material culture* (Oxford: Oxford University Press, 2019); Sarah Randles, 'The Material World', in Katie Barclay, Sharon Crozier-De Rosa and Peter N. Stearns (eds), *Sources for the History of Emotions: A guide* (London: Routledge, 2020), pp. 159–71.

49 Rob Boddice and Mark Smith, *Emotion, Sense, Experience* (Cambridge: Cambridge University Press, 2020); Boddice, *History of Emotions*, pp. 132–67; Joanne Begiato, 'Moving Objects: Emotional transformation, tangibility, and time-travel', in Downes, Holloway and Randles, *Feeling Things*, pp. 229–42; Joanne Begiato, 'Selfhood and "Nostalgia": Sensory and material memories of the childhood home in late Georgian Britain', *Journal of Eighteenth-Century Studies*, 42:2 (2019), pp. 229–46. For an introduction to the burgeoning literature on the senses, see: Mark M. Smith, *Sensory History* (Oxford: Berg, 2007); William Tullett, 'State of the Field: Sensory history', *History*, 106:373 (2021), pp. 804–20.

50 John E. Crowley, *The Invention of Comfort: Sensibilities and design in early modern Britain and early America* (Baltimore: Johns Hopkins University Press, 2001); Elizabeth Shove, 'Comfort and Convenience: Temporality and practice', in Trentmann, *Oxford Handbook*, p. 290; Jon Stobart (ed.), *The Comforts of Home in Western Europe, 1700–1900* (London: Bloomsbury, 2020).

51 Sasha Handley, *Sleep in Early Modern England* (New Haven: Yale University Press, 2016).

52 Thomas Sokoll (ed.), *Essex Pauper Letters, 1731–1837* (Oxford: Oxford University Press/British Academy, 2001), pp. 390, 410. My italics.

53 Ibid., pp. 617–8.

54 Woodruff D. Smith, *Consumption and the Making of Respectability, 1600–1800* (London: Routledge, 2002), pp. 189–204.

55 Geoffrey Crossick, 'The Labour Aristocracy and Its Values: A study of mid-Victorian Kentish London', *Victorian Studies*, 19:3 (1976), pp. 301–28; Robert Gray, *The Aristocracy of Labour in Nineteenth-Century Britain, 1850–1914* (London: Macmillan Press, 1981).

56 F. M. L. Thompson, *The Rise of Respectable Society: A social history of Victorian Britain 1830–1900* (Cambridge: Harvard University Press, 1988); Jennifer Davis, 'Jennings' Buildings and the Royal Borough: The construction of the underclass in mid-Victorian England', in David Feldman and Gareth Stedman Jones (eds), *Metropolis London: Histories and representations since 1800* (London: Routledge, 1989), pp. 11–39; Lynn MacKay, *Respectability and the London Poor, 1780–1870* (London: Pickering & Chatto, 2013); Patrick Joyce, *Visions of the People: Industrial England and the question of class, 1848–1914* (Cambridge: Cambridge University Press, 1991), p. 338.

57 Smith, *Making of Respectability*, pp. 195–6; Thompson, *Respectable Society*, pp. 353–4; Joyce, *Visions*, pp. 272, 338.

58 Sokoll, *Pauper Letters*, pp. 577–8.

59 This is similar to but distinct from Jan de Vries's ideas of 'social comfort', whereby people used consumption to mark and defend their social position. De Vries, *Industrious Revolution*, p. 22; Stobart, *Sugar and Spice*, pp. 271–5. Also see: Cohen, *Domestic Gods*.

60 Smith, *Making of Respectability*, p. 24.

61 However, there has been some work on the connection between the poor's clothing and respectability. Vivienne Richmond, *Clothing the Poor in Nineteenth-Century England* (Cambridge: Cambridge University Press, 2013), pp. 121–60.

62 Crowley, *Invention of Comfort*, p. 151.

63 Ibid., pp. 151–2; Shove, 'Comfort and Convenience', pp. 279–303; Oxford English Dictionary Online (www.oed.com).

64 Norman J. G. Pounds, *Hearth and Home: A history of material culture* (Bloomington: Indiana University Press, 1989), p. 198. On the development of the term, see: Patricia Meyer Spacks, *Privacy: Concealing the eighteenth century* (Chicago: Chicago University Press, 2003), pp. 1–26; Amanda Vickery, 'An Englishman's Home is his Castle? Thresholds, boundaries and privacies in the eighteenth-century London house', *Past and Present*, 199 (2009), pp. 147–73; David Vincent, *Privacy: A short history* (Cambridge: Polity Press, 2016); Oxford English Dictionary Online (www.oed.com).

65 MacKay, *Respectability*, pp. 22–3; Vickery, 'Englishman's Home', p. 173.

66 Vincent, *Privacy*, pp. 2–3.

67 Richard Gooch, *Memoirs, Remarkable Vicissitudes … of Cassiel, The Norfolk Astrologer* (Norwich: Benjamin Norman, 1852), p. 23. My italics.

68 John MacDonald, *Travels in Various Parts of Europe, Asia, and Africa, during a Series of Thirty Years and Upwards* (London: self-published, 1790), p. 50.

69 Lackington, *Memoirs*, p. 139.

70 Beverly Lemire, *The Business of Everyday Life: Gender, practice and social politics in England, c.1600–1900* (Manchester: Manchester University Press, 2005), pp. 82–109.

71 Such as: Lemire, *Business*, pp. 82–109; Styles, *Dress*; Richmond, *Clothing*, pp. 72–92; Alison Toplis, *The Clothing Trade in Provincial England, 1800–1850* (London: Pickering & Chatto, 2011), passim.

72 See, for instance, Sara Pennell, 'Material Culture in Seventeenth-Century "Britain": The matter of domestic consumption', in Trentmann, *Oxford Handbook*, p. 64; Janine Maegraith and Craig Muldrew, 'Consumption and Material Life', in Hamish Scott (ed.), *The Oxford Handbook of Early Modern European History, 1350–1750*, Vol. 1: *Peoples and Place* (Oxford: Oxford University Press, 2015), pp. 369–97; de Vries, *Industrious Revolution*, pp. 149–50.

73 Weatherill, *Consumer Behaviour*, p. 194; Pounds, *Hearth and Home*, p. 184; Overton et al., *Production and Consumption*, p. 170.

74 Tim Hitchcock, *Down and Out in Eighteenth-Century London* (London: Hambledon & London, 2004), p. 239.

75 Robert W. Malcolmson, *Life and Labour in England 1700–1780* (London: Hutchinson, 1981), p. 149; Thompson, *Making*, p. 351.

76 Researchers' use of the sources is discussed in Joseph Harley (ed.), *Norfolk Pauper Inventories, c.1690–1834* (Oxford: British Academy/Oxford University Press, 2020), pp. 1–9, 26–31.

77 For further information on these various inventories, see: Harley, *Norfolk Pauper Inventories*, pp. 26–31; Joseph Harley, 'Pauper Inventories, Social Relations, and the Nature of Poor Relief under the Old Poor Law, England, c.1601–1834', *Historical Journal*, 62:2 (2019), pp. 375–98; Joseph Harley, 'Material Lives of the English Poor: A regional perspective, c.1670–1834', PhD thesis (University of Leicester, 2016), pp. 33–5, 68–72; Harley, 'Material Lives of the Poor and their Strategic Use of the Workhouse', pp. 71–103.

78 I have critiqued the making of pauper inventories in detail in Harley, *Norfolk Pauper Inventories*; Harley, 'Pauper Inventories, Social Relations', pp. 375–98; Harley, 'Material Lives of the English Poor: A regional perspective', pp. 32–72. Here, I will only outline the most pertinent points.

79 Most studies on inventories tend to select no more than 30 items to analyse. Moreover, most focus on luxury and novel items, instead of basics such as furniture and fire irons. See, for instance, Weatherill, *Consumer Behaviour*; French, *Middle Sort*; David Hussey and Margaret Ponsonby, *The Single Homemaker and Material Culture in the Long Eighteenth Century* (Abingdon: Ashgate, 2012).

80 Muldrew, *Food*, pp. 172–3; Weatherill, *Consumer Behaviour*, p. 168; Sear and Sneath, *Consumer Revolution*, pp. 246, 262–3, 288.

81 For further information on the representativeness of pauper inventories, see: Chapter 2; Harley, *Norfolk Pauper Inventories*, pp. 47–53, 63–5; Harley, 'Consumption and Poverty', pp. 81–104; Harley, 'Pauper Inventories, Social Relations', pp. 375–98.

82 Differing survival rates of inventories largely stem from regional differences in poor relief. Harley, 'Pauper Inventories, Social Relations', pp. 375–98.

83 More specifically, the autobiographies and diaries number 112 and the pauper letters number approximately 1,500. The autobiographies and diaries used here are referenced in the bibliography. Most of the pauper letters are transcribed in Sokoll, *Pauper Letters*; Steven King, Thomas Nutt and Alannah Tomkins (eds), *Narratives of the Poor in Eighteenth-Century Britain*, Vol. 1: *Voices of the Poor: Poor law depositions and letters* (London: Pickering & Chatto, 2006); Peter Jones and Steven King, *Navigating the Old English Poor Law: The Kirkby Lonsdale letters, 1809–1836* (Oxford: British Academy/Oxford University Press, 2020). The majority of third-party accounts of the poor were made by the parson Richard Cobbold, who wrote about and painted the pictures of some 120 people in his home village of Wortham in Suffolk. Around a further 400 people are also mentioned incidentally in his accounts. SA HD 1025/1–2; SA HA 42/1–2; SA HD 1888/1; SA HD 368/1; SA HA 11/A13/10. For further context on Cobbold's records, see: David Dymond (ed.), *Parson and People in a Suffolk Village: Richard Cobbold's Wortham, 1824–77* (Ipswich: Wortham Research Group/Suffolk Family History Society, 2007); Ronald Fletcher (ed.), *The Biography of a Victorian Village: Richard Cobbold's account of Wortham, Suffolk* (London: B. T. Batsford Ltd, 1977).

84 Such as: Jonathan Rose, *The Intellectual Life of the British Working Classes* (New Haven: Yale University Press, 2nd edn, 2010).

85 The pros and cons of these narratives are discussed further in: Sokoll, *Pauper Letters*; King, Nutt and Tomkins, *Narratives of the Poor*, Vol. 1; King, *Writing the Lives*; John Burnett, David Vincent and David Mayall, *The Autobiography of the Working Class: An annotated critical bibliography*, Vol. 1: *1790–1900* (Brighton: Harvester, 1984); Griffin, *Liberty's Dawn*, pp. 5–10; Griffin, *Bread Winner*, pp. 8–23; Dymond, *Parson*.

86 For example, at times overseers would visit paupers who wrote letters to check their circumstances or ask officials from other parishes to do this. The publishers of autobiographies would sometimes ask people who knew the writers to check and verify their stories.

87 For an accessible introduction to the subject, see: Karen Harvey (ed.), *History and Material Culture: A student's guide to approaching alternative sources* (London: Routledge, 2009); Anne Gerritsen and Giorgio Riello (eds), *Writing Material Culture History* (London: Bloomsbury, 2015); Leonie Hannan and Sarah Longair, *History through Material Culture* (Manchester: Manchester University Press, 2017); Joseph Harley and Vicky Holmes, *Objects of Poverty: Material Culture in Britain from 1700* (London: Bloomsbury, forthcoming).

88 Exceptions to this include: Alastair Owens, Nigel Jeffries, Karen Wehner and Rupert Featherby, 'Fragments of the Modern City: Material culture and the rhythms of everyday life in Victorian London', *Journal of Victorian Culture*, 15:2 (2010), pp. 212–25; Jennine Hurl-Eamon, 'Love Tokens: Objects as memory for plebeian women in early modern England', *Early Modern Women: An Interdisciplinary Journal*, 6 (2011), pp. 181–6; V. A. Crewe and D. M. Hadley, '"Uncle Tom was there, in crockery": Material culture and a Victorian working-class childhood', *Childhood in the Past*, 6:2 (2013), pp. 89–105; Styles, *Threads of Feeling*; Styles, *Dress*; Styles, 'Objects of Emotion: The London Foundling Hospital Tokens, 1741–60', in Gerritsen and Riello, *Writing Material Culture*, pp. 165–71; Sally Holloway, 'Materializing Maternal Emotions: Birth, celebration, and renunciation in England, c.1688–1830', in Downes, Holloway and Randles, *Feeling Things*, pp. 154–71.

89 On using objects located from various collections, see: Hannan and Longair, *History through Material Culture*, pp. 95–120.

90 Cohen, *Household Gods*, p. xv.

91 Christiana Payne, 'Rural Virtues for Urban Consumption: Cottage scenes in early Victorian painting', *Journal of Victorian Culture*, 3:1 (1998), pp. 45–68; Tom Nichols, 'Motives of Control/Motifs of Creativity: The visual imagery of poverty in early modern Europe', in Hitchcock and McClure, *Routledge History*, pp. 138–63.

92 For contrasting views, see: John Barrell, *The Dark Side of the Landscape: The rural poor in English painting 1730–1840* (Cambridge: Cambridge University Press, 1992), pp. 89–129; K. D. M. Snell, 'In or Out of Their Place: The migrant poor in English art, 1740–1900', *Rural History*, 24:1 (2013), pp. 73–100; Diane Perkins, 'Morland, George (1763–1804)', *ODNB* (Oxford, 2004) (from: www.oxforddnb.com/view/article/19278, accessed 07/11/2014).

93 SA HD 1025/1–2; SA HA 42/1–2; SA HD 1888/1; SA HD 368/1; SA HA 11/A13/10; Dymond, *Parson*; Fletcher, *Biography*.

94 SA HD 368/1; SA HA 11/A13/10; SA HA 42/2. This building was called 'Ranter's Chapel'.

95 SA HD 368/1.

96 K. D. M. Snell, *Annals of the Labouring Poor: Social change and agrarian England, 1660–1900* (Cambridge: Cambridge University Press, 1985); J. L. Hammond and Barbara Hammond, *The Village Labourer*, ed. G. E. Mingay (London: Longman Group, reprint of 1911 edn, 1978); J. M. Neeson, *Commoners: Common right, enclosure and social change in England, 1700–1820* (Cambridge: Cambridge University Press, 1993); Jane Humphries, 'Enclosure, Common Rights, and Women: The proletarianization of families in the late eighteenth and early nineteenth centuries', *Journal of Economic History*, 50:1 (1990), pp. 17–42.

97 Regional dynamics of the eighteenth- and nineteenth-century textile industry are summarised in: Steven King and Geoffrey Timmins, *Making Sense of the Industrial Revolution: English economy and society 1700–1850* (Manchester: Manchester University Press, 2001), pp. 33–66.

98 E. A. Wrigley, 'A Simple Model of London's Importance in Changing English Society and Economy 1650–1750', *Past and Present*, 37 (1967), pp. 44–70; Overton et al., *Production and Consumption*; Weatherill, *Consumer Behaviour*, pp. 43–69; Lena Cowen Orlin (ed.), *Material London, ca. 1600* (Philadelphia: University of Pennsylvania Press, 2000); H. C. Mui and L. H. Mui, *Shops and Shopkeeping in Eighteenth-Century England* (London: Routledge, 1989); John Styles, 'Product Innovation in Early Modern London', *Past and Present*, 168 (2000), pp. 124–69; Danae Tankard, *Clothing in 17th-Century Provincial England* (London: Bloomsbury, 2020), pp. 73–98.

99 Snell, *Annals*, pp. 411–17; E. H. Hunt, 'Industrialization and Regional Inequality: Wages in Britain, 1760–1914', *Journal of Economic History*, 46:4 (1986), pp. 965–6.

100 Alan Dyer, 'Small Market Towns 1540–1700', in Peter Clark (ed.) *The Cambridge Urban History of Britain*, Vol. 2: *1540–1840* (Cambridge: Cambridge University Press, 2000), pp. 433–4.

1

Accommodating the poor

We have a much clearer picture of what the homes of the middling sort and the elite looked like compared with those of the poor. This is largely a result of there being many more sources through which to study these groups, such as surviving buildings and hundreds of thousands of probate inventories in archives.[1] Through the detailed study of poor homes in pauper inventories and the parson Richard Cobbold's descriptions and paintings of the buildings in his village of Wortham in Suffolk, this chapter helps to correct this imbalance.[2] It is argued that, largely as expected, the homes of the poor tended to be smaller than those of the wealthy and much more crowded. While some rooms were specialised according to function and people took pride in their dwellings, space was at a premium and so families would use the same rooms for a range of purposes, such as sleep, work and cooking.

The first half of this chapter focuses on pauper inventories which note rooms, and the second part considers contemporary writings and paintings. Inventories are powerful sources for studying rooms and household layout, as they offer the historian a systematic way of enumerating the number and types of rooms that people had. Moreover, by exploring the items found in these spaces – from cooking utensils to seating to fire irons and beds – one can infer how the rooms were used by householders and just how busy and cramped the spaces might have been. This allows us to get closer to the reality of how the homes of the poor functioned and were organised. The results will also occasionally be split into urban and rural samples (as defined in Chapter 7) where noticeable differences are found, but in general the results are remarkably similar whether the paupers lived in town or country.

Pauper inventories have limitations which must be kept in mind. Rooms are recorded in only 190 of the 645 pauper inventories. Of these, I have excluded 20 where rooms are noted only in passing, leaving a core

At home with the poor

sample of 170. The remaining inventories are distributed along unequal geographical lines. Most were made in Essex (91), while only eight and ten could be found for Dorset and Leicestershire/Rutland respectively. This means that regional comparisons are largely not undertaken here. Likewise, most of the inventories which record rooms were made in rural spaces (107) while only 47 could be categorised as urban, which again makes comparisons across locations challenging. The sizes and shapes of rooms and buildings are noted by appraisers, as are fixtures such as windows and doors and the building materials of abodes. This means that beyond impressionistic accounts, it is very difficult to uncover how insecure, damp and unsanitary dwellings were. Rooms could have been omitted from the inventories. Some spaces, especially passageways, might not have had goods in them and so were not worth naming by appraisers. Other rooms might have simply been forgotten about or merged with other spaces in the appraisers' notes. Householders could also have subdivided their abodes using makeshift partitions instead of walls, but only occasionally are these noted in sources.[3] The nomenclature for spaces can vary regionally. Indeed, the names of rooms in the inventories were ascribed by the appraisers and might not tally with the terms paupers used themselves.[4]

Number and size of rooms

Most of the indigent poor appear to have lived in two-roomed dwellings (26%), but almost as many inhabited a three- or four-roomed home (24% each) according to the pauper inventories (Table 1.1). Put another way, homes had an average of 3.3 rooms in them between 1670 and 1769, increasing to 3.5 for 1770–1835 (Table 1.2). A similar average of

Table 1.1 Average number of rooms in pauper homes, over time, 1670–1835

	1670–1769 (%)	1770–1835 (%)	All (%)
One-roomed home	3	8	5
Two-roomed home	28	25	26
Three-roomed home	29	21	24
Four-roomed home	24	24	24
Five-roomed home	9	12	11
Six-roomed home	5	5	6
Seven-roomed home or larger	1	5	4
Sample size	75	92	170

Accommodating the poor 33

Table 1.2 Average number of rooms in pauper homes, by county, 1670–1835

	1670–1769	1770–1835	All
Dorset (n=8)	2.8	4.3	3.4
Essex (n=91)	3.5	3.5	3.6
Kent (n=22)	3.9	4.6	4.3
Leics/Ruts (n=10)	7*	2.8	3.2
Norfolk (n=39)	2.7	2.8	2.7
All (n=170)	3.3	3.5	3.5
Sample size	75	92	170

*Only one inventory

3.7 rooms per abode can be seen in the 50 bastardy, debt, goods-given, rent and goods-taken inventories of paupers' goods which note rooms. Single-roomed dwellings feature in only 5 per cent of inventories, but they are undoubtedly under-represented in the results, as appraisers did not need to differentiate and name spaces in one-roomed abodes. At the other end of the scale, around one in ten and one in twenty inventories note five- and six-roomed homes, while homes with seven rooms or more are found in only six of the 170 pauper inventories. The two largest homes in the sample contained nine rooms. The overall number of people living in homes with five or more rooms appears to have slightly increased over time, while the number living in two- and three-roomed homes slightly declined (Table 1.1). However, the results overall indicate that most homes contained relatively few rooms across the period. The same trends can be seen in both urban and rural spaces: on average, rural homes had 3.3 rooms, whereas urban abodes had slightly more at 3.7 rooms.

Although it is difficult to draw definitive conclusions based on the small sample size, the poor in some counties appear to have experienced a relatively significant increase in room numbers, indicating that either homes got larger or existing rooms were sub-divided into additional spaces. In Kent and Dorset, house size increased from 3.9 and 2.8 to 4.6 and 4.3 rooms between 1670–1769 and 1770–1835 respectively (Table 1.2). It is possible that pauper abodes were smaller in Norfolk, Leicestershire and Rutland, as the inventories averaged 2.8 rooms per inventory post 1770. Compared with probate inventories, which mostly record rooms in middling abodes, pauper homes were relatively small. In Norwich, for instance, around 82 per cent of the middling sort lived in a house with four or more rooms between 1705 and 1730.[5] Similarly, the median number of rooms for 1720–49 was six and seven in Cornwall and Kent respectively.[6]

Room use

The names given to spaces could be highly divergent. Indeed, appraisers noted nearly 50 different room names in total. Nevertheless, of the 587 rooms recorded in the core sample of 170 pauper inventories, chambers were by far the most common (Table 1.3). The term was rarely coupled with adjectives such as 'bed' and 'sitting', and in most cases chambers were described according to their position or number in the house, such as 'chamber over kitchen' or '1st chamber'. Butteries, kitchens, parlours and dwelling rooms/houses also appear fairly regularly in the inventories. Most of the terms for rooms were used consistently throughout the long eighteenth century, but for some there were significant changes. Halls, for instance, fell out of use. The last pauper inventory to use the term was dated 1759, while for the 1670s–1750s halls were present in 37 per cent of sources. Butteries declined from 41 to 33 per cent between 1670–1769 and 1770–1835, while the term 'pantry' went from being unused to being used in 11 per cent of inventories between the same dates. This might suggest that there was a linguistic change in how some people described storage spaces. Generally, only the largest homes had more specialised service rooms and outbuildings such as brewhouses, washhouses, cellars, dairies and stables. Focusing on the two most common, brewhouses and washhouses, the average size of homes with either of these spaces was 5.3 and 5 rooms respectively. Drawing rooms and dining rooms are entirely absent in the sample.

It is clear that many rooms were spread across two floors by the late seventeenth century, as the terms 'upstairs' or rooms 'over' another appear in around one in five sources. It is probable that most householders accessed different floors by stairs, as ladders are noted in only 1 per cent of pauper inventories and most are listed alongside tools so were probably used for home maintenance. Around 14 per cent of the inventories note a 'yard', 'garden' or similar and 42 per cent include horticultural tools such as spades and sickles, suggesting that most people had an outside space of some kind. With enclosures taking place across large areas of the country in the long eighteenth century, most external areas probably took the form of some sort of garden adjacent to the home or an allotment close by.[7]

We now turn to studying the items found in rooms to ascertain their use. Seven categories are employed here: cooking, eating/drinking, heating, lighting, sitting, sleeping and working. The final category includes items associated with making products such as beer, bread and textiles but excludes goods related to general cooking and domestic chores such as washing, cleaning and ironing.[8] Measuring room use by looking at the goods located in rooms is, of course, problematic. Items such as candlesticks and lanterns, which are used to measure lighting, were

Table 1.3 Total number and percentage of pauper inventories which note particular rooms, 1670–1835 (extract)

	Number of rooms	Percentage of pauper inventories
Chamber	166	78
Buttery	68	37
Kitchen	59	35
Parlour	40	23
Dwelling room/house	34	20
Hall	21	12
Unnamed room	22	11
House	18	11
Low room	15	9
Brewhouse	13	8
Keeping room/chamber	12	7
Washhouse	12	7
Bedroom	10	6
Pantry	10	5
Shop	9	5
Closet	6	4
Cellar	5	3
Barn	4	2
Lodging room	4	2
Outhouse	3	2
Dairy	2	1
Fire room	2	1
Garret	2	1
Stable	2	1
Baking office	1	1
Cow house	1	1
Milkhouse	1	1
Scullery	1	1
Slaughterhouse	1	1
Woodhouse	1	1
Workshop	1	1

At home with the poor

transient and so moved between spaces depending on where people were and what time of day it was. Despite this, from this approach it is clear that most rooms in pauper abodes had multiple functions and were busy spaces. Being able to divide dwellings according to functions was an aim of many people, as can be seen with Francis Place and his wife, who after moving house remarked that 'for the first time' they 'enjoyed a truly comfortable residence in which we had rooms enough intirely to separate our domestic concerns, and get rid of the many inconveniences which had hitherto annoyed us'.[9] However, only occasionally were the poor able to achieve this.

Chambers

Chambers are by far the most common rooms in pauper inventories, being noted in 78 per cent of sources. Around one-fifth of the inventories record two chambers or more, but most homes only had one chamber. It is clear that some, perhaps most, chambers were located on the second floor, as they are often described as 'over' another room.[10] While in middling homes a growing number of houses had 'great' or 'best' chambers,[11] only four chambers in the pauper inventories are described along these lines. Despite the term 'chamber' being vague and a synonym for 'room', their purposes were remarkably consistent across the long eighteenth century. In most cases chambers functioned as a place for sleep, as 88 per cent contained beds or cradles (Table 1.4). Seating was also common, suggesting that comfort and rest were central functions of chambers. However, there is a limit to how far one can take these arguments. Most chambers appear to have had no form of heating, and artificial lighting was placed elsewhere, at least at the time of the inventory being

Table 1.4 Functions of chambers in pauper homes, 1670–1835

	1670–1769	1770–1835	All
Cooking (%)	13	8	10
Eating/drinking (%)	6	15	11
Heating (%)	5	8	7
Lighting (%)	3	6	5
Sitting (%)	56	53	54
Sleeping (%)	86	89	88
Working (any) (%)	24	30	27
Average number of activities (out of seven categories)	1.9	2.1	2

taken. Around 10 per cent also contained spinning wheels, and a similar percentage had woodworking or agricultural tools in them. In most cases the tools had probably been brought into the space for storage, but it does indicate that some goods and activities infiltrated and obscured the functions of chambers.

Halls

In wealthier abodes the hall was traditionally the largest and most important room of the home, accommodating varied activities such as sleep, work and dining. As the early modern period progressed, halls became less common as people increasingly divided them into separate rooms and newer buildings were made with more self-contained spaces.[12] The living quarters of the poor appear to have gone through a similar transition. Halls gradually feature less regularly in the pauper inventories and are entirely absent from the sample after 1759. Equally, in the 50 bastardy, debt, goods-given, rent and goods-taken inventories of paupers' goods which include rooms, the last hall noted in the sources is dated 1710.

Where present, halls were multifunctional spaces (Table 1.5). Around 90 per cent of halls had cooking equipment in them and at least 76 per cent contained a hearth. Once the meals were prepared, they would generally be eaten in the hall, as seating and tables as well as plates, cups and other vessels were almost universal in them. Work, such as baking and textile manufacture, appears to have regularly happened in this space, as 33 and 24 per cent of pauper inventories respectively note goods which relate to these activities. Halls might have also been a place of rest once meals were cooked and chores were completed. Most pauper homes contained just a single hearth and so the hall, with its fireplace and seating, was naturally a magnet for people who wanted to stay warm and relax.[13] Sleeping goods

Table 1.5 Functions of halls in pauper homes, 1670–1759

	1670–1759
Cooking (%)	90
Eating/drinking (%)	81
Heating (%)	76
Lighting (%)	48
Sitting (%)	100
Sleeping (%)	19
Working (any) (%)	52
Average number of activities (out of seven categories)	4.7

were found in 19 per cent of halls, but in three-quarters of cases the sleeping item was a cradle. Thus, most halls were only sleeping rooms in as much as they functioned as nurseries or accommodated snoozing infants while their parents went about their days.

Kitchens

Between the 1670s and 1710s, kitchens were entirely absent in pauper homes. After this date, 39 per cent of pauper inventories record a kitchen. This suggests that while halls declined over the early modern period, kitchens became more common.[14] The same can also be said of 'houses' and 'dwelling rooms/houses', which appear to have been used to denote a kitchen in Leicestershire/Rutland and Essex,[15] as they were not noted in the inventories until the c.1740s and 1759 respectively. Kitchens could also be referred to as low rooms, backrooms and fire chambers/houses, but these terms were used much less frequently (Table 1.3).[16]

Kitchens were a hub of activity (Table 1.6). As expected, food preparation was common, as 83 per cent of kitchens noted cooking utensils in them. According to the figures, there was a decline in cooking goods in kitchens over the long eighteenth century. This probably happened as over time these items were increasingly stored in pantries or butteries. Kitchens were spaces of domestic work. Around a third of kitchens included baking items. The making of butter and cheese was not widespread in pauper homes but where present it tended to be in kitchens.[17] Textile-making goods (usually spinning wheels) appear in around one in five kitchens, indicating that as meals were bubbling away many women would spin thread. Some kitchens contained agricultural tools. Outside spaces such

Table 1.6 Functions of kitchens in pauper homes, 1670–1835

	1670–1769	1770–1835	All
Cooking (%)	93	75	83
Eating/drinking (%)	70	75	73
Heating (%)	81	75	78
Lighting (%)	44	50	47
Sitting (%)	89	88	88
Sleeping (%)	19	16	17
Working (any) (%)	56	59	58
Average number of activities (out of seven categories)	4.5	4.4	4.4

Accommodating the poor

as outhouses and sheds are rarely noted in the inventories (Table 1.3) and with kitchens generally being situated downstairs with external doors, they were a convenient place to store tools.[18]

Meals were generally eaten in the kitchen, as tables, chairs and various eating and drinking utensils regularly feature in the space. This seating would have also been helpful for the women who cooked and engaged in domestic work, as these processes could be long and arduous. While the kitchens of most paupers were areas of labour, they could function as a living room and a place for congregating and socialising, as they were the most common location of the hearth and seating was almost universal there. The rooms might have been sub-divided, with cooking taking place on one side and rest and dining on another.[19] Kitchens were sometimes used for sleep, as 17 per cent of them contained items to this effect. Where present, these items were beds and not cradles, indicating that it was adults or older children who predominantly used kitchens for slumber, rather than young infants who slept while their mother worked. The majority of sleeping items were in kitchens in Norfolk. This is interesting, as in this county homes tended to be smaller and thus space was more constrained (Table 1.2).[20] When the inventories note single-roomed homes, the room was nearly always a kitchen or dwelling room/house. The kitchen, therefore, must have been a highly important space where people spent most of their time when at home, engaged in cooking and various chores, as well as resting after a day's work.

Parlours

During the 1500s, the parlours of the middling sort were multifunctional spaces used for a wide range of purposes. By the late seventeenth and early eighteenth centuries, they were rarely used for chores like cooking and work and most had shifted to being places of entertainment and dining.[21] In pauper homes, the use and incidence of parlours followed a different path. Parlours were the fourth most common room in poor dwellings; however, they appear to have declined over time. They are found in 35 per cent of the pauper inventories which note rooms between 1670 and 1769, but in only 12 per cent for 1770–1835. There was a movement towards comfort in the parlours of the poor, as indicated by the rise of hearths and seating and fall-off of working items (Table 1.7). Yet parlours continued to serve many purposes. Although the presence of beds and working goods declined, they still featured regularly in the space. As late as 1770–1835, working goods were found in 27 per cent of parlours and 73 per cent contained beds, denoting that there was simply not enough space for beds to be placed elsewhere. Thus, myriad activities often overflowed into parlours, making them multifunctional spaces.

At home with the poor

Table 1.7 Functions of parlours in pauper homes, 1670–1835

	1670–1730	1730–1769	1770–1835	All
Cooking (%)	14	25	18	20
Eating/drinking (%)	14	20	18	18
Heating (%)	0	0	45	13
Lighting (%)	0	15	0	8
Sitting (%)	57	65	82	68
Sleeping (%)	100	80	73	83
Working (any) (%)	57	55	27	45
Average number of activities (out of seven categories)	2.3	2.6	2.6	2.5

Table 1.8 Functions of pantries and butteries in pauper homes, 1670–1835

	1670–1769	1770–1835	All
Cooking (%)	65	74	68
Eating/drinking (%)	35	52	42
Heating (%)	0	2	1
Lighting (%)	3	5	4
Sitting (%)	19	21	19
Sleeping (%)	3	2	3
Working (any) (%)	61	76	68
Average number of activities (out of seven categories)	1.8	2.3	2.1

Pantries and butteries

Pantries and butteries were predictably more usual in larger homes. The average size of dwellings with one or both of these spaces was 4.4 rooms. In most instances, butteries and pantries were storage rooms, containing cooking, dining and working goods (Table 1.8). Pantries and butteries were one of the most common places in which to find working items such as kneading troughs and agricultural tools. Tubs for making and preserving foodstuffs also appeared frequently in them. This was probably because many were stored there while not in use or were placed there out of the way while beer was forming or meat was being salted. In each case the sleeping item in pantries and butteries was a cradle, suggesting that people did not sleep in there but used the space to store old cots when they were no longer needed. Similarly, it is unlikely that hearths were located in pantries or butteries, but rather the room accommodated spare fire irons that were no longer in use or were not needed to hand by the active hearth.

Frontstage and backstage activities

Identity is formed both by the individual and within social groups. As part of this, according to the sociologist Erving Goffman, people engage in 'impression management' along the dramaturgical lines of the 'frontstage' and 'backstage'. In the frontstage, people's 'public' profile is in full view and so they judiciously control their conduct and behaviour. Meanwhile, in backstage areas individuals revert to their 'private' selves. Away from the public gaze, there is no need to self-consciously act as they want others to see them.[22] This concept has been applied to the historical home with mixed results: that is, there is some debate as to whether people placed their finest items in frontstage areas of the home which received guests and less sought-after basic goods in backstage rooms.[23]

At a qualitative level, there is certainly evidence of paupers who might have acted along these lines. For example, in the 'Front Room' of the Dungays in Maidstone, Kent, there were elaborate items for receiving guests, including a 'Square Mahogany Dining Table & green cover' and '6. Ash. Rush bottom Chairs'. The room was further adorned with a '30hour Clock [with] Wainscot Case' and '6 small pictures' and was heated by a well-equipped fireplace. The Dungays were also tea drinkers, for in the room there were three tea tables, including '1. Wainscot Tea Table' and '1. Painted Roung [round] Deal Tea Table', a range of earthenware vessels, and '1 Japan [lacquered] Tea board & Tea Ware'.[24] Drinking tea in this well-furnished room with this extensive range of non-necessities would have been an experience that went beyond satisfying thirst. The Dungays appear to have wanted to present a certain respectable image of themselves and even engaged in a form of conspicuous consumption by hanging on to these markers of respectability. Elsewhere in the home, backstage activities appear to have taken place. There was a washhouse in the abode where washing and cooking was done, and beds, chairs, lighting and fire irons could be found upstairs.

The pauper inventories indicate that most people did not divide their goods into frontstage and backstage areas. The home was much more fluid than this. In fact, many of the items often associated with luxury or display were more likely to be found in functional rooms in which many activities took place than in spaces primarily devoted to receiving guests or entertainment, in both urban and rural spaces (Tables 1.9 and 1.10). Clocks, for instance, were commonly found in cooking spaces such as kitchens. Chambers, which were chiefly used for sleeping, were the most likely room to contain looking glasses, pictures and window curtains. Parlours, especially by the nineteenth century, have been portrayed as the main front-facing space in working-class abodes where many of these goods were located and where people showed their respectability and domesticity.[25] There is limited evidence for this in the period covered by this book.

A number of these coveted goods were found in spaces that had seating in them and where eating and drinking took place, which might account for their use in rooms that received guests. However, as noted above, the

Table 1.9 Types of rooms with various goods in them, 1670–1835

	Clock (%)	Looking glass (%)	Picture (%)	Tea items (%)	Window curtains (%)
Buttery	0	0	0	8	11
Chamber	0	30	20	6	39
Dwelling room/house	18	17	15	19	11
House	9	2	10	11	0
Keeping room	15	8	10	8	6
Kitchen	27	21	10	18	17
Low room	6	5	0	8	11
Parlour	6	3	10	2	0

Table 1.10 Functions of rooms with various goods in them, 1670–1835

	Clock (%)	Looking glass (%)	Picture (%)	Tea items (%)	Window curtains (%)
Cooking	67	54	35	75	39
Eating/ drinking	67	71	70	76	78
Heating	82	62	75	68	61
Lighting	48	40	55	47	39
Sitting	94	84	100	86	67
Sleeping	18	46	35	19	50
Working (any)	52	49	50	57	61

lines between rooms were clearly blurred and often these items appear to have been positioned in multifunctional spaces where they were most useful and convenient for homemakers. These spaces might have received visitors, but in general this was not their only purpose. Clocks were one of the most expensive items that paupers owned, yet they were most likely to be found in kitchens. Although many of these clocks were decorative and prestigious to own (Chapter 6), this suggests that impressing visitors was not their main function and that timing activities such as cooking was more important. By acquiring window curtains of a particular colour or pattern people could display their taste, but around half of the rooms with curtains had beds in them, indicating that their use in blocking light and preventing draughts was more important. Likewise, most looking glasses were found in chambers so were particularly useful in helping people to get dressed and check their appearances, rather than decorate the home. Tea became an important staple of the poor by the late eighteenth century and was customarily offered to guests (Chapter 5). Yet although tea might have been prepared in the kitchen and carried into another room, it is probable that at least some was consumed in busy cooking and working spaces, as these were often the main seating and resting areas.

Paintings and descriptions of buildings

Contemporaries almost universally claimed that the homes of the poor were of the lowest quality, being overcrowded, unsanitary, comfortless, insecure and vulnerable to the elements. The land valuer Nathaniel Kent, for instance, argued that labourers' 'shattered hovels' and 'miserable tenements' adversely affected their health and morals.[26] Thomas Davis, a steward, claimed that 'Humanity shudders at the idea of an industrious labourer ... being obliged to live, or rather to exist, in a wretched, damp, gloomy room ... without a floor',[27] while Benjamin Silliman went as far as to say that most homes in the south-west looked like they 'were constructed to shelter cattle [rather] than men'.[28] Historians too, often relying on interpretations like these, almost always paint the same picture.[29] Even the labouring sort could be critical of the abodes of their neighbours. Charles Whetstone called homes in the Peak District 'ancient *huts*', remarking that 'slaves in America enjoy better and more healthy accommodations' than families living in Sheffield.[30] Despite these views being by no means uncommon and repeated time after time, we must be wary of their veracity. A number of commentators were writing under the guise of promoting novel building plans and new ways of living.[31] Sometimes the accounts were written by journalists looking for a good story.[32] Others made these remarks to argue that the living conditions of labourers had declined as a result of industrialisation.[33] Without contextualising the abodes by finding out who lived there, it is difficult to ascertain just how representative these accounts are and the extent to which age, marital status, occupation and a host of other factors affected their experience of home.

The writings of Richard Cobbold are very different to these crude accounts and offer us a new way to address this well-trodden topic. As parson of Wortham village in Suffolk between 1824 and 1877, Cobbold painted the buildings in the parish and wrote descriptions of the people who lived there. He built up an encyclopaedic knowledge of everybody and claimed that there was only one building he had not been in. He did this as a hobby in his personal notes and not to promote an agenda.[34] Thus, by analysing his writings and paintings, and drawing on family reconstitution, we have a unique opportunity to test some of the conclusions drawn from the inventories and delve further into the buildings that labouring people occupied in a nineteenth-century rural parish.

The pauper inventories reveal that only around 4 per cent of paupers lived in abodes with seven rooms or more. Cobbold's paintings and writings similarly indicate that it was unusual for labouring people to occupy larger homes. When the poor did live in sizeable dwellings, it was generally the result of them enjoying some particularly prosperous years in earlier life but then falling on hard times as they grew older.[35] Benjamin Bobby, for instance, was a bricklayer who inherited his father-in-law's successful business and 'accumulated money'. However, in later life he became pauperised and committed suicide in 1857. His home was particularly large and included a yard and barn (Figure 1.1).[36] The building and barn still stand today. The barn is now a separate domestic space, but the main building includes two reception/sitting rooms, a kitchen, hall,

Figure 1.1 Green's Farm, the former home of Benjamin Bobby (b.1804, d.1857) and Susannah Bobby (b.1805–06, d.1858), painted by Richard Cobbold, 1860 (source: SA HD 1888/1; reproduced by kind permission of the owner)

pantry and six bedrooms spread across the ground, first and attic floors.[37] Although the functions of these rooms would have shifted in various ways over 150 years, the structure is considerable and largely the same as it was in Benjamin's time. This dwelling would have given Benjamin, his wife Susannah and their numerous children space and the opportunity to separate activities into different rooms.[38]

For the majority of people, living in a home the size of Benjamin Bobby's was beyond their means. Most inhabited much more humble surroundings. A number of these buildings, on the face of it, appear to have been reasonable structures that were probably sufficient for the needs of small families, and they were, in the words of Cobbold, often 'picturesque'.[39] An example of one of these buildings is the modest scenic abode of Madget's Cottage depicted in Figure 1.2. Inhabited by Cobbold's servant John Madget up until his death, by 1860 74-year-old bricklayer Robert Harbour and his wife and 'neat cheerful tidy daughter' lived in the building. Harbour was described as very industrious, yet he must have had difficulties in his final years as he suffered a fall, rendering him able to walk only with crutches.[40] However, since the family was small and Madget's Cottage did not appear to have a second floor beyond the attic, he would have been able to move around with relative ease.

Space must have been sparse for most large families. Figure 1.3 portrays Buck's Cottage, which would probably have been fine for a few people but cramped with several more. In 1851, it was occupied by John and Harriet Buck and their four children, as well as Harriet's 83-year-old mother Sarah Scott. Those who were of working age were agricultural labourers and Scott was a pauper. By 1860, four adults and three children

Figure 1.2 Madget's Cottage, the home of Richard Harbour (b.1786, d.1864) and Susan Harbour (b.1791, d.1873), painted by Richard Cobbold, 1860 (source: SA HD 1888/1; reproduced by kind permission of the owner)

Figure 1.3 Buck's Cottage, painted by Richard Cobbold, 1860 (source: SA HD 1888/1; reproduced by kind permission of the owner)

lived there.[41] It is unlikely that a structure the size of Buck's Cottage would have had many rooms to divide domestic activities into and to cultivate privacy. In a similar vein, Figure 1.4 shows the cottage of the gardener James Flatman, who occupied the dwelling sometime between the 1830s and 1850s with his wife and eight children. While it was picturesque, it must have been very difficult for the family to negotiate the restricted space. So crowded was the home that typhus spread among everybody 'like a plague', killing James and two to four of his children before a nurse could be found to help.[42]

It was not unusual for buildings to be sub-divided or repurposed into discrete domiciles, making some homes particularly small. Figure 1.5, for instance, shows an example of a house that was split into two. In 1860 one side was occupied by the widowed tailoress Mary Cock and three other adults,[43] and next door were the labourers John and Sarah Bush and one of their children.[44] Browne's Cottages were former storerooms that were converted into four homes for labouring families (Figure 1.6). In 1860, the residences had six, two, four and five people living in them respectively.[45]

Accommodating the poor 47

Figure 1.4 Gardener's Cottage, the home of James Flatman, painted by Richard Cobbold, 1860 (source: SA HD 1888/1; reproduced by kind permission of the owner)

Figure 1.5 The cottages of Mary Cox (b.1811, d.1877) and John Bush (b.1789, d.1870), painted by Richard Cobbold, 1860 (source: SA HA 42/2; reproduced by kind permission of the owner)

We can learn more about how cramped and difficult multiple occupancies could be from the writings of the labouring poet John Clare (b.1793). Throughout his childhood, he lived in a cottage in Helpston, Northamptonshire, with his parents and siblings (Figure 1.7). Clare described the home 'as roomy and confortable as any of our neighbours'

Figure 1.6 Browne's Cottages (right), painted by Richard Cobbold, 1860 (source: SA HD 1888/1; reproduced by kind permission of the owner)

Figure 1.7 John Clare Cottage, today (source: photographed by author, 2018)

and said that they 'never felt a desire to have a better' one. However, between 1813 and 1814 their landlord decided to raise the rent and split the building into four tenements, leaving him and his sister, parents and ageing grandmother 'a corner of one room on a floor for 3 Guineas a year and a little slip of the garden'.[46] In the period that followed, the family lived in overcrowded conditions and went into arrears, resulting in his father 'going on the parish' and their possessions being inventoried.[47]

Back to Wortham, some landlords were dutiful and took steps to ensure that their tenants lived in abodes that were fit for purpose. G. H. Wilson, for instance, authorised his steward to put his farmhouses 'into decent repair' and rebuild properties that were dilapidated.[48] Some labouring people even turned to making their own cottages, giving them the opportunity to tailor the structures to their own specifications and needs.[49] Other landlords let their properties become run down. The elderly trio Moll King, Billy Rose and John Mayhew cohabited at the end of their lives and made ends meet through poor relief, charity and odd jobs such as nursing and hawking. According to Cobbold, they lived in 'one of the poorest hovels' in Wortham, which 'will most likely be pulled down' at Moll King's death (Figure 1.8). The roof is clearly seen as sinking and the building appears to be in a poor state of general repair.[50] Despite various challenges, many people worked hard to make their homes as pleasant and clean as possible. By 1860, Harbour's Hut had become 'a poor miserable kind of a hut' as it had had 'very little landlord's work' (Figure 1.9). However, throughout much of the 1840s and 1850s (and possibly 1830s) it was inhabited by the agricultural labourer James Harbour and his wife Ann, who raised their children there. Throughout their tenure of the property, the Harbours were 'very cleanly tidy' and thus made the best of the abode.[51] In a similar vein, the agricultural labourer William Minter and his wife Maria occupied one half of the building depicted in Figure 1.10. They raised their twelve

Figure 1.8 The cottage of Moll King (b.1760s/70s, d.1862), Billy Rose (b.1792, d.1863) and John Mayhew (b.1797, d.?), painted by Richard Cobbold, 1860 (source: SA HD 1888/1; reproduced by kind permission of the owner)

Figure 1.9 Harbour's Hut, the home of James Harbour (b.1791, d.1863) and Ann Harbour (b.1791, d.1877), painted by Richard Cobbold, 1860 (source: SA HD 1888/1; reproduced by kind permission of the owner)

Figure 1.10 Minter's Cottage, the home of William Minter (b.1799–1801, d.1869) and Maria Minter (b.1805–07, d.1886), painted by Richard Cobbold, 1860 (source: SA HD 1888/1; reproduced by kind permission of the owner)

children there from the 1820s. Cobbold described it as 'a very poor cottage' and one which he was surprised had stood for so long, yet because the family were 'cleanly' and 'industrious', he said, 'I could go into the Minters Cottage and find the children and the old tottering table, with its patched cloth clean and decent'.[52]

Conclusion

Through the most detailed analysis of pauper inventories to date and the unique archive of Richard Cobbold, we have a clearer picture of what the homes of the poor looked like and how they were laid out and organised. The functions of rooms such as chambers and pantries were fairly consistent across households, while the roles of alternative spaces could be dynamic and change as needs shifted over the long eighteenth century. Kitchens, for instance, became more widespread, while halls and parlours were seen as less useful and were renamed and repurposed. Having said this, the most common and important rooms in pauper households tended to be multi-purpose spaces, and it was not unusual for eating, drinking, cooking, sleeping and work to infiltrate rooms with which they were not commonly associated. It is asserted throughout this book that poverty did not always equate to dwellings being messy, haphazard and unorganised. However, in this case it is likely that poverty – and the consequences of being unable to afford a larger home – meant that people needed to be pragmatic and did not have the space to separate activities into different rooms. The materials from Wortham broadly corroborate these trends. Although for most buildings in Wortham we can see them only from the outside, space would have been an issue for most people, especially when their families were particularly large. Nonetheless, it is clear that the poor took pride in their homes and worked hard to keep them as well turned out as they could.

By studying where possessions such as pictures and tea items were placed, this chapter has also shown that conceptualising the home into 'frontstage' and 'backstage' areas is too crude and simple a dichotomy. A much more nuanced view of abodes is necessary, as people would generally place sought-after items where they were needed most, rather than where they might have been seen most. In fact, the composition of many homes was the outcome of countless conscious and unconscious decisions and material adjustments.[53] Considering the individuality of people is, therefore, key to understanding their homes. It might be, for example, that paupers intentionally or unintentionally spread out their showier goods and did not concentrate them in a frontstage space to avoid giving a visiting overseer the wrong impression of how poor they were. The next chapter continues this theme of individuality by studying how personal and familial circumstances affected material life over the life-cycle.

Notes

1 For example, see: W. G. Hoskins, 'The Rebuilding of Rural England, 1570–1640', *Past and Present*, 4 (1953), pp. 44–59; R. Machin, 'The Great Rebuilding: A reassessment', *Past and Present*, 77 (1977), pp. 33–56; Christopher Christie, *The British Country House in the Eighteenth Century* (Manchester: Manchester University Press, 2000);

Ursula Priestly and P. J. Corfield, 'Rooms and Room Use in Norwich Housing, 1580–1730', *Post-Medieval Archaeology*, 16 (1982), pp. 93–123; Overton et al., *Production and Consumption*, pp. 121–36; Hamling and Richardson, *Day at Home*.

2   There are, of course, a handful of useful studies on the dwellings of the poor, such as John Broad, 'Housing the Rural Poor in Southern England, 1650–1850', *Agricultural History Review*, 48:2 (2000), pp. 151–70; McEwan and Sharpe, *Accommodating Poverty*; Joseph Harley, Vicky Holmes and Laika Nevalainen (eds), *The Working Class at Home, 1790–1940* (Cham: Palgrave, 2022).

3   The pauper inventory of Thomas Ratts' goods includes 'a partition'. ROLLR DE 2461/60. Francis Place had a room that was divided using a curtain. Francis Place, *The Autobiography of Francis Place (1771–1854)*, ed. Mary Thale (Cambridge: Cambridge University Press, 1972), p. 124.

4   On the difficulties of using inventories to study rooms and room use, see: Lena Cowen Orlin, 'Fictions of the Early Modern English Probate Inventory', in Henry S. Turner (ed.), *The Culture of Capital: Property, cities and knowledge in early modern England* (London: Routledge, 2002), pp. 51–83; Harley, *Norfolk Pauper Inventories*, pp. 55–71; Overton et al., *Production and Consumption*, pp. 121–36; Hannah Barker and Jane Hamlett, 'Living above the Shop: Home, business, and family in the English "industrial revolution"', *Journal of Family History*, 35:4 (2010), pp. 311–28; Priestly and Corfield, 'Rooms', pp. 93–123.

5   Priestly and Corfield, 'Rooms', p. 100.

6   Overton et al., *Production and Consumption*, p. 122. Overton et al.'s sums did not include outbuildings, but they are counted here.

7   Snell, *Annals*, pp. 138–227; Hammond and Hammond, *Village Labourer*; Neeson, *Commoners*, esp. pp. 158–84. On the agricultural activities of paupers, see: Harley, 'Domestic Production', pp. 42–4 and Chapter 5.

8   Naturally, this is problematic. As Jane Whittle has recently argued, these activities made up an important part of women's work and were highly valuable to households. Jane Whittle, 'A Critique of Approaches to "Domestic Work": Women, work and the pre-industrial economy', *Past and Present*, 243:1 (2019), pp. 35–70.

9   Place, *Autobiography*, p. 193.

10 Studies on probate inventories tend to also find that most chambers were found upstairs. Handley, *Sleep*, pp. 113–14; Priestly and Corfield, 'Rooms', p. 103.

11 Overton et al., *Production and Consumption*, pp. 133–4.

12 Hoskins, 'Rebuilding', pp. 33–56; Machin, 'Rebuilding', pp. 33–56; Hamling and Richardson, *Day at Home*, pp. 98–139; Priestly and Corfield, 'Rooms', pp. 104–6; Overton et al., *Production and Consumption*, p. 130.

13 The hearth is discussed further in Chapter 4.

14 The same trend can be seen in the homes of the middling sort. See: Hoskins, 'Rebuilding', pp. 44–59; Sara Pennell, *The Birth of the English Kitchen, 1600–1850* (London: Bloomsbury, 2016), pp. 41–2; Sara Pennell, '"Pots and Pans History": The material culture of the kitchen in early modern England', *Journal of Design History*, 11:3 (1998), pp. 201–16; Hamling and Richardson, *Day at Home*, pp. 71–94; Overton et al., *Production and Consumption*, pp. 130–1.

15 The terminology is difficult to pin down. For example, Lorna Weatherill suggested that a 'house' was a 'general living room' and Hannah Barker and Jane Hamlett found that the space generally contained mixed goods so was used for varied purposes. Weatherill, *Consumer Behaviour*, pp. 9–10; Barker and Hamlett, 'Living', pp. 315–16. Also see: Pennell, *Birth*, pp. 40–2; Pennell, 'Pots and Pans', p. 206; Priestly and Corfield, 'Rooms', p. 103. Evidence from pauper inventories suggests that they most closely resembled a kitchen; however, for clarity I will assess only spaces that were directly called kitchens in this section.

16 Pennell, *Birth*, pp. 40–2; Pennell, 'Pots and Pans', pp. 205–6; Priestly and Corfield, 'Rooms', p. 106.

17 On pauper domestic production, see: Harley, 'Domestic Production', pp. 25–49 and Chapter 5.

18 Pennell, 'Pots and Pans', pp. 202–4.

19 Pennell, *Birth*, pp. 40–1, 99–102.

20 On average, houses that had kitchens with sleeping goods in them contained 2.5 rooms.

21 Hamling and Richardson, *Day at Home*, pp. 177–217; Priestly and Corfield, 'Rooms', pp. 107–9; Overton et al., *Production and Consumption*, p. 131–3. Some middling homes did not experience this shift due to lack of space. See: Barker and Hamlett, 'Living', pp. 316–17.

22 Erving Goffman, *The Presentation of Self in Everyday Life* (London: Penguin, reprint of 1959 edn, 1990).

23 Weatherill, *Consumer Behaviour*, passim; Matthew Johnson, *Housing Culture: Traditional housing in an English landscape* (London: University College London Press, 1993); Overton et al., *Production and Consumption*, pp. 135–6; Stobart, *Sugar and Spice*, passim; Hussey and Ponsonby, *Single Homemaker*, esp. pp. 37–8, 124–9; Pennell, *Birth*, esp. pp. 10–11.

24 KHLC P347/18/10.

25 Such as: Martin Daunton, *House and Home in the Victorian City: Working-class housing 1850–1914* (London: Edward Arnold, 1983), pp. 276–80. Also see: Joyce, *Visions*, pp. 151–5.

26 Nathaniel Kent, *Hints to Gentlemen of Landed Property* (London: J. Dodsley, 1775), pp. 228–58.

27 Thomas Davis, 'Address to the Landholders of this Kingdom', in *Letters and Papers on Agricultural Planting*, Vol. 7 (London: R. Cruttwell, 1795), p. 295.

28 Benjamin Silliman, *A Journey of Travels in England, Holland and Scotland* (New Haven: S. Converse, 3rd edn, 1820), p. 170.

29 Most recently: John Agnew, 'Cottages for Farm Labouring Families: Plans, exhortations and realities', *Rural History*, 33:2 (2022), pp. 157–77.

30 Charles Whetstone, *Truths. No. I or the Memoirs of Charles Whetstone* (no place or publisher, 1807), pp. 5, 28.

31 Such as Nathaniel Kent and Thomas Davis, noted above.

32 The classic example is Henry Mayhew's articles in the *Morning Chronicle*, which later appeared in Henry Mayhew, *London Labour and the London Poor*, Vols 1–3 (London: George Woodfall and Son, 1851).

33 Such as William Cobbett in *Rural Rides* (London: self-published, 1830).

34 SA HA 42/2. This building was called 'Ranter's Chapel'.

35 The life-cycle of poverty and consumption is discussed further in the next chapter.

36 SA HD 1888/1.

37 Harrison Edge Estate Agents listing for Green Farmhouse, Little Green, Burgate (from: https://media.onthemarket.com/properties/2019551/doc_0_0.pdf, accessed 01/12/2022).

38 SA HD 1888/1; UK National Census, 1851. In 1851, Benjamin and Susannah Bobby had seven children under their roof.

39 See Crack's Cottage in SA HD 1888/1.

40 SA HD 1888/1; SA HA 42/2; Dymond, *Parson*, pp. 148–50.

41 SA HD 1888/1; SA HA 42/2; UK National Census, 1851; Dymond, *Parson*, pp. 210–12. See Figure 6.1 for a picture of part of the interior of the home.

42 SA HD 1888/1; SA HA 42/2; Fletcher, *Biography*, pp. 44, 130. Due to there being several Flatmans in Wortham I cannot be more precise on dates. Records also differ on whether two or four children died.

43 The 1861 census indicates that two of these were her sons (both agricultural labourers) and one was a lodger (a nurse). UK National Census, 1861; SA HD 1888/1; SA HA 42/2; Dymond, *Parson*, pp. 80–2.

44 SA HD 1888/1; SA HA 42/2; Dymond, *Parson*, pp. 75–7.
45 SA HD 1888/1; SA HA 42/2.
46 Jonathan Bate, 'New Light on the Life of Clare', *John Clare Society Journal*, 20 (2001), p. 45; Jonathan Bate, *John Clare: A biography* (London: Picador, 2003), pp. 13–14, 80–3; John Clare, *John Clare's Autobiographical Writings*, ed. Eric Robinson (Oxford: Oxford University Press, 1983), pp. 114–15. Note that accounts of the cottage are patchy and often contradictory, so I cannot be more precise on aspects such as size and number of rooms. A depiction of the cottage in 1821 can be found in John Clare, *The Village Minstrel, and Other Poems*, Vol. 2 (London: Taylor and Hessey, 1821); however, it is probable that this was an idealised representation and so it is not reproduced here. I would like to thank Simon Kövesi, Erin Lafford and Nic Wilson for sending me references and helping me to navigate the history of the home.
47 Clare, *Autobiographical Writings*, pp. 114–15; Bate, *John Clare*, pp. 80–3.
48 One was known as 'New Cottage' owing to this. SA HD 1888/1; SA HA 42/2.
49 See Scott's cottage in SA HD 1888/1; SA HA 42/2. Also see: Dymond, *Parson*, pp. 208–10.
50 SA HD 1888/1; SA HA 42/2; SA HD 368/1; SA HD 1025/1; SA HA 11/A13/10; Dymond, *Parson*, pp. 163–6, 169–71, 202–4.
51 SA HD 1888/1; SA HA 42/2; Dymond, *Parson*, pp. 145–8. See Figure 6.2 for a picture of part of the interior of the home.
52 SA HD 1888/1; SA HA 42/2; SA HD 1025/1; Dymond, *Parson*, pp. 173–6. Also see: Place, *Autobiography*, p. 193.
53 Adrian B. Evans, 'Enlivening the Archive: Glimpsing embodied consumption practices in probate inventories of household possessions', *Historical Geography*, 36 (2008), pp. 61–4.

2

Material wealth and material poverty

Before we consider the poor's ownership and use of items from beds to non-necessities, it is important to understand how people's material wealth varied and changed over their lifetimes. For example, how did old age shape the poor's ability to acquire consumer goods? To what extent did people amass belongings over their lives or sell and pawn them during times of difficulty? Were there particular periods in the life-cycle when people were more desirous of owning novel products? Beverley Lemire, Alexandra Shepard and others have shown that during more fruitful periods the poor were able to consume a wide range of items, but during difficult times they would often sell their possessions to make do. Their belongings were thus important stores of value which could be liquidated into cash or traded when needed.[1] However, most of this research has concentrated on clothing, and we have less sense of how the poor's ownership and consumption of other items including fuel, food and household goods could shift over the life-course.[2]

To look at changes in material wealth and material poverty, the chapter starts by examining aggregate changes in consumption using inventories and then moves on to consider material culture using the writings of the poor and multiple inventories which record people's goods over time. From a quantitative perspective, the results strongly suggest that the indigent poor's material wealth was on the rise over the long eighteenth century, with each new generation owning more and better goods than their predecessors. Yet this is only half of the picture. By analysing how consumer behaviour fluctuated over the life-course using first-hand perspectives, it is found that people went through periods of material wealth and material poverty according to the life-cycle of poverty. During relatively prosperous years when the poor were healthy and family sizes were small, they consumed a wide range of goods including various foodstuffs, fuels, clothing and household possessions. However, during difficult periods

At home with the poor

such as old age and sickness, people often went cold as they could not afford fuel, their children became malnourished and ill clothed, and their household goods were pawned or sold to make ends meet. Family priorities shifted at these points, and people redirected their resources to acquiring the most basic items, such as bread and medicine for their loved ones.[3] Similarly, this chapter shows how households could descend into material poverty as a result of unemployment, desertion, poor budgeting, imprisonment, or a sudden disaster such as a house fire, burglary or flood. Consumption was undoubtedly on the rise for the masses during the long eighteenth century, but the extent of change could vary from person to person according to individual and family circumstances.

Aggregate changes in consumption

Financial values

In contrast to probate inventories, valuations are rarely noted in the inventories of paupers' belongings. This is unfortunate for the historian, but for the overseers and churchwardens themselves it made little sense to go to the trouble of putting a figure on every item that they encountered. Pauper inventories were made as a record of ownership with the idea of taking the goods at a later date, so it was pointless for officials to value the possessions when the condition of them could change over time. Moreover, just as often as the items were sold when they were taken, they were kept for use in the workhouse or given to other paupers, further ensuring that there were few advantages to valuing them. In total, 78 of the 645 pauper inventories note the total value of goods in indigent abodes; however, the majority of these (58) come from Norfolk, meaning that any regional trends are tentative. To overcome this and tease out the findings further, the pauper inventories have been bolstered by a further 94 bastardy, debt-related, goods-taken and poorhouse/workhouse-admittance-related inventories (Table 2.1). The valuations are likely to have been what the parish expected to receive on selling the goods, rather than the prices that the owners originally paid.[4] Nonetheless, the low overall value of goods is striking. The average total value of items in the pauper inventories is £4 3s. 2d., and for the wider sample it is only slightly higher at £4 15s. 11d.

The low value of assets recorded in the inventories is even more stark when one compares them to probate inventories (Table 2.2). For example, the average value of goods in the 37 pauper inventories dated 1675–1725 is £2 7s. 4d., which pales in comparison with the results of Lorna Weatherill, who found an average probate inventory value of £128 between the same dates. To some extent this is unsurprising, since Weatherill's sample included people who were mostly from the middling sort, yet nevertheless the difference is vast. Even compared with labourers' probate inventories,

Table 2.1 Average total value of goods owned by paupers, 1670–1835

		1670–1769	1770–1835	All years
Pauper inventories	Dorset (n=1)	£4 1s. 3d.	-	£4 1s. 3d.
	Essex (n=13)	£8 13s. 7d.	£12 4s. 0d.	£10 10s. 4d.
	Kent (n=5)	£4 1s. 3d.	£13 6s. 3d.	£9 12s. 3d.
	Leics/Ruts (n=1)	£1 0s. 0d.	-	£1 0s. 0d.
	Norfolk (n=58)	£2 4s. 10d.	£4 8s. 4d.	£2 6s. 4d.
	All counties (n=78)	£2 14s. 2d.	£11 5s. 2d.	£4 3s. 2d.
	Sample size	64	13	78
Other inventories*	Dorset (n=11)	£2 4s. 0d.	£3 1s. 6d.	£2 12s. 0d.
	Essex (n=37)	£5 15s. 4d.	£8 7s. 4d.	£6 18s. 6d.
	Kent (n=36)	£5 5s. 6d.	£10 5s. 11d.	£6 13s. 4d.
	Leics/Ruts (n=6)	£1 13s. 6d.	£2 19s. 6d.	£2 6s. 6d.
	Norfolk (n=82)	£2 6s. 3d.	£3 19s. 7d.	£2 9s. 1d.
	All counties (n=172)	£3 7s. 11d.	£9 1s. 11d.	£4 15s. 11d.
	Sample size	129	42	172

*Pauper inventories and bastardy, debt-related, goods-taken and poor/workhouse-admittance-related inventories relating to paupers' goods

which albeit record the goods of wealthier people than the wider labouring population,[5] the differences from paupers are considerable. Craig Muldrew, Joseph Harley, and Joanne Sear and Ken Sneath calculated a mean value of £34, £35 and £29 respectively for their samples of labourers' probate inventories.

While one could draw pessimistic conclusions from these figures, the overall picture is more positive when the findings are studied across time and area. Even allowing for inflation, the material wealth of paupers appears to have increased in value in each county over the long eighteenth century (Table 2.1).[6] In Dorset and Leicestershire/Rutland, this increase is rather modest upon first inspection, but in percentage terms total household value in the counties increased by 28 and 44 per cent respectively according to the wider sample of inventories. The material contents of pauper homes in Norfolk approximately doubled in value over the long eighteenth century. Those who were resident in the home counties experienced the most pronounced expansion in household wealth. The wider sample of inventories reveals that in Essex and Kent the value of goods increased from £5 15s. 4d. and £5 5s. 6d. in the period 1670–1769 to £8 7s. 4d. and £10 5s. 11d. respectively for 1770–1835. These findings are admittedly

Table 2.2 Average total value of goods in probate inventories, 1675–1800

	Weatherill (1988) 1675–1725		Muldrew (2011) 1700–99		Harley (2018) 1700–49		Sear and Sneath (2020) 1675–1725	
	No. inventories	Average inventory value (£)	No. inventories	Average inventory value (£)	No. inventories	Average inventory value (£)	No. inventories	Average inventory value (£)
Wider sample	2,902	128	N/A	N/A	N/A	N/A	2,981	124
Labourers	28	16	205	34	49	35	143	29

Source: Weatherill, *Consumer Behaviour*, p. 168; Muldrew, *Food*, pp. 183–4; Harley, 'Consumption and Poverty', p. 90; Sear and Sneath, *Consumer Revolution*, pp. 262–3.

Material wealth and material poverty   59

based on relatively small numbers of inventories, but they nonetheless strongly suggest that over time, indigent dwellings were increasingly filled with new and better possessions that were worth more money.

Number of possessions

Historians have often found that while the prices of many individual items decreased over the long eighteenth century, the total value of people's entire collections of material assets often increased.[7] This strongly suggests that people were acquiring greater quantities of goods; however, little work on inventories (of any type) has been undertaken to test this assumption. Table 2.3 helps to address this gap by showing the average and median total number of items that people are listed by the pauper inventories as owning. Naturally, this method is fraught with difficulties. It is not uncommon, for example, for pauper inventories to record 'some' of something, to not mention certain items which we know were present, or to write possessions in the plural, such as 'tubs' or 'bedding'. As a result these figures are crude, but at the very least they show that after 1770, parishioners owned more noteworthy items, and they offer empirical evidence to suggest that as many goods declined in price, people acquired more belongings. Indigent populations in Essex and Kent appear to have experienced the largest growth in their ownership of possessions, but the data from the other counties is also significant. Pauper inventories from Dorset, Leicestershire/Rutland and Norfolk record similar numbers of items to one another between 1670–1769, but Norfolk and Leicestershire/Rutland appear to have grown apace from the late eighteenth century while Dorset experienced a comparatively smaller increase. Overall, then, it is highly probable that paupers across England filled their homes with

Table 2.3 Average and median number of items owned by paupers, 1670–1835

	Average			Median		
	1670–1769	1770–1835	All years	1670–1769	1770–1835	All years
Dorset	32	40	35	25	30	27
Essex	54	70	62	46	53	48
Kent	57	132	85	39	106	60
Leics/Ruts	26	50	39	20	39	30
Norfolk	30	56	34	24	50	27
All counties	38	68	49	30	48	36
Sample size	403	232	645	403	232	645

60 At home with the poor

more things over the long eighteenth century, but that there were regional differences in this.

Item conditions

As a final means to measure aggregate changes in consumption, the conditions of pauper goods are considered. This form of analysis is based on the quantitative assessment of the adjectives that inventory takers used to describe items, such as 'old', 'blue', 'new', 'oak', 'joined' and so on.[8] Here we focus only on the descriptors that appraisers used to describe item conditions; the terms which reveal the size, function, colour, shape and construction of belongings are analysed at various points throughout the rest of the book.

Linguistic analysis is tricky to do. It is dependent upon the level of detail and thoroughness of the appraiser in describing items and in distinguishing one item from another, such as an old oak box from a new blue deal box. As a result, the methodology is potentially flawed if appraisers' levels of detail differed between regions, which, unfortunately, appears to have been true for Dorset, where less detail is recorded than for the other regions. This was probably because paupers in the county tended to own fewer items than their peers elsewhere (Table 2.3), meaning that appraisers did not need to distinguish similar things from one another. The methodology is also dependent on the subjective opinions of appraisers. Parish officials who made the pauper inventories tended to own a greater range of goods than most middling people and may have even aspired to be more 'genteel' in their patterns of consumption, according to Henry French.[9] Consequently, their perceptions as to what was 'old', 'broken' and 'good' were probably very different to what paupers themselves thought. Additionally, it is important to note that just because something was described as 'old' or 'broken', this does not mean that the item was worthless or had no sentimental value to its owners.[10] The term 'old', for instance, was sometimes used to denote something that was old fashioned rather than old in age.[11] Likewise, as Sarah Randles has shown, the emotional value of objects can even increase as they age and they lose their aesthetic and economic value.[12]

It can be difficult to understand what appraisers meant in their more inexplicable descriptions of objects. For example, Widow Hill, living in Kenninghall almshouse in Norfolk, owned 'a *very meane* Bed', and Easter Turner from West Harling, Norfolk, owned 'two *very ordenry*' shifts.[13] Moreover, utilising a quantitative methodology to analyse the words appraisers used removes the context and emotional milieu from which the items came. A description of something as 'very old' suggests a greater level of poverty than just 'old'. An 'old sheet' is a much greater indicator of poverty than an 'old clock', but this nuance is missed when the words are enumerated.

Material wealth and material poverty 61

Table 2.4 Percentage of pauper inventories which use particular adjectives to describe items, 1670–1835

	1670–1769	1770–1835	All years
'Good'	3	4	4
'New'	2	<1	2
'Bad'	<1	0	<1
'Broken'	<1	1	1
'Old'	25	26	25
Sample size	403	232	645

The results show that the terms 'good', 'new', 'bad', 'broken' and other similar adjectives were infrequently used by inventory takers (Table 2.4).[14] This is not to say that paupers rarely owned new or broken items: appraisers probably just used the terms infrequently. The word 'old', on the other hand, is noted at least once in around a quarter of all of the inventories, suggesting that aged items were fairly common throughout the period. There is, however, one significant problem with this linguistic approach which other historians have not recognised. Because the total number of goods that were found in households increased over time (Table 2.3), it is probable that more people owned a greater number of 'old' items by the late eighteenth and early nineteenth centuries than their ancestors might have owned previously. Taking Kent as an example, the results indicate that the material lives of paupers there were declining, as the percentage of pauper inventories which recorded 'old' goods between 1670–1769 and 1770–1835 increased from 21 to 45 per cent. However, in fact, it is because Kent paupers owned on average more than double the quantity of goods after 1770 than they did before this date that the likelihood of owning 'old' items increased. Thus, using percentages in linguistic analysis can mask and distort the actual nature of material culture.

By dividing the total number of goods in every pauper inventory by how many times the word 'old' is used, it is possible to address this problem and uncover the ratio of items which were seen as 'old' by appraisers.[15] As noted above, the Dorset pauper inventories are less descriptive than those from elsewhere, meaning that the results from the county are too flawed to warrant any statistical meaning. Despite this, the data from the other counties is lucid and appears to suggest that between the late seventeenth and early nineteenth centuries, people gradually owned fewer 'old' items. In Essex, for example, 1 in 47 items was described as 'old' between 1670 and 1769, but for 1770 and 1835 1 in 72 items were labelled in the same way. Similar trends can be seen in every other county except Dorset (Table 2.5).

At home with the poor

Table 2.5 Ratio of items in pauper inventories described as 'old', 1670–1835

	1670–1769	1770–1835	All years
Dorset	1 in 295	1 in 98	1 in 161
Essex	1 in 47	1 in 72	1 in 60
Kent	1 in 31	1 in 62	1 in 44
Leics/Ruts	1 in 130	1 in 251	1 in 197
Norfolk	1 in 41	1 in 63	1 in 45
All	1 in 46	1 in 75	1 in 58
Sample size	403	232	645

The reason for this decline in 'old' items from the 1770s may stem from contemporaries using the term less often or differently to people from earlier decades; however, I have found little evidence to support this. Rather, one of the key reasons for this change appears to be from a shift in people's priorities, in which the resilience and longevity of products became seen as less important compared with appeal of less-durable goods, which were more fashion-sensitive and subject to be traded as tastes changed. In other words, by the later period people may not have kept items long enough for them to have become 'old' and may have swapped them when they did for newer and perhaps more fashionable goods.[16] Examples of this can be seen throughout the home. In Chapter 5, for instance, it will be shown that there was a long-term move from hard-wearing dinnerware made from pewter and wood to earthenware, which was more fragile but could be adorned in numerous ways.

Material wealth and material poverty 'from below'

From a quantitative perspective, the inventories clearly indicate that consumption was on the rise and that over the long eighteenth century, people owned better-quality goods that were worth more financially. It is, however, important to remember that poverty was a constant battle, and so we now turn to the personal testimonies of the poor themselves to consider how consumer behaviour changed over the life-cycle. It is argued that families would go through several periods of material wealth and material poverty during their lives. This is because goods acted as stores of value, which people would amass during prosperous years and then sell or pawn to pay bills and acquire basics such as food and drink during times of difficulty.[17] In general, this series of buying and selling followed the 'poverty life-cycle' model (Figure 0.1), in which people were most likely to own more possessions when they were young adults, had fewer children and

Material wealth and material poverty 63

were in good health, but were more prone to pawning or selling their belongings during old age and times of sickness and when they had lots of young infants to support. The chapter also shows how material wealth could change as a result of luck and chance, such as a windfall inheritance or a disastrous house fire, as well as financial mismanagement and alcohol abuse.

Prosperous years of the life-cycle

In *The Theory of Modern Sentiments*, Adam Smith tells the story of a 'poor man's son' who looks around and 'admires the condition of the rich'. Displeased with his position, he then sets out to acquire a host of 'conveniences' in the 'pursuit of wealth and greatness', only later 'in the last dregs of life ... to find that wealth and greatness are mere trinkets of frivolous utility'.[18] The writings of the poor clearly indicate that during youth many people were, indeed, motivated to own novel and fashionable goods, as Smith suggests. At seven years old, the orphan Robert Blincoe moved from St Pancras workhouse in London to a cotton mill near Nottingham on the promise of 'roast beef and plum-puddings ... silver watches, and plenty of cash in [my] pockets', only to be very disappointed by the conditions when he arrived.[19] In later life, Thomas Carter recounted how when he put on his new school clothes for the first time, 'I ... confess that my hitherto slumbering vanity suddenly started up and inspired me with rather lofty notions concerning my personal appearance'.[20] As a 24-year-old framework knitter, William Hutton wrote about how the watch he had bought was 'the pride of my life' and how disappointed he was when he had to downgrade to an inferior model when money was tight.[21] Goods might also be key components of rituals such as courting, as can be seen in the writings of Richard Gooch, who as a young man gave his sweetheart 'a stick and pocket handkerchief as a lover's relic'.[22]

The impetus was thus clearly there for many young people to acquire goods, and they were more able to do so, as pay was often linked to physical ability. Having moved to London, where he received higher wages as a shoemaker, James Lackington quickly made the 'important discovery' that he really wanted a greatcoat.[23] Looking back on young adulthood, William Hart wrote about how 'I was very comfortable and earned great wages' and 'was very industrious and ... saved twenty guineas or more'. He noted that bread prices were especially high at the turn of the nineteenth century, 'but being single and earning good wages I did not feel it like those who had families'.[24] Of course, not all people were so lucky, and the pay gap between one job to another could be considerable,[25] but for those without children and with just one mouth to feed, these years often proved to be some of the most affluent and materially richest of their lives. The prosperity of these years becomes even more apparent when we consider how material circumstances changed over the lifetime. William Hart, for example, despite being relatively well off during his early years, struggled in later life to support his many children and was sacked at 56 because he could not keep up with younger dockyard workers.[26] Unfortunately, the vast majority of autobiographies were written by men and so the picture is opaque for women, yet there is no reason to think that they would have been less desirous than men of owning various consumer goods when they were young and childless.[27] Nevertheless, as Emma Griffin has shown, the earnings of boys and young men were generally much higher than those of girls and young women, meaning that the latter could not afford to buy things like their brothers could and were less able to move out of their parents' abodes until they married.[28]

Difficult years of the life-cycle

People were naturally interested and motivated to obtain consumer goods outside of their single, younger childless years. The fact that pauper inventories – which tended to be made of the goods of the elderly – reveal that people could own a wide array of items shows that many continued to acquire goods throughout their lifetimes. But for most this could be very difficult to do during particular periods, even when they were earning and had access to a wide array of makeshift economies. This section will now focus on the more challenging years that people faced and the affect that these challenges could have on material wealth.

Some people assembled household goods during their single years, meaning that when they married they had most of the basics that they needed to establish a new domicile.[29] Through efficient budgeting and 'good knowledge of domestic economy', others, such as David Whitehead and his wife, were able to set up their matrimonial home at 'very little expense'.[30] A handful of individuals even avoided marriage entirely so that they had 'no burdens' and financial 'misery'.[31] Marriage might also adversely impact other loved ones, such as Eleanor Beck of Kirkby Lonsdale, Lancashire, who said that she was 'unable to support myself any longer' in part as a result of her 'Sons having married and left me'.[32]

More often than not, couples found themselves in material poverty at the start of their marital lives. These years could be particularly challenging when people wed young or were expecting. Hugh Constable was approximately 19–21 years old when he wrote to the overseer of Chelmsford, Essex in 1827 to ask for help to marry his fiancé Susan Rising, who was around the same age.[33] He said 'I am very willing to Marry her but am quite unable to defray the expences of marrying or Getting a few Household Goods'.[34] The Lancashire mechanic/turner Benjamin Shaw was still an apprentice when he wed his pregnant partner Betty in September 1793. Both were only 20 years old.[35] The costs of setting up a new home

Material wealth and material poverty 65

meant that they could not afford many goods, and Benjamin made some of the items himself:

> We went to [our] House by our selves & had nothing to put in it, But a bed that [was] my fathers and me at dophinholme, & Betty had a box for Cloaths, & a pair of tongs, & a fue pots, &c I made each of us a knife & fork, & 2 Stools, we got a pan, & a looking glass, & a few trifles.[36]

The couple moved into their home during the winter and struggled to keep warm and feed themselves. Benjamin remarked that 'coals were very dear … and turf was dear, & the house was very cold, we were nearly Starved'. The family resorted to 'gather[ing] sticks' and 'fetch[ing] seeds to burn &c'.[37]

Many newlyweds had little choice but to move in with one of their parents or live somewhere as lodgers. When Benjamin and Betty Shaw's 19-year-old son Thomas married his pregnant partner Ann in October 1826,[38] Thomas had been out of work for 11 months and so the couple were forced to live with his parents for 9s. a week. After Thomas found employment, the couple 'got a few thing & we [Benjamin and Betty] found them a few more and they went to house near the 3 tons north road'.[39] The cobbler James Lackington and dairymaid Nancy Smith married in 1770. Despite having courted for some time, they had saved up little to set up a home and resorted to hiring costly furnished lodgings when they married. They said that the 'expence of ready-furnished lodging, fire, candles, &c.' meant that they had 'little left for purchasing provisions'.[40] The early years of marital life could therefore be marked by owning few possessions, due to the high costs of setting up a new home, rent and the expense of the wedding. It was also not unusual for couples to rush marriage despite it not making economic sense as they were expecting a child.[41] People tended to make ends meet at this point by making their own furniture, foraging for materials, living in furnished accommodation and relying on parental assistance.

Husbands and wives were generally at the peak of their earning powers when they were in their 20s and 30s, but at these ages people had most of their children. When Benjamin and Betty Shaw's second child arrived in July 1795, Benjamin noted how 'I had 4 to keep with 14^s a week, and few good[s] in the house, & bread very dear, &c'.[42] Samuel White was around 36 years old and earning 15s. a week in 1825 when he wrote to the overseer to say that 'flour and other nessecerais' are 'dearer' since 'one Death and two Births in the house'.[43] By October 1828 he and his wife had eight children to support, including a newborn and six that were under ten years old.[44] He noted: 'I am quite unable to feed and Clothe so many by my own earnings'.[45] Writing in Springfield, Essex, in 1809, Thomas Sagger asked for 'a months pay' from parochial authorities as 'our Children all eat so very harty that it Costs me 15 shillings a weak for flowr' and 'I Cand do to fill their bellys'.[46] Some people even put their children in the local workhouse or let them live with friends and family as they could not meet their material needs.[47]

The problems that came with having a large family were often perpetuated by economic factors such as stagnating wages and irregular employment. Elizabeth Davey in 1833, for example, stressed how 'my Famileay Is very Large and my husbands Irnasings are so small that I find It hard to git my children brad'.[48] Owing to the 'largeness of my Family which consists of myself and Wife along with 7 children', 'lowness of wages' and 'scarcity of Work', Christopher Grime wrote to the overseer of Kirkby Lonsdale, Lancashire for relief.[49] Around the birth of his daughter in November 1825, 26-year-old Christopher Thomson struggled to find enough work. Beginning 'to despair of keeping my family alive', he hawked his goods and gathered acorns from woodlands to sell.[50] Most children did not enter employment until they were between 7 and 11 years old, and their wages tended to be around half of those of an adult.[51] Moreover, average family size was increasing from the late eighteenth century due to more people getting married at an earlier age.[52] Collectively, this put a lot of pressure on parents to provide for their families and could lead to material hardships.

Sickness is not technically part of the life-cycle of poverty, but it was more probable and more dangerous to people during certain stages of life, such as childhood and old age, and had a significant impact on material wealth. The stresses of sickness were particularly amplified when the main wage earner was unwell, leading to families having to make cutbacks. As a result of John Shinn's father's 'nervous break-down' which rendered him unable to work for three years, he said:

> We were terribly short of both food and clothing. Our food was of the plainest kind and at times very short. We seldom tasted meat more than twice or three times a week, frequently only a piece of bread and butter between breakfast and tea, and often bread without butter, only a little sugar sprinkled on the bread, and in the winter we were very short of fuel, and frequently had to do without a fire.[53]

The knock-on effects could also be particularly acute when other members of the family were unwell. During the 1820s, Samuel White's wife Ann appears to have had a stroke, which meant that she needed a nurse. Their young children also required assistance on several occasions for measles and various other conditions. Samuel wrote that as a result of Ann's 'late atack she has not the full use of her left arm and her mental faculties are in a very weak state'.[54] He said that she had been 'unable to Do for her Family … in such a state of stupidety and forgetfulness' and that 'her Paralattic attack Prevents her been able to earn any thing'.[55] This meant that Samuel struggled to feed and clothe his family, as well to as keep the fires in his house burning.[56]

It was simply beyond the means of many people to pay bills for doctors, nurses, carers and medicine themselves. Wages were not high enough in any part of the country.[57] In one letter from J. B. Crowest in Upminster, Essex, for example, he asserted that there was a 'late long, & serious affliction' on his family, meaning that 'The Doctor's Bill (which is only in part) amounts to more than £12'. He claimed that 'I find myself yet much insolved ... it will be impossible for me to extricate myself'.[58] For paupers who received a pension from the parish, this was almost never enough to cover medicine or healthcare. In 1824, Mary Baynes, approximately 32 years old, was under the care of her mother, Sarah, as she was 'suffering from deseased lungs'. This resulted in a prodigious bill of £4 12s. 6d. from the apothecary, which compelled her mother to ask for additional help from authorities, 'as I am unable to Discharge it, having an allowance of only 2ˢ pʳ Week from this Parish'.[59]

Household priorities shifted during times of sickness. Many would sell possessions and redirect funds from rent, fuel, poor rates and clothing to try and pay for healthcare for their loved ones. In 1826, the 59-year-old journeyman fellmonger John Hall wrote a letter to Chelmsford parish in Essex, indicating that as a result of his daughter being too sick to stay in service he had 'Sold all my things Except my bed'. He asked the overseer to 'Be so kind as to Send me A Something to buy her A Bed [and] I Will get A fue things'.[60] An unemployed navvy (whose name is unknown) was unable 'to pay a woman to help us', and he and his ill wife 'had to sleep in a barn' and pawn a number of possessions to make ends meet.[61] Some people sold their goods by peddling them, such as Mary Saxby, who said that while her husband was unwell, 'Our custom was, to go round the neighbouring villages, to sell our goods, and return at night'.[62] With people selling their goods and making cutbacks, families also risked their long-term health. George Salkeld of Manchester, for instance, wrote to his overseer worried that his wife and children might 'relapse' in their recoveries because of 'their emaciated frames' resulting from 'want of proper nourishment'.[63]

When people did not survive their illnesses, their families were left in both emotional and material turmoil. After the deaths of their husbands, women particularly found themselves in much reduced circumstances. Many widows were forced to downgrade their homes and material goods, as they had lost their partner's pay and were left to support themselves and any children they may have had on menial pay.[64] Mary Saxby recounted how she was left 'a poor disconsolate widow, with five children, four of them young' when her husband died. This meant that she fell 'deeply in debt' and 'sold what I had, and discharged all our debts'. Saxby 'then applied to the parish for assistance: and, for a short time, they gave me three shillings weekly, but soon reduced this allowance'.[65] Men too, of course, suffered after the deaths of their wives. When Joseph Jewell's mother died, his father started drinking more and his 16-year-old sister was left to budget and run the household. While his mother was alive, Jewell stated, they had been 'comfortably provided for', but when she died they got into debt with various shopkeepers and 'fared very hard' from 'want of bread and very much the want of nesessary cloathing'.[66]

Losing children was a common occurrence over the life-cycle, and many families would ask parishes for help with burial costs and other material expenses. In 1805, Hannah Wall wrote to the overseer of Rainham stating:

> my youngest Child Died this Morning ... the Child has been Poorly this month Back, and has run me to a deal of Expence with Doctor & Medecins, I hope you will send me what Money you Think will Bury him, as to my Other Child, he is almost Naked for want of Cloths, and what to do I dont know, I am So much Distrested as to myself, my Cloths are all in the Pawn Brokers I hope you will send me Relief as Soon as Possible as I am greatley Distrest.[67]

From this one example a number of facets relating to material poverty can be noted. First, the writer highlighted how sudden illness could strike and how quickly bills for medicine, healthcare and funeral costs could build up. Second, she revealed that these financial burdens had resulted in the pawning of goods and the neglect of other important material needs, such as clothing for her other child. Finally, and perhaps most strikingly, she wrote this letter on the morning of her son's death, so desperate was her financial need.

In recent decades growing numbers of historians have studied old age, revealing that although society was generally sympathetic to the plight of the elderly, many lived out their final years in destitution.[68] The writings of the poor indicate that most people had little expectation of retirement and laboured until they were physically incapable or died. They reveal that elderly people often felt a sense of shame as they could not work as intensely as they once had due to infirmity and their loss of strength and dexterity. These difficulties are best exemplified through the 53 letters William James wrote to ask for poor relief. He was around 67–69 when he wrote his first letter in 1818 and was 77–79 when he wrote the last in 1828.[69] Over the course of his letters he developed rheumatism and grew weaker, and his sight began to fail. He said that 'at our advanced Age, these things are hard' and that 'I experience the decays of Nature so much, that I cannot work as I have done'.[70] Unable to keep up with younger workers, he was paid less than them in his role as a bellhanger or labourer.[71] William's mental health suffered as a result of this, and he was less able to acquire basic necessities for his family. He stated 'my Spirits & strength are Quite worn down – Eye sight fail me so much, that I cannot see to do any thing by Candle light & work so little to do – & Strength failing me, that I cannot Earn enough to get bread'.[72] In 1822, he said that 'we live very scantily & hard' and 'my Earnings have been but small ... with which we cannot procure Necessaries, to support health nor Nature'.[73] On top of this, his elderly wife (born c.1748–49) and adult daughter (born c.1777) were often unwell.[74] This led to declining levels of material wealth and a growing dependence on the parish and friends to support their material needs. In 1818, for instance, William stated that 'the things we have, are only our Bed, & a few things bought in for us, by a friend or two, when my things were sold of ... so that none of them are mine'.[75] Such stories of multiple levels of struggle were common among the elderly.

Other factors

In this section, we continue to consider how material wealth changed over time but focus on reasons beyond the poverty life-cycle. Unemployment and under-employment are mentioned in around a quarter of pauper letters sampled here, but lack of work was probably more widespread than this and an issue for most at one time or another. This can be seen in a letter from Abraham Stuck of Upminster, Essex, which noted how 'I have walked all round this part and cannot get a Job'. He says 'The fact is, there are so many poor who belong to parishes, that ... can get no work'.[76] Periods of under-employment were particularly difficult for the labouring sort. People had *some* work, so parishes could be hesitant in offering support, but the poor themselves were left not knowing if they would have enough money for necessities week to week and were forced to sell off goods. John Balls wrote to the overseer of St Botolph, Colchester, Essex, to plead that 'our Trade is so bad that We have little or Nothing to Do ... we realy are in Great Distress and Cannot Get Work enough for Nessasary Food and Oblidge to go without Bread or any thing frequently by the Day tolgeter', meaning that their 'Hunger is so very Sharp'.[77] Breaks in work also occurred more often when people grew older and were let go for younger workers.[78] Sometimes people received material help from friends and kin when work was lacking, but not everybody had these connections. In 1819 John Hall stated that 'Work is verry Short ... I Cant get enougf for bread ... I have No Other friend but you [the parish] to go to for Any thing'.[79]

During the final decades of the old poor law, instances of hunger became more usual and acute following various harvest failures and sudden rises in the price of bread and flour.[80] Buckinghamshire labourer Joseph Mayett wrote about how one poor harvest meant that 'bread was very dear', which forced him into debt and left him to consider what to do with 'very few of my goods that I had to sell'.[81] The need to use pawnshops was especially pronounced during such downturns in the economy. After a particularly bad harvest, unemployed ordinance worker John Lincoln had so little food for his family that he 'sold and pawned all our furniture and all Sunday Clothes – for bread'. At another point they sold their bed.[82] During one 'great commercial depression' when food prices were especially high, the blacksmith Samuel Hick remarked that 'Many of the poor people ... sold part of their furniture, and whatever they could spare of other things, in order to procure food'.[83] In a similar vein, John Brown found that the Napoleonic wars 'had raised all articles of consumption up to famine price', meaning that 'the pawnbroker's store-rooms were crowded; families were reduced to the greatest misery, having parted with their beds, furniture, clothes, in fact anything and everything that would fetch money'.[84]

Material poverty could strike families for non-economic reasons outside of their control. Thomas Preston lost his possessions after his home was burgled. He said that he was robbed by 'a black-hearted wretch', who 'went to my lodgings, and ... contrived to get every useful article of my furniture, even my children's last bed, table, chair, knife and fork, in his possession'.[85] In her autobiography Mary Saxby recalled a house fire that killed one of her children and left her family destitute of belongings. She wrote:

> we lost, not only our child, but nearly every thing. We had not a garment left, to shift either ourselves or children; although before, we had some very good ones. A watch, and a large pair of silver buckles, which we had about us, was all that remained: and how gladly should we have given these to have restored the child![86]

The family subsequently struggled to furnish their next abode, stating that 'Our beginnings were very small, as we had little to furnish it with'.[87] Likewise, weaver William Heaton noted a catastrophic fire in 1835 which left his wife 'nearly burnt to death' and the family bereft of goods.[88] This was not the only time that disaster struck a household that Heaton was living in. When he was a child, his parent's home flooded. The family were saved only thanks to 'the kindness of the neighbours', who 'unroofed part of the house' to pull the parents and children out. This catastrophe left 'all our provisions ... completely spoiled, as well as the principle part of our household goods'.[89]

The actions and decisions of people themselves or their families affected material wealth. 'G. J.' of Ribchester in Lancashire, for example, chronicled how his father squandered a £500 inheritance on drink and 'wasted it in other ways' when he was a child, resulting in the family having to sell their belongings and move into a smaller cottage after the money ran out.[90] Retelling his life as a drunk, Charles Bent noted that at the height of his habit he spent the family finances on alcohol. He revealed that it 'left me without a home, without bread for my family, my wife without clothes, except what she had on her back, and myself the inmate of a prison'.[91] Francis Place remarked that there were around three occasions when his family became 'destitute' as a result of his father's gambling addiction. On one occasion, his father lost some £800 in savings and 'was obliged to sell the Lease and ... his house and [baking] business'.[92] A series of letters

Material wealth and material poverty 71

were sent between Romford and Mundon parishes in Essex regarding the 'worthless Pauper' John Thurtell during the 1830s. Thurtell, alongside his wife and seven children, had been afflicted with illnesses including smallpox, but his careless management of finances and his abusive nature was frequently highlighted in the letters. The overseer of Romford wrote about how Thurtell received a 'handsome allowance' from Mundon, but 'beats his wife tremendously' and had left her 'half naked – scarcly a shoe for her foot wet through – and not had – (if she tells the truth) one bit of food all day except a few potatoes'. Their neighbour announced that 'such a picture of distress and misery is rarely to be seen – the whole of them sleeping on a something called a bed – living in the greatest possible filth and dirt – the vermin crawling about them in a way that they may be scraped of in bunches'.[93]

The autobiographical writings of Benjamin Shaw illustrate examples of financial mismanagement. Benjamin complained about his wife Betty's lack of control of household resources. He claimed that 'her allowance has been more than the most of womans', but 'when she got any thing, Bedgowns, or hankerchiefs, or Stocking, or any article new, She gave the old ones away' and 'was allways in debt, without endeavering to get out'. Benjamin noted that through her overspending 'She hath robed me of money – sometimes taken my cloths to Pawn, & once my watch, &c, and frequently told lyes to deceive me'.[94] In early 1829, Benjamin and Betty's daughter Mary became pregnant out of wedlock at the age of 17. The father of the child, Robert Smith, was sent to prison soon after this for being involved in a brawl. Mary 'began to use all kinds of fraud' and 'Cheated every way' to support Robert while he was in prison, such as by stealing her father's money and building up debts in his name. Several months later, Benjamin's other daughter Agnes came home from Preston 'having left most of her cloths in the Pawn Shop'. This surprised Benjamin, as Agnes was in full employment and he had been helping her financially. Agnes had instead spent her money irresponsibly on goods including '7 or 8 gowns in a little more than 2 years'. Benjamin was disappointed with his daughters. He stated that 'both [Mary] & her sister Agness did badly for me by runing into Debt and Pawning their Clothes & my Bed Cloths & Book or any thing they Make Money off &c'. This amounted to Benjamin losing '7 or 8 Pound in Money by them & lost very many thing alltogether'.[95] Families would often pull together during challenging times, but these examples demonstrate that this was not always the case and that relatives could push people into material poverty.

People could go from being relatively well off to materially bereft almost overnight as a result of desertion. If this abandonment led to a partner and their children being unable to support themselves, poor law officials often distrained their goods to offset the costs of the relief they received. Sometimes the parish let forsaken families keep basic clothing and household goods, but on other occasions they were left with almost nothing.[96] When David Love was a child, his collier father deserted his mother and siblings. The parish subsequently 'sold all his household furniture, and all my mother's good clothes'. He remarked that 'not a single article was left, but what she had on her body'.[97] When Thomas Preston's wife absconded for America, the 'poor little family ... was frequently pinched with hunger and cold'.[98] People had to find new ways of meeting their material needs, as the help that abandoned families received in poor relief was rarely enough to live off. Love's mother turned to begging for bread to feed her family.[99] The abandoned mother of Edward Allen Rymer avoided using poor relief – and thus presumably did not have her goods taken by authorities – by feeding her family foraged 'young nettles' and 'Wild fruit and herbs'. Quite often, however, they 'went hungry to bed and breakfasted on nothing!'[100] It is difficult to ascertain how common desertion was, but in a time when divorce was not an option for most people it was probably not unusual, possibly affecting something like one in ten families.[101] Abandonment could end an unhappy marriage, but it frequently left a partner and their children in dire straits for many years to come. It was usually the husband who jumped ship, and with women earning less than men and having childcare duties, they particularly suffered and many swiftly became materially destitute.

The selling of goods and use of pawnshops for temporary financial relief was widespread. In most cases, individuals would sell or pawn their clothes and linen, but significant numbers of people also traded household goods such as tea items, timepieces and dinnerware.[102] Many contemporaries bemoaned the poor's reliance on pawnbrokers, and the writings of the labouring sort also acknowledge how treacherous they could be.[103] Between 1798 and 1803, William Brown worked at a pawnbroker's shop in Sheffield, only to lament that the working classes and poor 'too frequently habituate themselves to this kind of traffic, which proves very detrimental'.[104] He told the story of one woman who fell into a cycle of paying considerable sums in interest without ever being able to reclaim her possessions:

> a poor woman in her need, pawned her gown, petticoat, and stays at our shop, for fifteen pence, and for fourteen years successively payed the interest amounting to two guineas, besides ticket money, but unfortunately for her she could pay the interest no longer, and she had the mortification to see her clothes exposed for public sale.[105]

While there were undoubtedly people who lost out to pawnbrokers, the shops were an important part of the economy of makeshifts and many people used them to successfully alleviate short-term money problems.[106] Some individuals even used pawnshops to acquire funds for desired goods or leisure activities, rather than necessities such as food. The wife of

Material wealth and material poverty   73

Charles Bent, for example, took 'a bundle of clothes to a pawnbroker's' to exchange them for trousers 'as the pair I possessed were rather shabby … [for a] chapel and temperance meeting'.[107] George Calladine 'began to sell and pledge what few articles I had left in the jewellery way to meet my wants' at fairs and races.[108] In Dundee, weaver William Thom pawned 10s. worth of goods and used the funds to acquire basic provisions, as well as 4s. worth of second-hand books.[109]

Inventories over time

To build on the findings from the ego documents and to further under-stand the extent to which material wealth varied over people's lifetimes, we turn back to inventories. The inventories of people on outdoor relief are compared with those who were just about to enter the workhouse. Individuals who had multiple inventories made of their belongings at dif-fering times are also assessed in this section. In a similar manner to above, it is argued that as people became poorer due to various adversities, their material wealth accordingly declined.

Material life before entering poorhouses and workhouses

Conditions in pre-1834 workhouses were not as dire as one might ini-tially think. However, most people tried to avoid the workhouse and only entered it as a last resort, often when they were old and infirm and had nowhere else to turn.[110] People would sell or pawn their goods at times of desperation to make ends meet. As the workhouse was a place to avoid, many would have, in theory, sold their goods to try to avoid this fate. Therefore, by comparing pauper inventories, which record the goods of people on outdoor relief, with inventories which list people's belongings as they entered poorhouses/workhouses, we can analyse the extent to which people became materially poorer as their poverty overwhelmed them.

By focusing on Dorset and Essex between 1770 and 1835, where and when most of the poorhouse/workhouse-admittance-related inventories were made, we learn that in all likelihood people sold or pawned their belongings in an attempt to maintain some semblance of self-sufficiency before being forced to enter the poorhouse or workhouse. On average, admittance-related inventories for Dorset and Essex record 25 and 44 possessions, respectively, compared with 40 and 70 for the pauper inven-tories. Individuals who received outdoor relief were much more likely to own nearly every type of item compared with those entering the poor-house/workhouse (Table 2.6). While the differences in ownership are not considerable for items such as beds, boxes and chairs, there are stark dis-parities for goods that were less necessary for everyday life. For example, only 6 and 7 per cent of those in Dorset and Essex who were poorhouse/

74 At home with the poor

Table 2.6 Percentage of indoor and outdoor paupers who owned various items, 1770–1835

	Poorhouse/workhouse admittance-related inventories, 1773–1832			Pauper inventories, 1770–1835		
	Dorset	Essex	All counties	Dorset	Essex	All counties
Beds (any)	80	94	85	100	98	99
Beds (feather)	13	32	23	32	49	38
Boxes (any type)	68	59	68	73	69	73
Chests of drawers	3	18	12	0	41	33
Cupboards	23	50	38	41	69	59
Chairs	70	82	77	82	92	93
Tables (any type)	70	85	78	86	92	93
Frying pans	18	32	29	23	44	39
Saucepans	3	24	15	5	29	22
Tea items	45	50	49	59	69	65
Bellows	35	26	32	45	59	56
Tongs	28	35	30	45	59	57
Warming pans	8	21	14	18	46	41
Books	3	0	4	14	8	9
Looking glasses	0	9	7	32	33	33
Timepieces	3	6	6	9	26	23
Sample size	40	34	94	22	116	232

workhouse-bound appear to have owned timepieces and looking glasses, compared with 44 and 33 per cent of the indigent populations receiving outdoor relief. It is possible that individuals who knew they were entering the poorhouse/workhouse would hide their belongings or entrust them to relatives to stop the parish from taking them away. However, this is likely to have only had a minimal impact on the results, as authorities were well aware of this possibility and took steps to punish the poor who tried to deceive them. Officials would generally not tell people that their goods were about to be inventoried, so people had limited time to hide anything.[111] Moreover, the fact that the material wealth of paupers who

Material wealth and material poverty   75

were about to start indoor relief was low across the board strongly suggests that people would sell or pawn their goods in the long run before they entered the institution, in the hope of staying independent.

Case studies

As a final way to measure material wealth over time, individuals who had multiple inventories taken of their goods are analysed. It should never be assumed that inventories are complete, and appraisers may have prioritised inventorying some items over others. Items may have also become lost or broken. However, the later-dated inventories nearly always record fewer items than the earlier ones, indicating that people would, indeed, trade and sell their belongings as they became more impoverished. Poor relief and parish records show that in most cases the life-cycle of poverty was a central cause for people's declining material wealth.

In June 1731, a series of pauper inventories were made in Redenhall with Harleston and Wortwell in Norfolk. In the following years, the parish updated its records by making additional inventories of the possessions of the paupers who were still alive. Widow Todd and Elizabeth Trew were part of this process, and in both cases their updated inventories recorded fewer goods than the earlier ones (Figures 2.1 and 2.2). Todd and Trew received long-term pensions of 2s. to 2s. 6d. and 1s. to 1s. 6d. per week respectively and were given money and goods in kind on a fairly regular basis. Even with this assistance, both struggled to support themselves, resulting in the decline of their material goods. Todd was widowed, had three children to support and was often unwell during the 1730s. This may explain why her latter inventory recorded fewer goods than the first and

Figure 2.1   Pauper inventories of Widow Todd's goods, Redenhall with Harleston and Wortwell, Norfolk, 1731 and 1738

[Inventory] Of the Goods in ye Possession of Geo Todds Wid^w: (viz) taken by M^r. John Edwards overseer June ye 26th 1731.	An Inventory taken of ye Goods belonging Wid^w: Todd by M^r. Jno. Peck Overseer the 29th day of Sep^t: 1738 viz
One old Bed & two Bedstead, two Boltsters, three Spining-weels, one Reel, one wash-Killer, one Pottage-pot Six old Chairs, two Tables, one Cubbard and Shelves for Dishes, and a hanging Shelf, one Box Iron, one Gridiron, two handirons, one hake, one Salt Box, one Pare of Bellows.	one Bed a Boltster & Bedstead one Cubburd one Weel & Reel a Candle-stick a Dresser & Cole a Shelf an Iron-porridg pot four old Chairs .... a Cover Lid & a new Sheet –

Source: NRO PD 295/102.

Figure 2.2 Pauper inventories of Elizabeth Trew's goods, Redenhall with Harleston and Wortwell, Norfolk, 1731 and 1745

[Inventory] Of the Goods In the Possession of Eliz Trew taken by M[r]. John Edwards Overseer June 26th. 1731 (viz)	An Inventory taken on Aprill y[e] 15th 1745. of y[e] Goods belonging to Eliz Trew; by M[r]: John Edwards, M[r]. Wiseman and M[r]. John Jackson: (viz.)
One Bed and Bedstead, one Boltster, one Pillow, four Chairs, one Table, two Boxes, one Joynt stool, one Sive one Looking-Glass, one Cubbard, one Reel, one Spining-weel, two pots, 2 handirons one fire-Shovel & tongs pott-hooks, two Candle-sticks, one hake, two Larg stone Bottles, and some Earthen-ware, one warming pan, two skillets, three Killers, one Large wooden Bowl, two pails, and one Boxiron.	1 bed & bedstead, 1 Cubbard, 4 Chairs, 1 Coffer 1 Table & Stool 1 Desk, 1 Box-Iron, 1 pair of Cobirons, 1 pair of Tongs; 1 firepan, 1 hake & gridiron, 2 Candle sticks & a pair of Bellows, A Porrige pot & Kettle, 1 pail & Bowl, one pair of Old Sheets ....

Source: NRO PD 295/102.

Figure 2.3 Inventories of Daniel Drake's goods, Little Waltham, Essex, 1805 and 1816

Pauper inventory, 1805	**Workhouse admittance-related inventory, 1816**
Dan[l] Drakes Goods Oct[r]. 15 1805	1816 An Inventory of Dan[l] Drakes
1 Sacken Bedsted & flock Bed	Jan-y 3 articles Removed To the Workhouse
1 Blanket & Sheet	
1 Coverlet & Pilloes	3 Tables
3 Tables 3 Chairs	2 Cheers
1 Spinning Wheel 2 Boxes & Stool	Bedstead with Sacking Bottom
1 Tea Kettle & Tin Boiler	1 Hutch
1 Bellows fender & fire Shovel	2 Boxes
2 Candlesticks	Tea Kettle
Warming Pan	a five pint Bottle
Tongs Box iron	1 Tin Saucepan
1 old Saw & waterpot	1 Old flock Bed
1 Frying pan Dish & pan	1 Blacket & Coverlet
1 Saw Trammell	
1 Hammer	

Source: ERO D/P 220/18/7; ERO D/P 220/12/4

why it was missing various cooking equipment and fire irons. Trew, on the other hand, was unable to support herself and was under the care of a man named Robert Quantell by 1745. In a similar manner to Todd, her second inventory was missing goods from the former including a looking glass.[112]

The same patterns can be seen in the early nineteenth century. Figures 2.3 and 2.4 record the possessions of two paupers whose goods

Figure 2.4   Inventories of Rhoda Cook's goods, Tolleshunt D'Arcy, Essex, 1808 and 1809

Pauper inventory, 1808	Workhouse admittance-related inventory, 1809
Inventory Of Rhoda Cook's Goods taken 25th Feb[y]. 1808. – A sq[r]. Deal Table, a round Table & three Chairs, a kneading-trough, Scales & 1 p'r Weight, p[r]. Bellows, Trevett, Fender, poker, Tongs, Fry[g]. pan, Box Iron & 2 Heaters, 1 Iron Candle Stick & 3 broken ones, – a Spin[g]. Wheel, a pail & Wash tub, a Safe & small Tub, 2 Stools & Clothe Basket, a Small Chest of Drawers, 2 Feather Beds – 2 p[r]. Sheets, 2 p[r]. Blankets, & 2 Coverlets – 2 Stump Bed-Steads, 5 Curtain rods & 1 Curtain a hand Basket & an Old p[r]. Racks –	Acco[t]. of Rhoda Cooks Goods carried into the Workhouse Sept[r] 30th. 1809. Stump Bedstead, Feather Bed & 2 pillows – 2 Sheets, 1 Blanket & a Coverlet, a Deal Safe, 2 Chairs & a Linnen Basket, a Wash Tub and an Oak Box –

Source: ERO D/P 105/8/2.

were appraised in pauper inventories and workhouse admittance-related inventories. The first inventory of c.58-year-old Daniel Drake's possessions records 34 goods,[113] while the second inventory taken 11 years later only records 15. There is a similar decline in the number of items across the two inventories of spinster Rhoda Cook's belongings, from around 52 in 1808 to 14 in 1809. Both inventories also record smaller varieties of possessions over time. The second account of Drake's goods does not record candlesticks, various tools and fire irons that are listed in the first source. Likewise, the latter inventory of Cook's possessions is missing a feather bed, chest of drawers, chair, stools, tables, linen, cooking vessels and fire irons. Both paupers ended up in the workhouse but had previously received money and relief in kind from their parishes. Drake, for instance, received relief which included £1 6s. towards his rent in October 1805, and Cook collected 1–2s. per week along with flour, coal, clothing and shoes from the parish.[114] They were both thus struggling like their counterparts in the first-hand sources above and probably used their household goods to alleviate their problems.

Not everybody faced material hardship as the sole result of the life-cycle of poverty. Destitution could also be brought on or perpetuated by various personal and economic factors. Figure 2.5 shows the goods of John and Ann Clare which were temporarily stored in Beaminster workhouse in Dorset in 1822 and 1828. John was 42 years old when the first storage inventory was made, while his wife Ann was 27 and they had three children aged between 1 and 7.[115] John was a sailcloth weaver earning

At home with the poor

Figure 2.5 Workhouse storage inventories of John and Ann Clare's goods, Beaminster, Dorset, 1822 and 1828

1822	April Goods of Jn° Clares	Ann Clares goods Brought in 3ᵈ Decmbʳ 1828
Taken out By him 11ᵗʰ Septr	Brought in the House 1 Bedsted Round Table Square D° 4 Chairs 2 Small D° Pail & a Drepper Quart Cup 3 Half Pints D° 2 Oval Dishes 5 Broken plates Iron Pot ½ Doz Pot 1 Sail Cloth Lome & Part of Another	one BeadStead and Bed Tie, one paire of Sheets & one Blanket one Quielt & Two Fether Bolsters 3 Tables & 3 Chaires one Safe & one Sower Pan one Corner CupBoard
Novʳ 2ⁿᵈ	Both Loums taken away By Mʳ Demans Man	

Source: DHC PE-BE/OV/7/1.

around 7s. 6d. a week in 1820 and Ann was a mantua maker.[116] The Clares received occasional poor relief during the 1810s and early 1820s, including casual relief for sickness and money when work was scant. The family also probably received a pension of around 1s. to 1s. 6d per week from 1820 for around six months.[117] The Clares were thus struggling, but the tipping point into absolute poverty came when John and Ann were sent to prison for 'Stealing Shop Goods' in February 1822. This meant that their children moved into the workhouse, where they were eventually joined by their parents after they were acquitted around a month later. Poor law authorities put the possessions of the Clares into storage.[118] The storage inventory indicates that the family had most of the basic items needed to run a household, such as a bed, seating and cooking items, but that they were not well off.

The Clares left the workhouse in September 1822 and seem to have been generally self-sufficient in the following years, receiving only occasional casual relief which usually did not exceed 5s. per payment.[119] However, in July 1828 John was sent to prison for stealing yarn.[120] Ann subsequently received large sums of casual relief which totalled £5 6s. up to December 1828. This was not enough, and Ann and her children (including an extra child) entered the workhouse once more.[121] Another account of their possessions was made and fewer goods were recorded in this inventory compared with the first. John was eventually acquitted in March 1829 and joined his family in the workhouse, where he later received a sentence of 21 days of hard labour for 'Misbehaviour in a Workhouse'. When the family eventually left the institution in September 1830, they went onto casual relief.[122] John and Ann were clearly struggling

Material wealth and material poverty 79

on several fronts, as they experienced sickness in their household and had children to support and John could not find enough work. However, it was problems of their own making that ultimately drove the family from casual to indoor relief. When John and/or Ann were sent to prison, their family economy was decimated and they had few other options but to sell their goods and later move into the workhouse.

Conclusion

People could become materially impoverished as a consequence of simply growing old or having children, as well as poor budgeting, desertion and acts of God. Visiting pawnshops and selling belongings from clothing to tea goods were common ways in which families made ends meet during these times. Despite these challenges and the omnipresent nature of poverty, I would like to end on a positive note. Pauper inventories record the goods of one of the poorest groups in England. The fact that they clearly evidence improvements in the quality, value and conditions of the items that the dependent poor owned is important. Most people would experience periods of solvency and relative material prosperity when they were healthy, they had decent employment and their families were not too large. Even during old age, when many people struggled to keep a roof over their family's heads, the same home could contain an array of desirable consumer goods. These arguments are developed further in the next three chapters, which show how the ownership of various goods from clocks to feather beds to saucepans was on the rise over the long eighteenth century. It is argued that these changes helped to transform the lives of the poor and improve the quality of their domestic lives.

Notes

1 Lemire, *Business*, pp. 82–109; Tomkins, *Urban Poverty*, pp. 204–34; Styles, *Dress*, pp. 229–45; Shepard, *Accounting for Oneself*, pp. 277–302; Toplis, *Clothing Trade*, pp. 135–8, 146–9.

2 Exceptions include: Harley, 'Material Lives of the Poor and their Strategic Use of the Workhouse', pp. 71–103; Harley, 'Consumption and Poverty', pp. 81–104; Shepard, *Accounting for Oneself*, pp. 277–302.

3 These arguments were first developed in Joseph Harley, '"I can barely provide the common necessaries of life": Material wealth over the life-cycle of the English poor, 1790–1834', in Harley, Holmes and Nevalainen, *Working Class at Home*, pp. 25–45. The following chapter expands this analysis using hundreds more personal testimonies and inventories. I also consider non-life-cycle-related factors which were not explored in my previously published chapter.

4 Mark Overton, 'Prices from Probate Inventories', in Tom Arkell, Nesta Evans and Nigel Goose (eds), *When Death Do Us Part: Understanding and interpreting the probate records of early modern England* (Oxford: Leopard's Head Press, 2000), pp. 120–41.

5 Harley, 'Consumption and Poverty', pp. 81–104.

6 This statement is based on comparing the total value of items in pauper inventories with both 'optimistic' and 'pessimistic' price indices in E. H. Phelps Brown and Sheila V. Hopkins, 'Seven Centuries of the Price of Consumables, compared with Builders' Wage-Rates', *Economica*, 23:92 (1956), pp. 296–314; Elizabeth W. Gilboy, 'The Cost of Living and Real Wages in Eighteenth Century England', *Review of Economics and Statistics*, 18:3 (1936), pp. 134–43; Peter H. Lindert and Jeffrey G. Williamson, 'English Workers' Living Standards during the Industrial Revolution: A new look', *Economic History Review*, 36:1 (1983), pp. 1–25; Feinstein, 'Pessimism Perpetuated', pp. 625–58.

7 Carole Shammas, 'The Decline of Textile Prices in England and America prior to Industrialization', *Economic History Review*, 47:3 (1994), pp. 483–507; Overton, 'Prices from Probate Inventories', pp. 120–41; de Vries, *Industrious Revolution*, pp. 144–8.

8 This method of analysis was first developed in Mary C. Beaudry, 'Words for Things: Linguistic analysis of probate inventories', in Mary C. Beaudry (ed.), *Documentary Archaeology in the New World* (Cambridge: Cambridge University Press, 1988), pp. 43–50. Also see: Overton et al., *Production and Consumption*, pp. 114–6; Muldrew, *Food*, p. 200.

9 French, *Middle Sort*, pp. 141–200.

10 Sara Pennell, '"For a crack or flaw despis'd": Thinking about ceramic durability and the "everyday" in late seventeenth- and early eighteenth-century England', in Hamling and Richardson, *Everyday Objects*, pp. 31–9; Jon Stobart and Mark Rothery, 'Fashion, Inheritance and Family', *Cultural and Social History*, 11:3 (2014), pp. 385–406.

11 For example, an inventory of Staplehurst workhouse in Kent records '1 Old Fashion[ed] Tea Kettle'. In Hatfield Broad Oak, Essex, an old-fashioned trunk and sideboard are noted in the inventories of Widow Child and Widow Mary Searles respectively. ERO D/P 4/18/8.

12 Randles, 'Material World', p. 167.

13 NRO PD 108/84; NRO PD 27/21. My italics.

14 Other studies have also found that these terms were uncommon in inventories. Muldrew, *Food*, p. 200; Beaudry, 'Words for Things', p. 46; Overton et al., *Production and Consumption*, pp. 114–15.

15 This methodology cannot be used with 'new', 'good', 'bad' or 'broken' since appraisers used the terms too infrequently.

16 de Vries, *Industrious Revolution*, pp. 129–33; Maxine Berg, *Luxury and Pleasure in Eighteenth-Century Britain* (Oxford: Oxford University Press, 2005); Jon Stobart, 'Gentlemen and Shopkeepers: Supplying the country house in eighteenth-century England', *Economic History Review*, 64:3 (2011), pp. 895–7.

17 Lemire, *Business*, pp. 82–109; Tomkins, *Urban Poverty*, pp. 204–34; Styles, *Dress*, pp. 229–45; Shepard, *Accounting for Oneself*, pp. 277–302; Toplis, *Clothing Trade*, pp. 135–8, 146–9.

18 Adam Smith, *The Theory of Moral Sentiments*, ed. D. D. Raphael and A. L. Macfie (Indianapolis: Liberty Fund, reprint of 1759 edn, 1984), pp. 181–3.

19 Robert Blincoe, *A Memoir of Robert Blincoe, by John Broad* (Manchester: J. Doherty, 1832), pp. 13–16, 57.

20 Thomas Carter, *Memoirs of a Working Man* (London: Charles Knight & Co., 1845), p. 61.

21 William Hutton, *The Life of William Hutton* (London: Baldwin, Cradock and Joy, 1816), p. 64.

22 Gooch, *Memoirs*, p. 19.

23 Lackington, *Memoirs*, p. 208.

24 William Hart, 'The Autobiography of William Hart, Cooper, 1776–1857: A respectable artisan in the industrial revolution', Part I, ed. Pat Hudson and Lynette Hunter, *London Journal*, 7:2 (1981), pp. 153–5.

25 William Farish, for example, recounted how at 22 he was very poor. William Farish, *The Autobiography of William Farish: The struggles of a handloom weaver*, ed. Owen R. Ashton and Stephen Roberts (London: Caliban Books, 1996), pp. 41–2.

26 William Hart, 'The Autobiography of William Hart, Cooper, 1776–1857: A respectable artisan in the industrial revolution', Part II, ed. Pat Hudson and Lynette Hunter, *London Journal*, 8:1 (1982), pp. 69–70, 72.

27 Gendered differences in consumption are discussed further in Chapter 7.

28 Griffin, *Bread Winner*, pp. 31–2, 75–6, 84–5.

29 For example, Hart, 'Autobiography', Part II, p. 66.

30 Whitehead, *Autobiography*, p. 54. Also see Place, *Autobiography*, p. 111.

31 George Mitchell, 'Autobiography and Recollections of "One from the Plough"', in Stephen Price (ed.), *The Skeleton at the Plough, or the Poor Farm Labourers of the West* (London: G. Potter, 1874), p. 112.

32 Jones and King, *Navigating*, p. 57.

33 *UK National Census*, 1841.

34 Sokoll, *Pauper Letters*, p. 258.

35 Benjamin Shaw, *The Family Records of Benjamin Shaw Mechanic of Dent, Dolphinholme and Preston, 1772–1841*, ed. Alan G. Crosby (Stroud: Alan Sutton Publishing, 1991), pp. xvi, 120.

36 Ibid., p. 32.

37 Ibid., p. 32.

38 Shaw, *Family Records*, pp. lxxv–lxxvi.

39 Ibid., p. 97.

40 Lackington, *Memoirs*, pp. 196–7.

41 Ginger Frost, *Promises Broken: Courtship, class, and gender in Victorian England* (Charlottesville: University Press of Virginia, 1995), pp. 98–117.

42 Shaw, *Family Records*, p. 34.

43 ERO D/CR 164; Sokoll, *Pauper Letters*, p. 215.

44 ERO D/P 36/28/3; Sokoll, *Pauper Letters*, pp. 264, 270.

45 Sokoll, *Pauper Letters*, p. 270.

46 Ibid., p. 566.

47 For example, Ann Candler, *Poetical Attempts, by Ann Candler, a Suffolk Cottager; with a Short Narrative of her Life* (Ipswich: John Raw, 1803), p. 8; Leonard Wheatcroft, *The Autobiography of Leonard Wheatcroft of Ashover 1627–1706*, ed. Dorothy Riden (Chesterfield: Derbyshire Record Society, 1993), pp. 84–5.

48 Sokoll, *Pauper Letters*, p. 529.

49 Jones and King, *Navigating*, p. 157.

50 Christopher Thomson, *The Autobiography of an Artisan* (London: J. Chapman, 1847), pp. 203–4.

51 Griffin, *Liberty's Dawn*, pp. 60, 64, 68–78; Jane Humphries, *Childhood and Child Labour in the British Industrial Revolution* (Cambridge: Cambridge University Press, 2010), p. 176; Muldrew, *Food*, pp. 233–4.

52 E. A. Wrigley and R. S. Schofield, *The Population History of England 1541–1871: A reconstruction* (Cambridge: Cambridge University Press, 2nd edn, 1989), pp. 208, 431.

53 John Shinn, 'A Sketch of my Life and Times', in John Burnett (ed.), *Destiny Obscure: Autobiographies of childhood, education and family from the 1820s to the 1920s* (London: Penguin Books, 1982), p. 188.

54 Sokoll, *Pauper Letters*, p. 233.

55 Ibid., pp. 235, 264.

56 Ibid., pp. 241, 270.

57 Hunt, 'Industrialisation', pp. 935–66; Snell, *Annals*, pp. 411–17.

58 Sokoll, *Pauper Letters*, p. 624.

59 Ibid., pp. 195–6; ERO D/P 94/18/55.

60 Sokoll, *Pauper Letters*, p. 326; Pamela Sharpe, '"The bowels of compation": A labouring family and the law, c.1790–1834', in Hitchcock, King and Sharpe, *Chronicling Poverty*, p. 90.

61 Anonymous, 'Autobiography of a Navvy', in John Burnett (ed.), *Useful Toil: Autobiographies of working people from the 1820s to 1920s* (London: Penguin, 1976), p. 63.

62 Mary Saxby, *Memoirs of a Female Vagrant* (London: J. W. Morris, 1806), p. 25.

63 Jones and King, *Navigating*, p. 53.

64 Vicky Holmes, *In Bed with the Victorians: The life-cycle of working-class marriage* (Basingstoke: Palgrave, 2017), pp. 83–102; Julie-Marie Strange, *Death, Grief and Poverty in Britain, 1870–1914* (Cambridge: Cambridge University Press, 2005), pp. 195–203.

65 Saxby, *Memoirs*, pp. 51–2.

66 Joseph Jewell, 'Autobiographical Memoir of Joseph Jewell 1763–1846', ed. Arthur Walter Slater, *Camden Miscellany*, 22 (1964), pp. 127–8. Also see: William Smith, 'The Memoir of William Smith', ed. B. S. Trinder, *Transactions of the Shropshire Archaeological Society*, 58 (1966), pp. 184–5.

67 Sokoll, *Pauper Letters*, p. 562.

68 Such as: Pat Thane, *Old Age in English History: Past experiences, present issues* (Oxford: Oxford University Press, 2000); Susannah R. Ottaway, *The Decline of Life: Old age in eighteenth-century England* (Cambridge: Cambridge University Press, 2004); L. A. Botelho, *Old Age and the English Poor Law, 1500–1700* (Woodbridge: Boydell Press, 2004).

69 Sokoll, *Pauper Letters*, p. 390; ERO D/P 178/1/15; ERO T/R 300/1.

70 Sokoll, *Pauper Letters*, pp. 409, 413.

71 Ibid., pp. 411, 414, 417.

72 Ibid., pp. 483–4.

73 Ibid., pp. 414, 417.

74 Sokoll, *Pauper Letters*, p. 390; ERO D/P 178/1/15; ERO T/R 300/1.

75 Sokoll, *Pauper Letters*, p. 390.

76 Ibid., p. 135.

77 Ibid., p. 354.

78 See for example, Hart, 'Autobiography', Part II, p. 72.

79 Sokoll, *Pauper Letters*, p. 311.

80 Emma Griffin, 'Diets, Hunger and Living Standards during the British Industrial Revolution', *Past and Present*, 239 (2018), pp. 71–111; Carl Griffin, *Politics of Hunger: Protest, poverty and policy in England, c.1750–c.1840* (Manchester: Manchester University Press, 2020).

81 Joseph Mayett, *The Autobiography of Joseph Mayett of Quainton (1783–1839)*, ed. Ann Kussmaul (Chesham: Buckingham Record Society, 1986), p. 65.

82 Quoted from: Griffin, *Bread Winner*, pp. 199–200.

83 Samuel Hick, *The Village Blacksmith; or, Piety and Usefulness Exemplified* (London: Hamilton, Adams and Co., 5th edn, 1834), p. 191.

84 Brown, *Sixty Years' Gleanings*, p. 43.

85 Thomas Preston, *The Life and Opinions of Thomas Preston, Patriot and Shoemaker* (London: self-published, 1817), pp. 30–1.

86 Saxby, *Memoirs*, p. 26.

87 Ibid., p. 27.

88 William Heaton, 'A Sketch of the Author's Life', in William Heaton, *The Old Soldier; the Wandering Lover, and Other Poems* (London: Simpkin, Marshall, & Co., 1857), pp. xix–xx.

89 Ibid., p. xvi.

90 G. J., *The Prisoner Set Free: The narrative of a convict in the Preston house of correction, with a few remarks from the Rev. John Clay* (Preston: L. Clarke, 1846), p. 5.

Material wealth and material poverty 83

91 Charles Bent, *Autobiography of Charles Bent, a Reclaimed Drunkard* (Sheffield: D. T. Ingham, 1866), p. 17.
92 Place, *Autobiography*, pp. 23–4.
93 Sokoll, *Pauper Letters*, pp. 544–5, 550.
94 Shaw, *Family Records*, pp. 76–7.
95 Ibid., pp. xxxviii–xxxix, 104–5, 107.
96 Giles Jacob, *The Compleat Parish-Officer* (London, 10th edn, 1744), p. 187; Richard Burn, *The Justice of the Peace and Parish Officer*, Vol. 3 (London, 12th edn, 1772), pp. 505–7; Thomas Walter Williams, *The Whole Law relative to the Duty and Office of a Justice of the Peace*, Vol. 3 (London, 3rd edn, 1812), pp. 673, 740.
97 David Love, *The Life, Adventures, and Experience, of David Love. Written by himself* (Nottingham: Sutton and Son, 3rd edn, 1823), p. 3.
98 Preston, *Life*, p. 19.
99 Love, *Life*, p. 3.
100 Edward Allen Rymer, 'The Martyrdom of the Mine', ed. Robert G. Neville, *History Workshop Journal*, 1:1 (1976), p. 228.
101 Figure from Griffin, *Bread Winner*, pp. 147–52; Jonathan Healey, *The First Century of Welfare: Poverty and poor relief in Lancashire, 1620–1730* (Woodbridge: Boydell Press, 2014), pp. 191–201. Also see: Snell, *Annals*, pp. 359–64; Joanne Bailey, *Unquiet Lives: Marriage and marriage breakdown in England, 1660–1800* (Cambridge: Cambridge University Press, 2003).
102 YALH Accession 38; Alison Backhouse, *The Worm-Eaten Waistcoat* (York: self-published, 2003), pp. 77–81; Lemire, *Business*, pp. 82–109.
103 Tomkins, *Urban Poverty*, pp. 205–13.
104 William Brown, *A Narrative of the Life and Adventures of William Brown* (York: T. Weightman, 1829), p. 18.
105 Ibid., pp. 18–19.
106 Ibid., pp. 17–18.
107 Bent, *Autobiography*, p. 16.
108 George Calladine, *The Diary of Colour-Serjeant George Calladine, 19th Foot, 1793–1837*, ed. M. L. Ferrar (London: Eden Fisher & Co., 1922), p. 96.
109 William Thom, *Rhymes and Recollections of a Hand-Loom Weaver* (London: Smith, Elder & Co., 1844), pp. 13–14.
110 James S. Taylor, 'The Unreformed Workhouse, 1776–1834', in E. W. Martin (ed.), *Comparative Development in Social Welfare* (London: Allen and Unwin, 1972), pp. 57–84; Harley, 'Material Lives of the Poor and their Strategic Use of the Workhouse', pp. 71–103; Alannah Tomkins, 'Poverty and the Workhouse', in David Hitchcock and Julia McClure (eds), *The Routledge History of Poverty, c.1450–1800* (London: Routledge, 2021), pp. 234–49.
111 Harley, *Norfolk Pauper Inventories*, pp. 22–3, 67–9.
112 NRO PD 295/3; NRO PD 295/94; NRO PD 295/102–103.
113 ERO D/P 105/1/19.
114 ERO D/P 220/12/3; ERO D/P 105/8/1–2.
115 DHC PE-BE/OV/7/4.
116 DHC PE-BE/OV/9/1; DHC NG-PR/1/D/1/3; DHC NG-PR/1/D/2/1.
117 DHC PE-BE/OV 1/5–7.
118 DHC NG-PR/1/D/1/3; DHC NG-PR/1/D/2/1; DHC PE-BE/OV/7/4.
119 DHC PE-BE/OV/7/4; DHC PE-BE/OV 1/5–7.
120 DHC NG-PR/1/D/2/2; DHC PE-BE/OV/7/5.
121 DHC PE-BE/OV 1/5–7; DHC PE-BE/OV/7/5.
122 DHC NG-PR/1/D/2/2; DHC PE-BE/OV/7/5; DHC PE-BE/OV 1/7.

3

Building blocks of the home

Before the seventeenth century, most people possessed only limited items of furniture such as a bed, table, bench and a few boxes of some sort. Over the seventeenth and eighteenth centuries, the homes of the middling sort and the elite were transformed as new types and styles of furniture entered their homes. Chests of drawers grew in ownership to become a staple of many households. The growing use of dressers and various cupboards allowed families to display and store their goods ostentatiously, as well as more conveniently. Over time, chairs were progressively chosen over benches, forms and stools, and there was an upsurge in seats that were upholstered and lined with leather. Feather beds were recognised over flock or straw mattresses as the archetype of comfort. People were drawn more towards items made of exotic and decorative woods such as mahogany and walnut, while furnishings such as napkins and tablecloths were increasingly used alongside furniture. These changes collectively added comfort, convenience and decoration to the homes of the middling sort and the elite.[1]

This chapter traces the poor's ownership of various items of furniture to illustrate how they too witnessed a transformation in the range of furniture and furnishings that they possessed. These improvements were much smaller, delayed and limited compared with those of more affluent groups. Chests of drawers and feather beds, for example, became relatively common in indigent abodes only around the late eighteenth and early nineteenth centuries, but among the middling sort they were possessed in high numbers from around a hundred years earlier. There were distinct regional differences, as the homes of the poor in relatively remote areas such as Dorset, Leicestershire and Rutland were generally barer than those in more commercial and well-connected areas including Essex and Kent. Furniture was expensive: it was ultimately passed around, repaired, serviced and used until it became more useful as firewood.[2] Many items of

Building blocks of the home 85

furniture were acquired second-hand as cast-offs from the middling sort; children would receive hand-me-down furniture from parents; and the parish would grant paupers goods from the workhouse and deceased parishioners. Nevertheless, when these novel items of furniture and furnishings entered the homes of the poor, they helped to create dwellings that were more comfortable, practical and decorative. The items also had important ramifications on ideas of parenting, homeliness, privacy and convenience, to name but a few.

Beds and furnishings

Beds should be considered emotional objects and spaces in addition to material articles, as they were often centre stage in daily activities and key episodes of people's lives. The bed was where marriages were consummated, where children were conceived and later born. They were sites of pillow talk in which marital and conjugal relations were formed and maintained and where couples would bicker with one another. Religious bonds were renewed and reinforced in and around beds through morning and evening prayers. Parents would care for, nurse and play with their children in bed, serving to strengthen their attachments and evoke feelings of joy and safety. During times of ill health, they sheltered the sick and were the space where many people took their last breaths. Sleep is the most time-consuming daily activity we do. It plays a fundamental role in our mental and physical health, and without peaceful rest one's short- and long-term energy, health, and happiness can significantly deteriorate. Eating, drinking, relaxing, reading and exploring inner thoughts also regularly played out within the confines of the bed.[3] The importance of beds and their furnishings, therefore, in the homes of any social group cannot be overstated. The poor recognised this and increasingly invested in their sleeping environments over the long eighteenth century, such as through the acquisition of better beds and bed hangings. This helped to ensure that sleep and other activities were both physically and psychologically comfortable and that people felt content and safe when they laid their heads to rest.[4]

It was once not uncommon for people to sleep on the floor or on a straw pallet,[5] but by the late seventeenth century this was no longer the case for most. Beds were virtually ubiquitous at this point: only 2 per cent of the entire sample of pauper inventories do not record one (Table 3.1). Bedsteads were probably acquired only a handful of times over a lifetime. Many would have been bought second-hand or given to households by the parish. They could also be passed down through families and have key dates, initials and names carved into them, making them important carriers of family history.[6] This meant that the quality of beds could vary significantly within a single household. Some of the poor owned expensive and highly attractive beds. Labouring couple Judy and James Fuller were said, by the parson Richard

Table 3.1 Percentage of paupers who owned mattresses, 1670–1835

	1670–1769	1770–1835	All years
Feather	19	38	26
Flock	14	17	15
Straw/chaff	4	12	7
Any type/unspecified	98	99	98
Sample size	403	232	645

Cobbold, to have possessed a 'remarkable … old state bed' acquired at auction (Figure 3.1). It was described as 'Green maroon ornamented and edged with silver chord', with a 'coat of arms being worked at the head' by its previous owner. The bed became something of a talking point among neighbours in the Fullers' village of Wortham, Suffolk.[7] Others, however, owned beds that were worth very little and were uncomfortable. The pauper inventory of Ann Turner's goods in Ashwellthorpe, Norfolk, recorded a bed worth only 2s.[8] As a resident of Kenninghall almshouse in Norfolk and receiving casual relief, Widow Hill slept on 'a very meane Bed'.[9] While travelling in the 'company of Gipsys', Thomas Smith slept on a 'bag of straw' and his 'foster parents' bed consisted of canvas, stretched on four sticks, which were driven into the ground'.[10] The two children of pauper John Jump of Oldham, Lancashire, had 'a Bed Composed Chiefly of Rags &c with little or no Covering over them'.[11] Most of the poor possessed beds that fell somewhere between these two extremes.

Numerous sources point to the growing ownership of more-comfortable beds among the poorest. Inventories show that the average value of beds and mattresses together increased from £1 3s. 1d. each between 1670–1769 to £2 2s. 4d. for 1770–1835, indicating that paupers spent more money on them. Mattress stuffing is only intermittently recorded by appraisers, yet feather beds outnumbered flock or straw beds throughout the entire period and doubled in ownership over the period (Table 3.1). These alternative mattresses were seen as inferior to feather bases, but they appear to have slightly grown in ownership and they did have their uses. Flock beds, for instance, were prized for being cooler and were particularly useful for children who wet the bed, due to their absorbency.[12] The quality of mattresses was probably better in the home counties, as feather beds were more common there, but significant numbers also owned feather beds in Dorset and Norfolk by the late eighteenth century (Table 3.2). It was only in Leicestershire and Rutland where feather bed ownership appears to have been especially low. On occasion, paupers owned more mattresses than bedsteads, indicating that they stacked them for increased comfort or used

Building blocks of the home   87

Figure 3.1 Bed of Judy and James Fuller, painted by Richard Cobbold, c.1851-54 (source: SA HA 11/A13/10; reproduced by kind permission of the owner)

them as spares for overnight guests. People also appear to have acquired greater numbers of beds over time. From 1770, there is an average of 1.9 beds per pauper inventory, compared with 1.3 for the hundred years prior to this. The appraisers generally noted bedsteads only briefly, but some tentative points can be made. Most bedsteads were probably made from

Table 3.2 Percentage of paupers who owned feather mattresses, 1670–1835

	1670–1769	1770–1835	All years
Dorset	24	32	28
Essex	32	49	41
Kent	32	41	35
Leics/Ruts	9	6	7
Norfolk	11	32	14
All counties	19	38	26
Sample size	403	232	645

oak and had a sack- or cord-bottomed base to them. Trundle beds, which were pulled out from under a larger bedstead, are rarely singled out in the inventories. Yet they were probably more common than the inventories suggest due to the relative lack of space that many had in their homes.

Bed sharing was common, but its prevalence could vary over the life-cycle and shift according to personal circumstances. As a 24-year-old single journeyman, William Hart recounted how he moved home in 1800 to somewhere 'very comfortable, having a room and a bed to myself'. However, this lasted only around seven months when he was forced to relocate. This was 'very disagreable' to Hart, who now had to 'lodge with strange people after being so comfortable'.[13] Bed sharing may have particularly declined among parents and the young. From 1770, cradles were recorded in around one in ten pauper inventories, compared with one in twenty between 1670 and 1769. A handful of people even possessed 'child beds', suggesting that some beds were specifically designed to accommodate the young. The writings of the poor too indicate that separate spaces for the young were important by the early nineteenth century. In a letter written by pauper George Watson to the parish of St Botolph in Colchester, Essex, he mentioned how his daughter Hannah had used the money she received from the parish frugally and budgeted 'a Trifle ... for an old Cradle for her Child',[14] showing that for many, distinct sleeping spaces for the young were a necessary expense. Sometimes the poor used large food containers, drawers or boxes lined with pillows and textiles as improvised cots.[15] Elizabeth Twist's home, for instance, included 'One bed in fashing of a Chest of Draws wth a Pillow', and the autobiography of Benjamin Shaw detailed how as a baby he would 'lay in a box &c by the fire'.[16] Naturally, the experience of bed sharing varied among people. Dividing beds between individuals in boarding schools, workhouses and other establishments was seen as preferable to having no bed and advantageous for keeping warm.[17] On the other hand, bed sharing meant less privacy and could lead to frustrating sleepless nights through lack of space, fidgeting, snoring and bed wetting. The autobiography of the cabinet maker James Hopkinson describes one such night when he was 'ruthlessly awakened' by the man he was sharing a bed with, who trudged in drunk, shouted, vomited in a hat and snored 'like a steam engine'.[18] More seriously, bed sharing was sometimes connected to ideas of immorality and criminal cases involving sodomy, adultery, rape and pregnancy outside of marriage.[19] Accidental suffocation of children while sleeping with parents can also be found in coroners' inquests.[20]

With greater investment in beds, people became increasingly preoccupied with physical and psychological comfort, as well as privacy and respectability in the domestic sphere. During the early modern period, the marital bed was seen to be both a public and a sociable space; it could be found in various multifunctional rooms of the house and saw rituals such as the bedding ceremony. These ideas eroded over the Enlightenment as marriage evolved into a more private affair, with bodily functions being reconfigured to be hidden and a matter of personal conscience.[21] Ideas of privacy were probably less prevalent among poorer people compared with the middling sort owing to their limited resources, but they nonetheless became more central to their sensibilities.

Bed hangings can be particularly linked to these concepts of comfort, respectability and privacy. They had practical sensory purposes, as they helped to dull light, prevent draughts and keep the warmth in. Bed hangings also allowed privacy by offering those who could not afford a larger home a more cost-effective internal divide that could separate couples, children and lodgers from one another while sleeping, resting or having sex in the same room. The need for privacy in sleeping rooms was acknowledged by social commentators, especially from the second half of the eighteenth century. Writing in 1775, Nathaniel Kent argued that 'it is shocking, that a man, his wife, and half a dozen children should be obliged to lie all in one room together; and more so, that the wife should have no more private place to be brought to bed in'.[22] Likewise, in 1792 John Wood said that boys and girls should not sleep in the same room as their parents to avoid 'offence to decency'.[23] The privacy and modesty afforded by bed hangings was, of course, limited, as sound could still pass through them and the hangings were only a fabric divide that could easily be breached. Yet they would have at least allowed people to feel safe and like they had some control over their surroundings.

Bed hangings became more usual in poor abodes over the period (Table 3.3). Ownership increased particularly in Kent and Norfolk: half of paupers in these counties possessed at least one set after 1770. In Essex around one-third of the poor consistently owned bed hangings over the long eighteenth century, and hangings became especially common across Leicestershire and Rutland from the 1800s. It was only in Dorset

Table 3.3 Percentage of paupers who owned bed hangings, 1670–1835

	1670–1769	1770–1835	All years
Dorset	0	0	0
Essex	36	34	35
Kent	26	50	35
Leics/Ruts	11	29	20
Norfolk	17	51	23
All counties	21	34	26
Sample size	403	232	645

where the acquisition of material hangings appears to have been negligible. This suggests that although paupers in the south-west increasingly valued comfort with feather beds, they could not afford or did not desire hangings. Most pauper inventories listed no more than one set of bed curtains even if the inventory recorded multiple beds, possibly indicating that they were reserved for the head of household. The wider sample of inventories records 23 blue, 19 green, 4 yellow and 4 red hangings. Often the hangings were accompanied with valances and other material trims, which helped to create a more decorative, content and psychologically comfortable environment for users. The portrait of Judy Fuller discussed above illustrates just how prominent such hangings could be and how they could brighten and enhance the domestic space (Figure 3.1).[24]

As an alternative or supplement to bed hangings, people could use window shutters or curtains. It is not possible to uncover how widespread shutters were using inventories, since they were not moveable possessions and so were rarely recorded by appraisers. Window curtains, on the other hand, were noted by inventory takers but appear to have been relatively uncommon outside of Kent and to a lesser extent Essex (Table 3.4). Nevertheless, where present, window shutters and curtains helped to promote comfort in sleeping rooms by preventing draughts, softening outside light and noise, and maintaining privacy from on-looking passers-by. Through owning window curtains, people could decorate domestic spaces using various colours, patterns and trims.[25] This can be seen in the chambers of Joseph Lone and Widow Adams, who had 'Dimity Wi[n]dow Curtains' and 'a Sett of Striped Curtains' respectively.[26] How window curtains might have looked and adorned abodes can also be appreciated by looking at Cobbold's paintings of working people. Figure 3.2, for example, shows the front room of the spinster Dinah Garrod and a vibrant set of green stripped curtains and valances, along with flowers on the windowsill.

The possession of bed furnishings is arguably as important as that of the bed frame and mattress itself. Without sufficient bedding and

Table 3.4 Percentage of paupers who owned window curtains, 1670–1835

	1670–1769	1770–1835	All years
Dorset	0	0	0
Essex	3	11	7
Kent	0	23	8
Leics/Ruts	0	3	1
Norfolk	2	0	2
All counties	2	9	4
Sample size	404	231	645

nightwear, evenings would be cold, long, restless and uncomfortable for people no matter what mattresses and bedsteads they owned. Bedding, pillows and bolsters were common across society, even though the condition and quality of them was sometimes poor. They were commonly given to paupers as relief in kind by parishes.[27] When entering Sherborne almshouse in Dorset in the seventeenth century, many individuals brought only linen, pillows and bolsters with them.[28] Even the homeless probably had a blanket or covering of some sort to sleep with.[29] Unfortunately, bed furnishings are omitted in some inventories and inconsistently described in others, meaning that it is not possible to examine how ownership of different types of bedding such as duvets, blankets and sheets evolved over the long eighteenth century, but some important deductions can still be made.

Most bedding, pillows and bolsters are listed alongside beds in the inventories, suggesting that they were counted when the bed was made. On average, people owned 5.3 items of bedding each (Table 3.5). Only 11 per cent of the pauper inventories catalogue ten or more articles of bedding and a mere 0.58 per cent record fifteen or more. Calculated alongside bed ownership, this amounts to approximately 4.3 items of bedding per bed in Leicestershire/Rutland, 3.8 in Kent, 3.2 in Norfolk, 3 in Essex and 2.3 in Dorset. In a similar vein, most households contained only two or three pillows/bolsters on average. This equates to just one or two for every bed, indicating that they were commonly shared among sleepers. Bolsters would have been especially useful for sub-dividing among people as they were long and thin.

Barrie Trinder and Jeff Cox have contended that surplus sheets are 'one of the best indications' as to the 'steadily rising standards of comfort' in early modern homes,[30] and so it could be argued that the abodes of the poor were bleak and uncomfortable since spare bedding was scant. In reality, the low numbers of furnishings in pauper dwellings were largely the result of pragmatism, with the poor having pawned or sold possessions that were not immediately necessary to them before their goods were inventoried by the parish. In other words, it made more sense for

Figure 3.2 Portrait of Dinah Garrod, painted by Richard Cobbold, c.1848–49 (source: SA HA 11/A13/10; reproduced by kind permission of the owner)

people to sell excess bedding, pillows and bolsters than it did for them to go hungry or neglect pressing bills. In the pawnbroking account book of George Fettes of York, around four-fifths of the 10,906 pledges he received between 1777 and 1778 included at least one item of textiles, clothing or household linen. These were by far the most common categories of goods that were put into pawn.[31] Pauper letters also frequently mention selling bedding to make ends meet. In October 1832, William King wrote a

Building blocks of the home 93

Table 3.5 Pauper ownership of bedding and pillows/bolsters, 1670–1835

	Bedding (any type)		Pillows/bolsters	
	%	Average number	%	Average number
Dorset	70	3.9	40	2.1
Essex	86	5.8	57	2.9
Kent	83	6.7	55	2.6
Leics/Ruts	87	6.5	28	2.7
Norfolk	80	4.1	44	2.2
All counties	82	5.3	47	2.6

message to the overseer of Braintree, Essex, to stress that 'our Blanket and Meny other things are away [pawned] By Reason of want'.[32] Across several letters written to the overseer of Uttoxeter, Staffordshire, by a surgeon on behalf of John Jump between 1831 and 1832, money was requested on several occasions to release bedding from the pawnbrokers.[33] Jump even noted how he had become unwell from sleeping 'on Other Peoples Floors without House or Bedding'.[34] However, he ultimately never reclaimed his bedding, as the pawnshop 'with all its Contents was Burned to the Ground' in August 1832 'before the Money arrived' to redeem the goods.[35]

The materials of people's bedding are seldom mentioned in sources, but it is probable that most were made out of linen and wool, and by the late eighteenth century more were formed of cotton.[36] Likewise, the stuffing of pillows and bolsters was too rarely noted by appraisers to form clear conclusions.[37] Some paupers owned low-quality furnishings. 'Old' was a common adjective employed by appraisers to describe sheets, and occasionally the terms 'bad' or 'coarse' were used. Pauper Ann Tedder was even given '2 Blanketts almost wornout' by Beauchamp Roding, Essex parish, in 1748.[38] The prevalence of worn and aged bedding is perhaps unsurprising considering that the poor did not own much spare bedding and that it would have gone through a relentless cycle of being used and washed with little respite.[39] Nevertheless, just because something was old does not mean that it did not hold significant emotional, sensory and utilitarian value to their owners.[40] Furthermore, sources indicate that most people owned bedding that varied according to personal preferences in design, colour, quality and value. Inventories sometimes note blue, green, red or yellow coverlets, quilts or rugs. Pauperised couple Edward and Dorothy Bird of Hatfield Broad Oak, Essex, possessed four beds, one of which was accompanied with yellow furnishings and two with blue in 1802.[41] Rhoda Wretham from East Harling in Norfolk owned a 'Patch Work Coverlid' in 1821.[42] Cobbold's paintings of the poor in Wortham,

94 At home with the poor

Figure 3.3 Portraits of Mary Burrows (top left), Isaac Fake (top right), Anne Taylor (bottom), painted by Richard Cobbold, c.1840–60s (source: SA HD 1025/2; reproduced by kind permission of the owner)

Suffolk, equally illustrate how vibrant sets of bedding could add warmth and make a space appear more decorative, comforting and homely to residents. The beds and hangings in the rooms of Mary Burrows and Anne Taylor, for example, were coloured purple and white, while Isaac Fakes' bedding appears to have been a mix of green, cream and orange (Figure 3.3). The portraits show how rooms could have colour schemes which were contrasted and enriched through differing shades, colours and patterns that complemented each other.[43] People often had strong emotional attachments to their beds and bedding. The part of the bed left

Building blocks of the home   95

vacant by a deceased husband or wife must have evoked powerful feelings of sorrow, loneliness and melancholy for the spouse left behind. Textiles passed down through families as dowries or heirlooms, sometimes with names or initials embroidered into them, probably also aroused emotional responses, helping children to recall their parents and promoting feelings of safety and love. The making, cleaning and mending of sheets also likely encouraged thoughtful meditation and contemplation for the women undertaking these tasks.[44]

Research on the middling sort indicates that by the mid-eighteenth century most individuals had attire specifically for sleeping in, such as nightcaps and night-rails.[45] Clothing is perhaps the most inconsistently recorded category of goods in the inventories used here, yet on occasion references to nightcaps, 'night'/'bed' gowns and 'bed clothes' can be found in the sources.[46] Autobiographies offer further evidence that the poor wore specialised clothing for slumber, or at least got changed in some way before they went to bed. Lancashire alcoholic 'G. J.', for example, recounted how during the 1820s, he and his wife would often find themselves 'drunk in bed, *with their clothes on* – in the middle of the daytime', indicating that they usually wore bedclothes of some sort or slept with little on.[47] David Love noted how he knew many beggars who would deceive people with false infirmities. Love 'took particular notice when they were *undressing themselves for their beds*, that they had no lameness about them'. The same men also often got 'so drunk that they could not undress themselves for their beds'.[48] The need to be warm at night must have been especially important among the poor, as fuel could be expensive and most sleeping chambers did not contain hearths (Chapters 1 and 4). Thus, when individuals did not own nightwear, they probably slept in day clothes, perhaps with nightcaps, as can be seen in accounts of travelling vagrants who wore what they had on during the day when they slept and rested.[49] Of course, not everybody would have been worried about being cold (especially during the summer), but for most, homes must have been chilly for large parts of the year, and decent bedding and clothing of some sort was paramount to a peaceful night's rest.

Adjusting sleeping spaces to be cool and airy was viewed as important to eighteenth-century medical practitioners.[50] Whether the poor shared these attitudes is unclear, yet they would have had some ability to regulate their environment despite their limited resources, through using warming pans. Warming pans were particularly common in Essex and Kent, being recorded in 49 and 60 per cent of pauper inventories respectively (Table 3.6). In the other counties they were owned by around one-quarter to one-third of paupers. Most warming pans were valued at 1s. 6d. to 2s. 6d. meaning that they were relatively affordable. Copper warming pans, which heated more effectively than brass pans, also appear to have become slightly more common over the period. Indigent people would have benefited from the use of warming pans, as some, perhaps most, of their homes were badly insulated and draughty, resulting in damp bedsheets.[51] Warming pans also used less fuel than a lit hearth and so were a prudent investment, as well as one related to warmth and comfort. As an alternative to warming pans, people may have turned to ceramic bedwarmers. Though often just as cumbersome as warming pans (Figure 3.4), ceramic bedwarmers were safer, as they warmed beds using hot water and

Table 3.6 Percentage of paupers who owned warming pans, 1670–1835

	All years
Dorset	27
Essex	49
Kent	60
Leics/Ruts	24
Norfolk	34
All counties	40

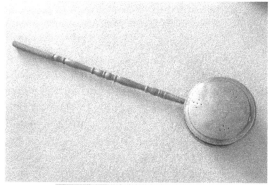

Figure 3.4 Warming pan (top) and ceramic bedwarmer (bottom), c. nineteenth century (source: privately owned; photographed by author, 2020)

did not need close supervision to avoid burning bedsheets. They could also be left in the bed throughout the night.

Although beds were common by the late seventeenth century, the enduring nature of poverty meant that many people slept under worn-out bedding, could not afford spare sheets and had to share beds in very trying conditions. Yet there were significant changes in the poor's use and possession of beds and furnishings over the long eighteenth century. Psychological and physical comfort became more important to indigent populations, as greater numbers of people invested in feather mattresses and acquired warming pans to regulate dampness and temperature. Bed hangings were increasingly used to make sleeping chambers more private and sensorially pleasing to residents, and many tried to make a feature of the area using colour schemes and different patterns on their hangings and bedding.

Storage units

Storage units had inherent practical purposes, but they also afforded people psychological comfort. Knowing where one's belongings were and that they were safe helped to create a sense of order and tidiness in a world that could be chaotic and difficult to negotiate. Frequently in daily use for clothes, storage units could also accommodate goods for longer periods of time. Spare items which might come in useful one day would be deposited in them, as well as a lifetime of sentimental sundries that individuals would revisit on occasion and could not bear to dispose of. A simple padlock on a storage unit could mean everything to people who shared rooms or slept in spaces that were trafficked by other members of the household, by way of giving them something that was theirs and a sense of privacy, independence and serenity.[52] By the late eighteenth century, ownership of a more diverse range of receptacles, including dressers, cupboards and chests of drawers, grew among the poor. These items were generally more convenient to use than boxes, allowing people to sub-divide their belongings into drawers and different compartments. In turn, those with meagre resources were able to elevate the appeal of their domestic spaces, as these articles of storage furniture could be used to display ornaments or plates and came in a variety of colours, materials and designs.

The most basic storage unit was a box, chest, trunk, coffer or ark of some sort.[53] Generally composed of five planks of wood to make the sides and base, these items were widely available and most were inexpensive and robust. Boxes (of any type) made up a constituent element of the home, being recorded in 79 per cent of pauper inventories at an average of 2.5 per home (Table 3.7). Appraisers tended not to describe stands or legs and used the adjectives 'little' or 'small' as often as 'large', suggesting that they tended to be placed on floors and came in various

Table 3.7 Pauper ownership of storage units, 1670–1835

		Average number	1670–1769 (%)	1770–1835 (%)	All years (%)
Box (any type)*	Dorset	2.9	84	73	80
	Essex	2.7	88	69	77
	Kent	3.6	92	91	92
	Leics/ Ruts	2.6	71	89	80
	Norfolk	1.9	79	62	77
	All counties	2.5	82	73	79
Chests of drawers	Dorset	1	3	0	2
	Essex	1.1	23	41	33
	Kent	1.2	13	41	23
	Leics/ Ruts	1	3	11	7
	Norfolk	1.1	13	43	18
	All counties	1.1	14	33	21
Cupboard (any type)~	Dorset	1.3	22	41	30
	Essex	1.4	69	69	69
	Kent	1.3	66	73	68
	Leics/ Ruts	1	23	49	35
	Norfolk	1.2	52	41	49
	All counties	1.3	52	59	55
Dresser	Dorset	1	14	32	20
	Essex	1.1	4	12	8
	Kent	1	16	55	30
	Leics/ Ruts	1.1	23	6	14
	Norfolk	1.1	10	19	11
	All counties	1.1	10	18	13
	Sample size		403	232	645

*Including arks, chests, coffers, hutches and trunks; specialised items such as hat and knife boxes are not included.
~Including pressers (i.e. press cupboards) and safes

Building blocks of the home   99

sizes. Sometimes the boxes were listed with locks and keys, helping people to feel content and safe knowing that their possessions were secure from trespassers. They acted as repositories of a wide range of belongings, such as clothing, linen, household goods and other valuables. The contents of Old Baidon's chest in Leeds, Kent, included 'a cote a hat and a Scarfe and a greene Apron 2 Blanketts more old Blanketts a pillocote and a Sheete 2 pot brasse scilletts a basting ladle a scimer [and] a brasse scimer'.[54] In Havering-atte-Bower, Essex, Widow Betts' deal box contained 'a Box iron and one Heatter one Flat Tin CandleStick ... one flanel Peticoat one Silk Bonnett one Pockett [and] one Sheet'.[55] Though most boxes were simple and unremarkable, on occasion they added a decorative element to rooms. William Pocock of Penshurst in Kent, for example, owned 'One large *handsom* Trunk'.[56] Isabella Brown, who used Fettes' pawnbroker's shop nearly 40 times between July 1777 and February 1778, pawned a box containing artificial flowers on one occasion.[57] Deal, ash, elm, leather-lined and painted boxes are also more commonly noted in the inventories from 1770, indicating that people became more interested in the appearance and colour of boxes according to personal taste over the eighteenth century.

Boxes remained the most popular storage unit that the poor owned well into the nineteenth century, but their use gradually declined in most regions as indigent populations increasingly acquired chests of drawers, cupboards and dressers (Table 3.7). The rise of chests of drawers is particularly notable. During the late seventeenth and early eighteenth century they were virtually unheard of in pauper abodes, but around a century later at least one-third of parishioners possessed one (Table 3.8).[58] Chests of drawers were not an insignificant investment. On average, they were valued at 8s. by appraisers, and they were more commonly constructed out of mahogany, elm and walnut than other storage units were. They were thus visually appealing and sought after and retained their value well. Growing ownership of chests of drawers was a practical development in comfort and convenience, allowing inhabitants to obtain their possessions more quickly and easily than from a box. More could be stored using less floor space, since drawers could be built one on top of another, whereas

Table 3.8   Percentage of paupers who owned boxes and chests of drawers, over time, 1670–1835

	1670–1709	1710–49	1750–89	1790–1834
Boxes (any type)	84	83	79	71
Chest of drawers	2	12	23	36
Sample size	45	163	270	145

the size of a box was constrained by how easy it was to reach items at the bottom.[59] While some drawers were messy and contained miscellaneous articles such as books, scissors and box irons, most were used to organise and sub-divide different types of linen and garments. This helped to structure and organise domestic spaces better.

Despite their practical advantages, there were significant regional differences in ownership of chests of drawers. In Dorset and Leicestershire/Rutland, only 2 and 7 per cent of the pauper inventories recorded chests of drawers respectively, while in Essex, Kent and Norfolk, ownership burgeoned and by the late eighteenth century around two-fifths of paupers in the counties possessed a set (Table 3.7). These regional differences probably resulted from myriad factors, including desire, location and availability. People in Essex and Kent were generally better connected to London, where chests of drawers were produced in significant numbers and where fashions for 'new' goods often emerged.[60] Meanwhile, Norfolk, especially Norwich, hosted some of the highest numbers of specialised furniture makers and brokers in the country,[61] which again probably made the items more visible and appealing to consumers.

Originally a surface where food was 'dressed', by the late seventeenth century dressers evolved into objects that had shelves for displaying tableware and enclosed compartments and drawers for other goods.[62] Ownership of dressers increased in nearly all the counties, especially in Kent (Table 3.7). Their large and specialised design gave people the practical means to store objects out of sight and display others for decoration. For instance, on the shelves of Widow Marchant's dresser in Chiddingstone, Kent, were '3 b[l]lue Edge plates 4 Bassons, ½ Dozen Cupps & Sawyers, 1 Rummer Glass, 2 wine Glasses, 3 b[l]lue Plates, one Queens wares bowl, 2 Quart, 2 pint [and] one ½ pint Pott'.[63] Most households contained only a single dresser for the kitchen, meaning that the ornamental positioning of items on shelves also facilitated quick access to plates, bowls and other vessels while cooking and dishing up food. The drawers of most dressers were probably used to store items for dining such as table linen and cutlery, along with other miscellaneous household goods. The majority of dressers were made from deal and some were even painted, adding a visually enhancing element and personal touch to rooms.

The term 'cupboard' was traditionally used to describe a side table in which cups and dishes were placed; hence the name *cup*-board. By the seventeenth century the term was associated with furniture that had cabinets and doors.[64] Cupboards were common in the home counties during the long eighteenth century, being recorded in around three in four pauper inventories (Table 3.7). They grew in ownership in Dorset and Leicestershire/Rutland and were possessed by around two-fifths to half of paupers there by the late eighteenth century. Ownership of cupboards appears to have slightly declined in Norfolk, but they are still recorded in

Building blocks of the home 101

41 per cent of pauper inventories between 1770 and 1835. Most cupboards were probably shared spaces for general household use, since locks and keys were infrequently listed with them. Their contents and use could vary considerably. A corner cupboard 'full of Cups Saucers plates Etc' was found in the keeping room of Thomas Waight of Thundersley, Essex, in 1796.[65] The cupboard of Sam Skeer in Pluckley, Kent, on the other hand, included a razor and tinder box, as well as plates, glass bottles, spoons, and knives and forks.[66] 'Bread and cheese' cupboards were mentioned in a handful of Essex inventories. Press cupboards, a predecessor to the wardrobe, are found in 15 and 12 per cent of Essex and Kent pauper inventories respectively. As with other items of storage, we see the gradual infiltration of cupboards that added a decorative element to rooms. By 1770, painted cupboards were more frequently listed in the inventories. Sometimes linen was used to cover cupboards and items were placed on them for adornment. The hall of Thomas Brown in Hatfield Broad Oak, Essex, contained a 'press cupbord with cupbord cloath with earthing potts and cups upon itt'.[67] In the same parish, '2 flower pots' were positioned on Catherine Barker's corner cupboard in 1782.[68]

Storage units made up fundamental building blocks of the home and went through important changes. Boxes were most common, even though with each generation the poor progressively invested in newer shapes and sizes of storage furniture. These items were often more expensive than boxes, but they helped to enhance the domestic sphere, make it more convenient for residents and allow people to display their goods in a more decorative and gratifying manner. The numbers of inventories which record decorative woods such as ash and elm also increases over time, and greater numbers of units appear to have been painted, to personalise them and make them more visually appealing. Thus, even the country's poorest invested in better and more divergent units to store and display what little they owned.

Seating

The need to sit is universal, and to be able to do this on an item of furniture that was specifically designed for this purpose and comfortable was important to the poor. Suitable seating was crucial for rest, as well as for facilitating chores and domestic production, such as washing and laundry. The ordered and appropriate positioning of seating was considered as a marker of respectability. This can be seen in the comments of pastor Richard Cobbold, who upon entering the home of labouring couple Thomas and Frances Garnham remarked how 'It was a pleasure to go into that cottage at all times', as 'Every chair was in its place … Her husband's easy chair in the corner of the fireplace, her boys' stools and form properly stationed, and her only daughter's footstool at her own feet'.[69] Before the seventeenth century, chairs were a marker of status, wealth and rank.

They would typically be used by heads of households and individuals in positions of authority, while others sat on stools, benches or forms.[70] As the example of the Garnhams above illustrates, components of this structure can be seen in the nineteenth century, and even today many households operate some sort of a hierarchy in seating. Children, for instance, might be swiftly removed from sofas if they encroach on their mother or father's spaces or be relegated to sub-standard stools when guests arrive.[71]

Seating could ignite powerful emotional responses in people. Working-class writers sometimes fondly recounted families and friends sitting around conversing. As a child, after 'the labours of the day were done', Thomas Carter and his family 'sat, much pleased with the novelty of the whole scene' by the fireplace.[72] In later life as a lodger, he recalled sitting in 'an easy chair by the side of a good fire', where he had 'a little pleasant chat with my host and hostess, together with my fellow-lodger'.[73] Frank Steele's most 'precious' memories from childhood were of his father coming home from work and telling his children stories from his chair:

> he [his father] would settle into that old mahogany-and-horsehair chair, so well worn and moulded to his convenience, and read – and discuss his readings with my mother, who sat knitting or sewing after clearing the tea-things away. And he would break off at times to tell us boys the most absurd tales. It was his humour to relate a funny story as though it were a fact and a personal experience, and leave it to Mother to reconcile his flights of fancy and square them (if she could) with the sober truth of everyday life.[74]

Seating was thus not just important for practical reasons but could also trigger sentimental and emotional responses in people. It played a central role in the formation of fond memories of loved ones and was the site where cherished pastimes such as reading, chatting and relaxing played out. Notions of fatherhood, motherhood and household structure were established, developed and imbedded in people's psyches through these recollections.

Ownership of seating was relatively common among the English poor by the late seventeenth century (Tables 3.9 and 3.10). Indigent dwellings located in the home counties were particularly well equipped: the majority of inventories from Essex and Kent record seating at a mean of around 6–7 per source. A high percentage of pauper inventories from Leicestershire/Rutland also note seats, but this may stem from there being no extant inventories for the counties prior to the 1760s, when seating ownership was lower. For paupers who appear not to have owned seating, this did not mean that they simply stood all day and did not rest until they slept. Items such as beds, boxes, tables and pails could be used as makeshift seating. For example, though undoubtedly embellished and adorned with messages of morality,[75] Figure 3.5 depicts somebody sitting on a pail, while others lean or sit on chairs. People could also sit on the floor, ledges and fixtures in the home.[76]

Table 3.9 Pauper ownership of seating, 1670–1835

	Seating (any type)		Chair		Stool		Bench/form		Settle		Upholstered seating	
	%	Average number	%	Average number	%	Average number	%	Average number	%	Average number	%	Average number
Dorset	75	4.2	70	2.9	42	1.7	22	1.6	12	1	2	1
Essex	92	6.8	89	5.5	48	2.2	18	1.7	1	1	3	3.7
Kent	97	6.1	90	5.2	35	1.6	32	1.7	7	1	3	1
Leics/Ruts	96	6	93	5.6	14	2.6	11	1.5	0	0	0	0
Norfolk	85	5.4	79	4.4	47	1.9	8	1.6	1	1	2	1.4
All counties	89	6	84	4.9	42	2	16	1.6	2	1	2	2.3

Table 3.10 Pauper ownership of seating, over time, 1670–1835

		1670–1729	1730–69	1770–1809	1810–35
Seating (any type)	%	78	88	95	97
	Average number	4.8	5.4	6.8	7.7
Chair	%	66	85	92	97
	Average number	3.6	4.4	5.8	6.2
Stool	%	43	41	38	52
	Average number	2.2	1.8	2.1	2.2
	Sample size	125	268	165	65

Figure 3.5 George Morland, *The Happy Cottagers (The Cottage Door)*, 1790 (source: Royal Holloway, University of London THC0046, George Morland, *The Happy Cottagers (The Cottage Door)*, oil on panel, 1790)

Chairs were the most common type of seats possessed by the poor (Table 3.9). Due to their backs, they helped individuals to sit with a better posture and were one of the most comfortable forms of seating available.[77] The ownership of chairs grew over the long eighteenth century in every county. Between 1670 and 1729, they are recorded in 66 per cent of the pauper inventories at an average of 3.6 per household. Nearly every inventory records chairs by the early nineteenth century (97 per cent) at a mean of 6.2 each (Table 3.10). This suggests that chairs were enjoyed by adults, children, lodgers and visitors, and that their use was no longer as deeply embedded in cultures of power and authority. From 1750, greater numbers of appraisers described chairs according to style, design, colour and material, indicating that they had become more diverse and decorative. Chairs made from elm, ash, mahogany, rush and walnut were increasingly noted by overseers. There was a growth in ownership of arm and elbow chairs, which allowed many to maintain a higher degree of comfort when resting. Some paupers even acquired arm or elbow chairs that matched other chairs. Michael Aggus from Earsham, Norfolk owned 'Five Elm hollow seat Chairs' and 'Two Elbow [chairs] to match'.[78] In Rhoda Wretham's East Harling home in Norfolk, there were '½ Doz[en] Hollow seat'd Chairs' and an 'Arm'd D⁰ [chair] to match'.[79]

Stools, benches, forms and settles were seen as more traditional items of seating due to their often simple construction and their use by non-heads of household. Each of these items appears to have been less common than chairs throughout the period, yet they were not entirely superseded and remained prominent in many dwellings (Tables 3.9 and 3.10). Stools were consistently owned by around two-fifths to half of paupers at an average of around two each throughout the long eighteenth century (Table 3.10). They continued to be important objects for at least four reasons. First, when using a spinning wheel or doing household tasks such as washing clothes, stools were the most ergonomic type of seating, as they allowed users to move more freely than a chair or settle. Some appraisers even listed a stool next to the entry for a spinning wheel, suggesting that the two were connected.[80] Second, stools, especially joint stools, were stackable[81] and so could be piled up in a corner when they were not needed or when space was scarce. Third, stools were particularly suitable for children, and could be used as footrests since they were often low-built.[82] Finally, most were small, unadorned and formed of oak, meaning that they were cheap alternatives to chairs and other seating.

Levels of ownership of benches and forms were low or declining for most counties over the eighteenth century. In Dorset and Essex, for example, benches/forms were recorded in 32 and 24 per cent of pauper inventories respectively between 1670 and 1769, but just 5 and 12 per cent of sources for 1770–1835. It was only in Kent where benches/forms remained a fairly frequent feature of poor homes, being noted in around one-third of inventories across the long eighteenth century. Settles are effectively benches with arms and high backs. They were helpful on long winter nights, as their large structures helped to keep the fireplace heat in and draughts out,[83] but they appear to have fallen out of favour for chairs and stools in every county.

From the second half of the eighteenth century, the standard of seating in poor dwellings was generally superior to that of the generations that came beforehand. Yet it is important to not take these arguments too far, as the quality of seating could still be inadequate or even unbearable. One night David Whitehead (b.1790) was locked out of his master's house, so he slept on the couch chair of his next-door neighbour. He remembered how 'sleep was out of the question, [because] there were so many of those little nimble blood suckers, fleas; I was constantly fidgeting and turning, and the old couch chair cracking'.[84] Significant numbers of people also possessed odd or old collections of seating alongside more valuable chairs. For example, Michael Aggus owned 'Two old Broken Chairs' and '4 old Chairs', in addition to his matching elbow chairs outlined above.[85] When Thomas Reece entered Redenhall workhouse in 1757, he brought '3 odd Chairs' with him.[86] In all, then, some people appear to have been able to retain decorative and comfortable chairs from more prosperous periods in their lives, while others had probably sold their better chairs and replaced them with cheaper ones that were unmatching, less fashionable and perhaps less comfortable.

To add to this, ownership of upholstered seating was negligible among the poor throughout the period (Table 3.9). Even for the poor living close to London, which was at the centre of the upholstery trade,[87] ownership did not exceed 3 per cent of pauper inventories. This was probably an added expense that the majority of people could not afford. The middling sort and the elite, on the other hand, increasingly acquired upholstered furniture from the early seventeenth century.[88] Cushions offered people a cheaper alternative, but only 9 of the 645 pauper inventories record one or more cushions. If additional padding and support was needed while seated, most people probably turned to spare clothing or pillows to line their backs.

Uncomfortable, broken, archaic and sometimes even vermin-ridden seating prevailed in poor homes. However, it would be unfair to paint too negative a picture. Chairs grew in ownership in every county and were increasingly found in higher numbers and in a greater range of styles, designs, colours and materials. More traditional forms of seating such as stools remained popular not just because people could ill afford an alternative, but because they were ergonomic choices for various household tasks and for children. Seating – a seemingly innocuous item – was an important building block in the construction of memories and emotional connections. It was when sitting down that familial bonds were often renewed and where new connections were formed. Chapter 4 develops these themes further by considering how families would sit around the fireplace, but for now we turn to tables.

Tables

Early modern tables were typically long, heavy and thick, making them particularly suitable for use alongside benches. Most were made from oak and were assembled to withstand rough everyday usage until they were no longer serviceable.[89] Marks, scuffs and faded colours were features of many tables from years of people dropping things on them and cups and plates being scraped across their surfaces. These abrasions also give clues as to the feelings of users, such as the anxious picking of loose threads and the impatient bouncing of feet on the beam (Figure 3.6). Over time, tables evolved to be smaller, lighter and thinner, and greater numbers were made to be square, round or oval. These designs were seen as more fashionable and further encouraged households to acquire chairs over cumbersome alternatives such as benches and settles.[90] Tables were increasingly used for particular purposes, resulting in the growth of specialised tables such as dining, tea and dressing tables.[91] Sometimes used in tandem with tablecloths and napkins, a further element of refinement, social manners and respectability was added to the use of tables. Collectively, this meant that tables were important objects for their convenience as they made various domestic tasks easier, but they also helped to shape various social rituals and added to the aesthetic appeal of homes.

Tables were common in the homes of the middling sort by the late seventeenth and early eighteenth century.[92] During the same period, they appear to have been owned in high numbers in poor homes, but they were probably not ubiquitous at this point, as 31 per cent of pauper inventories

Figure 3.6 Long oak table, c. eighteenth century (source: privately owned; photograph provided by and reproduced with permission of James Ribbons Antiques)

At home with the poor

Table 3.11 Pauper ownership of tables, over time, 1670–1835

		1670–1709	1710–39	1740–69	1770–99	1800–35
Table (any type)	%	69	70	81	92	93
	Average number	1.6	1.7	1.9	2.6	2.8
Round/ oval table	%	0	3	10	18	30
	Average number	0	1	1.2	1.2	1.4
Square table	%	0	2	13	20	24
	Average number	0	1	1.4	1.6	1.3
Long table	%	2	3	5	2	1
	Average number	1	1	1	1.3	1
Table board	%	4	4	9	8	5
	Average number	1	1	1.3	1.2	1.2
	Sample size	45	125	222	123	107

do not record one (Table 3.11). Of course, one should never assume that every inventory is complete, but over the period we do progressively see an increase in table ownership, indicating that it was during the eighteenth century that they became universal. By the turn of the nineteenth century, tables were clearly omnipresent, being recorded in 93 per cent of pauper inventories at an average of nearly three each. For those who did not possess a table, they could use fixtures, ledges and other makeshift surfaces around the home as elevated horizontal surfaces. For example, Figure 3.7 portrays a woman using a laid-down chair alongside planks of wood and a linen sheet as an improvised table surface to rest and cool her oatcakes. George Walker is well known for his sympathetic representations of the poor and so it is feasible that people made do without a table, as depicted here, if they needed to.[93]

Long tables are rarely noted in pauper inventories (Table 3.11), which is surprising as research conducted by other historians indicates that they were common.[94] Perhaps they were not described in this way by appraisers as they were so common that their shape was a given. In any case, from the mid- to late eighteenth century, growing numbers of people appear to have moved towards tables formed of new decorative shapes that were made using greater craft. By the early nineteenth century, round/oval and square tables are recorded in 30 and 24 per cent of pauper inventories. A similar pattern of growth can be seen in the bastardy, debt, rent and goods-taken inventories of paupers' goods. Only 5 and 3 per cent of these inventories note round/oval and square tables for 1668–1769; however, after 1770, 25 and 19 per cent of

Figure 3.7 George Walker, *Woman Making Oat Cakes*, 1814 (source: George Walker, *The Costume of Yorkshire*, London: T. Bensley, 1814, plate 9)

inventories record these shapes respectively. On occasion, other peculiarly shaped tables are recorded, such as that of James Gobbett in Norfolk, who owned a 'triangle table'.[95] Round, oval and square tables were generally seen as more sophisticated and fashionable by contemporaries. They tended to be smaller than long tables and were often decoratively placed in the corners and on the borders of rooms as side tables.[96] This switch to new shapes helped to make chairs more popular too, as round, oval and square tables were not well suited to use with benches and settles.

By the late eighteenth century, there was a growth in the number of inventory takers who labelled tables by material, colour, finish and use. This indicates that the tables of the poor had improved in quality and that appraisers found these properties worthy of note. There was a slight increase in ownership of tables made from decorative and relatively expensive woods, including wainscot (an imported high-quality oak), walnut and ash. When tables were painted, white was the most popular colour, and japanned (lacquered) tables were noted more often by the late eighteenth century. Dressing, dining and tea tables grew in ownership, showing that some tables moved from multifunctionality to being more specialised. Leaf tables and tables with drawers are also more frequently recorded in pauper inventories after 1770.

The move towards tables which came in a variety of shapes would have helped to alter social dynamics when friends and families gathered.[97]

These new tables were important to novel social rituals, including the drinking of tea and dining with new tableware such as knives and forks and earthenware plates. Eating, drinking, socialising and talking ultimately became more intimate, equal and satisfying for all.[98] People did not need to raise their voice to speak to someone at the other end of the table or reach a long way to pass them condiments or shared dishes. When playing games, participants could access communal piles of cards easily and circulate dice and other game pieces effortlessly. Owning tables that could be extended with leaves helped households to accommodate family and guests more comfortably. Dressing tables meant that people could get ready conveniently and efficiently, as they often had inbuilt drawers or small compartments for storing items.[99] Some even had looking glasses attached to them, allowing people to take further care and pride in their appearances.[100]

As with seating, it is important to not overstate changes in the consumption of tables in poor homes. While there was an increase in tables made of exotic woods and in decorative shapes, most of the poor seem to have favoured multi-purpose tables made of oak or deal which could withstand a range of uses. These limits are more apparent in some regions than others. In Dorset and Norfolk, paupers were slightly less likely to possess tables and owned them in lower numbers than elsewhere (Table 3.12). Those living in Dorset appear to have been among the least likely to own round, oval and square tables, and tables with removeable legs (table boards) were also especially common in the county. These were more archaic and traditional types of tables, as they allowed users to transform spaces which had multiple functions with relative ease and could be piled neatly into a corner when they were not needed.[101] Sometimes appraisers listed trestles (moveable legs) with table boards, but not as often as they did for the probate inventories of the middling sort.[102] This meant that the poor sometimes used makeshift legs, such as Robert Howell from Martham in Norfolk, who had '1 Small one [table] on the Stool'.[103] Similarly, when the pauper Mary Webbs had her goods sold by Lower Halstow parish in Kent in 1781, her inventory included 'One Joint Stoole with a table thereon'.[104]

It is unclear how regularly tablecloths and napkins were used alongside tables. On the one hand, writing in 1797, Frederic Morton Eden argued that 'not only the lowest peasant eats his meal at a table, but also has his table covered with a table-cloth'.[105] Old Bailey records too show that tablecloths and napkins were increasingly stolen from the labouring sort as their price declined from the second half of the eighteenth century.[106] However, there is much evidence to the contrary which suggests that significant numbers of the poor did not possess table linen or that they owned it only during relatively prosperous periods of their lives.

Table 3.12 Pauper ownership of tables, 1670–1835

		Average number	1670–1769 (%)	1770–1835 (%)	All years (%)
Table (any type)	Dorset	1.8	59	86	68
	Essex	2.5	88	92	90
	Kent	2.3	84	100	90
	Leics/Ruts	2.2	86	100	92
	Norfolk	1.8	69	86	72
	All counties	2.2	76	93	82
Square table	Dorset	1.2	8	14	10
	Essex	1.6	16	24	20
	Kent	1	13	18	15
	Leics/Ruts	1.6	0	20	10
	Norfolk	1.2	4	19	7
	All counties	1.4	8	21	13
Round/ oval table	Dorset	1	11	14	12
	Essex	1.3	7	23	16
	Kent	1.1	13	23	17
	Leics/Ruts	1.8	0	29	14
	Norfolk	1.2	5	22	8
	All counties	1.3	7	23	13
Board	Dorset	1.4	49	18	37
	Essex	1.1	2	5	4
	Kent	1	8	18	12
	Leics/Ruts	0	0	0	0
	Norfolk	1	3	3	3
	All counties	1.2	7	6	7
	Sample size		403	232	645

While linen of any kind is under-recorded in the inventories, napkins and tablecloths still only appear in 2 per cent of the pauper inventories. Bedding, on the other hand, is recorded in 82 per cent of the same sources (Table 3.5). The research of Lorna Weatherill shows that between 1675 and 1725, the poorer somebody was, the less likely they were to own table linen. In fact, only 7 per cent of the probate inventories she used with £1–2 worth of household possessions note table linen, compared with 74 per cent of inventories which list over £100 worth of goods.[107] Between 1777 and 1778, the pawnbroker's pledge book of George Fettes of York recorded 10,906 pledges. Of these, 179 and 181 were for tablecloths and napkins respectively. Clothing and linen of various sorts were the most common pledges that Fettes received and so one of the key items that people sold to make thrift during difficult periods.[108]

Unlike other types of furniture, tables were less necessary to everyday life. One could still eat a meal, converse with family or do various chores without a platform on which to rest one's elbows, plates or tools. Yet in each county the poor increasingly invested in tables, and some turned to ones which came in various shapes, sizes and materials according to personal taste. The fact that appraisers increasingly used adjectives such as 'dining', 'tea' and 'dressing' to describe tables from the late eighteenth century is also important. It shows just how far poor abodes had come, and how people could create a more satisfying space which had various items around it for specific purposes. These changes, of course, pale in comparison with those of the middling sort and the elite, but for indigent people they were significant and show that convenience and comfort had become more important to homemakers.

Conclusion

When studied, most research on furniture has focused on the construction, design, advertising and retailing practices of high-profile furniture makers in the capital, rather than the consumption of more ordinary furniture and its use in the provincial domestic sphere.[109] This is an unfortunate oversight, as these everyday items formed crucial building blocks of the home and not all items of furniture were meant to be showy. Furniture was placed around dwellings to create a sense of order and structure, and ultimately made the home more pleasing to be in. Alongside furnishings, it altered the appearance of interiors and allowed dwellings to function according to personal preferences. It was on items of furniture that pivotal and memorable moments of the life-cycle occurred. Beds played host to three of the most important parts in people's life – birth, marriage and death – and it was within their confines that activities such as reading, talking and sex played out. Being sat around a table was an important location where families gathered to hear about one another's days and renew their familial bonds. Storage units had practical purposes, but they were also repositories of cherished memories and their contents could reveal much about one's dreams, passions and hopes. The next chapter develops these topics further by focusing on the hearth and its importance.

Notes

1 Overton et al., *Production and Consumption*, pp. 90–8, 108–11; Sear and Sneath, *Consumer Revolution*, pp. 131–42; French, *Middle Sort*, pp. 141–200; Clive Edwards, *Eighteenth Century Furniture* (Manchester: Manchester University Press, 1996); Ralph Fastnedge, *English Furniture Styles from 1500–1830* (Harmondsworth: Penguin, reprint of 1955 edn, 1961); F. Gordon Roe, *English Cottage Furniture* (London: Phoenix House, 3rd edn, 1961).
2 In contrast, Cohen estimated that the nineteenth-century middle classes would change furniture around every seven years. Cohen, *Household Gods*, p. 33.
3 Laura Gowing, 'The Twinkling of a Bedstaff: Recovering the social life of English beds 1500–1700', *Home Cultures*, 11:3 (2014), pp. 275–304; Holmes, *In Bed*; Handley, *Sleep*; Angela McShane and Joanne Begiato, 'Making Beds, Making Households: The domestic and emotional landscape of the bed in early modern England' (unpublished paper, 2011); Hamling and Richardson, *Day at Home*, pp. 228–63; Katie Barclay, 'Making the Bed, Making the Lower-Order Home in Eighteenth-Century Scotland', in Stephen G. Hague and Karen Lipsedge (eds), *At Home in the Eighteenth Century* (London: Routledge, 2022), pp. 266–82.
4 Handley, *Sleep*.
5 Lawrence Wright, *Warm and Snug: The history of the bed* (Stroud: Sutton Publishing, reprint of 1962 edn, 2004), p. 18; Fastnedge, *Furniture Styles*, p. 2.
6 Handley, *Sleep*, p. 123; McShane and Begiato, 'Making Beds', pp. 4–5.
7 SA HD 368/1; SA HD 1025/1.
8 NRO PC 88/1.
9 NRO PD 108/84.
10 Thomas W. Smith, *A Narrative of the Life, Travels and Sufferings of Thomas W. Smith* (Boston: Wm C. Hill, 1844), pp. 18–19.
11 King, Nutt and Tomkins, *Narratives*, p. 251.
12 Handley, *Sleep*, pp. 46–7, 59–60.
13 Hart, 'Autobiography', Part I, p. 155.
14 Sokoll, *Pauper Letters*, pp. 317–18.
15 Vicky Holmes, 'Dangerous Spaces: Working-class homes and fatal household accidents in Suffolk, 1840–1900', PhD thesis (University of Essex, 2012), pp. 271, 303.
16 NRO PD 295/102; Shaw, *Family Records*, p. 22.
17 Tomkins, *Urban Poverty*, p. 67.
18 James Hopkinson, *Victorian Cabinet Maker: The memoirs of James Hopkinson 1819–1894*, ed. Jocelyne Baty Goodman (London: Routledge & Kegan Paul, 1968), pp. 90–1.
19 Gowing, 'Twinkling', pp. 288–95.
20 Holmes, 'Dangerous Spaces', pp. 281–91.
21 Gowing, 'Twinkling', p. 279.
22 Kent, *Hints*, p. 229.
23 John Wood, *A Series of Plans for Cottages or Habitations of the Labourer* (London: I. and J. Taylor, 2nd edn, 1792), pp. 4–5.
24 Also see Figure 3.3.
25 Weatherill, *Consumer Behaviour*, pp. 81–3; Overton et al., *Production and Consumption*, p. 113.
26 ERO D/P 300/12/3; ERO D/P 4/18/8.

27 For instance, bedding and pillows/bolsters are noted in 74 and 49 per cent of the goods-given inventories respectively.

28 Ann Clark (ed.), *Sherborne Almshouse Register* (Dorchester: Dorset Record Society, 2013), pp. 62–134.

29 On sleeping rough, see: Hitchcock, *Down and Out*, pp. 23–48.

30 Barrie Trinder and Jeff Cox (eds), *Yeoman and Colliers in Telford: Probate inventories for Dawley, Lilleshall, Wellington and Wrockwardine, 1660–1750* (London: Phillimore & Co., 1980), p. 36.

31 Unfortunately, it was not always possible to distinguish between clothing, textiles and household linen to give more precise figures. YALH Accession 38; Alison Backhouse, *Worm-Eaten*, pp. 77–81.

32 Sokoll, *Pauper Letters*, pp. 133–4.

33 King, Nutt and Tomkins, *Narratives*, pp. 238–48.

34 Ibid., p. 238.

35 Ibid., pp. 247–8.

36 Styles, 'Lodging at the Old Bailey, pp. 74–5; Helmreich, Hitchcock and Turkel, 'Rethinking Inventories', p. 23; Horrell, Humphries and Sneath, 'Consumption Conundrums', pp. 853–4; Lemire, *Fashion's Favourite*.

37 Two per cent of pauper inventories record feather pillows/bolsters, 1.7 per cent flock and 0.3 per cent straw.

38 ERO D/P 146/8.

39 Washing is discussed further in Chapter 4.

40 Randles, 'Material World', p. 167; Pennell, 'For a crack', pp. 31–9.

41 ERO D/P 4/18/8.

42 NRO PD 219/114.

43 On colour, see: Diana Young, 'The Colours of Things', in Chris Tilley, Webb Keane, Susan Kuechler, Mike Rowlands and Patricia Spyer (eds), *Handbook of Material Culture* (London: Sage, 2006), pp. 173–85; French, *Middle Sort*, pp. 179–85.

44 On emotion and textiles, see: Alice Dolan and Sally Holloway (eds), 'Emotional Textiles' special edition, *Textile*, 14:2 (2016), pp. 152–267; Holloway, 'Materializing Maternal Emotions', pp. 154–71; Styles, *Threads of Feeling*; Sara Pennell, 'Making the Bed in Later Stuart and Georgian England', in Jon Stobart and Bruno Blondé (eds), *Selling Textiles in the Long Eighteenth Century: Comparative perspectives from western Europe* (Basingstoke: Palgrave, 2014), pp. 30–45; Handley, *Sleep*, esp. pp. 131–48; Sasha Handley, 'Objects, Emotions and an Early Modern Bed-Sheet', *History Workshop Journal*, 85 (2018), pp. 169–94; McShane and Begiato, 'Making Beds'.

45 Handley, *Sleep*, pp. 52–7.

46 It is important to note that these items can also be associated with daywear.

47 G. J., *Prisoner Set Free*, p. 8. My italics.

48 Love, *Life*, pp. 20–1. My italics.

49 Such as: Josiah Basset, *The Life of a Vagrant or the Testimony of an Outcast* (London: Charles Gilpin, 1850), passim; Saxby, *Memoirs*, passim; Samuel Bamford, *Early Days* (London: Simpkin, Marshall, & Co., 1849), pp. 253–75.

50 Handley, *Sleep*, pp. 39–68.

51 On housing, see Chapter 1.

52 Vickery, *Behind Closed Doors*, pp. 38–48.

53 In theory, each of these boxes were slightly different to one another, but in practice the terms were interchangeable and flexible. This is why they are analysed collectively here. Oxford English Dictionary Online (www.oed.com); Lucy Razzall, *Boxes and Books in Early Modern England: Materiality, metaphor, containment* (Cambridge: Cambridge University Press, 2021), pp. 11–12.

54 KHLC P222/12/1.

55 ERO D/P 64/18/8.

56 KHLC P287/18/5. My italics.

57 YALH Accession 38.

58 The results from the bastardy, debt, rent and goods-taken inventories of people on relief corroborate this change. Between 1668 and 1769, 82 per cent of the inventories recorded boxes but after 1770, the proportion had fallen to 64 per cent. Meanwhile, the ownership of chests of drawers increased from 13 to 26 per cent over the same period.

59 Overton et al., *Production and Consumption*, pp. 90–2; Gertrude Jekyll and Sydney R. Jones, *Old English Household Life* (London: B. T. Batsford, 2nd edn, 1945), pp. 95–7.

60 Wrigley, 'Simple Model', pp. 44–70; Overton et al., *Production and Consumption*; Weatherill, *Consumer Behaviour*, pp. 43–69; Orlin, *Material London*; Mui and Mui, *Shops and Shopkeeping*; Styles, 'Product Innovation', pp. 124–69; Tankard, *Clothing*, pp. 73–98.

61 For example, using a key term search for 'furniture' in an 1839 trade directory covering six counties, 23 furniture traders of some kind were listed in Norfolk. The closest other county to this figure was Cambridgeshire, which had 13 furniture traders. Bedfordshire only had five and Huntingdon listed none. As for 'cabinet makers', around one-third of the total in the directory lived in Norfolk. *Robinson's Commercial Directory of the Six Counties forming the Norfolk Circuit: Beds, Cambridgeshire, Hunts, Norfolk, and Suffolk, with Oxfordshire* (London: William Robson & Co., 1839).

62 Francis W. Steer (ed.), *Farm and Cottage Inventories of Mid-Essex, 1635–1749* (Chichester: Phillimore & Co., 2nd edn, 1969), p. 12.

63 KHLC P89/12/17.

64 Steer, *Inventories*, pp. 14–15; Roe, *Cottage Furniture*, pp. 134–5.

65 ERO D/P 357/12/1.

66 KHLC P289/18/2.

67 ERO D/P 4/18/8.

68 Ibid.

69 SA HA 11/A13/10.

70 Ralph Edwards, *English Chairs* (London: HMSO, 1951), p. 5; Fastnedge, *Furniture Styles*, p. 8; Steer, *Inventories*, p. 13; Gerard Brett, *Dinner Is Served: A history of dining in England 1400–1900* (London: Rupert Hart-Davis, 1968), p. 92.

71 Megan Doolittle, 'Time, Space, and Memories', *Home Cultures*, 8:3 (2011), pp. 253–4; Julie-Marie Strange, 'Fatherhood, Furniture and the Inter-Personal Dynamics of Working-Class Homes, c.1870–1914', *Urban History*, 40:2 (2013), pp. 279–80.

72 Carter, *Memoirs*, pp. 50–1.

73 Ibid., p. 146.

74 Quoted from Doolittle, 'Time, Space', p. 254.

75 Payne, 'Rural Virtues', pp. 45–68; Barrell, *Dark Side*; Nichols, 'Motives of Control/ Motifs of Creativity', pp. 138–63.

76 Such as in: Laika Nevalainen, 'Flexible, Portable and Communal Domesticity: Everyday domestic practices of Finnish sailors and logging workers, c.1880s to 1930s', in Harley, Holmes and Nevalainen, *Working Class at Home*, p. 225.

77 Crowley, *Invention of Comfort*, p. 146.

78 NRO PD 295/106.

79 NRO PD 219/114.

80 See for instance the pauper inventory of Albine Davidge's goods in DHC PE-EST/ OV/1/1.

81 Roe, *Cottage Furniture*, pp. 110–11.

82 Ibid., p. 112.

83 Ibid., p. 109; Jekyll and Jones, *Old English*, p. 93.

84 Whitehead, *Autobiography*, p. 9.

85 NRO PD 295/106.

86 NRO PD 295/117.

87 For example: Overton et al., *Production and Consumption*, pp. 91, 95–6, 191.

88 Ibid., pp. 95–6.

89 Fastnedge, *Furniture Styles*, pp. 20–2; Roe, *Cottage Furniture*, pp. 127–8.

90 Margaret Visser, *The Rituals of Dinner: The origins, evolution, eccentricities, and meaning of table manners* (London: Viking, 1992), p. 122; Fastnedge, *Furniture Styles*, pp. 20–2.

91 Fastnedge, *Furniture Styles*, passim; Roe, *Cottage Furniture*, passim; Berg, *Luxury and Pleasure*, pp. 229–32.

92 Weatherill, *Consumer Behaviour*, pp. 26, 44; French, *Middle Sort*, pp. 141–200.

93 George Sheeran, 'Walker, George (1781–1856)', *ODNB* (Oxford, 2014) (from: www.oxforddnb.com/view/article/105621, accessed 07/11/2014); David Hill, *Turner and Leeds: Image of industry* (Leeds: Jeremy Mills Publishing, 2008), pp. 145–6.

94 Fastnedge, *Furniture Styles*, pp. 20–2; Roe, *Cottage Furniture*, pp. 127–8.

95 NRO PD 295/133.

96 Fastnedge, *Furniture Styles*, pp. 77–9; Brett, *Dinner Is Served*, p. 91.

97 Hints and anecdotal records of people congregating around tables can be seen in: Robert Story, *Love and Literature; Being the Reminiscences* (London: Longman, Brown, Green and Longmans, 1842), pp. 34–5; Joshua Marsden, *Sketches of the Early Life of a Sailor* (Hull: William Ross, 3rd edn, 1821), pp. 36–7; William Gifford, *Memoir of William Gifford, written by Himself* (London: Hunt and Clarke, 1827), p. 16; MacDonald, *Travels*, p. 97; Hick, *Village Blacksmith*, p. 233; Joseph Donaldson, *Recollections of an Eventful Life Chiefly Passed in the Army* (Glasgow: W. R. McPhun, 1824), p. 67; Gooch, *Memoirs*, p. 49.

98 Carter, *Memoirs*, pp. 50–1.

99 Fastnedge, *Furniture Styles*, pp. 121, 123.

100 Eating is discussed in Chapter 5. Games (particularly children's games) and looking glasses are assessed in Chapter 6.

101 Fastnedge, *Furniture Styles*, p. 9; Brett, *Dinner Is Served*, p. 90; Visser, *Rituals of Dinner*, pp. 148–9; Roe, *Cottage Furniture*, p. 123.

102 Steer, *Inventories*, pp. 11–12.

103 NRO PD 710/68.

104 KHLC P168/18/1.

105 Eden, *State of the Poor*, Vol. 1, p. 524.

106 Horrell, Humphries and Sneath, 'Consumption Conundrums', pp. 850–3.

107 Weatherill, *Consumer Behaviour*, pp. 108–9.

108 YALH Accession 38; Backhouse, *Worm-Eaten*, pp. 77–81.

109 Margaret Ponsonby, 'Consumption of Furniture and Furnishings for the Home in the West Midlands using Local Suppliers 1760–1860', PhD thesis (University of Wolverhampton, 2001), pp. 20–4, 35.

4

Comforts of the hearth

The hearth was the heart of the home. It was central to the wellbeing and comfort of inhabitants through the warmth and light that it provided. Hours would have been spent preparing and cooking meals by it, and to perform household activities such as brewing, ironing and laundry, heat and hot water from the fireplace was necessary. The hearth also became a location for rest and relaxation for families. People would often read and chat with their loved ones by the fire, or enjoy solitary time daydreaming and pondering the day's events to the sights and sounds of a crackling fire. The hearth could, however, equally be a scene of discomfort, anxiety, fear and danger. When families argued it frequently took place by the hearth, and out-of-control fires and poorly maintained fireplaces were not uncommon throughout the period, sometimes resulting in severe injuries and even death.

The chapter starts by examining the number of hearths that poor abodes contained, before moving on to consider fuel, domestic chores such as laundry and washing, memories of the fireplace, and artificial lighting. It is argued that although most pauper homes contained only a single hearth, it was nevertheless *the* key site where families gathered and where various household chores were carried out. The fuel used in the hearths of the poor varied considerably according to location. In areas close to coalfields, such as Lancashire, Leicestershire and Rutland, coal was in use throughout the period, whereas counties further afield continued to use a mix of wood and peat well into the nineteenth century. Cleanliness became much more important to people, and the variety of laundry- and washing-related items in people's homes grew. By exploring indigent recollections of the hearth, the emotional and symbolic importance of the area is considered, along with how fireplaces could be a site of danger or conflict. The hearth was undoubtedly the most important form of illumination in poor homes, but people also used candles for lighting and to make dwellings appear brighter and more spacious. The practice of

Number of hearths

Before examining the importance and uses of the hearth, it is important to establish the number of fireplaces that tended to be found in poor dwellings. One of the most important yet most problematic sources through which to research this is hearth taxes, which note the number of hearths that abodes contained to determine how much tax each household paid. Keith Wrightson and David Levine have suggested that households with six or more hearths were likely to have been occupied by the gentry and that those with one hearth or that were exempt were the homes of the labouring sort.[1] While there is clearly some correlation between number of hearths and social standing, this approach oversimplifies household structure, ignores the influence of location and perpetuates the old myth that being poor equated to having very little. Research on various settlements shows that it was not unusual for the gentry to have far fewer hearths than six, and that the poorer sort did not always just have one fireplace.[2] Regionally, households in the north also tended to contain fewer hearths than those in the south irrespective of social standing or wealth.[3] An alternative approach for studying fireplaces is to use pauper inventories.

The majority of pauper inventories record only one set of bellows, tongs and other fire irons each, which suggests that most homes had only one hearth. Of course, people may have divided or shared the items between different fireplaces, but this was probably not widespread, especially with andirons, fire pans and grates, since these items held the fuel in place and so were not moveable when the fire was lit. One can more reliably estimate hearth numbers by focusing on the 170 pauper inventories which record rooms from Chapter 1, since these sources reveal which rooms the fire irons were in and thus where people's hearths were most likely located. Although the inventories which record rooms are heavily skewed towards Essex, the results are remarkably consistent and indicate that most paupers around the country lived in abodes which contained a single hearth (Table 4.1). The average number of hearths in pauper abodes appears to have increased over time, but not significantly so. In fact, the results show that only two people in the sample had three hearths and only fifteen had two. As an alternative, people could have turned to a stove, yet only 3 per cent of the pauper inventories note one. Most stoves were recorded in the Essex pauper inventories dated 1810–35, which may suggest that they were starting to become more common from the early nineteenth century, but without inventories for the rest of the century it is impossible to tell.

Table 4.1 Average number of hearths in pauper homes, 1670–1835

	1670–1769	1770–1835	All years
Dorset (n=8)	1	1	1
Essex (n=91)	1	1.2	1.1
Kent (n=22)	1.3	1.4	1.3
Leics/Ruts (n=10)	1	1.3	1.2
Norfolk (n=39)	1	1.1	1.1
All (n=170)	1	1.2	1.1
Sample size	76	91	170

Table 4.2 Location of hearths in pauper homes, 1670–1835

	%
Kitchen	27
Dwelling room/house	18
House	10
Hall	10
Chamber (unspecific)	7
Lower room	5
Other	22

As noted in Chapter 1, the terms used to denote a kitchen vary considerably. In Essex and Leicestershire/Rutland, the term 'house' or 'dwelling room/house' might have predominated for kitchens. 'Lower room', 'backroom', 'fire room' and 'parlour' could also be used to signify a kitchen. With this in mind, the vast majority of hearths appear to have been in kitchens of some sort (Table 4.2), and they witnessed myriad activities such as cooking, drinking, eating, sitting and various forms of domestic production, including baking (Table 4.3). This is largely unsurprising, since cooking, washing and other activities required heat from the hearth, but these results nonetheless help to illustrate how and why the hearth became a focal point where residents would gather. With most homes containing only a single hearth, there was only one location where people could warm themselves. It was situated by the fireplace, where seating was often placed, where cooking needed to be done, where ovens were located for breadmaking and where hot water was produced.

At home with the poor

Table 4.3 Functions of pauper rooms with hearths in them, 1670–1835

	%
Cooking	76
Eating/drinking	74
Lighting	53
Sitting	93
Sleeping	26
Working	52

Fuel

We have some two centuries' worth of studies on the importance of coal and its use in technologies of the industrial revolution.[4] Yet while this literature has understandably grown apace, there remains less work on people's use of more traditional forms of energy such as wood and peat, and on how fuel was utilised in the domestic setting.[5] The poor are particularly under-researched in this area, which is unfortunate, as fuel had a direct impact on quality of life. Indigent populations could use a considerable range of substances as fuel, including dung, furze and even seaweed,[6] but the three main choices at their disposal were usually coal, wood or peat.[7] Choosing one of these over another had ramifications on the quality and efficiency of cooking, how well illuminated abodes were, the ability to keep a household warm and how smoky dwellings were. By examining the hearth-related goods found in pauper inventories alongside poor relief records, this section considers the types of fuel that the poor tended to use and the extent to which coal superseded peat and wood over the long eighteenth century.

Fire irons have been grouped into coal- and wood-related hearth items to research the types of fuel that paupers used (Table 4.4). This form of analysis is problematic, and several issues must be kept in mind. First, there are no fire irons which can be directly connected to the use of peat, and so for this fuel we must rely on poor relief records. Second, the table is based on the assumption that the poor tended to use certain fire irons with particular fuels. For coal, we have two estimates from the pauper inventories. The first is conservative and reliant on the presence of grates (which were almost always used with coal), records of coal reserves and the term 'coal' being used. The second calculation is more speculative and based on a wider range of goods which tended to be, but were not always, used with coal over other forms of firing.[8] The poor could be very resourceful and so some will have used these items with other fuels.[9] Third, it is possible

Table 4.4 Percentage of paupers who owned hearth items related to coal and wood use, 1670–1835

		1670–1769	1770–1835	All years
Coal (Estimate 1)*	Dorset	0	5	2
	Essex	5	14	9
	Kent	3	0	2
	Leics/Ruts	9	20	14
	Norfolk	3	24	7
	All counties	3	14	7
Coal (Estimate 2)**	Dorset	0	5	2
	Essex	13	43	28
	Kent	5	14	8
	Leics/Ruts	11	26	18
	Norfolk	4	43	11
	All counties	7	34	17
Wood (any type) ***	Dorset	0	5	2
	Essex	50	27	38
	Kent	50	77	60
	Leics/Ruts	11	6	8
	Norfolk	25	22	24
	All counties	30	26	29
	Sample size	403	232	645

*Grates, coal and the word 'coal' being noted
**Fenders, grates, pokers, coal and the word 'coal' being noted
***Andirons, wood and the words 'wood', 'faggots' etc. being noted

that increases in coal use in the second estimate may stem from people using pokers and fenders with other fuels. Fourth, sometimes grates were fixtures of the home and so were not noted in the inventories, since they were not moveable property. Fifth, just because somebody owned hearth items connected to particular fuel use, this does not mean that they used them from day to day. The poor may have kept old fire irons as spares for when they had to switch to alternative fuels due to shortages or financial restraints. Finally, it is possible that changes in fuel use in the table may stem from the poor buying more-specialised items which are easier to identify in the inventories, rather than actual shifts in the types of fuel that people used. Because of these issues, the results are imperfect and

122 At home with the poor

indefinite in areas. Nevertheless, by studying fire irons alongside the fuel that was granted to paupers by poor law authorities, revealing and suggestive trends are uncovered.

Coal was, undoubtedly, the most superior form of fuel available to consumers throughout the long eighteenth century. It burned for long periods of time and provided more heat and light than alternative fuels.[10] Despite this, evidence indicates that the switch to coal was a long-drawn-out process, with significant regional differences (Tables 4.4 and 4.5). In some regions there were remarkable continuities in traditional fuel consumption, while elsewhere energy use changed considerably within a relatively short space of time. Wood was the most common form of firing

Table 4.5 Types of fuel used by paupers, c.1650s–1830s

County	Types of fuel used
Dorset	Little evidence of specialised fire irons, and paupers tended to be given firewood or peat by authorities. Coal use was rare.
Essex	Significant rise in ownership of coal-related items and coal being given to paupers by poor law authorities after 1770. Before this date, it was usual for wood to be provided for recipients of relief and around half of the pauper inventories recorded wood-related hearth items. Peat use was atypical.
Kent	Little evidence of ownership of coal-related items or coal being given to paupers. Peat use was also rare. Wood eclipsed all other forms of fuel during the long eighteenth century.
Lancashire	Coal consumption prevailed: 61% of the pauper inventories and debt-related, poorhouse/workhouse-admittance and bastardy-related inventories which record the goods of paupers note coal-related hearth items (31 inventories in total). Coal was also commonly given to paupers as relief in kind. No record of wood or peat use was found.
Leicestershire/ Rutland	Coal was commonly given to paupers during the eighteenth century and some paupers owned specialised hearth items connected to coal use. Wood was used less frequently and no record of peat burning has been uncovered.
Norfolk	Wood use was most common between c.1650 and 1770, while peat and coal were used less frequently by paupers. After 1770, coal was used more often by indigent populations, resulting in a prolonged decline in wood and peat use. Peat appears more frequently in Norfolk than the other counties owing to its proximity to the Fens. The peat appears to have often been collected using 'flag' or 'turf' spades, which are occasionally noted in the inventories.

Source: All inventories of paupers' goods and c.2,500 records of fuel given to inventoried paupers in various poor relief records.

used by indigent populations in Kent, and paupers in Dorset used a mix of wood and peat throughout the entire period. In Leicestershire, Rutland and Lancashire, on the other hand, coal use was widespread, while coal only started to surpass other forms of fuel in Essex and Norfolk from the late eighteenth century. These results are important. They show that traditional forms of fuel continued to be important over the industrial revolution and that their decline was more gradual and prolonged than some historians have suggested.[11]

The widespread use of coal in Lancashire, Leicestershire and Rutland was the simple consequence of it being widely available and relatively cost-effective to acquire, since people lived close to coalfields.[12] Meanwhile, in the south and east of the country there were no known coal reserves during the period, meaning that the switch to coal was much more prolonged, fragmented and expensive for the poor who lived there. Most coal came into southern and eastern regions of the country through costly coastal shipping from the north east, Gloucestershire and south Wales.[13] There were also considerable natural resources in some of the regions, which would have put people off buying coal. Kent had some of the most widespread woodlands in England and the poor could exploit this by gathering firewood for free or by buying it at a more economical price than coal.[14] Likewise, those living to the west of Norfolk could access peat from the Fens.[15] The decision to change to coal may have also been influenced by the designs of people's fireplaces. If somebody were to use coal on a wood-burning hearth, for example, the thick and dirty smoke from the coal would have been primarily drawn into the room rather than up the chimney.[16] With coal being expensive and there being abundant cost-effective alternatives in some regions, there was little incentive for people to make the necessary alterations to fireplaces and chimneys to accommodate coal.

In spite of these obstacles, the poor were pushed into using coal. Woodlands came under pressure from urbanisation and demand from the shipbuilding industry during the Napoleonic wars.[17] Enclosure also grew apace, which meant that greater numbers of people had limited access to commons and waste lands to freely gather fuel themselves.[18] The move to coal appears to have been particularly marked in Essex and Norfolk. By the early nineteenth century, coal was recorded in one-fifth to half of the pauper inventories from the counties, while evidence of wood use was only found in 14 per cent of the sources (Table 4.6). The same trends can be seen among those who were resident in urban and rural areas of Essex and Norfolk. Using the first estimate of coal use, 14 and 18 per cent of the urban and rural pauper inventories respectively recorded coal goods, while the second estimate indicates that at least 38 and 44 per cent of people in urban and rural areas respectively used coal between 1770 and 1834.[19] Coal was thus very important from the closing decades of the

124   At home with the poor

Table 4.6 Pauper ownership of hearth items related to coal and wood use in Essex and Norfolk, 1670–1835

	1670–1729	1730–69	1770–99	1800–35
Coal (Estimate 1)	1	5	15	18
Coal (Estimate 2)	2	10	40	47
Wood	21	41	36	14
Sample size	101	184	78	74

eighteenth century, being utilised by the poor in large parts of East Anglia as well as areas close to coalfields.

Wealthier members of society increasingly switched to coal even when they lived far away from collieries. It was often the more expensive option, but they saw the benefits of using coal over other forms of fuel and had the means to buy it and to alter their fireplaces accordingly.[20] The poor, on the other hand, had to base their decisions on a number of factors, such as cost, accessibility and what their chimneys were designed for. This appears to have led to a highly fragmented and regionalised picture of coal consumption. It was probably not until after railways covered the country that the poor switched to coal on a national level.[21] Nonetheless, whatever the reason that the poor moved to coal, the change was ultimately beneficial as it was the most efficient form of fuel available. Sometimes the switch also came at the time when coal started to decline in price and firewood grew in cost, as can be seen in Essex and Norfolk.[22]

Laundry, washing and cleaning

An important function of the hearth was drying clothes and heating water for washing and laundry. It was once commonly believed that large proportions of the population devoted little time and resources to housework and washing,[23] yet recent research has helped to change our ways of thinking about these practices. Susan North's work in *Sweet and Clean* has eroded long-held notions that people rarely washed their bodies and that cleanliness primarily came from wearing white linen undergarments during the early modern period.[24] Likewise, Louise Falcini has shown that to be part of the eighteenth-century 'respectable' poor one needed to have both clean clothes and bodies.[25] Here we use ego documents and inventories to reveal an interesting but incomplete picture of washing, laundry and cleaning. Narratives of the poor, for example, rarely mention these practices, since the tasks were so unremarkable that they were not worth noting. Through inventories, we learn about the items people used for housework, such as tubs and clothes irons, but little about soap or other cleaning agents, how often laundry, washing and cleaning was done, or how long the tasks took.

The English weather would have left many people's clothes damp, muddy and sweaty from a hard day's labour in the fields or being out and about. The first place that many people went after the toils of the day was the hearth. On William Cobbett's travels around England in the early nineteenth century, on several occasions he arrived at his destination wet through and went straight to the hearth to recuperate and to get dry and warm up.[26] On one evening in October 1796, the shoemaker James M'Kaen sat by the kitchen fire 'drying my stockings, which I had wet when I walked into the river'.[27] After a 'wet day', Samuel Bamford and his friends 'sat drinking until our clothes were dry on our backs' in the public house.[28] Miners, according to Edward Allen Rymer, would finish work 'black, and covered by sweat and foam'.[29] Even when somebody worked domestically, the conditions could vary between being swelteringly hot and humid to bitterly cold.[30] Laundry must have therefore been a frequent and laborious task for poor householders.

From the mid-eighteenth century, the labouring sort were increasingly labelled as foul-smelling and filthy compared with their social superiors.[31] Yet while the poor naturally had fewer resources and implements for maintaining cleanliness compared with the well-to-do,[32] sources indicate that the poor were far from universally smelly and dirty. The pauper inventories show that the indigent poor owned a considerable and diverse range of tubs, which could be used for a host of tasks, including washing and laundry (Table 4.7). Furthermore, as with many other household goods, the poor's ownership of tubs increased from 1770, suggesting that the capability for washing increased as the century went on. It would be useful at this point to quantify the receptacles which relate only to washing bodies or clothing (such as lye letches, washing tubs and bucking tubs), but this is highly problematic as it was not unusual for everybody – even the wealthy – to use the same tubs for multiple functions.[33]

Despite the difficulties studying tubs, the inventories show that paupers increasingly possessed other specialised laundry- and

Table 4.7   Percentage of paupers who owned tubs and washing-/laundry-related items, 1670–1835

	1670–1709	1710–49	1750–69	1770–89	1790–1835
Basin (any type)	2	5	5	25	17
Clothes/linen basket	0	1	3	8	13
Clothes horse	0	0	1	5	8
Clothes iron (any type)	18	23	17	38	37
Tub (any type)	56	63	66	78	77
Sample size	45	163	185	85	145

washing-related goods. Basins, the majority of which would have been used for washing parts of the body such as hands and armpits, were possessed by around four to five times more people from 1770 compared with the preceding years. Many households even contained significant quantities of basins, especially in the home counties, such as William Land and William Nottage of Essex, who owned nine each.[34] Regarding laundry, there was a slight growth in the possession of clothes/linen baskets and clothes horses. Neither item was strictly necessary to the process of cleaning clothes, but they helped to make laundry easier and more organised. Without a clothes horse, people were creative and would dry their clothes on string which reached across the hearth and household beams (Figure 4.1). Sometimes people also laid their clothes out on trees or across the grass.[35]

Most notably, clothes irons doubled in ownership from the late eighteenth century. Sometimes they were listed alongside ironing boards, stands and rests. Box irons, which were heated through an iron wedge (heater) being placed in their cavity, were the most common type of clothes iron among the indigent poor. Most owners of box irons possessed multiple numbers of heaters, which had the advantage of allowing the user to iron for prolonged periods of time, as one heater could be on the fire while the other was in use. In George Fettes' pawnshop in York, most clothes irons

Figure 4.1 George Cruikshank, *A Distressed Father*, 1824 (source: John Wight, *Mornings at Bow Street: A selection of the most humourous and entertaining reports which have appeared in the Morning Herald*, London: Charles Baldwin, 1824, pp. 224–5)

Comforts of the hearth 127

were pledged to Fettes for less than a shilling, showing that they were not expensive and that even the most impoverished could ensure that their clothes were ironed and respectable by the later decades of the eighteenth century.[36] Clothes irons were, however, also the fourth most pawned item in Fettes shop,[37] indicating that as bills mounted many people forwent ironing their clothes and their appearance suffered.

The proliferation of these various items suggests that cleanliness became more important to the poor over time and indicates that house-holders could wash, dry and iron their clothes to a higher standard from the late eighteenth century than their parents or grandparents could have. Nonetheless, homes must have been the site of a constant battlefield for cleanliness. The hearth would have been particularly difficult to keep in order, as it required constant vigilance to clean up soot, grease, and spilled liquids and foods. Many labouring people were meticulous and ensured that the hearth and other areas of the home remained spotless. Thomas Carter, for example, describing his aunt, said that:

> She was a very industrious woman, and quite remarkable for her love of clean-liness. In her person she was one of the most neatly attired women I have ever seen; while the floor and walls of her cottage, together with every article of her household furniture, were kept in the cleanest possible condition. She carried her dislike to dirtiness so far as to request every person coming into her house to be careful not to soil, or otherwise put out of order, the well scrubbed and 'neatly sanded floor'.[38]

Being a clean, industrious and reliable homemaker appears to have been at the forefront of many people's ideas of what made a decent woman. Autobiographers Benjamin Shaw and Samuel Bamford complimented some of the women in their lives for being 'cleanly'.[39] David Love's first and second wives were described as 'good' and 'famous' at washing respec-tively.[40] Almost inevitably, others hated housework and would do it only reluctantly, such as William Ablett, who 'dislike[d] cleaning very much'.[41]

Pauper inventories reveal that people owned a considerable range of brushes to keep homes and attire clean, such as dustpans and brushes as well as clothes, hand, hat, hearth, scrubbing, sweeping and table brushes. Between 1810 and 1835, around one-in-three pauper inventories recorded at least one brush of some kind, compared with one-in-twenty dated 1670–1749. Mops and tubs for washing dishes were also occasionally noted in the inventories dated post-1790. Such items were fairly cheap and thus probably more widespread than the inventories suggest, as they were not a priority of appraisers. Susan Parker of Canterbury, Kent, for instance, owned 'Brushes & [a] mop' worth 1s.,[42] while paupers John Smith and John Welch from Lancashire owned one brush each, worth 1d. and 4d. respectively.[43] Therefore, just because somebody was poor, this did not mean that they took little pride in their homes or that they were happy liv-ing in a dusty, dirty and unhygienic space. Being able to maintain a clean house was key to being seen as respectable, and many people strived for this even on meagre budgets.

Cherished and upsetting hearthside memories

Beyond work and chores, the hearth was central to the comfort of householders as a location of recreation, relaxation and rest. Indeed, seating was the most common type of item to be found in the same rooms as hearths (Table 4.3). Sitting by the fire was a multisensory and absorptive experience, which calmed nerves and facilitated social interaction.[44] People would sit there and have a few quiet moments to themselves, or use the space to converse with friends and family about the day's events and future plans. Paintings of the poor commonly depict families and pets around the fireplace, talking and enjoying each other's company (Figure 4.2). These pictures were made to breed morality among the poorer sort and satisfy wealthier consumers, who sometimes had little idea of what poor abodes looked like,[45] but the frequency with which these types of pictures survive suggests that there is some truth to them.[46] Moreover, ego documents identify the hearth as a focal point of treasured memories. Born in Middleton, Lancashire, in 1788, the writings of Samuel Bamford contain a

Figure 4.2 Thomas Vivares, *A Family at Home*, 1800 (source: Wellcome Collection, 28669i, soft-ground etching)

Comforts of the hearth 129

wealth of information about how he and his siblings and cousins would sit around the hearth to hear stories. By the fireplace 'on a winter's night', his aunt Elizabeth would:

> set her wheel aside, take a pinch of snuff, hutch her chair towards the other hob, and excite our curiosity and wonder by strange and fearful tales of witches, spirits, and apparitions, whilst we listened in silence and awe, and scarcely breathing, contemplated in imagination, the visions of an unseen world, which her narratives conjured up before us.[47]

These stories etched themselves into the mind of young Samuel, who as an adult could vividly recall colourful fables of human and feline spirits.[48] Guests too would sometimes grace the home and entertain the children with hearthside tales. Occasionally, when 'days became short, and cloudy, and stormy, and we had long nights to sit by the fire', an old lady would visit Samuel's home for shelter. Samuel remarked that she was 'rather out of her mind', but 'had plenty of tales, chiefly of an admonitory and religious turn', which delighted the children.[49] It was not just ghost or religious stories that were told by the fireplace. While serving an apprenticeship in weaving, Samuel noted how during one evening with his master's cook and housemaid, 'the subject of fortune-telling was talked about as we sat on the hearth'.[50]

The pastimes that individuals and families enjoyed by the hearth were varied. Autobiographies and other first-hand sources over-represent the numbers of people who loved reading, since they capture the literate poor, yet when this pursuit is noted it appears to have often been enjoyed adjacent to the hearth. *Chevy Chase*, a popular ballad of the early modern period, was 'read over with great delight at our fire-side' by Thomas Holcroft during the 1750s,[51] while James Watson spent his teenage years as an apprentice 'reading by the kitchen fire, during the long winter nights'.[52] John Bethune similarly enjoyed reading by the fire, but would also spend long hours writing poetry there 'with an old copy-book, upon which his paper lay, resting on his knee … [as a] writing-desk'.[53] Towards the end of his life, Bethune was seldom healthy and one of his few comforts was 'the pleasure of taking his accustomed seat by the fire'.[54] Others enjoyed singing or playing musical instruments next to the hearth. Benjamin Shaw fondly recounted how, when he was a child, a lodger used to play his fiddle in the evenings at his grandfather's home 'while I lay in a box &c by the fire'.[55] During the winters, Samuel Bamford and his childhood friends 'sat singing carols and hymns, playing at "forfeits", proposing riddles, and telling "fyerin tales"' by 'a warm, comfortable hearth'.[56] To relax when the sun set, many would smoke. On the night of 25 October 1812, Snowhill Dunhill was arrested for allegedly stealing wheat from a neighbour's farm. Before being reprimanded by a justice of the peace, he noted having been 'seated in my chair by the fire, taking my accustomed pipe', which was 'an indulgence I never omitted the last thing at night'.[57] Because the fireplace was warm and allowed people to see what they were doing, it is perhaps unsurprising that it was habitually frequented by inhabitants. Nevertheless, these accounts clearly indicate that the hearth was valued by people for reasons other than its applications. It was a site that comforted people and allowed them to relax and unwind from the day's labours. The hearth was an important space for solitary reflection and for family interactions, while gazing into the flicking and crackling embers and enjoying the fire's light and heat.

Even today, in an era when central heating is universal and hearths are no longer necessary, many fireplaces remain focal points of homes. Occupants often make features of the space and display gifts, ornaments and ephemera on or around the mantelpiece out of habit, sentimentality, convenience and a desire to decorate.[58] The veracity of contemporary paintings is always questionable, yet with some regularity artists and engravers depicted items around fireplaces of the past. They nearly always include some combination of ornaments, ornate plates, pictures and books to adorn and frame the hearth, in addition to a number of items that were needed nearby, such as cooking utensils, dinnerware and fire irons. Figure 4.3, for instance, shows the hearths of two elderly widows in Wortham, Suffolk. Painted by the pastor Richard Cobbold, the mantelshelf of 'tidy' 91-year-old Barbara Batley is fairly minimal, displaying a few items for decoration,[59] while that of Poll Parker, aged 95, displays a more

Figure 4.3 Portraits of Barbara Batley (left) and Poll Parker (right), painted by Richard Cobbold, c.1848–52 and c.1852 (source: SA HA 11/A13/10; reproduced by kind permission of the owner)

haphazard sequence of various goods that were decorative and might be needed to hand.[60] We also see occasional glimpses of mantelpieces in inventories of paupers' goods. On Mrs Vince's mantelshelf, there were '6 Stone Pleates a Pestle with mortar A Coffe Pot [and] 3 Paire of Brass scals'.[61] Widow Goulding's inventory listed '16 Sundries on Mantel Piece' and Nicklas Haworth had 'five Candlesticks [and] Chimney Ornaments' above his fireplace.[62] The mantelpiece was also a convenient surface on which to place the contents of one's pockets and various itinerant items such as letters, pipes and tobacco, alongside its more permanent fixtures.[63] With people spending many hours by the hearth, the mantelpiece served as both a handy storage space and a way for people to embellish their homes.

It is important to not over-romanticise hearths of the past, and to remember how they could be difficult spaces. Fireplaces could be contested areas where families argued or ignored each other. They were sometimes the site of aggression and physical assaults between spouses, as can be seen in prints of the period such as Figure 4.4. One violent hearthside incident stemmed from strangers breaking into the home of Poll Parker in 1797. Her husband was away on duty with the volunteer corps when three soldiers entered her home and tried to assault her. Showing 'spirit ... few women possess', she grabbed a poker from the fireplace and 'levelled them all'. The men were subsequently carried to hospital in a publican's cart, where they 'became the laughing stock of the regiment'.[64]

Figure 4.4 *Family Argument*, c.1810 (source: courtesy of the Lewis Walpole Library, Yale University 810.00.00.36, unknown artist, skimmington on woodcut wove paper)

The hearth was a bitterly uncomfortable space when households did not have adequate firing. As William Cobbett remarked, 'Fire is a capital article. To have no fire, or a bad fire, to sit by, is a most dismal thing.'[65] In a similar vein, William Thom said that the only light from an unlit hearth is 'the light of despair'.[66] The necessity of fuel for warmth features prominently in the writings of the poor. Pauper letters suggest that a number of people would make do with little fuel during milder times of the year, but they became particularly desperate for firing during the winter months. In September 1811, Mary Mayden requested 'a sufficient quantity of Firing' from the overseers of St James, Colchester, Essex, for 'when the cold weather sets in'.[67] Two years earlier, Ann Prigg wrote Rayleigh's officials in Essex to ask for 'some Firing for the Winter' in November 1809.[68] For those who went through winters with little fuel, this often left dark marks on their memories. Elizabeth Ann Manning noted how the winter of 1829/30 was a 'verry trieng Winter for me as fireing have been verry dear'.[69] As a child of five, George Mitchell worked as a bird scarer. He often came home 'wet through' from his labours and would sleep in his clothes so that 'the heat of my body dried them ... for there was often no fire to dry them by'.[70] At a similar age, Joseph Terry recalled one particularly harsh turn in the seasons which left him with long-term health problems:

> In the winter season my feet, and especially my heels and toes, were much frostbitten, swollen and sore – so much so that after we were in a better circumstance, and my parents could afford to clothe me better, it took years of care, scrubbing and washing to bring my feet into a proper and natural state.[71]

Hearths must have been desperately demoralising places when they were ignited only for short periods of time or left void of fires entirely. The dark open space of the fireplace would have been a constant reminder of what might have been, while people were left struggling to get warm with whatever extra clothes and blankets they could find.

Even when there was ample fuel, rooms with hearths could become unpleasant spaces. The ash and soot that came from the fireplace must have been voluminous, resulting in regular and laborious cleaning for homemakers. Chimneys also needed regular maintenance and would intermittently become blocked. When this happened, smoke would have nowhere to go but to re-enter the room, leading to continual annoyance for residents and sight and breathing difficulties. The didactic penny newspaper *British Workman* records one such example in 1857 (Figure 4.5). In it, the Graves family noted how their hearth was 'a sad enemy to their peace' and 'continually annoyed them', as smoke went 'every direction, except up the chimney'. Mrs Graves found it 'unbearable' to 'sit in such a smoke as she did, all day' and noted that the room 'was not fit for any human creature to live in'. It was a cause of arguments between her and her husband Abel. When he returned home from work expecting 'his meal

Comforts of the hearth 133

Figure 4.5 *Story of a Smoky Chimney*, 1857 (source: J. Johnson, *British Workman*, 36, p. 141)

in a clean house … by a bright fire', he instead 'had to listen a long time to the complaints of his wife' and endure 'a scolding' from her until he fixed it.[72] It is unclear whether this parable was true or concocted to promote a particular moral – that one should promptly deal with one's troubles – but this amusing story nevertheless reveals how hearths could be uncomfortable and frustrating spaces when they did not work properly.

More alarmingly, fireplaces could be a source of considerable danger to families. Out-of-control domestic blazes were not uncommon throughout the period, and many arose from the hearth. William Hutton recalled playing by the fire as an infant when his sister gave him 'a piece of cap paper, plaited in the form of a fan' which caught alight and 'set fire to my petticoats, frock, and bib'. The children's mother was mercifully close by. Upon hearing the cries of her dismayed children, she extinguished the fire and put an end to this 'tragi-comedy'.[73] Other families were not as fortunate as the Huttons. Mary Saxby wrote about one house fire which resulted in the loss of all her possessions and her daughter:

> whilst my husband, myself, and four children, were gone out, the poor man [looking after Mary's baby] went from the huts … and left my dear baby by a little fire. When he returned, the huts were in flames, and he could not find

her. He ran about, like a mad man, to seek her, but in vain; till, in his fright, he, threw himself into the midst of the fire, and pulled her out alive … and he, almost senseless, threw her on his back, leaving the clothes and huts to burn; and ran, as fast as he could … He had much difficulty to find me; and when he did, he cried out, 'Mary, your child's burnt to death!' Oh my God! It was thou, and only thou, that sustained my senses through this awful scene. As my dear child was not quite dead, they provided us a lodging in the town. I believe every means was made use of to preserve her; but in a few days she died: and we lost, not only our child, but nearly every thing. We had not a garment left.[74]

There are numerous examples of adults injuring themselves in fires too. William Heaton's wife was nearly 'burnt to death' when her clothes caught alight as she was heating an oven.[75] In 1826, pauper Ann White experienced a fit which meant that 'she has not the full use of her left arm'. Her husband Samuel noted how she was left 'in such a state of stupidety and forgetfulness' that she caught fire and her clothes 'were burnt very much but through Mercy it was Put out before it Burnt her body'.[76]

Growing numbers of the poor are likely to have taken steps to protect themselves and their families by investing in better fire irons (Table 4.8). Lighting hearths could be difficult, tedious and dangerous, but from the 1730s at least half of all pauper households appear to have contained bellows. Bellows were especially helpful in lighting fires, as they allowed people to feed air to the fire from a distance where they were less likely to burn themselves (Figure 4.6). By the turn of the nineteenth century, fenders are noted in around a fifth of pauper inventories. Fenders, which were metal frames placed in front of fires, helped to prevent objects from catching fire if burning fuel rolled out of the hearth. Pokers also rose in ownership and tongs were fairly common throughout the period. These various items allowed people to heat and light the home more safely and efficiently, but there is a limit to how far fireplaces became more secure. Items such as fire screens, which covered the hearth with a protective grid, were uncommon. They were viewed as an unnecessary expense that was out of the

Table 4.8 Percentage of paupers who owned various fire irons, 1670–1835

	1670–29	1730–69	1770–99	1800–35	All years
Bellows	29	50	58	53	48
Fender	1	3	13	21	7
Fire screen	0	<1	2	0	1
Fire shovel	9	16	26	19	16
Poker	1	4	13	23	8
Tongs	50	59	63	51	56
Sample size	125	268	123	107	645

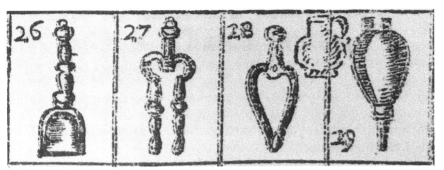

Figure 4.6 Randle Holme, picture of a fire shovel, two pairs of tongs and a pair of bellows, 1688 (source: Randle Holme, *The Academy of Armory*, Vol. 2, ed. I. H. Jeayes, London: Rorburghe Club, reprint of 1688 edn, 1905, pp. 18–19)

financial means of many people, even as late as the 1900s.[77] Sometimes the poor used makeshift items instead, such as Roger Riches of Martham, Norfolk, who used 'a Lafe [leaf] of a Table for a [fire] Skreen'.[78]

Since fireplaces were of central importance to households, it is likely that everybody had both cherished and upsetting memories of the space. On one day, the hearth could be where families took pleasure in each other's companies and where people enjoyed the solitary comforts of smoking and reading. Many writers fondly remembered how formative experiences of their childhood took place by the fireplace. However, on other days the hearth hosted events a person would rather forget, such as an out-of-control fire, the demise of a dying relative, or seeing their parents bicker and fight.

Lighting

The most important form of illumination in poor abodes was undoubtedly the fireplace. A lit hearth meant that people could do things outside of daylight hours and allowed homemakers to create a more comfortable and respectable domestic environment.[79] The poor sometimes used very emotive language to describe how soothing burning hearths could be. On one occasion Samuel Bamford encountered a 'red cheerful fire glowing', and John Brown described a room that was comfortable in part because 'the fire was burning brightly'.[80] However, when in other rooms away from the hearth, other forms of lighting were needed, and owing to insufficient funds or inadequate supplies, as noted above, it was not unusual for the poor to be unable to light their hearths. During milder times in the year, it might have also been viewed as not sensible to keep the hearth lit for prolonged periods, in order to save fuel for when it was really needed.

As an alternative to the hearth, the poor could choose between a range of items from pricey beeswax or tallow candlesticks to inexpensive rushlights, which were made from long rushes dipped into fat, oil or grease. They could also turn to oil derived from fish, whales and other sources in lamps. According to social reformer William Cobbett, the rural poor favoured rushlights as they 'cost next to nothing', meaning that the labourer could 'have as much light as he pleases'. He even alleged that they gave 'a *better light* than a common small dip-candle'.[81] Other sources, however, give little evidence as to oil use and the types of candles or rushlights that the poor used, as the terms are often used ambiguously and interchangeably.[82] Pauper inventories note the ownership of candlesticks and lanterns throughout the long eighteenth century, but these figures cannot be used as a reliable measure of oil, candle or rushlight use. Many homes also contained fixtures such as wall brackets and sconces for candles and rushlights as well as makeshift holders, but the inventories rarely note these.[83] James Lackington, for example, one evening used 'the handle of a pewter pot' to position a candle while he read. This almost led to disaster, as Lackington fell asleep and woke to find 'the candle burned down to the handle of the pot' and 'melted' off with 'part of the chair consumed' with fire.[84] People also probably used bottles to hold candles, as can be seen in the top-left corner of one fictional print from 1751 (Figure 4.7).

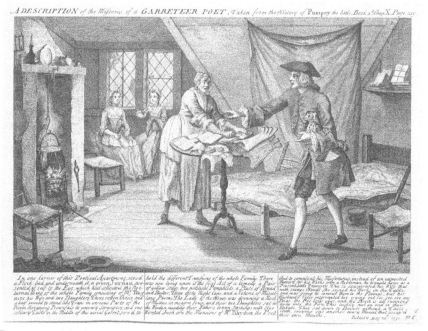

Figure 4.7 John June, *Miseries of a Garreteer Poet*, 1751 (source: courtesy of the Lewis Walpole Library, Yale University 751.02.00.01, print on paper)

Although the findings from the inventories are limited since they do not note fittings or makeshift items that were used as candleholders, they are nonetheless revealing. Candlesticks, lanterns and lamps appear to have grown in ownership over the long eighteenth century (Table 4.9). The indigent poor of Kent were once again most likely to possess these items compared with paupers elsewhere. The increase in ownership of lanterns and lamps was especially important to homemakers since they were designed to protect flames and prevent accidents (Figure 4.8). Nearly two-thirds of the paupers who owned a candlestick owned more than one, which suggests that people may have burned several rushlights or candles at once. Most candlesticks, lanterns and lamps had the advantage of being mobile, while others were clearly intended to be static. Thomas Cullam of Forncett in Norfolk, for instance, owned '2 Candle Stands', while John Tadgell of Hatfield Broad Oak, Essex owned 'a Stable Lanthorn'.[85]

Research on time suggests that most labouring people stayed awake for a few hours after the sun set and woke before the sun came up throughout much of the year.[86] Consequently, although it is very difficult to determine how long the poor kept hearths and candles alight, this analysis of artificial lighting suggests that they did not rely on fireplaces and neither sat in the dark nor went straight to bed when the hearth embers died. The homes and lives of the poor thus appear to have become more comfortable over the period following their rising ownership of candlesticks, lanterns and lamps, as people had some flexibility and their days were not totally dictated by

Table 4.9 Pauper ownership of lighting goods, 1670–1835

		Average number	1670–1769 (%)	1770–1835 (%)	All years (%)
Candlestick	Dorset	1.9	22	32	25
	Essex	2.6	35	47	42
	Kent	2.4	42	68	52
	Leics/Ruts	2	11	51	32
	Norfolk	1.7	27	46	30
	All counties	2.2	29	48	36
Lantern/lamp	Dorset	1	8	14	10
	Essex	1.1	5	9	7
	Kent	1.1	11	27	17
	Leics/Ruts	1	0	14	7
	Norfolk	1	5	22	7
	All counties	1.1	5	14	8

Figure 4.8 Randle Holme, picture of lantern, 1688 (source: Holme, *Academy of Armory*, pp. 18-19)

Table 4.10 Functions of pauper rooms with lighting in them, 1670-1835

	%
Cooking	76
Eating/drinking	75
Heating	81
Sitting	91
Sleeping	29
Working	63

the rhythms of day and night. The growing ownership of artificial lighting would have changed people's day-to-day rituals and allowed them to work longer hours or do household chores. Lighting meant that people could sit and relax during dark evenings, as well as play cards or read a book. In fact, seating was the most common category of item found alongside artificial lighting (Table 4.10). Lighting made straightforward tasks such as changing clothes and using a commode much simpler and opened up new opportunities for entertaining guests and conversing with fellow household members. Candlesticks and lanterns were also increasingly used alongside looking glasses from the late eighteenth century. Used together, these items

Comforts of the hearth 139

helped to make homes appear more spacious, bright and pleasant and could enhance the aesthetic qualities of furniture and fittings, with flickering candlelight dancing off them and bringing the pieces to life.[87]

Conclusion

The bulk of literature on consumption and material culture has tended to emphasise how comfort became more important to people over the early modern period.[88] Some scholars have even argued that the eighteenth century witnessed a 'comfort revolution'.[89] This chapter has too shown just how important comfort was to the poorer sort. Fireplaces brought people warmth and contentment during cold winter nights. With ample fuel, a bright space could be created in which people cooked food, did their household chores and relaxed in the evenings. Hearths also became more convenient and safer to use over the period with better fire irons, and there was a growth in the use of artificial lighting alongside or instead of hearths. There is, however, another side to the story that has been hitherto unconsidered: discomfort. Most homes contained one only hearth, and many continued to use relatively inefficient forms of firing into the nineteenth century. For those who lived in unhappy households, who could not acquire sufficient firing or who had a poorly maintained fireplace, the hearth could be a source of considerable unease or even danger to families. It is important to find balance between these two dichotomies and realise that what happened in one household could differ from what happened in another. The next chapter considers hearths further by examining the cooking practices of the poor, in addition to aspects related to eating, such as tableware, drink and food production.

Notes

1 Keith Wrightson and David Levine, *Poverty and Piety in an English Village: Terling, 1525–1700* (London: Academic Press, 1979), p. 35.
2 Sneath, 'Consumption, Wealth', pp. 188–94; Tom Arkell, 'Identifying Regional Variations from the Hearth Tax', *Local Historian*, 33:3 (2003), pp. 148–74; Chris Husbands, 'Hearths, Wealth and Occupations: An exploration of the hearth tax in the later seventeenth century', in Kevin Schürer and Tom Arkell (eds), *Surveying the People: The interpretation and use of document sources for the study of population in the later seventeenth century* (Oxford: Leopard's Head Press, 1992), pp. 65–77.
3 Arkell, 'Identifying', pp. 148–74; Husbands, 'Hearths', pp. 75–7.
4 Such as: W. Stanley Jevons, *The Coal Question: An inquiry concerning the progress of the nation, and the probable exhaustion of our coal mines* (London: Macmillan and Co., 1865); J. U. Nef, *The Rise of the Coal Industry* (London: Routledge, 1932); Michael W. Flinn, *The History of the British Coal Industry*, Vol. 2: *1700–1830: The industrial revolution* (Oxford: Oxford University Press, 1984); Kenneth Pomeranz, *The Great Divergence: China, Europe, and the making of the modern world economy* (Princeton: Princeton University Press, 2000); Robert C. Allen, *The British Industrial Revolution in Global Perspective* (Cambridge: Cambridge University Press, 2009).

5 There are exceptions, such as: Paul Warde, *Energy Consumption in England & Wales 1560–2000* (Naples: CNR, 2007); Donald Woodward, 'Straw, Bracken and the Wicklow Whale: The exploitation of natural resources in England since 1500', *Past and Present*, 159 (1998), pp. 43–76.

6 Caroline Davidson, *A Woman's Work Is Never Done: A history of housework in the British Isles 1650–1950* (London: Chatto & Windus, 1982), pp. 74–7.

7 Writers such as Caroline Davidson have argued that cow or horse dung was the main fuel used by the poor. Ibid., pp. 76–7. I have, however, found little evidence of this. Horses and cows were rarely owned by the poor, so they might have had limited access to dung.

8 Pokers, for example, are included in the second method of measuring coal use, as they were particularly suitable for stoking coals. Coal needs to be compacted to burn, and the thin design of pokers would have allowed people to get between the coals and rearrange them much more easily than would tongs.

9 The mechanic/turner Benjamin Shaw, for instance, noted using both coal and turf in his home. Shaw, *Family Records*, p. 32.

10 E. A. Wrigley, *The Path to Sustained Growth: England's transition from an organic economy to an industrial revolution* (Cambridge: Cambridge University Press, 2016), pp. 7–18; John Hatcher, *The History of the British Coal Industry*, Vol. 1: *Before 1700: Towards the age of coal* (Oxford: Oxford University Press, 1993), pp. 37–9.

11 For example, see: Warde, *Energy Consumption*; Paul Warde, 'Woodland Fuel, Demand and Supply', in John Langton and Graham Jones (eds), *Forests and Chases of England and Wales c.1500–c.1850: Towards a survey and analysis* (Oxford: St John's College Research Centre, 2005), pp. 85–6; Allen, *British Industrial Revolution*, p. 96.

12 Nick von Tunzelmann, 'Coal and Steam Power', in John Langton and R. J. Morris (eds), *Atlas of Industrializing Britain, 1780–1914* (London: Methuen & Co., 1986), pp. 72–5; Allen, *British Industrial Revolution*, pp. 80–105; Thomas Holcroft, *Memoirs of the Late Thomas Holcroft, Written by Himself* (London: Longman Brown, 1852), p. 22.

13 Hatcher, *Coal*, pp. 2–3, 6–8, 10–14, 34, 135–41, 173–84, 479–504; Flinn, *Coal*, pp. 10–14, 18–19, 21, 146–89, 213–15, 220–1, 297–311, 442; von Tunzelmann, 'Coal', p. 75; Eden, *State of the Poor*, Vol. 1, pp. 524–5, 547–8.

14 H. A. Wilcox, *The Woodlands and Marshlands of England* (London: University Press of Liverpool, 1933), map B; Cobbett, *Rural Rides*, pp. 291–2; Jane Humphries, 'Enclosure', pp. 32–3.

15 Wilcox, *Woodlands*, map B.

16 Hatcher, *Coal*, pp. 37–9, 409, 412; Allen, *British Industrial Revolution*, pp. 90–6; Lawrence Wright, *Home Fires Burning: The history of domestic heating and cooking* (London: Routledge, 1964), pp. 65–6, 106; Overton et al., *Production and Consumption*, p. 98

17 Paul Warde, 'Fear of Wood Shortage and the Reality of the Woodland in Europe c.1450–1850', *History Workshop Journal*, 62:1 (2006), pp. 28–57; Hatcher, *Coal*, pp. 5–8, 31–7; Wilcox, *Woodlands*, map B.

18 Snell, *Annals*, pp. 138–227; Hammond and Hammond, *Village Labourer*; Neeson, *Commoners*, esp. pp. 158–84.

19 Urban areas have been categorised as having a population of 1,000 or more. See Chapter 7 for further information.

20 Overton et al., *Production and Consumption*, pp. 98–9.

21 Roy Church, *The History of the British Coal Industry*, Vol. 3: *1830–1913: Victorian pre-eminence* (Oxford: Oxford University Press, 1986).

22 Hatcher, *Coal*, pp. 308–11; Warde, 'Fear', p. 38.

23 Most notably, see: Georges Vigarello, *Concepts of Cleanliness: Changing attitudes in France since the Middle Ages*, trans. Jean Birrell (Cambridge: Cambridge University Press, 1988).

24 Susan North, *Sweet and Clean? Bodies and clothes in early modern England* (Oxford: Oxford University Press, 2020).

25 Louise Falcini, 'Cleanliness and the Poor in Eighteenth-Century London', PhD thesis (University of Reading, 2018).

26 Cobbett, *Rural Rides*, pp. 76–7, 151–2.

27 James M'Kaen, *The Life of James M'Kaen, Shoemaker in Glasgow* (Glasgow: Brash and Reid, 2nd edn, 1797), p. 49.

28 Bamford, *Early Days*, p. 226.

29 Rymer, 'Martyrdom', p. 229.

30 Ruth Mather, 'Politicising the English Working-Class Home, c.1790–1820', in Harley, Holmes and Nevalainen, *Working Class at Home*, p. 53.

31 Smith, *Sensory History*, pp. 66–7; Holly Dugan, '*Coriolanus* and the "Rank-Scented Meinie": Smelling rank in early modern London', in Amanda Bailey and Roze Hentschell (eds), *Masculinity and the Metropolis of Vice, 1550–1650* (Basingstoke: Palgrave, 2010), pp. 139–59; Constance Classen, David Howes and Anthony Synnott, *Aroma: A cultural history of smell* (London: Routledge, 1994), pp. 165–9; Jonathan Reinarz, *Past Scents: Historical perspectives on smell* (Urbana: University of Illinois Press, 2014), pp. 145–75.

32 Lesley Hoskins, 'Household Inventories Reassessed: A "new" source for investigating nineteenth-century domestic culture in England and Wales', *Home Cultures*, 11:3 (2014), pp. 344–7.

33 North, *Sweet and Clean*, pp. 212–13.

34 ERO D/P 194/18/4; ERO D/P4/18/8.

35 Davidson, *Woman's Work*, p. 154; Lackington, *Memoirs*, p. 452.

36 YALH Accession 38.

37 Backhouse, *Worm-Eaten*, pp. 77–81. This sum is based on clothing and linen being grouped together in one category.

38 Carter, *Memoirs*, pp. 18–19.

39 Shaw, *Family Records*, pp. 3, 12; Bamford, *Early Days*, p. 99.

40 Love, *Life*, pp. 28, 159.

41 William Ablett, *Reminiscences of an Old Draper* (London: Sampson Low, Marston, Searle & Rivington, 1876), p. 6.

42 CCAL U3/100/12/B/30.

43 WAS TR/Ath/C/2/37–58; LRO QSP/2348/3.

44 Christopher Dana Lynn, 'Hearth and Campfire Influences on Arterial Blood Pressure: Defraying the costs of the social brain through fireside relaxation', *Evolutionary Psychology*, 12:5 (2014), pp. 983–1003.

45 Payne, 'Rural Virtues', pp. 45–68; Barrell, *Dark Side*; Nichols, 'Motives of Control/ Motifs of Creativity', pp. 138–63.

46 Also see Figures 4.3, 5.6, 6.2 and 6.3.

47 Bamford, *Early Days*, p. 162.

48 Ibid., pp. 162–9.

49 Ibid., pp. 182–4.

50 Ibid., p. 202.

51 Holcroft, *Memoirs*, p. 24.

52 James Watson, 'Reminiscences of James Watson', in David Vincent (ed.), *Testaments of Radicalism: Memoirs of working class politicians 1790–1885* (London: Europa Publications Limited, 1997), p. 109.

53 John Bethune, *Poems by the Late John Bethune; with a Sketch of the Author's Life, by His Brother* (Edinburgh: Adam and Charles Black, 1840), p. 45.

54 Ibid., p. 84.

55 Shaw, *Family Records*, p. 22.

56 Bamford, *Early Days*, p. 135.

57 Snowden Dunhill, *The Life of Snowden Dunhill of Spaldington, East Riding* (1766–1838), ed. David Neave (Howden: Mr Pye Books, 1987), pp. 17–18.

58 Rachel Hurdley, *Home, Materiality, Memory and Belonging: Keeping culture* (Basingstoke: Palgrave, 2013).

59 SA HD 1888/1.
60 For other pictorial examples of mantelpieces, see Figures 3.7, 4.1, 4.2, 4.4, 4.5, 4.7, 5.6, 6.2 and 6.3.
61 ERO D/P 219/12/29.
62 ERO D/P 157/8/3; LRO PR 2392/6.
63 Hurdley, *Home, Materiality*, pp. 51–78.
64 SA HD 368/1.
65 Cobbett, *Cottage Economy*, p. 201.
66 Thom, *Rhymes*, p. 101.
67 Sokoll, *Pauper Letters*, p. 376.
68 Ibid., p. 567.
69 Ibid., p. 597.
70 Mitchell, 'Autobiography', p. 97.
71 Joseph Terry, 'Recollections of My Life', in John Burnett (ed.), *Destiny Obscure: Autobiographies of childhood, education and family from the 1820s to the 1920s* (London: Penguin Books, 1982), p. 71.
72 *British Workman*, 36 (1857), pp. 141–2.
73 Hutton, *Life of*, p. 3.
74 Saxby, *Memoirs*, pp. 25–6.
75 Heaton, 'A Sketch', pp. xix–xx.
76 Sokoll, *Pauper Letters*, pp. 233, 235.
77 Vicky Holmes, 'Absent Fireguards and Burnt Children: Coroners and the development of Clause 15 of the Children Act 1908', *Law, Crime & History*, 2:1 (2012), pp. 41, 54–5.
78 NRO PD 710/68.
79 Crowley, *Invention of Comfort*, pp. 111–40; Witold Rybczynski, *Home: A short history of the idea* (New York: Penguin, 1987), pp. 122–43.
80 Bamford, *Early Days*, p. 81; Brown, *Sixty Years' Gleanings*, p. 143.
81 Cobbett, *Cottage Economy*, pp. 193–7. Also see: Jekyll, *Old West Surrey*, pp. 101–7; Steer, *Inventories*, pp. 21–2.
82 F. G. Emmison (ed.), *Jacobean Household Inventories* (Aspley Guise: Bedfordshire Historical Record Society, 1938), p. 31.
83 Rupert Gentle and Rachael Feild, *English Domestic Brass 1680–1810 and the History of its Origins* (London: Paul Elek, 1975), pp. 94–5.
84 Lackington, *Memoirs*, p. 173.
85 NRO PD 421/133; ERO D/P 4/18/8.
86 Hans-Joachim Voth, *Time and Work in England 1750–1830* (Oxford: Oxford University Press, 2000), pp. 67–72, 94–9, 151–4; Vicky Holmes, 'Death of an Infant: Coroners' inquests and the study of Victorian domestic practice', *Home Cultures*, 11:3 (2014), p. 321.
87 Ann Smart Martin, 'Lustrous Things: Luminosity and reflection before the light bulb', in Gerritsen and Riello, *Writing Material Culture*, pp. 157–63.
88 Crowley, *Invention of Comfort*.
89 Sara Horrell, Jane Humphries and Ken Sneath, 'Cupidity and Crime: Consumption as revealed by insights from the Old Bailey records of thefts in the eighteenth and nineteenth centuries', in Mark Casson and Nigar Hashimzade (eds), *Large Databases in Economic History: Research methods and case studies* (London: Routledge, 2013), pp. 246–67.

5

Eating and drinking

The subject of food and poverty is one of the most enduring topics in history. To name but a few examples, economic historians have long studied food and agricultural change to understand the industrial revolution, population change, urbanisation and the extent to which working people had the energy to be industrious.[1] Numerous issues linked to diet, such as nutrition, calories, height, the cost of food and hunger have been used as measures of change throughout the 'standard of living' debate.[2] For decades, social and political historians have considered the effects that food shortages and enclosure had on welfare, class consciousness, protests and ideas of a 'moral economy'.[3] In a similar vein, commentators during the long eighteenth century itself wrote extensively on food, including the repeatedly cited Thomas Robert Malthus, who lamented that the country would struggle to feed itself as a result of rapid population growth.[4] This chapter is less concerned with these older historiographical issues, focusing instead on how people cooked and consumed their meals in the domestic sphere. Namely, I consider the pots and pans that the poor used to cook with, the extent to which they engaged in domestic self-provisioning, the types of plates and cutlery that they used, whether eating became more of a pleasurable pursuit rather than one of necessity, and the nature of tea and coffee drinking. These areas are much less well trodden than the topics noted above but just as important to consider.

The evidence reveals that although many people had the means to cook in diverse ways, such as roasting and frying, most meals were boiled or stewed. This does not, however, mean that the poor only ate out of necessity and were content with boring dishes. Rather, many would flavour their meals with herbs and spices and it is important to remember that liquid-based dishes remained a staple of people's diets because they enjoyed them. Many people also had the means to bake their own bread and grow their own vegetables to add to these dishes, but they sourced foodstuffs such as cheese, beer, butter and meat from outside the home.

When it came to serving the finished meal, earthenware dishes, which could come in a wide array of colours and patterns, were the norm. As in middling homes, there was a decline in pewterware and woodenware as people's tastes and needs changed, but these dishes continued to be found in some spaces for everyday use. Knives and forks grew in ownership, indicating that there was a move away from communal eating to personal dishes and new dining rituals. The chapter ends by considering tea, coffee and chocolate consumption. Perhaps more so than any other product, tea took off on an unprecedented scale and was a universal staple of labouring diets by the 1770s. Some people used a range of tea paraphernalia such as tea caddies and tea tables along ceremonial and ritualistic lines while they drank tea. Yet for most, tea drinking was not emulative of wealthier people and was much more restrained, involving a range of multi-purpose goods which could be used alongside various other drinks. Although less popular than tea, coffee also became fairly widespread, while chocolate was probably only an occasional treat for most.

Cooking and food preparation

Boiling and stewing

The most basic and common form of cooking was boiling and simmering meat and vegetables in liquid to form dishes such as stews, broths, porridge and soups. It is difficult to precisely ascertain how these methods of cooking were conducted using inventories – or any other sources, for that matter. The descriptors for boiling and stewing cooking items are often opaque, regionally diverse and difficult to distinguish from one another. For example, boilers can be synonymous with kettles, posnets synonymous with skillets, and cauldrons synonymous with cooking pots.[5] Regionally, a crock was a metal cooking pot in the south east but a small earthenware pan in the north.[6] Even for items which appear to have had a specific function, such as a porridge or pottage pot, it is probable that they were used with other foods and it is difficult to tell how different they were to a boiler or a cooking pot.[7] Equally, it is generally not possible to examine surviving artefacts to uncover how these items might have looked and functioned, since many were melted down once they were no longer needed.[8]

Despite these difficulties, the pauper inventories reveal important trends (Table 5.1). In all, boiling and stewing items were common in the inventories and these appear to have been the chief way in which people cooked, but there were changes in the types of vessels that the poor owned. The results suggest that over the long eighteenth century, boilers and saucepans became especially common in poor homes while alternative cooking vessels such as cooking pots, kettles and skillets gradually

Eating and drinking 145

Table 5.1 Percentage of paupers who owned various boiling and stewing goods, 1670–1835

	1670–1729	1730–69	1770–1809	1810–35
Boiler	2	19	31	35
Cauldron	0	0	0	0
Cooking pot	42	39	31	23
Crock	1	6	6	5
Kettle	45	31	28	15
Porridge pot	13	12	9	5
Pottage pot	9	6	9	2
Posnet	2	0	1	0
Saucepan	0	3	19	29
Skillet	46	41	17	0
Sample size	125	268	165	65

declined in ownership. Cauldrons and posnets were almost entirely absent in the sample, indicating that by the late seventeenth century, most people had moved away from them.

Like with many items covered in this book, one might expect the variety of boiling and stewing implements in pauper homes to increase as the period progressed, but conversely the range narrowed. This decline in some boiling- and stewing-related cooking vessels does not mean that paupers were moving away from this form of cooking. Nor can the falling off of numbers of these items be completely explained through semantic reasons. Instead, the results from the inventories indicate that the poor increasingly owned only *one* type of boiling or stewing cooking vessel (usually a boiler or saucepan) rather than several types. Before 1770, around three-fifths of paupers owned at least two types of cooking vessel related to boiling and stewing food, whereas after 1770 around two-fifths of people owned multiple types of vessels.

Hidden in these numbers are regional differences, so Table 5.2 breaks the figures down by county. The results suggest that in the home counties the poor generally possessed the greatest variety of boiling and stewing items. Cooking pots were the most common vessels that people owned everywhere except in Essex, but it was not unusual for them to be supplemented by kettles and skillets. The same trends from a much smaller sample of inventories can also be seen in Lancashire.[9] In Essex, boilers appear most frequently in the sources, but this might be the result of there being more inventories from the county for the late eighteenth and early nineteenth centuries, when boilers were more widespread.

Table 5.2 Percentage of paupers who owned various boiling and stewing goods, by county, 1670–1835

	Dorset	Essex	Kent	Leics/Ruts	Norfolk	All
Boiler	2	44	13	0	10	20
Crock	13	0	30	6	0	5
Cooking pot	65	12	40	54	46	36
Kettle	32	38	33	38	24	32
Porridge pot	0	11	25	7	11	11
Pottage pot	0	12	7	0	7	7
Saucepan	2	16	10	10	4	9
Skillet	20	39	33	1	36	31

Despite having similar functions, these boiling and stewing vessels were used in different ways. When in use, larger round-bottomed vessels such as cooking pots tended to be suspended over the fire using pot-hooks, hakes or cranes of some kind (Figure 5.1).[10] Most of these pot-hooks were probably adjustable, allowing the user to place the pot at a height which would either slowly stew the food or quickly boil it. Skillets and posnets, on the other hand, had three legs and a long handle and were placed over the burning fire or to the side of it (Figures 5.1 and 5.2). Cooking pots also had three small legs, but these were instead used to firmly set the pot down from the pot-hook once the food was cooked (Figure 5.1).[11]

The majority of cooking pots were described as iron pots, while most boilers, kettles and skillets appear to have been made from iron or brass, and increasingly copper or tin from the late eighteenth century. Copper was the best conductor of heat, meaning that any cooking utensils created from this metal would have heated quicker, reducing cooking time and the amount of fuel that was needed.[12] Some of these cooking vessels were described with covers or lids of some sort, and a number were labelled 'small' or 'large' by appraisers, suggesting that they could be used to cook varying quantities of food depending on who was eating. Various householders had several cooking vessels for different purposes, such as 'Old' Goodman Brown, who, in 1670, possessed 'Three brase catles [kettles] one a litle bigger then an other'.[13] On occasion, the appraisers were more specific regarding the size of paupers' pots. William Hunt, for example, was given a '2 Gallon Iron pot' by Speldhurst, Kent parish, when he left the workhouse in 1818 and Robert Ward of Wethersfield, Essex, possessed 'one Kettle containing about 3 pails full, one Boiler about 1½ pail, one Gall[on] Skillet, [and] one ¾ of a pint Skillet'.[14] Skillets were usually identified as pint- or quart-sized by appraisers so were probably

Figure 5.1 Randle Holme, picture of a brass pot (left), adjustable pot-hook (centre) and posnet (right), 1688 (source: Holme, *Academy of Armory*, Vol. 2, pp. 18–19)

Figure 5.2 Skillet, c.1700–1900 (source: Metropolitan Museum of Art, New York 10.125.599w, Skillet, iron, c.1700–1900)

mostly used to cook smaller amounts of food. The value of these boiling and stewing items was generally a few shillings but on occasion they were worth more than a pound each. Value was clearly assigned to the vessels according to size as well as material. This can be seen in the inventory of Dame Beddles' goods in Canewdon, Essex, which notes 'A Boiler for 3 pailfuls' worth 10s. and a 'one pailful' boiler valued at 4s.[15] It was also not unusual for cooking items to be described as 'old' by appraisers, yet this did not necessarily mean that the items were sub-standard and had limited use. Cooking vessels often had personal significance and continued to be valued when they were old because of the years of trusted service that they had given to their owners.[16] With some cooking implements being relatively expensive, there was also little point in replacing old utensils when they still worked. Even when they were broken, many people would sooner repair than replace them.[17]

One of the most important changes in cooking came from the poor's growing use of saucepans from the later eighteenth century (Tables 5.1 and 5.2). Saucepans can be linked to the boiling and stewing of food but they were much more versatile than this, as they enabled people to make sauces and even foreign-influenced meals. Saucepans were also more efficient than larger pots, as they were smaller and heated quicker. They were flat-bottomed so particularly suited to use with enclosed cooking ranges, or they could be placed on trivets which held items in place next to or in the fire (Figure 5.3).[18] In Kent, for example, between 1770 and 1835, 27 per cent of the pauper inventories recorded trivets.

Although the eighteenth-century rich and poor knew little about the nutritional value of food, producing boiled meals had various advantages over alternative forms of cooking such as roasting, frying and grilling. Making stews and soups was one of the more nourishing ways to prepare meals, as the vitamins and juices from the ingredients would have generally stayed in the water. When roasting these nutrients and juices would have been lost, unless they were gathered in a dripping pan and then consumed

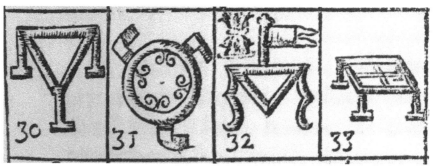

Figure 5.3 Randle Holme, pictures of trivets, 1688 (source: Holme, *Academy of Armory*, Vol. 2, pp. 18–19)

somehow. Cooking broths and stews meant that cheaper cuts of meat could be used, as the boiling process helped to make the meat tenderer than if it were roasted. Boiling was the safest way to prepare older meat and was essential for cooking salted meat.[19] Following the scarcity of wood and lack of inexpensive alternative fuels in some areas,[20] boiling could also have the advantage of needing less fuel than roasting, and pudding could be boiled at the same time.[21] While a meal was boiling it could be left with minimal observation as people busied themselves with other household tasks. Finally, and perhaps most importantly, it is vital to stress that boiled dishes were common as people liked them. Stews, soups, porridge and many other liquid-based dishes were loved by the English and so remained a staple in the face of a world where rival cuisines, new ingredients, cookbooks and novel cooking techniques became more well known and widespread.[22]

Grilling, roasting, frying and toasting

Boiling and stewing was not the only cooking technique open to people. Families could also engage in methods such as grilling, roasting, frying and toasting. Table 5.3 records the frequencies of pauper inventories which note cooking implements linked to these activities. Spits, for instance, roasted meat, and gridirons could be used to grill, roast and toast food (Figure 5.4). Gridirons and frying pans appear to have been owned by people for long periods of time, and there is no real discernible increase or decline in their ownership. Spits too were possessed by people for a prolonged period, but the data indicates that they declined in ownership, while dripping pans and jacks (a mechanical device used for turning spits) were possessed only in negligible numbers. Ranges are likely to have been under-recorded in the pauper inventories since some appraisers may have viewed them as fixtures rather than moveable possessions. Nevertheless, they appear to have been owned by only a minority of paupers.

Table 5.3 Percentage of paupers who owned various cooking items, 1670–1835

	1670–1729	1730–69	1770–1809	1810–35
Dripping pan	4	4	4	0
Frying pan	35	41	38	43
Gridiron	26	28	25	22
Jack	2	1	2	0
Range	0	2	3	3
Spit	22	20	13	5
Sample size	125	268	165	65

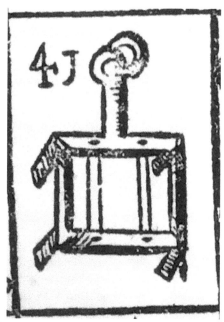

Figure 5.4 Randle Holme, picture of a gridiron, 1688 (source: Holme, *Academy of Armory*, Vol. 2, pp. 18–19)

Taking all types of cooking items into account, the results indicate that the poor owned relatively fewer items related to grilling, roasting, frying and toasting food compared with boiling and stewing implements. In total, around four-fifths of paupers owned at least one cooking item related to boiling and stewing food, whereas three-fifths owned one or more goods related to grilling, toasting, frying or roasting food.[23] These figures remained relatively static throughout the long eighteenth century, suggesting that there were few changes in the cooking techniques of the poor over the period and that the consumption of food cooked in diverse manners was possible but remained less common than cooking meals in a single pot of some sort.

It has been argued throughout this book that the material lives of the poor broadly improved over the long eighteenth century. Yet with food, which made up the majority of families' expenditure,[24] the results from the pauper inventories strongly suggest that cooking techniques changed little. This might stem from a general reticence in relation to new types of food and the desire to cook traditional stews and other liquid-based dishes, as noted above. It could also be the simple consequence of people not having the time to cook diverse meals or being too poor to regularly purchase foods that could be fried, roasted and grilled, such as meat and eggs. There were slight regional differences in this, however. In Dorset,

Eating and drinking 151

Leicestershire and Rutland, the poor appear to have been among the least likely to own frying pans, gridirons and spits compared with their counterparts who lived elsewhere (Table 5.4), suggesting that cooking in these counties might have been particularly rudimentary. The same can also largely be said of the indigent population located in Lancashire.[25] Meanwhile in Essex, Kent and Norfolk, paupers owned slightly higher numbers of grilling, roasting, frying and toasting items.

Although we do see some improvements in cooking practices, largely as a result of the growing use of copper and saucepans, the results largely corroborate the arguments of contemporary commentators who contended that the quality of the poor's food could be inadequate and scarcely improved over time. Writing in 1831, social reformer William Cobbett argued that 'All of you who are sixty years of age can recollect that bread and meat, and not wretched potatoes, were the food of the labouring people'.[26] In a similar vein, social investigators David Davies and Frederic Morton Eden claimed that the diets of the labouring population had declined in a number of areas.[27] Comparable accounts can also be seen in the writings of the poor. Working-class autobiographies are littered with references to hunger,[28] as are the letters sent by paupers to parishes asking for relief. Robert Beck of Kirkby Lonsdale in Lancashire, for instance, noted how he 'had nothing … nether Bread nor Buter But few Potatoes and Salt' owing to lack of work and his wife's illness.[29] Equally, when Samuel Parker wrote to the overseer of Uttoxeter in Staffordshire, he asked for relief, as his family were 'in a state of Starvation for potatoes and Salt [h]as been our chiefest Diet'.[30] Paupers frequently emphasised the lack of meat in their restricted fares, such as William James of Chelmsford who claimed that 'it have not been in my power, to purchase any meat, these 6 weeks past, we have now a piece of Bread only'.[31]

Any improvements in the cooking practices and food of the poor pale in comparison with those of people from the lower middling sort and above, who moved away from boiling and stewing at a much faster pace

Table 5.4 Percentage of paupers who owned various cooking items, by county, 1670–1835

	Dorset	Essex	Kent	Leics/Ruts	Norfolk	All
Dripping pan	2	6	8	0	2	4
Frying pan	28	46	38	28	41	40
Gridiron	17	33	35	0	29	27
Jack	0	1	2	1	1	1
Range	0	1	0	0	4	2
Spit	3	21	27	0	20	17

152 At home with the poor

than paupers.[32] Vessels such as saucepans were owned by much smaller numbers of the poor than other groups. They grew in ownership among the middling sort from the late seventeenth century, and by the 1800s they were probably owned by the majority of people from the group.[33] By the second quarter of the eighteenth century, around half of the middling sort in Kent owned jacks, meaning that around two out of three of the middling sort in Kent had a jack to use with their spit.[34] In contrast, according to the pauper inventories only one in sixteen paupers who owned a spit in Kent also possessed a jack. This indicates that the small number of paupers who spit roasted their food had to manually turn it, sometimes for many hours. This was an uncomfortable job, as people had to be close to the heat of the fire and risked burning themselves.

Taste and flavouring food

Even if cooking techniques remained rudimentary and the poor dined on much the same meals as their forebears, this did not mean that they ate only bland food and did not enjoy what they consumed.[35] Recalling his life as a child, Samuel Bamford remarked that 'Our fare was of the simplest kind, and far from profuse', but he fondly noted the milk, bread and dumplings that he had which were 'so entirely delicious, that of anything more excellent we could not form an idea'.[36] The shoemaker Thomas Holcroft similarly noted how his father was always 'satisfied with [his] plain, wholesome diet'.[37] Others were adventurous and tried new things when they could. While serving as a soldier in Portugal, John Green sampled new foods such as olive oil, which was 'a good substitute for butter, and tastes very well' and 'has no unpleasant taste whatever'.[38] Sometimes the soldiers complained about their fare, suggesting that they were used to better and that flavour was important to them. While onboard a hulk with some 700 French prisoners, John Brown stated that although the salt fish of the French was 'pretty good', their 'food was not of first-rate quality' and was 'unwholesome' to an Englishman.[39]

One of the main ways in which the poor could improve their meals was through herbs and spices. These could be purchased from the market or foraged and grown in gardens and allotments. Thomas Carter had a 'miniature garden' which bordered his father's and included 'several kinds of herbs, such as mint, thyme, rosemary, and southernwood'.[40] Meanwhile, Samuel Bamford's grandfather Daniel had a garden which was poorly maintained but included 'sprouts of sweet herbs shooting amongst struggling weeds'.[41] Even workhouse inmates were provided with herbs and spices from the market or gardens adjacent to the institution.[42] Additionally, as noted in the pauper letters above, those who could only afford potatoes still added salt to them, and the household budgets of even the poorest of people often note buying salt.[43] Our craving for salt

Eating and drinking   153

is widespread across humans and animals and without it people who are used to seasoned dishes suddenly find their food bland and flat. Salt had the power to elevate the flavour of even the blandest of dishes.[44]

We can also see glimpses of flavouring in inventories. Rather unusually, there survives one pauper inventory for Clayton-le-Moors in Lancashire which notes the 'Groceries' of Thomas Webster, including sugar, currants and nutmeg.[45] Salt and pepper boxes were inexpensive purchases that were easily missed by appraisers, but they were still recorded in 4 and 10 per cent of pauper inventories respectively.[46] Spice drawers, along with pestles and mortars used to grind spices for medicine and food, are also occasionally recorded in the inventories, as are items related to mustard, nutmeg, sugar and vinegar. In 1775 John Playne from Staplehurst in Kent, for instance, owned '1 Spoon w[i]th a Nutmeg Grater in the Handle' and '1 vinegar Bottle',[47] while John Osborne of Sandhurst, Kent, possessed '1 China Mustard Pot' in 1783.[48] Both of these paupers also owned items related to sugar, which significantly grew in per capita consumption over the eighteenth century and became more affordable.[49] Much of this sugar would have been used with tea, but it could also be used to flavour sauces, porridge and other dishes.[50] Monotony and lack of flavour was therefore not the case for all.

Baking and self-provisioning

Another important way in which people might prepare and acquire consumables was through baking, and through self-provisioning such as brewing and the rearing of livestock. By quantifying the items from the pauper inventories which are closely tied to these various activities, one can ascertain how common they were in pauper homes. The results should, however, be taken with a pinch of salt. Ovens, for instance, indicate that people were involved in baking of some kind, yet because ovens were fixtures they were rarely recorded in inventories.[51] Various tubs and other large vessels could be used for salting, pickling, brewing and many other pursuits, but unless their use is described by the appraiser it is impossible to determine their purpose. Growth in particular activities might also stem more from people using more specialised equipment which is easier to categorise than from actual increases in self-provisioning.[52] In spite of these difficulties, the results clearly suggest that although households were busy spaces engaged in baking and vegetable growing, the poor largely sourced foodstuffs such as cheese, beer, butter and meat from outside the home (Table 5.5).

Baking was common among paupers. Kneading troughs and peels were the most usual baking items noted in the inventories, indicating that the poor were primarily engaged in breadmaking. However, rolling pins, baking stones and pastry pans occasionally appear in the sources, which

At home with the poor

Table 5.5 Percentage of paupers who owned various food and drink processing goods, 1670–1835

	1670–1729	1730–69	1770–1809	1810–35	All years
Agricultural/outdoor tools	18	21	35	38	26
Animals (actual)	5	2	7	3	4
Animals (actual and potential)	10	7	22	23	14
Baking	19	29	45	46	33
Brewing	20	9	20	3	14
Cider making	0	<1	1	0	<1
Crops	2	2	1	3	2
Dairy work	5	3	8	5	6
Distillation	0	<1	1	0	<1
Food preservation (e.g. brining and salting)	6	3	12	5	6
Sample size	125	268	165	65	645

shows that some households could also make cakes, pastries, biscuits and oatcakes. The baking items were generally owned in small numbers and so were probably used for personal consumption. Some working people nonetheless baked products to sell, such as Betty Shaw, who made oatcakes for neighbours 'for hire'.[53] It has been argued that as the country industrialised, people bought more bread and ready-made products from the market.[54] A number of contemporaries too bemoaned how domestic breadmaking declined.[55] These results show clear evidence that baking remained important as the country transitioned from a pre-industrial to an industrial economy. People could be very pragmatic, though. Many families continued to source bread from the market in addition to making their own, in accordance with the cost and availability of ingredients and fuel.[56]

It has – quite rightly – been argued that as more land was enclosed in England during the early modern period, the labouring sort had fewer opportunities to forage materials as well as to farm crops and raise animals.[57] In spite of this, the pauper inventories suggest that domestic arable farming remained important and grew over the long eighteenth century. In the majority of cases the poor owned hand tools such as spades, hoes and mattocks in small numbers, indicating that it was farming for personal consumption in gardens or allotments that they were primarily engaged in. Sometimes these outdoor tools were used to maintain hedges and lawns

Eating and drinking   155

or for gathering peat and wood. Where noted, the crops tend to be modest quantities of wheat, hay, barley, or produce such as potatoes, beans and peas. The autobiographies of the poor show that growing food could supply families with a variety of produce. In Benjamin Shaw's childhood home there was a 'good' garden which had several beehives and 'Plenty of Berry trees &c'.[58] Selling fruit and vegetables could be a lifeline for people when there were surplus yields. John Clare's parents in Helpston, Northamptonshire, for example, had an apple tree in the garden which 'generaly made the [40s.] rent' that they paid annually. When their landlord increased their rent to three guineas a year, the apples from the tree still made up 'the greater part of our rent', until 'the old tree faild to bear fruit and left us unable to get up the rent'.[59] The land surveyor John Tuke even went as far as to say that the 'gardens of the labourers may frequently be seen better cultivated than those of the farmers; because the labourer occupies no other land, and his garden is appropriated to the cultivation of potatoes, and other useful vegetables, for his family'.[60]

While around 14 per cent of pauper inventories note animal-related items such as saddles and troughs, only 4 per cent of sources list livestock of some sort. It is probable that these goods associated with animal ownership were left over from more prosperous times, before people entered relief lists. If animals were present, there was every incentive for appraisers to document them, since they were expensive saleable assets or could be put to use in the poorhouse/workhouse if taken by parochial authorities. The only exception to this might be leased animals, as they were not technically owned by the poor themselves.[61] Where animals are recorded in the inventories, it is generally only a single animal for food that is noted rather than one for transport. In total, 42 various poultry such as chickens and geese, ten cows, ten pigs, seven sheep, six beehives, three asses and two horses are mentioned across 29 of the 645 pauper inventories. These numbers are very small and are dwarfed by the livestock of the middling sort.[62] With most people having access only to gardens or allotments of some sort, many people simply would not have been able to accommodate animals which needed space to graze.[63] It was common for families to not have enough to eat themselves, so having animals to feed would have been too much of a strain for many. Livestock could also be a risky investment. A cow, for instance, cost several pounds to purchase and if it died young it would have had limited time to repay its owner's investment in milk.[64] As noted above, some people might have turned to leasing a cow to protect themselves from sudden loss, while in some parishes there was an element of sharing. In Wortham, Suffolk, thatcher James Jolly had a pony which was a 'slave of the parish', carrying women to their place of service, transporting the sick, and even playing with children and helping people to go on holiday (Figure 5.5).[65] For most, however, livestock ownership was rare, so meat and milk, as well as by-products such as feathers and wool, had to be sourced elsewhere.

Figure 5.5 Portrait of James Jolly and his horse, painted by Richard Cobbold, c.1840s–1862 (source: SA HA 11/A13/10; reproduced by kind permission of the owner)

Alternative forms of food and drink self-provisioning appear to have been uncommon in indigent households. Evidence of cheese, milk and butter production could be found in only around one in twenty pauper inventories. Some people, such as Thomas Swan of Osgathorpe in Leicestershire, were clearly engaged in dairying on a considerable scale; Swan owned several churns, a number of cheese containers and '43 cheeses'.[66] However, this was far from typical, and most families who involved themselves in dairying possessed only a single item such as a churn or a milk pot. Food preservation, such as salting, smoking, brining and pickling, was also found in only around one in twenty pauper inventories, but it was probably more widespread than this, since many of these processes could be done with only a multi-purpose container of some sort. It is unclear which meats, fish, vegetables and fruits paupers treated most often, but where produce was noted it was nearly always pork. Most inventories note a solitary powdering or brine tub, suggesting that only modest quantities of food were preserved in pauper homes. Domestic drink production was equally scarce. Beer and ale were a necessity to people of the past. Cider was especially important in the south west, and there was a growth in the consumption of spirits over the long eighteenth century.[67] Nonetheless, brewing appears to have been present in only around 14 per cent of pauper households, while cider production and distillation could only be detected in three and two of the inventories respectively. When it came to acquiring drinks other than water, as well as butter, cheese and processed foods such as smoked meats and jams, many people therefore had no option but to turn to the market.

Finally, we consider regional differences in baking and self-provisioning. In sum, the inventories indicate that it was not in rural areas such as Dorset and Leicestershire where these pursuits were most common but in the more commercial areas of Essex and Kent (Table 5.6). This runs counter to what one might expect, as in the home counties there were many more shops and a greater variety of retail spaces in which people could purchase foodstuffs rather than produce their own.[68] Further research is needed to explain why some poor people continued to self-provision in these areas, but the same trends can be seen in wealthier households.[69] It might be that these families associated home production with quality and so even when there was a wide choice in shops, people still chose to make their own when they could.[70] Through self-provisioning, families could keep a better eye on ingredients and reduce their chances of consuming adulterated groceries.[71] Making one's own food and drink might also have been cheaper than procuring it from the market.

These results have important implications for Jan de Vries's highly influential 'industrious revolution' theory, which claims that households specialised and moved away from modest domestic production to acquire new consumer goods over the eighteenth century.[72] I have argued elsewhere that because households remained active spaces while they acquired new consumer goods, the theory does not work in practice.[73] In a similar vein, the results here do not support the concept, since domestic

158   At home with the poor

Table 5.6 Percentage of paupers who owned various food and drink processing goods, by county, 1670–1835

	Dorset	Essex	Kent	Leics/Ruts	Norfolk
Agricultural/outdoor tools	10	39	30	14	19
Animals (actual)	5	7	8	1	2
Animals (actual and potential)	10	21	27	6	7
Baking	5	56	52	34	15
Brewing	3	17	23	0	15
Dairy work	3	6	17	4	3
Food preservation	2	6	33	1	2

production was especially prominent in Essex and Kent, where rates of consumption were generally higher. If the theory were accurate, we would expect poor households in these counties to have been reliant on wages to buy foodstuffs as new goods entered their homes.

Dining and drinking

While assessing cooking, food preparation and self-provisioning allows the historian to gauge the poor's wellbeing through the quality of their food, evaluating the ways in which indigent people consumed their fare allows us to consider its cultural and social significance.[74] Unsurprisingly, the majority of research on dining has focused on the middling sort and the elite, who epitomised a number of changes to social rituals and behaviours over the eighteenth century, including the refinement of manners, politeness and civility.[75] Overall, the evidence indicates that the poor had some rituals when eating and drinking. For example, many families would alternate between wooden and earthenware dishes according to what they were consuming, and the eating of meals with knives and forks became more usual. It would be wrong to assume that because people were poor or did not own certain types of tableware, they had no eating manners and few social rituals when eating.[76]

This research on tableware and dining has wider implications for our understanding of the industrial revolution, as the tea, coffee and sugar trades and ceramic, glass and cutlery production were key players in British economic growth,[77] while more 'traditional' enterprises such as pewter production declined.[78] Likewise, the development and success of regions and cities such as the Potteries and Sheffield came largely from their expanding industries in these areas. By assessing the poor's consumption of various items of tableware, this work adds to this literature by

Eating and drinking   159

uncovering how far down the social ladder people consumed goods from these industries, and where and when they reached people.

Tableware

The materials of the poor's eating and drinking vessels, such as plates, bowls and cups, are assessed in this section. Unfortunately, this category of goods appears to have been under-recorded by appraisers, as two-fifths of pauper inventories fail to note any receptacles. Of course, it is possible that some dwellings simply did not contain any. If people ate bread with most meals, for instance, then they may not have seen the need to own plates. However, it is likely that no more than a minority of paupers would have done this, since people still needed containers to hold drinks and bowls for liquid-based foods. The analysis of eating and drinking is made more difficult by appraisers who were vague in their descriptions, noting 'some' earthenware or naming plates and bowls but not materials. Inventories also often miss the great variety of designs and colours that can be found in ceramic remnants from archaeological sites.[79]

The pauper inventories show that people could own a diverse range of eating and drinking vessels from the late seventeenth to the early nineteenth centuries (Table 5.7). Earthenware was the most common material for much of the period, followed by pewter and wood. China, delftware, glassware, stoneware and tinware implements grew slightly in ownership from the second half of the eighteenth century, while leather vessels are recorded in only a handful of inventories. The quantity of eating and drinking utensils that people possessed also appears to have grown for a number of materials. For instance, the number of vessels with an unspecified material increased from an average of 3.2 items per household between 1670 and 1709 to 11.5 items by 1790–1835. In Table 5.8 the results are broken down by region. The data continues to point to earthenware, pewterware and woodenware as the most usual materials of tableware around the country. However, it is the poor in Kent, and to a lesser extent Essex, who owned the greatest quantities and varieties of dinnerware.

As earthenware became more important, pewterware and woodenware appear to have declined in ownership.[80] Pewter was the most common dining material in pauper inventories for 1670–1709, yet by 1790–1835 only around one in ten sources note the material (Table 5.7). Woodenware was used for longer periods than pewter, but from the 1810s it is recorded in only 9 per cent of sources. In spite of this, it is important to not overstate the switch to earthenware, as pewter and wood remained prominent for long periods of time. In fact, 58 per cent of pauper inventories which list earthenware also include pewter and/or wooden vessels, and 72 per cent

160 At home with the poor

Table 5.7 Pauper ownership of various dinnerware, 1670–1835

		1670–1709	1710–49	1750–89	1790–1834	All years
Chinaware	%	0	0	3	6	3
	Average number	0	0	5.6	13.6	9.6
Delftware	%	0	2	3	6	3
	Average number	0	7	9.9	8.5	9
Earthenware	%	11	31	30	30	29
	Average number	4.5	5.5	9.8	7.6	8.3
Glassware	%	4	7	11	13	10
	Average number	3.5	11.1	6.6	6.2	7
Leatherware	%	4	1	<1	1	1
	Average number	1	1	1	1	1
Pewterware	%	36	26	23	10	22
	Average number	4.4	4.5	5.2	7.6	5.1
Stoneware	%	2	5	10	12	9
	Average number	1	2.9	3	2.3	2.7
Tinware	%	0	0	3	8	3
	Average number	0	0	2.9	2.4	2.6
Woodenware	%	11	24	25	15	22
	Average number	7.6	5.6	5.6	2.4	5.6
Unspecified	%	24	36	36	50	39
	Average number	3.2	3.4	6.5	11.5	6.9
	Sample size	45	163	270	145	645

of the paupers who owned earthenware owned eating and drinking vessels made from any material. This suggests that the poor alternated between various bundles of dinnerware depending upon what they were eating. Pewterware and woodenware were especially important in this process.

Eating and drinking 161

Table 5.8 Pauper ownership of various dinnerware, by county, 1770–1835

		Dorset	Essex	Kent	Leics/Ruts	Norfolk
Chinaware	%	0	9	18	0	3
	Average number	0	14.9	2.3	0	4
Delftware	%	5	6	14	11	0
	Average number	5	8.7	13.3	19.5	0
Earthenware	%	41	34	73	26	38
	Average number	4	10.6	14.4	15	7.4
Glassware	%	5	16	45	3	19
	Average number	12	8.4	6.7	1	5.9
Leatherware	%	0	2	0	0	0
	Average number	0	1	0	0	0
Pewterware	%	32	15	45	23	5
	Average number	6.7	7.3	6.1	4.8	5.5
Stoneware	%	0	15	27	3	24
	Average number	0	2.5	6	1	2.2
Tinware	%	5	9	18	6	0
	Average number	3	3.4	1	2.5	0
Woodenware	%	14	21	41	26	16
	Average number	6.3	4.1	7	6.1	4.3
Unspecified	%	32	53	73	37	46
	Average number	7.3	12.7	17.9	7.5	3.9
	Sample size	22	116	22	35	37

Both were hard-wearing and were thus ideally suited for 'everyday use', whereas earthenware might have been used for particular meals or 'best use' as it was fragile and seen as more respectable. While living with his aunt and uncle as a child, Samuel Bamford (b.1788) noted how meals and vessels changed depending on what they were eating. At breakfast, 'a brown earthen dish' was placed in front of everybody and 'water porridge was poured into the dish, hot from the pan'. When dinner was meat and potatoes, the family would have 'an allowance of the meat on a piece of oat cake', while the potatoes were 'poured into a [communal] dish' and they 'all stood round and with spoon or knife ... [to] eat from the dish'. With broth, 'each received a mess for himself, to which he added as much oaten cake as he chose; the potatoes were eaten out of the [communal] dish, and the meat being served in portions'.[81]

The decline in pewterware and woodenware and rise in earthenware suggest that the poor's outlook towards eating and drinking progressively changed over the eighteenth century. Earthenware, which was closely linked to respectability and the refinement of tableware and decoration, was increasingly valued by the poor, as the longevity and function of hard-wearing products such as pewter and wooden vessels was gradually seen as less important. Earthenware was cheap, widely available and did not scratch as easily as pewter. It came in a number of shapes and sizes and could be decorated with colour and patterns.[82] Widow Piercon from Martham, Norfolk, for instance, owned 'Six earthen Blue & white Plates [and] 1 yellow earthen dish',[83] while Mary Woolfry of Bere Regis in Dorset possessed 'blew and White' earthenware.[84] Cheap ceramic homeware could even be designed to illustrate people's political leanings or commemorate major events such as the Peterloo Massacre.[85] With pewter and wood, on the other hand, there was limited scope to differentiate the product and make it more appealing to consumers on a decorative level.[86] Earthenware was also heavily associated with tea drinking, as teapots and cups and saucers were often made from the material. Thus, despite the fragile nature of earthenware and the fact that it had to be replaced more often than pewter or wooden receptacles, the poor increasingly acquired earthenware in a similar way to the middling sort and the elite. [87]

Glassware, stoneware and tinware saw modest increases in ownership as the period progressed, allowing people to differentiate and change between dinnerware as they saw fit. When people owned glassware, they tended to possess it in fairly high numbers. Interestingly, the inventories list wine glasses and drinking vessels that were linked to spirits. Dame Austin from Staplehurst in Kent, for example, possessed '1 Tumbler' and '3 Glass Bottles' among other glassware; while Michael Aggus from Redenhall in Norfolk owned two wine glasses, 'one Beaker Glass' and '10–12 Glass Bottles'.[88] This increase in alcohol-related glassware indicates that the vessels used to drink certain beverages had started to become more specialised. Stoneware was fired at a higher temperature than earthenware, making it more hard-wearing, and it was also cheaper to acquire, but it could be a sought-after ceramic, often decorated with various colours and prints.[89] White stoneware is found in some of the inventories. One pauper even had six stone plates on her mantelpiece, indicating that they were used to adorn and enhance the domestic space.[90]

A small number owned notable items such as china and delftware, especially in Kent. Some paupers even owned highly fashionable refined earthenware, such as Widow Marchant from Chiddingstone, Kent, who possessed 'one Queens wares bowl' in 1811 and Widow Adams of Hatfield Broad Oak, Essex, who owned 'Fourteen pieces of QueenWare'.[91] These are particularly remarkable examples, since Queen's ware was made by Wedgwood and became very fashionable from the second half of the

Eating and drinking 163

eighteenth century after Josiah Wedgwood supplied Queen Charlotte with it.[92] Delftware grew in ownership among the poor especially between the 1770s and 1800s. The delftware collection of Mrs Buckwell of Canterbury in Kent was particularly impressive. Spread across several rooms, her home contained 'fower Delf Jars', '26 Delf Plats', '23 P[iece]^s of Delf & Ston wear' and '2 Delf' bowls in 1780.[93] China was equally viewed as fashionable by consumers and could be purchased relatively inexpensively on the second-hand market. The pawnbroker's pledge book of George Fettes of York, for example, shows that a lot of china was pawned for less than pewterware and could be bought for around a shilling apiece if left unredeemed by its owners.[94]

Cutlery

The quantitative results from the pauper inventories indicate that spoon and knife and fork ownership was low but increasing over the long eighteenth century (Table 5.9). However, the figures are misleading. It is probable that spoons were universal and that knives and forks became more widespread as the period progressed. Most cutlery was worth only a few pence as it was made from wood or cheap metals, so for most appraisers it was not worth the bother of counting and listing it.[95] Likewise, spoons made from inexpensive materials are common finds in archaeological digs from settlements dated well before the period of study here.[96] In part, the apparent rise in cutlery ownership comes from parochial officials noting more expensive and unusual sets from the late eighteenth century.[97] The recorded words of the labouring sort corroborate the idea that knives and forks were more common by the late eighteenth century and that expendable ones were the norm. Mechanic/turner Benjamin Shaw, for instance, noted that he lacked various basics such as fuel upon moving into a new home in 1793, yet one of his first priorities was to make himself and his wife a set of knives and forks.[98] Perhaps more telling, autobiographies of numerous working people such as apprentices, soldiers and labourers mention knives and forks in passing, indicating that they were customarily used up and down the country.[99]

Spoons, knives and forks are not necessary for the consumption of food. People can handle bread and other solid foods with their hands,

Table 5.9 Percentage of paupers who owned knives, forks and spoons, 1670–1835

	1670–1729	1730–69	1770–1809	1810–35
Knives and forks	0	1	7	15
Spoons	2	4	10	8
Sample size	125	268	165	65

164   At home with the poor

break off pieces with their hands and teeth, and drink stews without them. Traditionally, the majority of people ate their meals with their hands and used few or no items of cutlery except a spoon and/or a multi-purpose knife that they carried around with them.[100] Thus, with the growing use of knives and forks there was a transformation in people's eating habits and dining rituals, as people desired to be self-contained and began to use personal cutlery to cut up food and bring it to mouth. This meant that the rules and systems to which people conformed at the table had significantly changed.[101]

The poor probably started to use knives and forks at a later date than the middling sort and the elite.[102] Yet this does not mean that there were no eating manners or social etiquette among those who did not own cutlery. People who did not wash their hands before eating, seized food with both hands or licked their fingers, for instance, were seen as particularly rude in some households during the Middle Ages.[103] Moreover, it is important to note that just because people owned knives and forks, this does not mean that they used them for every meal. As we saw above, the poor commonly ate boiled and stewed meals which needed spoons. It is also possible that some people reverted to the same eating habits and manners that they were taught as children, meaning that they continued to habitually pick up food even when they owned knives and forks.[104] For these reasons, the move to knives and forks among the poor was gradual, with the practice of using hands only slowly being phased out across the generations.

Hot drinks

Tea and coffee first came to England around the second quarter of the seventeenth century.[105] Both were initially only consumed by the very rich and royalty as they were very expensive and seen as exotic and novel luxuries.[106] By the early to mid-eighteenth century, both had become widespread among the middling sort but tea had overtaken coffee in popularity.[107] We know much less about the poor's drinking of tea and even less about their intake of coffee. Most of what we know about the poor is based on subjective contemporary comments, household budgets and workhouse records and has often focused on the impact that tea had on labouring diets.[108] Consequently, in this section we consider the types of tea and coffee goods that poor people owned, how they used them, and the wider economic, social and cultural contexts behind the poor's consumption of hot drinks.

There are considerable differences in opinion as to when tea became universal among the poor. Frederic Morton Eden found that tea was mass-consumed by the poor in the south in 1797,[109] whereas David Davies, writing just two years before Eden, said that 'though the use of tea is more common than could be wished, it is not yet general among the labouring poor'.[110] There is also a wide spectrum of views among historians. Ralph

Davis claimed that 'by 1750 the poorest English farm labourer's wife took sugar in her tea'.[111] John Rule, on the other hand, said that 'tea had become by 1800 a near universal essential' and Woodruff Smith that it was 'the nineteenth century, [when] tea with sugar became an important part of the British working-class diet'.[112]

Evidently, there is no definitive consensus among contemporary and historical writers. Thus, my analysis starts by using pauper inventories to measure the prevalence of tea-related items such as tea kettles and teapots to examine when the consumption of tea became widespread (Table 5.10). The results suggest that from the late seventeenth century to the first quarter of the eighteenth century, tea was consumed primarily by the affluent, as no paupers owned tea items. From the 1730s to the 1760s, tea items gradually start to appear in the pauper inventories. By the 1770s, there was a major increase in tea items in pauper abodes, indicating that this was the key decade when tea was in general use across society. The consumption of tea among the poor continued to grow and from the 1790s, 70 per cent of paupers owned goods connected to tea use. There were slight regional differences in tea consumption, as tea items are less common in inventories from Dorset, Leicestershire and Rutland compared with Norfolk and the home counties (Table 5.11). Nevertheless, the results show that tea had become widespread across England by 1770. Even in Leicestershire and Rutland, where tea goods were least common in the sample, nearly half of the inventories list tea items for 1770–1835.

There are a number of economic, social and cultural reasons why tea came to be consumed en masse across all levels of eighteenth-century society within a relatively short space of time. I will start with the economic factors. Tea was heavily taxed by the government throughout much of the seventeenth and eighteenth centuries and these levies were intermittently increased.[113] This meant that during the first half of the eighteenth century, tea was very expensive and it was largely only the rich and the middling sort who could afford it. By the second half of the eighteenth century, tea

Table 5.10 Percentage of paupers who owned tea items, 1670–1835

	1670–1729	1730–49	1750s	1760s	1770s	1780s	1790–1835
Tea items	0	6	10	16	55	66	70
Sample size	125	83	59	126	44	41	145

Table 5.11 Percentage of paupers who owned tea items, by county, 1770–1835

	Dorset	Essex	Kent	Leics/Ruts	Norfolk	All
Tea items	59	69	73	49	68	65

started to become more affordable and accessible to all social groups. It was increasingly adulterated by tea dealers, which meant that it could be sold at a lower cost than if left pure.[114] There were informal avenues through which the poor could obtain tea cheaply or even for free. Some masters would give tea to their servants as part of their pay, and there was also a network of suppliers who sold used tea leaves at budget prices.[115] Most importantly, tea became more affordable due to an increase in smuggling during the second half of the eighteenth century.[116] Though the scale of smuggling is difficult to quantify, at their height smugglers brought in around double the volume of tea that the East India Company legally did.[117] It is, therefore, perhaps no coincidence that tea consumption was lowest in inland Leicestershire and Rutland and highest in the counties positioned on the coast. Tea appears to have become so affordable that shoemaker James Lackington said that he only consumed bread and tea during the late 1760s to *save* money.[118]

Tea appealed to people for reasons other than price and availability. When tea first came to England in the seventeenth century, it was often used for ailments such as headaches, fevers and colds.[119] It was gradually seen as less important for its medicinal properties but continued to be regarded as a restorative and calming drink. For example, while smallpox ravaged one workhouse, the staff had a 'comfortable cup of tea' to ease the tension and ready themselves for dealing with a corpse.[120] One of the reasons James Lackington drank only tea during the 1760s was to 'purge my mind, and make it more susceptible of intellectual pleasures'.[121] People also clearly liked the taste of tea. Once associated with gluttonous sin and Adam and Eve's fall from Eden, taste had become a positive which people sought not just for sustenance but for enjoyment as new foods and drinks became more widespread.[122] Tea tasted very different to alternatives on the market. It gave people a caffeine lift and was a thirst-quenching drink. During the colder months it helped to warm people up and offered them an alternative or supplement to blankets and extra clothing. On this basis, tea became the essence of comfort and a staple of people's diets.

Tea was related to social rituals which added to its appeal and meant that it was inextricably linked to contemporary ideas of domesticity and respectability.[123] The middling sort and the elite epitomised this ritualised taking of tea. Groups of people, especially women according to contemporary stereotypes, would sit around a tea table and use bundles of goods such as china, tea caddies and silverware to distribute and display tea to family and guests. They used certain hand gestures and modes of speech to denote their civilised, polite, respectable and sophisticated manners. Of course, it would be wrong to assume that the middling sort and the elite drunk every cup of tea in this ritualised manner. Sometimes people drank tea alone and so may not have wanted the paraphernalia that was associated with social display.[124] Nevertheless, for many middling and elite people this was a new form of hospitality and formed an increasingly important part of their lives.[125]

Eating and drinking 167

There has been little empirical research to assess the extent to which the poor may have consumed tea in a similar way. It is difficult to use pauper inventories to gauge this, as people did not necessarily use their tea goods in the same ways. Silver teaspoons may have primarily been used as stores of wealth, which could be sold or pawned to quickly raise money.[126] Sewing materials and other small items might have been stored in tea chests and caddies rather than tea. Despite these issues, by measuring pauper ownership of tea paraphernalia such as tea caddies, tea tables and teaspoons, it is possible to find some indication as to whether the poor took tea in a ritualised manner, since these bundles of tea goods were heavily associated with these behaviours and activities. Teaspoons, for instance, could be positioned in or across a teacup to politely indicate whether somebody wanted more tea.[127]

Table 5.12 records the percentage of paupers who owned tea paraphernalia. This category includes any items which can be related to some form of ritualised taking of tea, comprising tea tables, tea chests, tea trays, teaspoons, tea caddies, tea waiters, tea boards, tea canisters, and teacups and saucers. It is also important to note that earthenware, silverware and china can also be linked to the ritualised drinking of tea, though they are not quantified here unless something like 'earthenware tea goods' was noted by appraisers. The inventories indicate that there was some element of ritualised tea drinking among the poor, as by the 1790s one-third of sources noted at least one item of tea paraphernalia. This shows that tea drinking could be an enjoyable activity which went beyond thirst and taste. More precisely, the most common items of tea paraphernalia between 1770 and 1835 were tea tables (9 per cent), tea trays/boards (9 per cent) and tea cannisters (6 per cent). Regionally, tea paraphernalia was most common in the home counties, closely followed by Norfolk (Table 5.13). In Dorset, Leicestershire and Rutland, the numbers of paupers who owned tea paraphernalia were smaller than elsewhere but are not insignificant.

Table 5.12 Percentage of paupers who owned tea paraphernalia, over time, 1670–1835

	1670–1729	1730–49	1750–69	1770s	1780s	1790–1835
Tea paraphernalia	0	5	4	14	24	33
Sample size	125	83	185	44	41	145

Table 5.13 Pauper ownership of tea paraphernalia, by county, 1770–1835

	Dorset	Essex	Kent	Leics/Ruts	Norfolk	All
Percentage	18	33	36	14	27	28
Average number	2.7	4.0	5.8	3.2	1.5	3.8

A number of pauper inventories chronicle a rich array of tea paraphernalia, allowing us to glean how some paupers may have drunk tea. In the 'Keeping Room' of John Whale in Little Wakering, Essex, there was a range of sought-after non-necessities such as 'A Day Clock', a 'Round Looking Glass', '2 Pictures' and 'A Watch'. Of the tea goods, there were '2 Tea Pots', '1 Tea Kittle', 'a Tea board' and '1 Small Tea Caddy', as well as several tables and chairs in the room which people could sit upon to use these goods. Accompanying the tea items were a 'Sugar Pot', 'Sugar Nipers', 'Silver Sugar Nipers' and a 'Cream Nogon [vessel]'.[128] Similarly, in the 'Dwelling Room' of John Tadgell of Hatfield Broad Oak in Essex, there was a range of non-necessities, 'a Round Tea Table', numerous chairs and 'a Mahogany Tea Chest', 'a Gepand [lacquered] Tea board' and '67 Pieces of Tea=cups Glasses and Crokery Ware'.[129] These two well-furnished rooms with their extensive range of tea items made drinking tea something that was beyond quenching thirst. Clearly, these paupers wanted to make these rooms as nice as possible and present an image of respectability to whoever might have entered their abodes.[130] Even when people owned only one item of tea paraphernalia, they had the potential to engage in some form of ritualised tea drinking as their better-off peers did.

While some paupers drank tea in a ritualised manner that mirrored other social groups, it is important to not take this point too far. Most of the impoverished appear to have drunk tea in a much more restrained and simple way, involving earthenware instead of china, no tea waiters or tea chests, and a multi-purpose table instead of a tea table. Most paupers owned no more than a tea kettle. For many, teapots were the closest that they could get to owning decorative tea items, as they came in a variety of colours, materials and patterns.[131] The inventories list teapots made from tin, pewter, stoneware and earthenware, and several are described as black, white, cream and patterned. One pauper from Norfolk even owned a 'Mock Silver Tea pot'.[132] When people owned items of tea paraphernalia, they were often among the first items that were sold off when times were tough. In George Fettes' pawnshop in York, tea items were the third most common type of object to be pawned by customers.[133] Out of the 314 people who pledged one or more tea-related items between 1777 and 1778, 243 of them pawned at least one teaspoon and 12 and 15 individuals handed over their tea tongs and tea boards/trays respectively. Meanwhile, 31 people pledged a tea kettle and only four a teapot. This indicates that tea paraphernalia was seen as expendable to paupers, as they would generally sell off these items before tea kettles and teapots, which of course were more important in the actual making of tea.[134] Tea drinking had clearly become popular by this time, and people knew that there was an extensive ready market that they could use to sell their goods to quickly realise capital.

Many of the poor probably owned little in the way of tea paraphernalia, as they simply wanted to drink tea in their own ways and not emulate those of the rich.[135] They may have been more interested in drinking tea as an individual experience and as something that accompanied meals and so did not want the tea paraphernalia that was associated with ceremony and display.[136] Though a somewhat idealised image of the poor, Figure 5.6 offers an excellent representation of this simpler way in which many of the poor are likely to have prepared and drank tea. It portrays a lone elderly woman who has placed a tea kettle onto the fire. There is also a teapot and a cup and saucer on the table. She is in a comfortable armchair next to a fire and about to relax and enjoy a warm cup of tea. Whenever the woman prepared her tea, she would have always placed the kettle on the fire, fed the flames with bellows and used her tongs to stoke the fire. Once the kettle had boiled, she would then pour the water into the teapot and from there into her cup. This is not the stereotypical image of the tea drinking that some of the middling sort and the elite were engaged in, involving guests, polite conversation and silverware, but it was still a ritualised form of taking tea which followed similar repetitive actions geared towards comfort and enjoyment.

Pertaining to the actual tea itself, the poor appear to have generally used the cheapest tea leaves that they could acquire and only occasionally

Figure 5.6 William Redmore Bigg, *Poor Old Woman's Comfort*, 1793 (source: © Victoria and Albert Museum, London 199-1885, oil on canvas)

purchased higher grades of tea.[137] David Davies contended that the tea of the poor was generally made from 'Spring water, just coloured with a few leaves of the lowest-priced tea'.[138] During times of difficulty, tea was reluctantly off the menu for many. While in Middlesex Hospital in London, Francis Freeman asked for help from his parish of settlement as he did not have enough to eat and drink. He said 'wee have so litel in the hospitel to live on', including 'no tee no suger'.[139] When Edward Allen Rymer's father deserted his family and his mother 'managed to pull us through the storm without seeking relief from the Poor-law authorities', he said that 'flour, tea, sugar, &c., were luxuries hardly to be thought of'.[140]

Over the long eighteenth century, the per capita consumption of sugar increased considerably and its price declined, outpacing even tea.[141] This probably meant that sugar became widespread among the poor and that its use in tea was common. For some, sugar was irresistible. In 1757, 12-year-old Thomas Holcroft was given a trial as a stableboy. Upon entering his master's house, he saw tea things and a sugar basin set out on the parlour table. Thinking that no one was looking, he ventured 'step by step, on tip-toe' and seized 'a fine lump of sugar', only to see a seated gentleman in the room reading. Holcroft returned the 'delicious bait' to where he found it and 'slunk away, most heartily mortified', as the gentleman laughed at the young boy's escapades.[142] On occasion, the pauper inventories show glimpses of sugar consumption, as a handful note sugar nippers and sugar basins. These are generally listed next to tea items, suggesting that the two were used together. Similarly to tea, many people were unable to obtain even the cheapest sugar during times of difficulty. The labouring population in 1790s Blandford Forum in Dorset, for example, often used treacle instead of sugar to sweeten their tea.[143] Other people used molasses, a by-product of the sugar refining process,[144] or simply went without.[145]

The addition of milk to tea became common practice in England around the 1720s, resulting in black tea overtaking green tea in popularity.[146] However, it is probable that milk was less common among working people, whether for tea, as a beverage or as part of a meal in itself. While common in workhouses,[147] milk was difficult to acquire for labouring people and those on outdoor relief. For much of the eighteenth and nineteenth centuries it was expensive and did not decline in price as many other products did.[148] Frederic Morton Eden and David Davies were in agreement that milk was not ubiquitous among the poor, as most did not have the land or money to keep a cow and because there was a lack of outlets from which to buy milk.[149] The pauper inventories tell us little about the markets people could use to purchase milk, but they too show that domestic milk production was low, as only 6 per cent note dairy-related items (Table 5.5). Various other historians corroborate this picture, arguing that cow ownership declined among the poor as enclosure swept across Britain.[150]

The data from the pauper inventories indicates that, at least at a domestic level, coffee was relatively uncommon among the poor across

Eating and drinking 171

Table 5.14 Percentage of paupers who owned coffee items, 1670–1835

	1670–1729	1730–49	1750s	1760s	1770s	1780s	1790–1835
Coffee items	0	0	5	2	5	7	6
Sample size	125	83	59	126	44	41	145

the country (Table 5.14). However, coffee is also noted in passing in the autobiographies of some of the very poorest people sampled here, especially from the late eighteenth century.[151] Consequently, it is probable that coffee drinking was less popular than tea but was nevertheless not unusual. When the bricklayer John Holloway was jailed for the murder of his wife Celia in 1831, he noted in one letter to his mother that 'we have nothing but bread and water; and I assure you that we are [not] allowed to have any thing in reason, such as tea and sugar, or coffee'.[152] While 'in the midst of misery and poverty' due to his alcohol addiction, Charles Bent ate 'some dry bread and coffee' while his wife pleaded with him to change his ways.[153] Edward Allan Rymer described himself as 'half clad' early in his career as a miner, stating that the 'only food' he had was 'treacle and bread or apple pasty, with a pint bottle filled with coffee'.[154] Coffee was even given to inmates in some workhouses and to soldiers as part of their rations.[155] So memorable was a good cup of coffee that the soldier John Green remarked that 'the best coffee I had ever tasted' was while serving as a soldier in Lisbon.[156] Some people were so eager for coffee that they created alternatives when they could not afford any. Christopher Thomson 'roasted some of the acorns' he collected to sell 'as a substitute for coffee' in 1825, but said that 'I cannot recommend the substitute to those who can purchase the real coffee berry'.[157] In 1770 newlywed couple James and Nancy Lackington could not afford tea or coffee, so they 'fried some wheat, which when boiled in water made a tolerable substitute for coffee'.[158] People, therefore, clearly loved their coffee and would take steps to obtain some even when they were especially destitute.

Why, then, is coffee not noted in inventories very often, and why was tea more popular than coffee? Once again, the answer lies in economic, social and cultural factors. During the second half of the seventeenth century, coffee was initially cheaper than tea; however, this trend was reversed in the early eighteenth century, as plantation owners increasingly switched their attention to sugar cultivation at the expense of coffee. This meant that coffee became less plentiful and that its pre-tax price was much higher than that of tea.[159] On a practical level, coffee was difficult to prepare inexpensively, as it required a number of processes and specialised items to grind, roast and brew the coffee. In contrast, boiling water was all that was needed to make tea.[160] Consequently, it is probable that most people bought pre-prepared coffee for domestic use or consumed most of their coffee outside the home, such as in a coffeehouse.[161] This meant that

172   At home with the poor

the social and ceremonial rituals that surrounded drinking coffee were entirely different to those surrounding tea. A significant appeal of tea was that it could be drunk at home with relative ease and could be used to entertain guests. To serve coffee in the domestic sphere was much more difficult and time consuming.

Chocolate came to England around the same time as tea and coffee. It never reached the same levels of consumption as tea or coffee, but it was nevertheless not uncommon among the more affluent.[162] For the poor, none of the pauper inventories record any items related to chocolate drinks, and chocolate is almost entirely absent in their personal writings. Chocolate was expensive to acquire throughout the period and was difficult to prepare at home, as it required a number of processes to make, which often included adding ingredients such as eggs, milk and alcohol.[163] This made the drink even more difficult to prepare than tea and coffee, and more expensive. For these reasons, chocolate was probably only a rare treat for the poor.

Conclusion

Although relatively little can be said about ingredients, the evidence indicates that most cooked meals remained fairly basic over the long eighteenth century, consisting of boiled dishes such as stews, soups and porridge. Items linked to grilling, roasting, toasting and frying were present in many homes, but they were probably used irregularly and saved for meals such as Sunday dinner.[164] Overall, then, the results most closely resemble those of scholars such as Carole Shammas and Robert Fogel, who have argued that the quality of the poor's food largely remained inadequate over the period.[165] There were some improvements, such as with the growing use of copper and saucepans, as well as the emergence of tea and coffee and growing use of herbs and spices, but these changes fall far short of more optimistic accounts of labouring diets.[166] Nevertheless, even small changes could have a profound effect on people's lives. The ability to season food with spices and herbs allowed people to transform a meal that was bland into one that was full of flavour. Copper meant that pots heated quicker, saving fuel and speeding up the cooking process. Tea and coffee became a love of the British during the period and helped to redefine people's ideas of comfort. There were significant changes in how food was presented and consumed. Earthenware dishes were often coloured and patterned, allowing people to eat off decorative plates which conveyed their owner's tastes. The growing use of cutlery transformed the practice of eating from something that was communal to something that was personal and individual. New dining rituals came with new goods. The next chapter adds to this by focusing on novel 'non-essential' items and the impact that they had on people's lives.

Eating and drinking   173

Notes

1 Such as: Robert C. Allen, 'Economic Structure and Agricultural Productivity in Europe, 1300–1800', *European Review of Economic History*, 4:1 (2000), pp. 1–26; Roderick Floud, Robert W. Fogel, Bernard Harris and Sok Chul Hong, *The Changing Body: Health, nutrition, and human development in the western world since 1700* (Cambridge: Cambridge University Press, 2011); Shammas, *Pre-Industrial Consumer*, pp. 121–56; Robert Fogel, 'New Sources and Techniques for the Study of Secular Trends in Nutritional Status, Health, Mortality, and the Process of Aging', *Historical Methods*, 26:1 (1993), pp. 5–43; Nathan Nunn and Nancy Qian, 'The Potato's Contribution to Population and Urbanization: Evidence from a historical experiment', *Quarterly Journal of Economics*, 126 (2011), pp. 593–650; de Vries, *Industrious Revolution*; Muldrew, *Food*.
2 Summarised across: Hans-Joachim Voth, 'Living Standards and the Urban Environment', in Roderick Floud and Paul Johnson (eds), *The Cambridge Economic History of Modern Britain*, Vol. 1: *Industrialisation, 1700–1860* (Cambridge: Cambridge University Press, 2004), pp. 268–94; David Meredith and Deborah Oxley, 'Nutrition and Health, 1700–1870', in Floud, Humphries and Johnson, *Cambridge Economic History*, pp. 118–48; Griffin, 'Diets, Hunger', pp. 71–111.
3 Such as: Thompson, *Making*; E. P. Thompson, 'The Moral Economy of the English Crowd in the Eighteenth Century', *Past and Present*, 50 (1971), pp. 76–136; Neeson, *Commoners*; Griffin, *Politics of Hunger*.
4 Thomas Robert Malthus, *An Essay on the Principle of Population as It Affects the Future Improvement of Society* (London: J. Johnson, 1798).
5 Joy Bristow, *The Local Historian's Glossary of Words and Terms* (Newbury: Countryside Books, 3rd edn, 2001), pp. 24, 104, 142, 165; Oxford English Dictionary Online (www.oed.com).
6 Bristow, *Local Historian's Glossary*, pp. 49–50; Oxford English Dictionary Online (www.oed.com).
7 Pennell, *Birth*, pp. 71–2.
8 Ibid., p. 74.
9 Cooking pots are noted in 6 of the 11 Lancashire pauper inventories (55 per cent).
10 Fifty-one per cent of the pauper inventories record pot-hooks of some sort kind.
11 Samuel Harman's inventory from Redenhall in Norfolk, for example, notes 'a Large Iron pot w[i]th 3 Liggs'. NRO PD 295/102. Also see: Bee Wilson, *Consider the Fork: A history of invention in the kitchen* (London: Particular Books, 2012), p. 43; Wright, *Home Fires*, p. 41.
12 Wilson, *Consider the Fork*, pp. 56–7.
13 ERO D/P 153/12.
14 KHLC P344/18/8; ERO D/P 119/12/1.
15 ERO D/P 219/12/29.
16 Sara Pennell, 'The Material Culture of Food in Early Modern England c.1650–1750', in Sarah Tarlow and Susie West (eds), *The Familiar Past? Archaeologies of later historical Britain* (London: Routledge, 1999), pp. 35–50; Amanda Vickery, 'Women and the World of Goods: A Lancashire consumer and her possessions, 1751–81', in Brewer and Porter, *World of Goods*, p. 292.
17 Overseers' and workhouse accounts, for instance, sometimes record the repair of cooking utensils. Also see: Ben Jervis and Alison Kyle, *Make-Do and Mend: Archaeologies of compromise, repair and reuse* (Oxford: Archaeopress, 2012).
18 On the advantages and uses of saucepans, see: Pennell, *Birth*, pp. 73–4; Wilson, *Consider the Fork*, p. 49; Overton, *Production and Consumption*, pp. 100–1; Weatherill, *Consumer Behaviour*, p. 205.
19 Muldrew, *Food*, p. 100.
20 See Chapter 4.
21 Muldrew, *Food*, p. 100; Weatherill, *Consumer Behaviour*, p. 147.

22 Pennell, *Birth*, pp. 12–15, 61, 68–70; David Howes and Marc Lalonde, 'The History of Sensibilities: Of the standard of taste in mid-eighteenth century England and the circulation of smells in post-revolution France', *Dialectical Anthropology*, 16:2 (1991), pp. 126–8; Eden, *State of the Poor*, Vol. 1, pp. 496–7.

23 Around one-tenth of pauper inventories do not list cooking-related items, so these figures are a slight under-representation.

24 Davies, *Case of Labourers*; Horrell, 'Home Demand', pp. 561–604; Muldrew, *Food*, p. 29; Wrightson and Levine, *Poverty and Piety*, p. 40.

25 In total, frying pans, gridirons and spits are found in 36, 18 and 9 per cent of the 11 Lancashire pauper inventories. According to Eden, lower frequencies of these items may stem from the poor in the north preferring to boil and stew their meals. Eden, *State of the Poor*, Vol. 1, pp. 496–7.

26 William Cobbett, *Two-Penny Trash: Politics for the poor* (London: self-published, 1831), p. 195.

27 Davies, *Case of Labourers*; Eden, *State of the Poor*, Vols. 1–3.

28 Griffin, 'Diets, Hunger', pp. 71–111; Griffin, *Bread Winner*, pp. 193–226. Also see: Griffin, *Politics of Hunger*.

29 Jones and King, *Navigating*, p. 59.

30 King, Nutt and Tomkins, *Narratives*, p. 267.

31 Sokoll, *Pauper Letters*, p. 409.

32 Overton et al., *Production and Consumption*, pp. 98–102; Peter Earle, *The Making of the English Middle Class: Business, society and family life in London* (Berkeley: University of California Press, 1989), p. 297. Also see the diary of the Sussex shopkeeper Thomas Turner, which often details the diverse foods he ate: David Vaisey (ed.), *The Diary of Thomas Turner, 1754–1765* (Oxford: Oxford University Press, 1984).

33 Weatherill, *Consumer Behaviour*, p. 26; Overton et al., *Production and Consumption*, p. 99; Hussey and Ponsonby, *Single Homemaker*, p. 39.

34 Overton et al., *Production and Consumption*, pp. 99, 101.

35 Sensory historians argue that taste became more important over the eighteenth century. See, for instance, Howes and Lalonde, 'History of Sensibilities', pp. 126–30; Smith, *Sensory History*, pp. 75–91. For an excellent introduction to taste, see: Carolyn Korsmeyer (ed.), *The Taste Culture Reader: Experiencing food and drink* (Oxford: Berg, 2005); Priscilla Parkhurst Ferguson, 'The Senses of Taste', *American Historical Review*, 116:2 (2011), pp. 371–84.

36 Bamford, *Early Days*, pp. 52–3.

37 Holcroft, *Memoirs*, p. 11.

38 John Green, *The Vicissitudes of a Soldier's Life, or a Series of Occurrences from 1806 to 1815* (Louth: J. and J. Jackson, 1827), pp. 72–3.

39 Brown, *Sixty Years' Gleanings*, p. 175.

40 Carter, *Memoirs*, pp. 62–4.

41 Bamford, *Early Days*, p. 13.

42 Peter Collinge, '"He shall have care of the garden, its cultivation and produce": Workhouse gardens and gardening, c.1780–1835', *Journal of Eighteenth-Century Studies*, 44:1 (2021), pp. 21–39.

43 Davies, *Case of Labourers*; Eden, *State of the Poor*, Vols. 1–3.

44 Margaret Visser, 'Salt: The edible rock', in Korsmeyer, *Taste Culture Reader*, pp. 105–9.

45 LRO UDCL/9/7.

46 Pennell, 'Pots and Pans', p. 209.

47 KHLC P347/18/10.

48 KHLC P321/12/3.

49 Sidney W. Mintz, *Sweetness and Power: The place of sugar in modern history* (New York: Penguin Books, 1985); Stobart, *Sugar and Spice*, pp. 48–9.

50 On using spices and sugar in food, see: Mintz, *Sweetness*, pp. 79–87, 117–21, 131–9; Stobart, *Sugar and Spice*, esp. pp. 30–3, 222–37; Smith, *Making of Respectability*, pp. 96–7, 100–2. Sugar could also be used to preserve food.

Eating and drinking   175

51 Some people used a communal oven or an earthenware pot as an oven. Pennell, *Birth*, pp. 65–6; Pounds, *Hearth and Home*, p. 205; Davidson, *Woman's Work*, p. 50.
52 For further information on the difficulties of using pauper inventories to measure domestic production, see: Harley, 'Domestic Production', pp. 25–49.
53 Shaw, *Family Records*, p. 50.
54 Most notably, de Vries, *Industrious Revolution*.
55 Such as: Thomas Postans, *Letter to Sir Thomas Baring* … (London: Michael Staunton, 1831), p. 4.
56 This can be seen in poor law accounts, as overseers would sometimes switch between giving paupers flour and bread. Also see: Griffin, *Bread Winner*, pp. 206–11.
57 Snell, *Annals*, pp. 138–227; Hammond and Hammond, *Village Labourer*; Neeson, *Commoners*, esp. pp. 158–84.
58 Shaw, *Family Records*, p. 21.
59 Clare, *Autobiographical Writings*, pp. 114–15.
60 John Tuke, *General View of the Agriculture of the North Riding of Yorkshire* (London: B. McMillan, 1800), p. 180.
61 Shammas, *Pre-Industrial Consumer*, pp. 42–3.
62 Such as: ibid., pp. 17–51; Overton et al., *Production and Consumption*, pp. 39–47; French, *Middle Sort*, p. 53; Steer, *Inventories*, pp. 53–8.
63 Overton et al., *Production and Consumption*, pp. 40–1.
64 Shammas, *Pre-Industrial Consumer*, pp. 42–3.
65 SA HD 1025/1; SA HA 11/A13/10; Dymond, *Parson*, pp. 159–60.
66 ROLLR DE 1668/86.
67 For an introduction on the history of drink, see: Paul Jennings, *A History of Drink and the English, 1500–2000* (London: Routledge, 2016).
68 Mui and Mui, *Shops and Shopkeeping*.
69 Overton et al., *Production and Consumption*.
70 Ibid., p. 63. The opposite argument is made in Shammas, *Pre-Industrial Consumer*, p. 43.
71 John Burnett, 'The History of Food Adulteration in Great Britain in the Nineteenth Century with Special References to Bread, Tea and Beer', PhD thesis (University of London, 1958).
72 de Vries, *Industrious Revolution*.
73 Harley, 'Domestic Production', pp. 25–49.
74 Social rituals are defined as the repetitive ways in which practices such as eating or drinking were done.
75 See for instance: Visser, *Rituals of Dinner*.
76 Sarah Richards, *Eighteenth-Century Ceramics: Products for a civilised society* (Manchester: Manchester University Press, 1999), p. 127; Weatherill, *Consumer Behaviour*, pp. 154–5.
77 Mintz, *Sweetness*; Stobart, *Sugar and Spice*, pp. 48–9; Lorna Weatherill, *The Pottery Trade and North Staffordshire 1660–1760* (Manchester: Manchester University Press, 1971); Berg, *Luxury and Pleasure*.
78 John Hatcher and T. C. Barker, *A History of British Pewter* (London: Longman, 1974).
79 Suzanne Findlen Hood, 'Broken Objects: Using archaeological ceramics in the study of material culture', in Gerritsen and Riello, *Writing Material Culture*, pp. 67–72; John Bedell, 'Archaeology and Probate Inventories in the Study of Eighteenth-Century Life', *Journal of Interdisciplinary History*, 31:2 (2000), esp. pp. 231–40.
80 Hatcher and Barker, *Pewter*, pp. 81–141, 279–301; Overton et al., *Production and Consumption*, pp. 102–6; Hussey and Ponsonby, *Single Homemaker*, p. 39; Richards, *Ceramics*, p. 94.
81 Bamford, *Early Days*, pp. 103–5.
82 Weatherill, *Consumer Behaviour*, pp. 109–11; Richards, *Ceramics*; Overton et al., *Production and Consumption*, p. 104.
83 NRO PD 710/68.
84 DHC PE-BER/OV/1/9.

85 Ruth Mather, 'Remembering Protest in the Late-Georgian Working-Class Home', in Carl Griffin and Briony McDonagh (eds), *Remembering Protest in Britain since 1500: Memory, materiality and the landscape* (Basingstoke: Palgrave, 2018), pp. 142–7.

86 Hatcher and Barker, *Pewter*, p. 280.

87 Overton et al., *Production and Consumption*, pp. 102–4; Weatherill, *Consumer Behaviour*, p. 26; Hussey and Ponsonby, *Single Homemaker*, p. 39.

88 KHLC P347/18/10; NRO PD 295/106.

89 David Gaimster, 'Material Culture, Archaeology and Defining Modernity: Case studies in ceramic research', in Gerritsen and Riello, *Writing Material Culture*, pp. 59–72; Berg, *Luxury and Pleasure*, p. 132.

90 See the pauper inventory of Mrs Vince's goods in ERO D/P 219/12/29. Also included in her home was china and glassware, yet she still chose to place the stoneware on the mantelpiece.

91 KHLC P89/12/17; ERO D/P 4/18/8.

92 Neil McKendrick, 'Josiah Wedgwood: An eighteenth-century entrepreneur in salesmanship and marketing techniques', *Economic History Review*, 12:3 (1960), pp. 408–33; Berg, *Luxury and Pleasure*, passim; Smith, *Making of Respectability*, pp. 240–2.

93 CCAL U3/100/11A/2.

94 For instance, one person pledged three china plates for 2s. 6d., one six china plates for 3s. 6d., and another six china cups and saucers for 4s. YALH Accession 38. Also see: Weatherill, *Consumer Behaviour*, pp. 109–11.

95 On price, see: Weatherill, *Consumer Behaviour*, pp. 110–11; Sneath, 'Consumption, Wealth', p. 254.

96 Bedell, 'Archaeology', pp. 240–1.

97 Widow Beal from Lenham in Kent, for instance, owned 'one Pap Spoon. Silver' in 1771 and John Playne from Staplehurst in Kent owned '1 Spoon w[i]th a Nutmeg Grater in the Handle' in 1775. KHLC P224/8/1; KHLC P347/18/10. Teaspoon ownership also grew slightly.

98 Shaw, *Family Records*, p. 32.

99 Such as: ibid., p. 32; Preston, *Life*, p. 31; Donaldson, *Recollections*, p. 169; Gooch, *Memoirs*, p. 50; Bamford, *Early Days*, pp. 56, 212, 259; John Shaw, *A Narrative of the Life and Travels of John Robert Shaw, the Well-Digger* (Lexington: Daniel Bradford, 1807), p. 8; Brown, *Sixty Years' Gleanings*, p. 28; Carter, *Memoirs*, pp. 50, 73, 179; Blincoe, *Memoir*, pp. 30, 32, 48. Also see: Adam Smith, *An Inquiry into the Nature and Causes of the Wealth of Nations*, Vol. 1, ed. R. H. Campbell and A. S. Skinner (Indianapolis: Liberty Classics, reprint of 1776 edn, 1981), pp. 22–3.

100 C. T. P. Bailey, *Knives and Forks: Selected and described with an introduction* (London: Medici Society, 1927), pp. 1–2; J. F. Hayward, *English Cutlery: Sixteenth to eighteenth century* (London: HMSO, 1956), pp. 1–3; Brett, *Dinner Is Served*, pp. 60–4, 73–4; Wilson, *Consider the Fork*, pp. 78–82; Visser, *Rituals of Dinner*, pp. 183–4; Overton et al., *Production and Consumption*, p. 106.

101 Visser, *Rituals of Dinner*, p. 57; Richards, *Ceramics*, pp. 152–3; Overton et al., *Production and Consumption*, pp. 105–6.

102 Hussey and Ponsonby, *Single Homemaker*, p. 39; Overton et al., *Production and consumption*, pp. 99, 106; Weatherill, *Consumer Behaviour*, pp. 26, 168; Sneath, 'Consumption, Wealth', pp. 253–60; Sear and Sneath, *Consumer Revolution*, pp. 77–8.

103 Wilson, *Consider the Fork*, pp. 268–9; Bailey, *Knives and Forks*, pp. 1–2, 5–6.

104 On teaching children dinner manners, see Visser, *Rituals of Dinner*, pp. 40–56.

105 Sneath, 'Consumption, Wealth', p. 261; Helen Saberi, *Tea: A global history* (London: Reaktion Books, 2010), p. 91.

106 Robin Emmerson, *British Teapots and Tea Drinking 1700–1850* (London: The Stationery Office, 1992), p. 2; Woodruff D. Smith, 'From Coffeehouse to

Parlour: The consumption of coffee, tea and sugar in north-western Europe in the seventeenth and eighteenth centuries', in Jordan Goodman, Paul E. Lovejoy and Andrew Sherratt (eds), *Consuming Habits: Drugs in history and anthropology* (London: Routledge, 1995), pp. 148–50; Overton et al., *Production and Consumption*, p. 99; Weatherill, *Consumer Behaviour*, p. 26.

107 Overton et al., *Production and Consumption*, p. 99; Weatherill, *Consumer Behaviour*, p. 26; Shammas, *Pre-Industrial Consumer*, pp. 84–5.

108 See, for example, Rule, *Labouring Classes*, pp. 60–2; Shammas, *Pre-Industrial Consumer*, pp. 136–7, 144–6; Stobart, *Sugar*, pp. 219–21; Mintz, *Sweetness*, esp. pp. 74–150; Eden, *State of the Poor*, Vols. 1–3.

109 Eden, *State of the Poor*, Vol. 1, esp. pp. 496–547.

110 Davies, *Case of Labourers*, p. 39.

111 Ralph Davis, *The Rise of the Atlantic Economies* (Ithaca: Cornell University Press, 1973), p. 251.

112 Rule, *Labouring Classes*, p. 61; Smith, *Making of Respectability*, p. 121.

113 There were short intervals when taxes were reduced, such as in 1745 and 1784, but these were short lived. On tea taxes and trade, see: William J. Ashworth, *Customs and Excise: Trade, production and consumption in England, 1640–1845* (Oxford: Oxford University Press, 2003), pp. 176–83; Troy Bickham, *Eating the Empire: Food and society in eighteenth-century Britain* (London: Reaktion Books, 2020), pp. 32–8; Mui and Mui, *Shops and Shopkeeping*, pp. 250–87; Denys Forrest, *Tea for the British: The social and economic history of a famous trade* (London: Chatto & Windus, 1973), pp. 33–44.

114 John Burnett, 'Food Adulteration' pp. 157–291; Ashworth, *Customs and Excise*, pp. 307–14.

115 Ashworth, *Customs and Excise*, p. 311; Emmerson, *British Teapots*, p. 301; Nancy Cox, *Retailing and the Language of Goods, 1550–1850* (Farnham: Ashgate, 2015), pp. 136–8.

116 Ashworth, *Customs and Excise*, pp. 176–83; Forrest, *Tea*, pp. 68–74; Mui and Mui, *Shops and Shopkeeping*, pp. 160–4.

117 Mui and Mui, *Shops and Shopkeeping*, p. 250.

118 Lackington, *Memoirs*, p. 178.

119 Bickham, *Eating the Empire*, pp. 29–32; Smith, 'From Coffeehouse', pp. 152–4; Brian Cowan, *The Social Life of Coffee: The emergence of the British coffeehouse* (New Haven: Yale University Press, 2005), pp. 22–5, 47–53.

120 Bamford, *Early Days*, p. 61.

121 Lackington, *Memoirs*, p. 178.

122 Elizabeth Swann, *Taste and Knowledge in Early Modern England* (Cambridge: Cambridge University Press, 2020).

123 Smith, *Making of Respectability*, pp. 121–30, 171–87; Smith, 'From Coffeehouse', pp. 148–64. An exception to this is tea drinking in the workhouse: Stobart, *Sugar and Spice*, pp. 263, 273.

124 Stobart, *Sugar and Spice*, p. 273.

125 On the rituals of middling tea drinking, see: Smith, *Making of Respectability*, esp. pp. 121–31, 171–81; Smith, 'From Coffeehouse', pp. 148–64; Elizabeth Kowaleski-Wallace, *Consuming Subjects: Women, shopping, and business in the eighteenth century* (New York: Columbia University Press, 1997), pp. 19–36; Berg, *Luxury and Pleasure*, pp. 229–32; Emmerson, *British Teapots*, pp. 13–27; Stobart, *Sugar and Spice*, pp. 242–57; Vickery, *Behind Closed Doors*, pp. 271–6.

126 See, for example, Sokoll, *Pauper Letters*, p. 196; G. J., *Prisoner Set Free*, p. 5. Also see: YALH Accession 38.

127 Emmerson, *British Teapots*, p. 23.

128 ERO D/P 194/18/4.

129 ERO D/P 4/18/8.

130 Also see the example of the Dungays in Chapter 1.

178 At home with the poor

131 In total, tea kettles and teapots feature in 51 and 20 per cent of pauper inventories respectively for 1770–1835.
132 NRO PD 219/114.
133 Backhouse, *Worm-Eaten*, pp. 77–81; YALH Accession 38. This sum is based on clothing and linen being grouped together in one category.
134 Backhouse, *Worm-Eaten*, pp. 77–81; YALH Accession 38.
135 Stobart, *Sugar and Spice*, pp. 219–21.
136 Ibid., p. 273; Eden, *State of the Poor*, Vol. 1, p. 535.
137 Stobart, *Sugar and Spice*, pp. 195–6.
138 Davies, *Case of Labourers*, p. 39. Also see: Friedrich Engels, *The Condition of the Working Class in England*, eds Victor Kiernan and Tristram Hunt (London: Penguin, reprint of 1845 edn, 2009), p. 107.
139 Sokoll, *Pauper Letters*, p. 622.
140 Rymer, 'Martyrdom', p. 228.
141 Stobart, *Sugar and Spice*, pp. 48–9; Shammas, *Pre-Industrial Consumer*, pp. 81–2.
142 Holcroft, *Memoirs*, p. 35.
143 Eden, *State of the Poor*, Vol. 2, p. 148. Also see: Bamford, *Early Days*, p. 105.
144 Shammas, *Pre-Industrial Consumer*, pp. 82–3; Cox, *Retailing*, pp. 134–6; William Howitt, *The Rural Life of England*, Part II (London: Manning and Smithson, 1838), p. 150.
145 Sokoll, *Pauper Letters*, p. 622; Rymer, 'Martyrdom', p. 228.
146 Saberi, *Tea*, p. 91.
147 See, for instance, Tomkins, *Urban Poverty*, pp. 50–65. I have also collected hundreds of workhouse dietaries which I have not yet analysed thoroughly, but that on the face of it show that milk was commonly given to inmates.
148 Hannah Velten, *Milk: A global history* (London: Reaktion Books, 2010), p. 57; Eden, *State of the Poor*, Vol. 1, p. 532.
149 Eden, *State of the Poor*, Vol. 1, esp. pp. 531–2; Davies, *Case of Labourers*, pp. 37–8.
150 Such as: Snell, *Annals*, pp.174–9; Leigh Shaw-Taylor, 'Labourers, Cows, Common Rights and Parliamentary Enclosure: The evidence of contemporary comment c.1760–1810', *Past and Present*, 171 (2001), pp. 95–126.
151 The autobiographies indicate that there may have been regional differences in coffee consumption. The autobiography of Joseph Donaldson, for instance, notes one story in which a highlandman ended up eating coffee beans, as he had never seen coffee before and did not know how to properly consume them. Donaldson, *Recollections*, pp. 164–5.
152 John William Holloway, *An Authentic and Faithful History of the Atrocious Murder of Celia Holloway* (Brighton: W. Nute, 1832), p. 186.
153 Bent, *Autobiography*, pp. 13–14.
154 Rymer, 'Martyrdom', p. 229. Also see p. 239.
155 See for example, Bamford, *Early Days*, p. 74; Donaldson, *Recollections*, pp. 162, 164–5; Green, *Vicissitudes*, p. 78.
156 Green, *Vicissitudes*, p. 142.
157 Thomson, *Autobiography*, p. 204.
158 Lackington, *Memoirs*, pp. 197–8. Also see: Mather, 'Remembering Protest', p. 149.
159 S. D. Smith, 'Accounting for Taste: British coffee consumption in historical perspective', *Journal of Interdisciplinary History*, 27:2 (1996), pp. 183–214; Cowan, *Social Life of Coffee*, pp. 55–77; Ashworth, *Customs and Excise*, pp. 182–3; Smith, 'From Coffeehouse', pp. 148–50.
160 Smith, 'Accounting', p. 187; Saberi, *Tea*, p. 102; Hussey and Ponsonby, *Single Homemaker*, pp. 124–5.
161 Ready-made coffee is noted in Brown, *Sixty Years' Gleanings*, p. 69. Although first used by the middling sort and elite, over time coffeehouses were increasingly frequented by working people. For instance, see: Carter, *Memoirs*, pp. 117,

186, 191; Thomson, *Autobiography*, pp. 101, 105–6; Jewell, 'Autobiographical Memoir', p. 148; Holcroft, *Memoirs*, pp. 141, 215; Holloway, *Authentic*, p. 149; Green, *Vicissitudes*, p. 142. Also see: MacKay, *Respectability*, p. 21; Cowan, *Social Life of Coffee*.

162 Kate Loveman, 'The Introduction of Chocolate into England: Retailers, researchers, and consumers, 1640–1730', *Journal of Social History*, 47:1 (2013), pp. 27–46; Sarah Moss and Alexander Badenoch, *Chocolate: A global history* (London: Reaktion Books, 2009).

163 Ashworth, *Customs and Excise*, pp. 182–3; Hussey and Ponsonby, *Single Homemaker*, pp. 124–5; Cowan, *Social Life of Coffee*, p. 80.

164 Muldrew, *Food*, p. 100.

165 Shammas, *Pre-Industrial Consumer*, pp. 121–56; Floud et al., *Changing Body*; Fogel, 'New Sources', pp. 5–43.

166 Most notably: Muldrew, *Food*.

6

Non-essential goods

'Non-essential' goods, or 'luxury' goods as they were often labelled by contemporaries, are slippery terms. At one extreme, Bernard Mandeville broadly defined 'luxury' to include anything that was not necessary 'to keep a Man alive' in 1732.[1] Renowned economist Adam Smith agreed with Mandeville's definition but added that 'whatever [items] the custom of the country renders it indecent for creditable people, even of the lowest order, to be without', such as white linen shirts, leather, soap and candles, were not luxuries.[2] The issue is further complicated when items are assessed over a long period of time. As we have just seen, in the late seventeenth century tea was seen as a non-essential 'luxury' item, as it was expensive, novel and consumed only by the very rich. However, as the eighteenth century drew to a close and tea had become widespread and affordable, it was seen as an everyday necessity.

It is beyond the scope of this book to consider the use, semantics and applicability of the terms 'non-essential' and 'luxury' at length. In fact, the matter has already been discussed elsewhere.[3] The point is that the issue is complex and that definitions can vary widely and be subjective. With this in mind, this book uses the terms in their broadest sense and does not claim to offer a definition that is completely robust or infallible across all contexts. Thus, 'luxury' or 'non-essential' goods are loosely defined here to include items which were not necessary to the running of the home and the basic physical wellbeing of owners. This includes goods that were strongly linked to decoration, status, vanity, novelty, display and imitation, and items that were owned in superfluous numbers. It also encompasses possessions which were primarily geared towards pleasure, convenience and comfort, and goods that might have primarily been acquired when people had some disposable income at a relatively affluent stage in their lives. Included in this, therefore, are possessions such as timepieces and looking glasses, as well as items as varied as saucepans, chests of drawers, jacks and lanterns. Necessities, on the other hand, were everyday, mundane and rudimentary items that were often required for the support of life, such as food, water, blankets and basic cooking items. Some of these goods have already been covered in earlier chapters and so here we focus on printed materials, pictures, looking glasses, timepieces, gold, silver, jewellery, musical instruments, toys and bird cages.

With some regularity, academics have argued that the early modern period witnessed an unprecedented uptake in the consumption of luxury goods. However, despite such items being one of the most popular topics in material culture studies, the poorer sort have rarely been at the centre of this research. This is surprising considering that the issue certainly caught the imagination of contemporaries. In 1833, for instance, Alexis de Tocqueville argued that England was one of the richest and most prosperous nations in the world. Yet because people's material expectations had risen so much, he claimed, the poor *felt* much more destitute than they actually were and were therefore worse off than their European neighbours.[4] There were also a number of moral panics following the poor's apparent out-of-control splurging on gin, tea, white bread, ready-made clothing and other items deemed unnecessary.[5] This chapter offers empirical evidence to show that, indeed, many forms of non-essential consumption were on the rise among poor and working people, especially from the late eighteenth century. This spending can be seen around the country, but once again it was the poor in the home counties, especially Kent, who acquired these goods in the largest numbers. These possessions could have a profound impact on families. Items such as clocks allowed people to organise their lives better and were prestigious to own. Reading books entertained individuals and could provide people with a temporary or permanent escape out of their poverty. Pictures helped to decorate the home and create a space that was more visually appealing.

Books and the printed word

It was once generally thought that illiteracy, especially among the labouring sort and women, was widespread until the late nineteenth century. By counting the number of people who were unable to sign their names, David Cressy estimated that around 70 per cent of men and 90 per cent of women in Tudor and Stuart England were illiterate.[6] Other scholars have employed a similar methodology for the mid-eighteenth century and found that around 40 per cent of men and 60 per cent of women were unable to sign their names.[7] Research in recent decades has started to erode these long-held beliefs and show that more people than previously thought had access to the written word in some form or another and probably had some reading or writing skills. Using tens of thousands of letters written by paupers, Steven King's research has shown that more could write than was previously supposed.[8] Literacy had multiple levels: some people could read and write fluently, while others could not read handwritten texts or write but could decipher printed texts. Others only recognised odd passages from the Bible or simply knew the alphabet.[9] Even those who had no literacy whatsoever often had access to the written word as they knew someone who could act as a scribe or read to them.[10] An oral culture continued throughout the period which meant that the illiterate could consume texts and ballads by hearing them.[11]

The written word was thus clearly important to everybody by the eighteenth century. Yet pauper inventories indicate that although growing numbers of paupers owned books, only a minority were engaged with printed materials (Table 6.1). Similarly, books were recorded in only 4 per cent of the bastardy, debt, goods-taken and poorhouse/workhouse-admittance-related inventories of paupers' goods. There are, however, multiple reasons to suppose that inventories considerably under-represent the actual nature of ordinary people's engagement with printed materials. First, the early modern period witnessed what some have termed a 'printing revolution', whereby people across society engaged with printed media on an unprecedented scale, including so-called 'cheap prints' such as broadsides, chapbooks, ballads, pamphlets, almanacs and newspapers.[12] Printed materials (including books) became relatively easy to acquire and much more ephemeral by the eighteenth century, meaning that appraisers did not prioritise such goods, as they might have limited resale value, and much of them found use as toilet paper, fuel or wall insulation once they were finished with. Researchers have found that probate inventories also under-record printed matter.[13] Second, the plethora of autobiographies, diaries and pauper letters used in this study shows that reading and collecting printed material held great significance among large proportions of the poor. Naturally, first-hand sources are problematic since they were written by a sub-group of the poor who were able to read and write. Those who were completely illiterate or could only read have left little trace in this type of historical record. Nevertheless, the autobiographies and diaries used here show that the literate poor worked hard to gain these skills, loved reading, and would tirelessly collect new books and prints throughout their lifetimes using many creative strategies. Many of the voices in first-hand sources are from a male perspective, but it is important to note that women were also heavily engaged with written materials. For example, it is intriguing just how often poor women are depicted in pictorial

Table 6.1 Percentage of paupers who owned books, 1670–1835

	1670–1729	1730–69	1770–1809	1810–34
Book	2	4	6	15
Sample size	125	268	165	65

material reading or in possession of books, perhaps as a display of their piety, and how often it was mothers and not fathers who taught their children to read.[14]

The poor learned how to read through an array of methods. Their education was almost always haphazard and inconsistent and would stop and start according to circumstances. Some were lucky enough to live in an area that had a free school of some sort or to have parents who paid for them to go to school for short periods. Many recalled in adult life how they were grateful for the opportunity and made the most of it,[15] but there was also a sizeable number who were not interested and forgot much of what they learned. Josiah Basset, for instance, 'frequently played the truant, and were several times expelled by the master', despite how his father 'endeavoured to give us an education'.[16] Meanwhile, William Heaton was 'too fond of play' so 'did not ... make much progress' at school.[17] Some children and adults had a relative or friend who tutored them, such as John Bethune and Benjamin Bangs, whose mothers taught them how to read and write.[18] While serving in the army, Joseph Mayett relied on a fellow soldier to help him read.[19] William Farish learned 'to distinguish the letters of the alphabet' from 'an old cripple' his father knew.[20] Other autobiographers received help from their employers or their master's wives and servants.[21] Some people did not have these connections, and to teach themselves they turned to using self-help books such as Daniel Fenning's *Universal Spelling Book* (1756), as well as *Child's First Book*, *Jones's Pronouncing Dictionary* and *Dilworth's Spelling Book*.[22] Allen Davenport was especially creative. He learned to read by memorising ballads and then matching the words to those on a printed song sheet.[23]

By far the most commonly owned book was the Bible. Of the 32 pauper inventories which recorded books, seventeen specifically noted bibles and 7 listed prayer books. No other titles were highlighted by appraisers, apart from one other religious book entitled *A Call to Delaying Sinners* (1683) by Thomas Doolittle, which stressed that readers should make peace with God before it was too late.[24] Several bibles owned by the poor were small and fairly cheap copies worth no more than a few shillings. Others owned bibles which were both financially and sentimentally significant. Widow Thrower from Shelton in Norfolk, for example, owned 'A Great Bible',[25] which was probably worth around £1 or £2.[26] Some paupers owned family bibles which were passed down the generations and contained handwritten notes of births, marriages and deaths.[27]

Bibles could be owned for many reasons, such as for their perceived power to ward off spirits, to swear oaths on or to heal sick people,[28] but it was for religious knowledge and spiritual devotion that most people possessed them. A number of writers compared their reading of the Bible with that of other books, often noting how the former was always better. Joseph Mayett claimed that 'I have read many authors ... and always prefer the bible before any other book'.[29] Despite being 'very fond of reading', Samuel Sholl read 'little else' other than the Bible and knew it 'almost by heart' by around 10–12 years old.[30] The Bible acted as an emotional crutch for people during times of ill health. While suffering from frequent bouts of sickness, John Clare found the Bible to be 'an antidote to my deepest distresses' and 'the one book that makes the carnallitys of life palatable & ... supplys soul & body with happiness'.[31] During John Bethune's slow deterioration from tuberculosis, he was weak but conserved most of his energy to read his small pocket bible.[32] There was also a pleasurable aspect to bible reading. Between the ages of 16 and 21, the Methodist James Lackington spent 'every spare hour I enjoyed dedicated to the study of the Bible' and 'often privately took the Bible to bed with me, and in the long summer mornings read for hours together in bed'.[33]

Many books were read by people for entertainment and enjoyment. As a teenager, Thomas Wood would 'Get into bed for warmth' and then for a 'treat' read to be 'lifted ... for the time being, into another world'.[34] Similarly, William Hart said that he was 'passionately fond of reading',[35] while Charles Crocker remarked that 'reading became my favourite amusement, and books my dearest, and generally my only companions'.[36] Large numbers of the autobiographies include lists and descriptions of the authors' favourite books. John Clare, for instance, noted the library he amassed as a child with the odd shilling, which included, among others:

'Abercrombies Gardiners Journal,' 'Thompsons Seasons,' A Shatterd Copy of 'Miltons Paradise lost,' 'Wards Mathematics,' Fishers 'Young mans companion,' 'Robin Hoods Garland,' 'Bonnycastles Mensuration,' and 'Algebra,' 'Fennings Arithmetic,' 'Death of Abel,' 'Joe Millers Jests,' A 'Collection of Hymns,' with some odd Pamphlets of Sermons by the Bishop of Peterborough.[37]

Clare's list and those of other autobiographers show that the labouring sort read books on a huge range of topics, such as history, science, law, poetry, literature, novels, astronomy, astrology, mathematics, philosophy, theology, travel, geography and botany.

There are several books which came up repeatedly in autobiographies, showing that they had a wide reach and influence. Written by John Bunyan, *Pilgrim's Progress* (1678 and 1684) tells the story of one man's journey to escape sin and find salvation. The book 'pleased' John Clare 'mightily' and 'delighted' Charles Crocker so much that he 'read it again and again with undiminished pleasure'.[38] Several writers even noted that the book inspired them to follow a better path in life to save their souls like the book's protagonist.[39] The same could also be said of other titles with religious themes to them, such as Joseph Alleine's *An Alarm to Unconverted Sinners* (1671). When Joshua Marsden's grandmother read the book she was 'awakened' by it.[40] Mary Saxby stated that the volume had a long-term impact on her life and religious beliefs:

Non-essential goods   **185**

> I had never heard of this book; but going into a neighbour's house, I saw it lie on the table, and took it up to read it: I had not power to put it down again, for it so exactly described my case, that, before I had read many lines, I was bathed in tears. I begged the owner to lend it me, which she readily did. I took it home, and found I had got a treasure of more solid worth than the mines of both the Indies ... This book, the Lord was pleased to make of singular use to my soul; for many a time have I laid it before me, and wept, and prayed in bitterness of soul, because I feared that I was unconverted.[41]

Famous novels of the period, such as *Gulliver's Travels* (1726), *Pamela* (1740) and *Tom Jones* (1749), are recorded in the writings of the poor. Of particular note is Daniel Defoe's *Robinson Crusoe* (1719), which several autobiographers said was a formative text of their youth. Christopher Thomson asserted that 'like most juveniles, [I] felt a deep interest in the reading of Robinson Crusoe'.[42] After collecting 'an old imperfect copy' of the volume, William Heaton 'never ceased till I read it again and again',[43] while as a child of around five or six, Thomas Carter perused the classic 'with much eagerness and satisfaction'.[44] Samuel Bamford and his 'inseparable companion' pored over *Robinson Crusoe* together and were 'awed and fascinated by the discriptions of sea-dangers, shipwrecks, and lone islands with savages, and far-off countries teeming with riches and plenty'.[45]

People's reading habits went beyond religious devotion or pleasure and were geared towards learning new skills and self-improvement. Shoemaker Richard Buxton had a great love for learning. He taught himself how to read, later becoming a leading botanist by perusing one book after another on the subject.[46] William Hart purchased Dr William Buchan's *Domestic Medicine* (1769) on the advice of a friend. From the volume, he was able to find that it was 'the weakness of my nerves' that 'was the matter with me'.[47] Charles Bent's autobiography records the life of a man who was once fond of drink and debauchery. However, 'Being desirous of improving myself', Bent used his leisure time 'learning to read and write' so that he could study books which would help him 'settle accounts when required' and enrich his soul.[48] Richard Gooch, who in later life became an astrologer, first discovered his love for the topic upon reading *Astronomy and Navigation*. Costing only 4d., the book meant that his 'mind began to expand' and 'was the source, the germ, that planted science in my mind, it expanded my ideas, and at once led me'.[49] Ownership of these books gave people a greater purpose in life and even a potential route out of poverty.[50]

Autobiographies and diaries reveal that the poor used a considerable range of methods to acquire print. Purchases of books from shops, fairs and itinerant sellers feature throughout the ego documents. As a child, Allen Davenport 'saved all my halfpence' to buy printed materials,[51] while John Clare used 'every shilling I coud save' to purchase 'books and paper with'.[52] On one occasion, at 13, Clare 'teazd my father out of the 1ˢ/6ᵈ' to purchase James Thompson's *Seasons* (1730) and 'woud not let him have any peace till he consented to give it me'.[53] Itinerant sellers sold a huge range of goods, including printed materials. Benjamin Shaw lamented in his writings that his wife Betty spent far too much money buying goods from such street sellers that the family fell into debt.[54] There was also a vibrant second-hand industry which meant that people could buy books cheaply. In the pawnshop of George Fettes of York, for instance, there were bibles, hymn books, prayer books and even one book on the history of Scotland. When the books were not redeemed by their owners, most were probably sold by Fettes for only small amounts.[55]

Individuals would exchange and borrow books to 'mutually assist' one another.[56] When Charles Whetstone was poor and struggled to buy books, he relied on 'reading what accident put into my hands'.[57] As well as buying print from shops, fairs and hawkers, John Clare borrowed books from school and was lent books by friends and Mr Gee, a local farmer.[58] He stated that 'From these friendships I gathered more acquaintance with books which chances oppertunitys were but sparing'.[59] At one point, Timothy Claxton's main source of books was his 'poor friend Tom, the journeyman', but when Tom died there was also 'the departure of his books'.[60] Many people were given books by charities or by benevolent individuals. Philanthropic organisations such as the British and Foreign Bible Society and Society for Promoting Christian Knowledge gave bibles to the poor,[61] as did well-meaning individuals from the church and gentry.[62] Taverns, coffeehouses and many other public places also offered people access to a wide range of publications.[63] When Claxton arrived in London in 1810, he noted how coffeehouses for working people, where 'publications are to be had gratis by the customers', were becoming more common.[64] Some people were fortunate enough to have access to libraries or societies of some sort. Christopher Thomson, an apprentice shipbuilder, found the choice in the circulating library he joined 'bewildering'.[65] With the 'first trifling sum' that Charles Campbell got his hands on, he 'laid out ... subscription money at a circulating library in a neighbouring town'.[66] He also joined a society where he debated literary subjects. He recalled that it 'was a cheap school of pleasure ... well supplied with books, and almost conducted without any expense'.[67] The weaver William Heaton even formed a library with his friends to study 'the school of nature' using 'the best books we could find on the subject'.[68]

Clearly, print was of central importance to large numbers of indigent people. It offered them an escape from their often very tough lives and a way to better themselves. The books noted in the ego documents, from the Bible to *Pilgrim's Progress* to *Robinson Crusoe*, were of central importance to people, helping to shape their outlook on the world. Many worked tirelessly to learn the skills to read and would use whatever spare pennies and shillings that they had to acquire reading materials. When short of cash or hungry for more literature, they used a wide array of methods such as

Non-essential goods   187

borrowing, credit and the second-hand market to acquire print. Indeed, it is difficult to overstate the importance of books and the printed word to the autobiographers.

Pictures

Pauper inventories indicate that the ownership of pictures was low but slightly increased over the long eighteenth century (Table 6.2). Likewise, only 4 per cent of the bastardy, debt, goods-taken and poorhouse/workhouse-admittance-related inventories note pictures. Despite this, the numbers of people who possessed pictures were much higher, for similar reasons to books and other printed materials.[69] There was simply little motive for appraisers to go to the trouble of itemising pictures. Most were only worth a few pence when valued by officials or were described as 'pictures' or 'prints', indicating that the majority were probably mass-produced cheap copies. No pictures at the high end of consumption, such as paintings, are found in the inventories. They also had limited value in being given to other paupers or repurposed for parish institutions.

We can still learn about picture ownership using various sources. The inventories sometimes describe framed pictures with glass fronts to them, while other homemakers simply positioned unframed prints on their walls. The contents of the pictures were diverse. On the eve of entering Market Harborough workhouse in Leicestershire, Thomas Freeman possessed '1 large Picture of y[e] 10 Comandm[en][ts] & one Picture in Colours – Glased. Both in frames'.[70] Isabella Brown, who used George Fettes' pawnbroker's shop in York nearly 40 times in eight months, pawned a small picture of a nun for 6d. on one occasion.[71] Some pictures could be informative as well as decorative. Sam Skeer from Pluckley in Kent, for example, owned one 'Old Map' and Widow Doe of Wethersfield, Essex possessed '1 Large picture of London'.[72] Richard Cobbold's paintings of the interiors of people's homes in Wortham, Suffolk, are fairly accurate, as he was keen to ensure that they show 'genuine specimens of the features they record'.[73] In the bedroom of elderly widow Bet Mattock, Cobbold found 'two paper portraits of but little worth' hanging above her bed, one of which featured 'her husband and his terrier bitch' and the other 'the celebrated highwaymans portrait' of '[Dick] Turpin flying o'er a ditch' (Figure 6.1).[74] Having a picture of her deceased husband and dog in her bedroom must have

Table 6.2   Percentage of paupers who owned pictures or prints, 1670–1835

	1670–1729	1730–69	1770–1809	1810–34
Picture/print	1	3	8	14
Sample size	125	268	165	65

Figure 6.1 Portraits of Bet Mattock (left) and Sarah Scott (right), painted by Richard Cobbold, c.1862 and c.1849–55 (source: SA HA 11/A13/10; reproduced by kind permission of the owner)

helped to conjure up memories and feelings of love.[75] In the second depiction, Sarah Scott shows her strong Methodist beliefs through a picture of an angel.[76] Various other paintings and drawings of labouring homes by Cobbold show rural scenes, landscapes, cityscapes, religious imagery and portraiture in the backgrounds.[77]

Nearly every inventory which recorded pictures noted multiple numbers of them. This would have meant that the poor were able to spread the pictures around the home and make different rooms and areas more decorative and visually appealing according to individual preferences. Mrs Buckwell from Canterbury in Kent, for instance, owned 24 'prints' spread across her garret, low room and chamber.[78] People swapped or moved their pictures around as their tastes and ideas changed. Upon 'looking at the two pictures that hung on the wall' of a 'coloured engraving of a celebrated game cock' and 'sparring booth in London', shoemaker Charles Bent said that 'a feeling of disgust crept over me'. He set about replacing these pictures with 'others, containing a moral and important lesson'.[79] Some of these pictures might have been placed in the frames of other pictures or simply placed onto walls as ephemeral prints.

Looking glasses

Looking glasses (mirrors) had a wide range of purposes. First and foremost, they enabled people to check and maintain their hair and appearance.

Shaving at home was much easier with them, meaning that men could save money as they would not need to regularly visit a barber. Looking glasses could be used to enhance the domestic space if they were of a decorative design or placed in eye-catching areas such as above the fireplace. By combining mirrors with artificial lighting, users could brighten their homes and make abodes appear more spacious.[80] Looking glasses from the past sometimes even incorporated holders for candles or rushlights.[81] In folk law and popular culture, looking glasses were alleged to offer a passageway to spiritual and mystical worlds. Though these beliefs were probably less prevalent by the late seventeenth century,[82] a number of people still believed that mirrors could be used to tell the future, to find lost objects and to protect residents from witchcraft. It was also believed by some that looking glasses could be used as an instrument of the Devil and could capture the souls of the dying.[83] Thus, a mirror was not just an opulent item reserved for vanity and appearance but could also serve various other purposes.

Looking glasses went from being a rare luxury during the late seventeenth and early eighteenth centuries to being found in at least one-third of pauper abodes from the late eighteenth century (Table 6.3). They appear to have been most widespread in Kent, where nearly half of pauper inventories record them between 1770 and 1835, and least likely in Leicestershire and Rutland, where only one-fifth of the sources list one between the same dates (Table 6.4). The indigent poor generally possessed a single looking

Table 6.3 Percentage of paupers who owned looking glasses, over time, 1670–1835

	1670–1729	1730–69	1770–1809	1810–34
Looking glass	6	15	32	34
Sample size	125	268	165	65

Table 6.4 Percentage of paupers who owned looking glasses, by county, 1770–1835

	1770–1835
Dorset	32
Essex	33
Kent	45
Leics/Ruts	20
Norfolk	38
All counties	33

glass. Only three pauper inventories record three looking glasses, and eight list two.

The poor found use and value in a wide variety of looking glasses. Some paupers possessed mirrors that were clearly large and expensive and were used for a variety of purposes. The home of Widow Hincock in Smarden, Kent had a 'Wooden Candlestick' next to a 'Dressing Glass', indicating that the two were used together to help her get ready.[84] Jon Millbank had a 'Swing glass' worth 5s. in his 'Best Chamber' in Little Waltham, Essex,[85] while Mrs Buckwell from Canterbury in Kent possessed three looking glasses including '1 Swing Glas' and two pier glasses.[86] These mirrors would have added a decorative quality to the home. Pier glasses, for instance, were long and rectangular and were generally ornately positioned between two windows or above the chimney piece. Swing looking glasses were suspended on pivots, which allowed people to adjust them to a convenient angle and position.[87]

It was not only showy and costly looking glasses that the poor valued. Appraisers generally described paupers' looking glasses as 'small', which probably meant that most were fairly cheap compared with large mirrors and were either hand-held or only big enough to show a person's head and perhaps their shoulders. Valuations of looking glasses are noted in only eight inventories, yet in seven cases they are valued at no more than 1s. each. The pawnbroker's pledge book of George Fettes from York equally shows that looking glasses were pledged at a modal value of 1s. 6d. If left unclaimed by their owners, these mirrors would have probably been relatively inexpensive to buy from Fettes.[88] Even broken mirrors held their worth. The inventory of Richard Hammond's goods taken before he entered Redenhall workhouse records 'a Broken Looking-Glass'.[89] In David Love's autobiography he recounted how he slipped over and broke all the looking glasses that he was hawking. Yet he 'picked up the largest pieces of glass' and set about 'selling the cracked and damaged ones at any price'.[90] Looking glasses could thus be cherished and useful to the poor despite being cheap, plain or even broken.

Looking glasses were important possessions to people by the turn of the nineteenth century. While a struggling 20-year-old apprentice at a local mill, Benjamin Shaw married his pregnant partner Betty in September 1793.[91] The couple could not afford many goods to set up their new home, meaning that Benjamin made some of the items himself and that they were given goods by family. Yet Benjamin still listed a looking glass as one of the first and most important items he acquired, alongside 'a box for Cloaths, & a pair of tongs, & a fue pots ... a knife & fork, & 2 Stools ... a pan ... & a few trifles'.[92] The fact that the family appears to have prioritised attaining a looking glass indicates that they were important for home life and that they might have become more central to how people constructed and understood the self from the late eighteenth century.

Timepieces

The history of time has attracted the attention of a number of scholars, helping us to augment and revise our understanding of a host of topics. Jan de Vries, Hans-Joachim Voth and others, for instance, have surmised that the rise of capitalism came from people working harder and longer hours.[93] In a similar vein, E. P. Thompson claims that over the industrial revolution there was a fundamental change in people's lives as work went from being task- to time-orientated in the new punitive factories of the era.[94] Key to these arguments is the idea that people became more time-aware. We know that the middling sort increasingly acquired clocks and watches from the late seventeenth century,[95] yet we know surprisingly little about how common these items were among the poor beyond the capital and home counties.[96] Considering the huge emphasis put on watch and clock ownership by leading historians and its connection to the emergence of a capitalist economy, research is long overdue.

The pauper inventories indicate that the ownership of timepieces was initially very low among the poor, but that from the 1790s at least one-third of people possessed one (Table 6.5). At this point, it does not appear to have been unusual for paupers from the home counties to more distant areas such as Dorset, Leicestershire and Rutland to possess them (Table 6.6). This is an important finding: it shows that as the poor in London and the

Table 6.5 Percentage of paupers who owned timepieces, over time, 1670–1835

	1670–1709	1710–29	1730–49	1750–69	1770–89	1790–1809	1810–34
Timepiece	0	1	1	3	13	29	31
Sample size	45	80	83	185	85	80	65

Table 6.6 Percentage of paupers who owned timepieces, by county, 1790–1835

	1790–1835
Dorset	18
Essex	27
Kent	100
Leics/Ruts	29
Norfolk	25
All counties	30
Sample size	145

192   At home with the poor

home counties (especially Kent) increasingly acquired timepieces from the late eighteenth century, their peers in other parts of England were not left behind. This can probably be said of Lancashire, as 28 per cent of the pauper inventories and wider sample of inventories of paupers' goods for the county note timepieces for 1770–1835. As an alternative to a mechanical timepiece, people could also use sundials or hourglasses. However, only 6 per cent of the pauper inventories list an hourglass, and sundials are entirely absent in the sources.

The majority of inventories record timepieces in the form of a clock, while watches are conspicuously rare. This might suggest that watches were simply not owned by many people, yet there is much evidence to the contrary, especially when watch ownership is studied over the lifecycle. Naturally, some paupers would have concealed their watches when appraisers came knocking at the door, since they were small and easy to quickly tuck away out of sight. Most others, conversely, appear to have owned watches before their goods were inventoried by the parish, when they were in a better financial position. In fact, watches were so highly desired that they were often one of the first items that individuals acquired when they had some disposable income.[97] Watches were, however, also one of the first items that people would sell during difficult times, as they retained their value well and could be used to quickly realise reasonably large sums of money to pay bills or purchase food. E. P. Thompson even characterised watches as 'the poor man's bank'.[98] The pawnbroking records of George Fettes of York show that watches were the fifth most common type of good pawned in his shop,[99] fetching approximately 17s. 10d. on average per customer.[100] The writings of the poor show how and why people pawned or sold their watches. In December 1824, Thomas Smith wrote to the overseer of Chelmsford in Essex to ask for relief. He said that he had 'been out of employ for about a month' and so had 'pledged what furniture we can possibly spare ... [including] my own wearing appearel – all our Silver Spoons and my Watch'.[101] Likewise, the autobiography of William Hutton notes how he downgraded and traded two silver watches and later a brass one as they broke and he needed cash. Hutton eventually 'went without a watch thirty years' after he parted with his last one.[102]

Owning a timepiece had practical advantages, as it allowed people to tell the time without having to ask somebody else or use a public clock. Further to this, the pride, prestige and symbolic power of owning a timepiece was an important incentive. William Hutton described his first silver watch, costing £1 15s., as 'the pride of my life'.[103] So great was the gratification associated with owning a watch that Robert Blincoe even agreed to move from St Pancras workhouse in London to a cotton mill in Nottingham on the promise of luxuries such as 'silver watches'. These hopes did not quite materialise and to Blincoe's great disappointment 'there were no plum-pudding – no roast beef, no talk of the horses they were to ride, nor of the watches and fine clothing that they had been promised'.[104]

Clocks helped to decorate and adorn the homes of dwellers. Several pauper inventories list clocks with cases, which were probably self-standing clocks that had wooden cases covering the mechanisms. Over time, this type of clock became increasingly fashionable, and clockmakers created and decorated a range of sought-after timepieces.[105] Some inventories note clocks made out of decorative woods such as wainscot and deal, while in the 'Dwelling House' of John Marrable of Hatfield Broad Oak, Essex, there was 'A thirty Hour Clock wth blue Case'.[106] Several paintings by clergyman Richard Cobbold show just how prominent and eye catching clocks in cases could be. The first painting in Figure 6.2 depicts the home of the agricultural labouring family of James and Ann Harbour; in the background is a beautiful wooden standing clock. Similarly, the second painting shows a striking adorned wooden clock in the abode of pauper Widow Mary Ann Goodard. Clocks were among the costliest items that paupers owned. On average, they are valued at £1 10s. 9d. across 16 various inventories which note the values of paupers' goods. The most expensive clock was £3 3s. and the cheapest was 2s. Some inventories note 12-, 24- and 30-hour clocks, whereas others note eight-day clocks. The latter were worth more, as they needed winding less often.[107]

Memories, feelings and experiences can lodge themselves into objects, meaning that goods take on a life of their own and become important to

Figure 6.2 Portrait of Ann Harbour (left) and Mary Ann Goddard (right), painted by Richard Cobbold, c.1863–65 and 1855–63 (source: SA HA 11/A13/10; reproduced by kind permission of the owner)

194 At home with the poor

people beyond their practical or financial components.[108] When soldier Robert Butler lost his watch overboard in 1807, he noted that it 'cost me upwards of four pounds' but was most concerned with losing something that was sentimentally important. He noted that the watch had 'a seal attached to it' which had been given to him by his 'affectionate comrade … as a token of remembrance'. Butler said that they were 'much attached to each other' and hoped to see his friend again.[109] The autobiography of James Ashley records the history of the family's clock, which was passed down through the generations. It was first acquired by his grandparents in 1784 but was later distrained for debt in 1838 when his parents owned it. Upon seeing the clock for sale at auction in 1847, James' mother was determined to get it back and entered into a bidding 'duel' with other prospective buyers. She eventually won with a bid of £4 15s., bringing 'joy in the family' as the heirloom was restored to its rightful place.[110] Widow Water had her goods inventoried by parochial officials in Otford, Kent, in 1835. Included in the list was a clock. Rather than let the parish take the item, her son Richard 'advanced One pound Eight Shillings for the said Clock'.[111] No other items in the pauper inventory were redeemed in such a way, suggesting that the clock must have had significant symbolic ties to the family for Richard to spend such a large amount of money to save it. Therefore, whether for practical purposes, financial savings, decoration, sentimentality or pride, clocks and watches were important possessions for the poorer sort by the late eighteenth century.

Gold, silver and jewellery

The probate inventories and wills of the middling sort and the elite document gold, silver and jewellery ownership on a regular basis.[112] In contrast, only 1 per cent of pauper inventories record items made from precious metals or stones. Although they are rarely noted in inventories, some paupers in the sample amassed a decent range of items. Widow Beal from Lenham, Kent, for example, owned 'one Pap Spoon. Silver', 'one Pair of Sleve Bottons. Stone Set in Silver' and 'one Gold Ring',[113] while Susanna Brookman from Thundersley, Essex, possessed 'a Silver spur' and '1 silver tee spoon'.[114] The goods-taken inventory of Elizabeth Hutchford of Wrotham, Kent, listed seven rings, including two 'fancy' rings, one 'mourning' ring, '3 Plain Gold' rings and one ring with '2 brilliant' stones.[115]

Several historians have argued that labouring people did not have the status or money to acquire precious metals.[116] However, in spite of these claims and the evidence from the inventories, there is much evidence to suggest otherwise. Studies based on court records indicate that silver watches were the most common type of watches that labouring people owned.[117] Most importantly, wedding rings made from precious metals appear to have been especially common even though they were rarely listed in inventories.[118] In one letter to the overseer of Braintree, Essex, William King stressed that 'I Cannot Do without Soume Help. Every thing of My Wearing apparel and *Even* My wifes Ring is Put of [pawned] to Procure food'.[119] In a similar manner, Samuel Balls said that he 'had Pledged all our weairing Aparril and *Even* my wifes Ring',[120] while Frances James of Leicester stressed in a letter how her poverty had led her to 'pledge about every thing ... *even* to my ring off my finger'.[121] In his auto-biography, Charles Bent recounted how he was fined by the police one day for a drunken fight. To raise the 12s. 6d. that he needed to avoid prison, his wife pawned 'the wedding ring from her finger ... whilst the tears flowed down her cheeks as if her heart would break'.[122] The fact that each writer highlighted their wedding rings suggests that they were com-mon objects, but ones that were highly prized and should not be parted with. Some parishes even went as far as to purchase wedding rings for single female parishioners to incentivise marriage.[123] People also appear to have acquired inexpensive jewellery made from non-precious materials. Institutions such as Beaminster workhouse in Dorset, for instance, banned inmates from wearing earrings and hair ornaments.[124] It is likely, then, that jewellery and precious metals were more common than pauper inventories suggest, but that they tended not to be recorded by appraisers when they had little value or due to the conjugal, religious and emotional connections that they held for owners and families.

Precious metals and stones were often bought during more prosper-ous years and then pawned or sold during times of difficulty. Thomas Smith, for instance, wrote to the overseer of Chelmsford in Essex in 1824 to ask for relief. He said he had 'pledged ... all our Silver Spoons' as well as the family's clothing, furniture and a watch since he had no work and his family was so large.[125] The soldier George Calladine noted that when he had leave he got into the costly 'habit of going out to the different fairs or races', so he 'began to sell and pledge what few articles I had left in the jewellery way to meet my wants, and it was not long before all were gone'.[126] So common was the pawning of precious metals and stones that in George Fettes' pawnshop in York, gold, silver and jewellery were the second most common type of items pledged by customers, numbering over 1,000 deposits between July 1777 and February 1778.[127]

The poor had a clear interest in gold, silver and jewellery and would attach meaning to these goods. When noted in George Fettes' pledge book, items such as silver spoons and silver cups were often inscribed with initials when they were pawned, which suggests that owners had senti-mental ties to these objects as they also had to rings.[128] Some people even owned replica items to emulate precious metals, such as Rhoda Wretham of East Harling, Norfolk, who possessed one '*Mock* Silver Tea pot'.[129] If silver had not been sought after then Wretham could have easily acquired an earthenware teapot which would have cost much less.

Miscellaneous items

Insights can be gleaned into various other non-necessities, including musical instruments, toys and bird cages. Some of these items were sold to make ends meet before the inventories were taken, while others were omitted by appraisers since they had little financial value or were not worth reclaiming due to their limited use beyond entertainment. Nevertheless, where present, these articles were cherished by owners and show that daily life was not devoted solely to work and chores.

Musical instruments

Musical instruments are rarely noted in the inventories, but the writings of the poor clearly show that many people became transfixed with music and played various instruments. Violins, fiddles and flutes appear to have been particular favourites. Most individuals acquired and learned how to play their first instruments during childhood. For example, while working as a farmhand during the early 1780s, 14-year-old James Hogg saved up 5s. to buy an 'old' violin. He noted how it 'occupied all my leisure hours, and has been my favourite amusement ever since', and how he would spend 'an hour or two every night' playing.[130] When Thomas Holcroft was around five years old, his father 'indulged another whim' by putting his son 'under the tuition of a player on the violin'.[131]

Instruments tended to be played for simple enjoyment and to pass the time. William Thom even loved his 'faithful flute' so much that he wrote an ode to it.[132] They could also help to form and shape personal, familial and national identities.[133] James Hogg would often play his 'favourite old Scottish tunes' on his violin, and Thom claimed that he knew 'every Scotch song that is worth singing'.[134] Weaver David Whitehead of Rawtenstall, Lancashire, formed a band with his brothers and friends, which meant that they had the 'pleasure of enjoying each others company' and that they 'got on famously'. Helped by the rise of cheap prints such as ballads, Whitehead and his band were able to engage with music despite having little prior experience of singing and playing instruments.[135] Particular songs, or even the chirping of birds, could rouse cherished and despairing memories. The earliest memory of Christopher Thomson was when his mother 'placed me upon a chair ... directing me to the full clear song of a cuckoo that was there saluting the opening day', while she sang him a nursery rhyme.[136] It is possible that when Robert Butler played his violin he was taken back to the frontlines of Europe, as he used to play it during the Napoleonic wars 'to drown the painful sound of that cursing and swearing which abounds' and dying soldiers.[137]

Even among the most destitute, individuals found a way to make instruments such as flutes from scrap metal or bones.[138] Others used creative avenues to access instruments. David Love's friend would often borrow his violin, 'for he sold his'. The relationship was mutually beneficial, as from his companion Love 'learned to play slow tunes, which was an amusement for me in my leisure hours'.[139] Robert Butler, on the other hand, gave people lessons on the German flute and used the money to pay for music and his own violin and clarinet lessons.[140] In 1845, eight-year-old John Shinn witnessed the start of his father's three-year 'nervous break-down', which resulted in the family having to go without food, clothing and fuel for long periods. Yet around the same time his father 'came into possession of a violin' and gave it to John, who 'for a small sum ... purchased a cheap tutor and set to work to teach myself'. Two years later, a Swiss gentleman asked John's father to store a piano at their home. It was placed in the kitchen, where John 'set to work at once to teach myself' and 'made fair progress'. Soon after this, he was granted permission to practice the organ at his local chapel once a week.[141] Regardless of whether people owned an instrument, the poor thus found ways to engage with music.

Children's toys

Research on children often emphasises how the young were important contributors to the family economy and would start work at early ages.[142] Ego documents too remind us that fathers and mothers could be emotionally distant, choosing instead to prioritise work, household chores or even the pub over their young.[143] Nevertheless, children still had some sort of childhood, even if they were expected to work and be obedient to their parents. Autobiographers often fondly recounted how during their early years they would spend enjoyable evenings playing football, cricket and other games with friends. Paintings of the labouring sort, albeit highly idealised and littered with messages of morality,[144] would sometimes depict children playing with dolls, wooden horses, toy boats, and bats and balls of some sort.[145] Dice, marbles, toy teacups, ceramic dolls and gaming pieces have also been found in archaeological excavations of peasant and working-class areas.[146] Dolls even survive today which were created by poor families by dressing up objects such as skittles, wood, bones, clothes pegs and shoes in rags.[147] On occasion, inventories record toys, such as the Colchester rent-arrears inventory of pauper Edward Ladbrook's goods, which included a 'Childs toy'.[148] Toys could even be found in workhouses. In the workhouse in Staplehurst, Kent, 'some Child's Playthings & Toys' are noted in an inventory from 1806.[149] Further to this, the autobiographical writings of Samuel Bamford note how as a child he played with workhouse children 'at ball, or at hide-and-seek', while his father acted as governor of the institution.[150] If children could play with toys in the workhouse, it is highly probable that most of the young on the outside did the same.

Naturally, most toys were given to children as gifts by parents and families. While serving as a soldier in the Napoleonic wars, George Calladine 'bought a number of different toys and curious things made by the French prisoners, to distribute to my relations'.[151] William Brown noted how his parents had 'been in the habit of giving their children halfpence, to purchase fruit, sweetmeats, and toys'.[152] In the 1780s, wagon driver Robert Errington made his son Anthony 'a small waggon with 4 wood wheals'. Anthony loved the toy wagon, taking 'dilight to trale [it] after me', and used it to mimic his father at work.[153] Memories of these exchanges clearly evoked feelings of love and contentment, as well as wistful pining for a simpler time.[154] John Bethune recollected how happy he was at school as he 'painted ... myself many fine toys' and learned 'many fine games' with 'many fine friends'.[155] In a similar vein, Francis Place reminisced at length about the many 'boyish games' and 'kinds of sports and exercises' that he participated in as a child, which included swimming, flying kites, fishing and sailing model boats.[156]

Bird cages

It is difficult to ascertain how common bird cages were, but they do appear to have become more widespread in poor abodes from the eighteenth century. They were cheap to buy and fairly easy to make, so they were within the means of most people. The rent-arrears inventory of Elias Bygrave's goods, for instance, includes a 'Caniree bird and Cage' worth only 1s. 6d.,[157] while as a teenager William Farish earned small amounts of money 'making birdcages for sale'.[158] Pictures of abodes must always be viewed with caution, but surprisingly often they depict bird cages in the interiors and exteriors of labouring homes (Figure 6.3). A number of autobiographies also include discussions or poems about the writer's love of birds,[159] and many others note bird catchers,[160] showing that birds were popular and that there was a ready market for them. Some people kept their bird cages empty and used them for ornamentation, but when birds were present they were important pets. With minimal maintenance and food, owners had a pet that could sing or talk. The birds were seen as beautiful and interesting to observe, bringing joy to people during working hours and times of recreation.[161]

Conclusion

Over the long eighteenth century the poorer sort became more engaged in the consumption of goods which were not necessary to the support of life, whether described as 'luxuries', 'non-necessities', 'conveniences' or something else. Articles such as books, looking glasses and timepieces became more usual in people's abodes and often had a profound effect on

Figure 6.3 Thomas Heaphy, *Inattention*, 1808 (source: Yale Center for British Art, Paul Mellon Collection, B1975.3.175, watercolour)

their ways of life, influencing how individuals saw themselves, organised their daily activities and spent their leisure times. In a number of cases these items were fairly cheap, so people with even the most meagre of budgets could get involved. It is by the latter decades of the eighteenth century that most of these goods became more common in poor homes. This is an important finding. It suggests that many goods of the period

At home with the poor

were consumed not just by people with money, but also by the impoverished who were once thought to have little inclination or ability to acquire anything other than basic provisions. Although some of these items were acquired informally or second-hand, it is likely that demand for these possessions among the poor, who easily made up the majority of the population, would have had a considerable knock-on effect, stimulating production in new and expanding industries.

Notes

1 Bernard Mandeville, *The Fable of the Bees or Private Vices, Publick Benefits*, Vol. 1., ed. F. B. Kaye (Oxford: Clarendon Press, reprint of 1732 edn, 1988), p. 108.
2 Smith, *Wealth of Nations*, Vol. 2, pp. 869–73.
3 Werner Sombart, *Luxury and Capitalism*, trans. W. R. Dittmar, ed. Philip Siegelman (Ann Arbor: University of Michigan Press, reprint of 1913 edn, 1967); Christopher J. Berry, *The Idea of Luxury: A conceptual and historical investigation* (Cambridge: Cambridge University Press, 1994); Maxine Berg and Helen Clifford (eds), *Consumers and Luxury: Consumer culture in Europe 1650–1850* (Manchester: Manchester University Press, 1999); Maxine Berg and Elizabeth Eger (eds), *Luxury in the Eighteenth Century: Debates, desires and delectable goods* (Basingstoke: Palgrave, 2003); Berg, *Luxury and Pleasure*; Linda Levy Peck, *Consuming Splendor: Society and culture in seventeenth-century England* (Cambridge: Cambridge University Press, 2005); Johanna Ilmakunnas and Jon Stobart (eds), *A Taste for Luxury in Early Modern Europe: Display, acquisition and boundaries* (London: Bloomsbury, 2017).
4 Alexis de Tocqueville, *Memoir on Pauperism*, trans. Seymour Drescher, ed. Gertrude Himmelfarb (London: Civitas, 1997).
5 Jonathan White, 'Luxury and Labour: Ideas of labouring-class consumption in eighteenth-century England', PhD thesis (University of Warwick, 2001).
6 David Cressy, *Literacy and the Social Order: Reading and writing in Tudor and Stuart England* (Cambridge: Cambridge University Press, 1980), passim.
7 Roger S. Schofield, 'Dimensions of Illiteracy, 1750–1850', in Harvey J. Graff (ed.), *Literacy and Social Development in the West: A reader* (Cambridge: Cambridge University Press, 1981), pp. 206–8; Lawrence Stone, 'Literacy and Education in England 1640–1900', *Past and Present*, 42 (1969), p. 105.
8 King, *Writing the Lives*, p. 56.
9 Ibid; Mark Hailwood, 'Rethinking Literacy in Rural England, 1500–1700', *Past and Present*, 260:1 (2023), pp. 38–70; Keith Thomas, 'The Meaning of Literacy in Early Modern England', in Gerd Baumann (ed.), *The Written Word: Literacy in transition* (Oxford, 1986), pp. 98–104; David Cressy, 'Literacy in Context: Meaning and measurement in early modern England', in Brewer and Porter, *World of Goods*, pp. 311–13.
10 King, *Writing the Lives*, pp. 116–44; Sokoll, *Pauper Letters*, pp. 62–67; Cressy, *Literacy and the Social Order*, p. 14; Thomas, 'Meaning of Literacy', pp. 106–10.
11 Adam Fox, *Oral and Literate Culture in England 1500–1700* (Oxford: Oxford University Press, 2000); Adam Fox and Daniel Woolf (eds), *The Spoken Word: Oral culture in Britain 1500–1850* (Manchester: Manchester University Press, 2002); King, *Writing the Lives*; Cressy, *Literacy and the Social Order*, pp. 13–14; Thomas, 'Literacy', pp. 113–4.
12 Most notably: Elizabeth L. Eisenstein, *The Printing Revolution in Early Modern Europe* (Cambridge: Cambridge University Press, 2nd edn, 2012).
13 Overton et al., *Production and Consumption*, p. 113; Sneath, 'Consumption, Wealth', p. 293.

Non-essential goods 201

14 See Figures 3.2, 3.3, 3.7, 4.3, 5.6, 6.1, 6.2 and 6.3. Also see Chapter 7.
15 Such as: Charles Campbell, *Memoirs of Charles Campbell, at Present Prisoner in the Jail of Glasgow* (Glasgow: James Duncan & Co., 1828), p. 2; Charles Crocker, *The Vale of Obscurity, the Lavant, and Other Poems* (Chichester: W. Mason, 1830), p. ix; Samuel Sholl, *A Short Historical Account of the Silk Manufacture in England* (London: M. Jones, 1811), pp. 37–8.
16 Basset, *Life of a Vagrant*, p. 2.
17 Heaton, 'A Sketch', p. xvi. Also see: Jewell, 'Autobiographical Memoir', pp. 126–7.
18 Bethune, *Poems*, p. 4; Benjamin Bangs, *Memoirs of the Life and Convincement of that Worthy Friend Benjamin Bangs* (London: Luke Hinde, 1757), pp. 7–8.
19 Mayett, *Autobiography*, pp. 34, 41.
20 Farish, *Autobiography*, p. 10.
21 Lackington, *Memoirs*, pp. 98, 181; MacDonald, *Travels*, p. 42.
22 See, for example: Carter, *Memoirs*, pp. 28, 59; Clare, *Autobiographical*, p. 15; G. J., *Prisoner Set Free*, p. 4; Richard Buxton, *A Botanical Guide to the Flowering Plants … together with a Sketch of the Author's Life* (London: Longman and Co., 1849), p. iv; Gifford, *Memoir*, p. 7; Gooch, *Memoirs*, p. 8; Place, *Autobiography*, pp. 30, 40–1.
23 Allen Davenport, *The Life and Literary Pursuits of Allen Davenport*, ed. Malcolm Chase (Aldershot: Scolar Press, 1994), p. 4.
24 Owned by William Catley of Great Chishill, Essex. ERO D/P 210/18/4.
25 NRO PD 358/42.
26 Estabrook, *Urbane and Rustic*, p. 169.
27 Ibid., p. 169.
28 Cressy, *Literacy and the Social Order*, pp. 50–1.
29 Mayett, *Autobiography*, p. 72.
30 Sholl, *Short Historical Account*, p. 38.
31 Clare, *Letters of John Clare*, pp. 515–16.
32 Bethune, *Poems*, p. 81.
33 Lackington, *Memoirs*, pp 136, 139.
34 Thomas Wood, 'The Autobiography of Thomas Wood, 1822–1880', in Burnett, *Useful Toil*, p. 308.
35 Hart, 'Autobiography', Part I, p. 151.
36 Crocker, *Vale of Obscurity*, p. x.
37 Clare, *Autobiographical Writings*, p. 14.
38 Ibid., p. 13; Crocker, *Vale of Obscurity*, p. ix.
39 Joseph Barker, *The Life of Joseph Barker, Written by Himself*, ed. John Thomas Barker (London: Hodder and Stoughton, 1880), pp. 26–7, 53–4; Holcroft, *Memoirs*, p. 175; Brown, *Narrative*, p. 136; Mayett, *Autobiography*, p. 41.
40 Marsden, *Sketches*, p. 13.
41 Saxby, *Memoirs*, pp. 31–2.
42 Thomson, *Autobiography*, p. 65.
43 Heaton, 'A Sketch', pp. xvi–xvii.
44 Carter, *Memoirs*, p. 40.
45 Bamford, *Early Days*, p. 94.
46 Buxton, *Botanical Guide*, pp. iv–v.
47 Hart, 'Autobiography', Part I, p. 154.
48 Bent, *Autobiography*, p. 21.
49 Gooch, *Memoirs*, p. 14.
50 MacKay, *Respectability*, p. 8.
51 Davenport, *Life*, p. 4.
52 Clare, *Autobiographical Writings*, p. 14.
53 Ibid., p. 9.
54 Shaw, *Family Records*, pp. 41, 77.
55 YALH Accession 38.

56 Whetstone, *Truths*, p. 84.

57 Ibid., p. 85.

58 Clare, *Autobiographical Writings*, pp. 15–17, 46, 56.

59 Ibid., p. 46.

60 Timothy Claxton, *Hints to Mechanics, on Self-Education and Mutual Instruction* (London: Taylor and Walton, 1839), pp. 9–10.

61 John James Bezer, 'The Autobiography of One of the Chartist Rebels of 1848', in Vincent, *Testaments of Radicalism*, p. 178; Scott Mandelbrote, 'The English Bible and Its Readers in the Eighteenth Century', in Isabel Rivers (ed.), *Books and Their Readers in Eighteenth-Century England: New Essays* (London: Leicester University Press, 2001), pp. 47–50.

62 Dymond, *Parson*, pp. 55, 78; SA HD 1025/1–2; SA HD 368/1.

63 Cowan, *Social Life of Coffee*.

64 Claxton, *Hints*, p. 17.

65 Thomson, *Autobiography*, p. 65.

66 Campbell, *Memoirs*, p. 3.

67 Ibid., pp. 3–4.

68 Heaton, 'A Sketch', pp. xviii–xix.

69 Others have made similar claims, such as: Rembrandt Duits (ed.), *The Art of the Poor: The aesthetic material culture of the lower classes in Europe 1300–1600* (London: Bloomsbury, 2020).

70 ROLLR DE 1212/7.

71 YALH Accession 38; Backhouse, *Worm-Eaten*, p. 29.

72 KHLC P289/18/2; ERO D/P 119/12/1.

73 SA HD 368/1.

74 SA HA 11/A13/10; SA HD 1025/1; Dymond, *Parson*, pp. 167–9.

75 Handley, *Sleep*, pp. 139–40.

76 SA HA 11/A13/10; SA HD 1025/1; Dymond, *Parson*, pp. 210–12.

77 SA HD 1025/1–2; SA HA 42/1–2; SA HD 1888/1; SA HD 368/1; SA HA 11/A13/10. It is not possible to reproduce all these pictures here, but some appear in Dymond, *Parson*, pp. 59, 70, 73, 123, 140, 157, 168, 170, 176, 186, 191, 211, 219.

78 CCAL U3/100/11A/2.

79 Bent, *Autobiography*, pp. 21–2.

80 Crowley, *Invention of Comfort*, pp. 122–30.

81 Sear and Sneath, *Consumer Revolution*, p. 161.

82 Keith Thomas, *Religion and the Decline of Magic: Studies in popular beliefs in sixteenth- and seventeenth-century England* (London: Weidenfeld & Nicolson, 1971).

83 On these beliefs, see: Sabine Melchior-Bonnet, *The Mirror: A history*, trans. Katherine H. Jewett (London: Routledge, 2001), pp. 101–269; Margaret J. M. Ezell, 'Looking Glass Histories', *Journal of British Studies*, 43:3 (2004), pp. 326–8.

84 KHLC P339/8/1.

85 ERO D/P 220/18/7.

86 CCAL U3/100/11A/2.

87 Fastnedge, *Furniture Styles*, pp. 79–80, 216–17; Oxford English Dictionary Online (www.oed.com).

88 YALH Accession 38.

89 NRO PD 295/102.

90 Love, *Life*, pp. 34–5.

91 Shaw, *Family Records*, pp. xvi, 120.

92 Ibid., p. 32.

93 De Vries, *Industrious Revolution*; Voth, *Time and Work*. On work and time in the early modern period, see: Mark Hailwood, 'Time and Work in Rural England, 1500–1700', *Past and Present*, 248 (2020), pp. 87–121.

Non-essential goods 203

94 E. P. Thompson, 'Time, Work-Discipline and Industrial Capitalism', *Past and Present*, 38 (1967), pp. 56–97.

95 Overton et al., *Production and Consumption*, pp. 111–12; Weatherill, *Consumer Behaviour*, p. 26; Hussey and Ponsonby, *Single Homemaker*, p. 39; Sear and Sneath, *Consumer Revolution*, p. 207.

96 Helmreich, Hitchcock and Turkel, 'Rethinking Inventories', pp. 14–15, 18–21; Horrell, Humphries and Sneath, 'Consumption Conundrums', pp. 845–7; King, 'Pauper Inventories', p. 179. An important exception to this is Styles, *Dress*, pp. 96–107, which uses court records from the north and London to assess watch ownership.

97 Styles, *Dress*, pp. 96–107; Thompson, 'Time', pp. 69–70.

98 Thompson, 'Time', p. 70.

99 Backhouse, *Worm-Eaten*, pp. 77–81; YALH Accession 38. This sum is based on clothing and linen being grouped together in one category.

100 YALH Accession 38.

101 Sokoll, *Pauper Letters*, p. 196.

102 Hutton, *Life of*, p. 64.

103 Ibid., p. 64.

104 Blincoe, *Memoir*, pp. 13–16, 57.

105 R. W. Symonds, *A Book of English Clocks* (London: Penguin, 2nd edn, 1950), pp. 42–4, 52–4, 64–7.

106 ERO D/P 4/18/8.

107 Paul Glennie and Nigel Thrift, *Shaping the Day: A history of timekeeping in England and Wales 1300–1800* (Oxford: Oxford University Press, 2009), p. 36.

108 Cohen, *Household Gods*, pp. 153–6, 163–7; Randles, 'Material World', pp. 163–4; Leora Auslander, 'Beyond Words', *American Historical Review*, 110:4 (2005), p. 1020.

109 Robert Butler, *Narrative of the Life and Travels of Serjeant B – Written by Himself* (Edinburgh: David Brown, 1823), p. 43.

110 James Ashley, 'Account of Life', pp. 2–4 in The Burnett Archive of Working Class Autobiographies, Brunel University, London (from: http://bura.brunel.ac.uk/handle/2438/9356, accessed 12/06/2020).

111 KHLC P279/8/2.

112 Berg, *Luxury and Pleasure*, pp. 154–92; Weatherill, *Consumer Behaviour*, pp. 26, 44; Hussey and Ponsonby, *Single Homemaker*, p. 39; Sear and Sneath, *Consumer Revolution*, pp. 147–50.

113 KHLC P224/8/1.

114 ERO D/P 357/12/1.

115 KHLC P406/12/6.

116 Such as Sear and Sneath, *Consumer Revolution*, pp. 122, 149–50; Weatherill, *Consumer Behaviour*, p. 66; Sneath, 'Consumption, Wealth', pp. 287–90.

117 Styles, *Dress*, pp. 98–9; Helmreich, Hitchcock and Turkel, 'Rethinking Inventories', pp. 19–20; Horrell, Humphries and Sneath, 'Conundrums', p. 847.

118 In England, the exchange of rings was common. See: Love, *Life*, p. 25. Most rings appear to have been made from precious metals. For instance, the rings pawned to Fettes were nearly always made of gold. Less often they had stones in them or were made from silver. YALH Accession 38.

119 Sokoll, *Pauper Letters*, pp. 121–2. My italics. Also see p. 143.

120 Ibid., p. 299. My italics.

121 King, Nutt and Tomkins, *Narratives*, p. 281. My italics.

122 Bent, *Autobiography*, p. 12.

123 Steven King, 'Too Poor to Marry? "Inheritance", the poor and marriage/household formation in rural England 1800–1840s', in Anne-Lise Head-König (ed.),

Inheritance Practices, Marriage Strategies and Household Formation in European Rural Societies (Turnhout: Brepols, 2012), p. 134.

124 DHC PE-BE/OV/7/10.

125 Sokoll, *Pauper Letters*, p. 196.

126 Calladine, *Diary*, p. 96.

127 Backhouse, *Worm-Eaten*, pp. 77–81. This sum is based on clothing and linen being grouped together in one category.

128 YALH Accession 38.

129 NRO PD 219/114. My italics.

130 James Hogg, *Memoirs of the Author's Life and Familiar Anecdotes of Sir Walter Scott*, ed. Douglas S. Mack (Edinburgh: Scottish Academic Press, 1972), p. 7.

131 Holcroft, *Memoirs*, p. 9.

132 Thom, *Rhymes*, pp. 10, 24–5.

133 Begiato, 'Selfhood and "Nostalgia"', pp. 234–6, 238.

134 Hogg, *Memoirs*, p. 7; Thom, *Rhymes*, p. 29.

135 Whitehead, *Autobiography*, pp. 27–8, 31.

136 Thomson, *Autobiography*, pp. 27–8.

137 Butler, *Narrative*, pp. 255–6.

138 Chris Dyer, 'The Material World of English Peasants, 1200–1540: Archaeological perspectives on the rural economy and welfare', *Agricultural History Review*, 62:1 (2014), pp. 20–1.

139 Love, *Life*, p. 62.

140 Butler, *Narrative*, pp. 23–4.

141 Shinn, 'Sketch', pp. 188–9.

142 Such as: Sara Horrell and Jane Humphries, '"The Exploitation of Little Children": Child labour and the family economy in the industrial revolution', *Explorations in Economic History*, 32 (1995), pp. 485–516; Humphries, *Childhood*; Griffin, *Liberty's Dawn*, pp. 57–83.

143 Griffin, *Bread Winner*, pp. 227–61; Emma Griffin, 'The Emotions of Motherhood: Love, culture, and poverty in Victorian Britain', *American Historical Review*, 123:1 (2018), pp. 60–85.

144 Payne, 'Rural Virtues', pp. 45–68; Barrell, *Dark Side*; Nichols, 'Motives of Control/ Motifs of Creativity', pp. 138–63.

145 Such as Figures 3.5 and 4.4.

146 Owens et al., 'Fragments', p. 216; Crewe and Hadley, "Uncle Tom", pp. 92–4; Dyer, 'Material World', pp. 20–1.

147 Emily Cuming, 'Makeshift Dolls and Working-Class Childhood', in Harley and Holmes, *Objects of Poverty*.

148 ERO D/P 203/18/1.

149 KHLC P347/18/1.

150 Bamford, *Early Days*, p. 69.

151 Calladine, *Diary*, p. 14.

152 Brown, *Narrative*, p. 7.

153 Anthony Errington, *Coals on Rails or the Reason of My Wrighting: The autobiography of Anthony Errington*, ed. P. E. H. Hair (Liverpool: Liverpool University Press, 1988), p. 31.

154 Emily Cuming, 'Spaces of Girlhood: Autobiographical recollections of late nineteenth- and early twentieth-century working class', in Harley, Holmes and Nevalainen, *Working Class at Home*, pp. 99–121; Begiato, 'Moving Objects', pp. 229–42.

155 Bethune, *Poems*, p. 3.

156 Place, *Autobiography*, esp. pp. 47–55, 59–60, 68–70.

157 NRO PD 216/90.

158 Farish, *Autobiography*, p. 15.

159 Such as William Heaton, who 'used to go out in the fields and woods around the village at meal-times, and listen to the songs of the summer birds'. Heaton, 'A Sketch', p. xxiii.
160 Ablett, *Reminiscences*, p. 49; Shaw, *Family Records*, pp. 20, 73; MacDonald, *Travels*, p. 159; Holcroft, *Memoirs*, p. 212.
161 Michael Guida, 'Songbirds in East London Homes, from Henry Mayhew to Charles Booth', in Harley, Holmes and Nevalainen, *Working Class at Home*, pp. 123–43.

7

Contrasting genders and locations

A number of historians of the middling sort and the elite have argued that women and populations in urban spaces were at the centre of fashion and consumption. This chapter explores the extent to which the same was true of the poor. Overall, the pauper inventories indicate that gender was not a significant factor in determining the poor's levels of material wealth. While on the one hand men appear to have owned greater quantities of goods and women were more likely to engage in tea consumption, there were far more similarities between the genders than differences. As for urban and rural location, the results show that people in rural areas were not excluded from the consumer market but tended to own most items in smaller numbers than their urban counterparts. This is because goods were more visible and available to consumers in towns, meaning that they were adopted by the indigent urban poor sooner than by those in the country.

Gender

Women have often been placed at the centre of consumption. When Neil McKendrick claimed that the late eighteenth century witnessed a 'consumer revolution', he argued that women's contributions to the household economy and their desire to emulate their social superiors was fundamental to this. McKendrick's interpretation drew upon contemporary commentators who claimed that women had an insatiable desire to consume, keep up with fashion and emulate the rich.[1] These desires could ultimately lead to the ruin of the family. In 1732, for instance, Bernard Mandeville claimed that the 'poorest Labourer's Wife in the Parish, who scorns to wear a strong wholesom Frize … will half starve her self and her Husband to purchase a second-hand Gown and Petticoat … because, forsooth, it is more genteel'.[2] Subsequent studies on gender and consumption have toned down these arguments,[3] yet historians are still trying to understand the extent to which

Contrasting genders and locations 207

the act of buying various goods followed gender-defined lines or whether status, location, wealth and other factors were more important.

Even in the face of 40 years of research since Neil McKendrick's thesis, it is difficult to determine the extent to which gender impacted consumer behaviour. Some studies have found that women were responsible for making mundane and repetitive purchases such as food, whereas in other homes men took a more active role in this. Likewise, with furniture and non-necessities some historians have argued that men made most of these procurements and others have contended that women predominantly bought these items.[4] We are thus left with as many questions as we have answers. As for the poor, we know that men and women, in both obvious and more subtle manners, owned different types of clothing to one another but were both interested in fashion and appearance.[5] However, with non-necessities and household items, the literature is almost entirely absent. It might be that men were more engaged in consumption, since they were better positioned in society and had the financial means, but more work is needed to confirm this. Beverley Lemire, for example, has found that sailors played an important role in shaping and influencing new fashions, since they were often the first people to own, use and sell various commodities from abroad.[6] Similarly, Emma Griffin has noted how boys and young men often had much more spending power than their sisters as they went into employment quickly, while girls and young women were torn between their paid and domestic responsibilities.[7]

Research is clearly needed to determine if poor men and women had different relationships to material goods. To this purpose, the pauper inventories have been divided by gender to quantitatively examine differences in consumption. Eleven inventories have been omitted as it was not possible to discern whether they were made of a man or woman's belongings, leaving a sample of 634 inventories. While for 1670 to 1769 the pauper inventories are fairly evenly matched between men and women, for 1770 to 1835 around three-fifths of the inventories are for households that were male-headed and two-fifths households that were female-headed.[8] With Dorset, Kent and Leicestershire/Rutland, the sample sizes are relatively small for some time periods (Figure 0.2), especially when divided by gender, so what they reveal must be taken with a pinch of salt. Nevertheless, there are more than enough inventories to reveal gendered trends, especially for Essex, Norfolk and the sample as a whole.

At least 78 per cent of the women in the sample were widows or spinsters and 2 per cent were married when their goods were inventoried. It is likely that the remaining 20 per cent of women were widows and spinsters, since the majority of pauper inventories made of married couples' belongings were in the husbands' name. The 2 per cent of married women had pauper inventories made in their names only because their husbands were living away, in a poorhouse or lunatic asylum. Unfortunately, I was able to determine the marital status of only 41 per cent of the men in the sample, since parish officials tended not to describe men in this way. Nonetheless, of these around 19 per cent were widowers or bachelors and 81 per cent were married.

This analysis of pauper inventories is based on the supposition that consumption can be said to have been influenced by gender if one gender owned more than the other. Of course, this is a problematic assumption. The wives of the married men might have made all the decisions on what to buy, and the widowed women may have continued to own their deceased husbands' goods. There is no way around these problems, but similar analyses by Lorna Weatherill using probate inventories and Maxine Berg using wills have revealed interesting trends, despite being subject to the same criticisms.[9] Moreover, most of the women in the sample had been widowed for a number of years and only around 10 per cent of them had lost their husbands a year or less before the inventory was made of their belongings. This figure is an under-representation but does suggest that most women in the sample had been widowed for long enough to have exerted sole influence on what items to keep and buy. Likewise, this form of analysis tells us little about the emotional attachment that men and women had to their possessions.[10] The section will mostly examine items which were typically seen as 'feminine' by contemporaries and scholars, especially tea goods and non-necessities. I would have also liked to have assessed 'masculine' goods such as coffee, tobacco and guns; however, because these belongings are rarely recorded in the inventories, any statistics on the goods would be meaningless. But first, we explore the average number of items recorded in inventories of male- and female-headed households.

Number of possessions

Counting the number of goods in inventories is crude, as appraisers were sometimes vague on the quantities of items that paupers owned. For example, officials might note 'some' of something or use unspecific terms such as 'bedding' and 'fire irons'. Despite this, as noted in Chapter 3, this is a revealing method of analysis which gives us a top-down view of changes. Overall, the inventories indicate that both men's and women's consumption grew over the long eighteenth century, but they also show that there were clear differences between the genders: at nearly every interval, inventories of male-headed households list more items than those of female-headed households (Table 7.1). This might be the simple result of male-headed households generally being larger than female-headed ones, since most of the men were married while most of the women were widowed or spinsters. Conversely, the results might indicate that husbands and wives had the greater desire and means to consume more. In either instance, while

Table 7.1 Average number of items owned by male and female paupers, 1670–1835

	Men			Women		
	1670–1769	1770–1835	All	1670–1769	1770–1835	All
Dorset	59	41	46	26	39	28
Essex	59	79	70	45	56	51
Kent	62	135	93	53	128	76
Leics/Ruts	29	51	41	18	49	33
Norfolk	35	64	41	27	46	29
All	45	73	58	32	60	40
Sample size	184	144	332	213	85	302

useful, we need to look further than aggregate changes as owning a large quantity of goods does not necessarily mean that somebody lived a materially richer life than somebody who had few belongings.

Tea

Tea has commonly been portrayed as a feminine commodity due to its connection to the 'private' sphere, feminine sociability, respectability and civility.[11] A key component of each of these concepts was that tea was taken by middling women in the domestic space using a large range of tea items. Groups of women would gather around the tea table, make polite conversation and conform to the unwritten rules regarding how they should present themselves.[12] To many contemporary minds, tea drinking had a positive impact on the lives of middling and elite women, as it was seen as healthy and promoted civility and sobriety.[13] Conversely, contemporaries often portrayed the poor's drinking of tea in a very negative manner.[14] Gender was at the centre of these views. Women were stereotyped as trying to copy their social superiors, often to the detriment of their bodies, husbands and children. In 1745 Simon Mason argued that:

> Tea in an Afternoon ... is an Expence they [the poor] cannot afford ... I beg the Women's Pardon, for, amongst the lower Set, the Men are excluded to partake, if at Home ... Wives are regaling with their Tea ... These poor Creatures, to be fashionable and imitate their Superiors, are neglecting their Spinning, Knitting, &c. spending what their Husbands are labouring hard for; their Children are in Rags, gnawing a brown Crust, while these Gossips are canvassing over the Affairs of the whole Town, making free with the good Name and Reputation of their Superiors ... And by these Meetings much Gossiping, Lying, Backbiting, is broached and carried on, and proves often destructive to others more sober and industrious.[15]

Just over a decade after this, Jonas Hanway, in 'An Essay on Tea', took these arguments further and claimed that drinking tea adversely affected mothers' and wet nurses' milk, harming the young and creating a future weak military in the process.[16] Meanwhile, husbands were emasculated as their wives wasted household resources on tea and used speech, in which they were well versed from idle chat at the tea table, to tame and manipulate their partners.[17] These views were both exaggerated and contradictory in numerous ways, yet the important point to take from them is that in the minds of contemporaries, tea and the ritualistic drinking of it were seen as gendered among both the rich and the poor.

Lorna Weatherill's research on probate inventories has suggested that there were few differences between men and women in their ownership of hot drinks utensils.[18] Her data, however, only covers 1675 to 1725 so it misses the following decades when tea was mass-consumed among the poor and increasingly tied to cultural practices such as feminine sociability. Table 7.2 records the tea-related items that men and women owned according to the pauper inventories. Inventories dated before 1770 are omitted, since few paupers owned tea items then. In contrast to the results found by Weatherill, these figures suggest that the drinking of tea was more closely associated with women than it was men in nearly every county. The largest difference between men and women was in Kent regarding tea paraphernalia, such as tea tables, tea caddies and teaspoons, as over four

Table 7.2 Percentage of paupers who owned tea items, by gender, 1770–1835

		Men	Women
Tea item (any type)	Dorset	56	67
	Essex	70	68
	Kent	62	89
	Leics/Ruts	46	50
	Norfolk	60	75
	All	63	69
Tea paraphernalia (any type)	Dorset	19	17
	Essex	32	34
	Kent	15	67
	Leics/Ruts	8	20
	Norfolk	25	31
	All	24	34
	Sample size	144	85

times as many women in the county appear to have owned these goods compared with men.

While these broad findings suggest that tea drinking was more commonly associated with women, it is important not to overstate this, as tea goods were also relatively common in households headed by men. Moreover, the practice of drinking tea using tea paraphernalia was not just something that predominantly happened in female-headed households, as stereotypical contemporary representations of the eighteenth century suggest.[19] Of course, these tea goods may have been used by wives, yet the results suggest that in Dorset, Essex and Norfolk, men and women were equally likely to own tea paraphernalia. It was only in Kent, and to a lesser extent Leicestershire/Rutland, where the sample indicates that there may have been pronounced gendered differences in the ownership of tea paraphernalia.

Non-necessities

Eighteenth-century contemporaries perceived women as less rational than men, having little control over their innate desire to buy luxuries and fashionable items.[20] Recent historical work has demonstrated that these contemporary ideas are misleading, as men too bought non-necessities and gained much enjoyment from doing so.[21] Yet in spite of this, research has revealed that there were subtle gendered differences. For example, Maxine Berg has found that eighteenth-century middling women had greater emotional attachments to their possessions, as they described their goods in greater detail and bequeathed larger numbers of household goods in their wills than men.[22] David Hussey and Margaret Ponsonby have compared the probate inventories of husbands with those of their widows to examine how the domestic environment changed when the wife became the head of household. They find that widowed women owned greater numbers of non-necessities and decorative goods than when their husbands were alive.[23] This section will now assess whether pauperised men and women owned different numbers of non-necessities to one another, and whether the results can be taken to infer that women had a greater desire than men to make their homes more comfortable and decorative.

Between 1670 and 1769, most men and women owned similar numbers of non-necessities to one another (Table 7.3). This is unsurprising, since possession of most types of non-necessities was relatively low among all the poor during this period. From 1770, the numbers of various non-necessities in inventories of male- and female-headed households increased, but the differences between the two sexes are not sizeable. With the genders owning similar numbers of goods to one another, this might suggest that in some areas women's lives were not always as bleak as some historians have argued, since even the poorest woman could

At home with the poor

Table 7.3 Percentage of paupers who owned non-necessities, by gender, 1670–1835

	Men			Women		
	1670–1769	1770–1835	All	1670–1769	1770–1835	All
Book	3	9	5	3	8	5
Chest of drawers	15	28	21	12	41	21
Gold/silver	0	1	<1	<1	5	2
Looking glass	16	32	23	9	35	17
Mahogany	0	3	2	0	7	2
Picture	2	11	6	2	7	4
Timepiece	3	24	12	<1	24	7
Sample size	184	144	332	213	85	302

make a home and have some comforts.[24] Moreover, the results in part break down our ideas as to what was seen as 'masculine' or 'feminine'. For example, clocks and watches have generally been portrayed as 'masculine' items, linked to manhood and display by contemporaries and historians alike.[25] Yet when clocks were in the domain of the house, they appear to have assumed a different meaning and to have been used to decorate the home and time household tasks, rather than functioning as displays of masculinity and distinction as watches did outside the home. Timepieces might have also been gendered in how they were used, with men taking charge of winding them and women polishing them.[26]

All the same, the results from the inventories are contradictory. On the one hand, it appears that men generally possessed greater quantities of goods, but women were more likely to own tea-related items. As for most non-necessities, the differences between the genders are negligible. These results suggest that men and women were both interested in new goods and that no one gender had a greater affinity for consumption than the other. More research is needed to find whether there were differences in consumption at an emotional, sensory or other level, but, at least in regard to ownership, gender was not a significant factor in dictating what possessions the poor acquired.

Urban–rural differences

In the late seventeenth century, there were just over 850 towns in England, containing between one-fifth and one-third of the population. By 1841, around another 100 towns emerged and approximately half of the English population lived in these spaces.[27] Following a relatively recent growth in

Contrasting genders and locations   213

work on retailing, we have a decent understanding of the importance of such urban areas as fashion centres and markets and shops.[28] Additionally, Carl Estabrook, Mark Overton et al., and others have shown that this concentration of activities and people in built spaces helped to lead to greater spending on both old and new goods among wealthier consumers.[29] However, for the poorer sort we know relatively little about whether the material face of poverty looked different in town and country. We know that the poor engaged in greater spending in London,[30] but without comparisons with other towns and rural locations it is difficult to gauge the extent to which the capital was extraordinary. The objective of this section is thus simple: it seeks to examine whether the poor had greater material wealth when they lived in towns.

The pauper inventories have been split into urban and rural samples to determine if consumer behaviour differed by location. Unfortunately, this is not a straightforward task, as there are numerous ways to define an area as urban or rural. These include population size, how nucleated the settlement was, the local economy, the numbers of people who were employed inside and outside of agriculture, the possession of a market, and whether the area had administrative and legal powers.[31] Of these, population is the most practical method to use, but this too is fraught with difficulties, since writers have employed a wide range of population limits to define towns. Some contemporaries saw places with only 200–300 inhabitants as towns.[32] Gregory King, Lorna Weatherill and Ken Sneath define a town as anywhere which had around 500 people in it.[33] Penelope Corfield and C. M. Law define an eighteenth-century urban area as possessing 2,500 people or more.[34] E. A. Wrigley uses 5,000 people as a limit and Jan de Vries excludes any areas which had fewer than 10,000 people in his study on European urbanisation.[35] With such a wide variation of opinion among contemporaries and historians, and because I am studying over 150 years of history in which there was significant urban change, I have defined any areas that possessed 1,000 or more people as urban.[36] Having consulted a wide range of sources to determine settlement sizes,[37] 35 inventories have been excluded as they were on the borderline between the two, leaving a sample of 114 urban and 496 rural pauper inventories. Of these, a further 61 inventories dated 1670–1709 have been excluded from the rural sample so that the rural inventories more closely match the urban inventories, which start from 1708.

Number of possessions

The analysis starts by assessing the numbers of goods that people in urban and rural areas owned. Between the late seventeenth century and first three-quarters of the eighteenth century, the results for town and country are similar, with urban paupers averaging 43 items each and rural paupers 36 (Table 7.4). However, after 1770, urban paupers appear to

Table 7.4 Average number of items owned by paupers, by urban–rural location, 1708–1835

	Rural			Urban		
	1710–69	1770–c.1834	All	1708–69	1770–1828	All
Dorset	32	45	36	-	-	-
Essex	53	56	54	-	-	-
Kent	50	120	72	-	-	-
Leics/Ruts	25	50	38	-	-	-
Norfolk	27	56	34	-	-	-
All	36	59	45	43	93	64
Sample size	262	173	435	64	48	114

have overtaken their rural peers by some degree and owned an average of 34 more items per inventory. At a regional level, the results suggest that paupers in rural Kent possessed higher quantities of goods than those who lived in other rural areas. After Kent is Essex, further suggesting that the poor in the home counties tended to consume goods in higher numbers than those who lived elsewhere. County-level urban variations are not included here, since the sample is too small to reliably calculate these differences.

Household goods

In this section we consider various household goods, starting with furniture. The pauper inventories indicate that paupers in urban spaces were more likely to own various items of furniture, such as chairs, cupboards and tables, than those who lived in rural areas (Table 7.5). However, the differences are not sizeable, including with chests of drawers, which one might have expected to have been owned in much higher numbers by paupers in urban areas since they were relatively new and fashionable in the eighteenth century.[38] Likewise, there appear to have been few urban–rural differences regarding some food- and drink-related items. Spits declined in both urban and rural spaces at comparable rates to one another, and saucepans increased at virtually identical rates between the two spaces. Knives and forks were possessed in similar numbers in town and country. Tea items were 10 per cent more common in urban spaces, but they were nevertheless still widespread in the country by 1770.

Other goods in Table 7.5 show starker differences in ownership. In both urban and rural spaces, earthenware became more common over time, but it was much more usual among urban paupers throughout the

Contrasting genders and locations 215

Table 7.5 Percentage of paupers who owned furniture and items related to eating, drinking and cooking, by urban–rural location, 1708–1835

	Rural			Urban		
	1710–69	**1770–1835**	**All**	**1708–69**	**1770–1829**	**All**
Chair	77	95	84	89	88	89
Chest of drawers	15	33	22	17	35	25
Cupboard	47	58	51	61	60	61
Dresser	10	15	12	14	25	18
Table	74	92	81	80	94	86
Earthenware	20	29	24	42	56	48
Glassware	6	13	9	8	27	16
Knives and forks	1	10	5	0	8	4
Saucepan	2	21	9	3	21	11
Spit-related item	21	10	17	22	15	20
Tea items	9	63	31	8	73	35
Sample size	262	173	435	64	48	114

eighteenth and nineteenth centuries. Glassware also became more widespread in towns and cities than in villages and hamlets. This suggests that earthenware and glassware first reached people who lived in towns, whereas those in rural areas kept to more traditional eating and drinking vessels made from pewter and wood until the later eighteenth century.

Likewise, with regard to non-necessities, urban paupers generally owned a wider range of goods than their rural counterparts (Table 7.6). Pictures helped to decorate and make the home more pleasant. They were recorded in 21 per cent of urban inventories compared with only 6 per cent of rural ones for 1770–1835. Looking glasses were functional and helped in domestic comfort, as they made the home appear more spacious, bright and pleasant. They appear to have been owned by roughly one-third of urban and rural paupers by the later eighteenth century; however, the results clearly indicate that they reached the urban poor first. Between 1710 and 1769, only 8 per cent of paupers in the country owned a looking glass compared with 30 per cent in towns. Although mahogany items were owned by few paupers, they also appear to have been slightly more common in urban areas. Interestingly, timepieces (mostly clocks) were

At home with the poor

Table 7.6 Percentage of paupers who owned non-necessities, by urban-rural location, 1708-1835

	Rural			Urban		
	1710–1769	1770–1835	All	1708–1769	1770–1829	All
Book	3	8	5	5	10	7
Looking glass	8	29	17	30	38	32
Mahogany	0	2	1	0	8	4
Pictures	1	6	3	5	21	11
Timepiece	3	25	12	0	19	8
Window curtains	0	5	2	23	13	11
Sample size	262	173	435	64	48	114

slightly more common in rural spaces, yet this was to be expected as there was less need for them in towns, where there were more public clocks for people to use.[39]

Recent studies have started to argue that a simple urban–rural dichotomy is misleading, since there was considerable overlap between the two spaces in aspects such as size, population and green spaces.[40] The results from this section have added to this literature by showing that paupers in the town and country could own similar types of furniture and other goods to one another and that items like clocks were not uncommon in rural areas. This indicates that one should not always assume that urban populations were more motivated to own certain goods than their rural neighbours, or that the availability of goods in urban areas meant that levels of consumption were highest in towns. Nevertheless, the results indicate that it is still important to analyse urban and rural trends, since the poor's ownership of most goods was slightly higher in urban spaces and significantly higher for items such as dishware and non-necessities.

The reasons for these differences are numerous but fairly obvious. People lived in close proximity to each other in towns, so the desire to distinguish oneself and follow contemporary fashions was probably greater. Moreover, these goods were more widely available to purchase in towns and visible to people in shop windows, as well as in the homes of friends and pubs. This meant that people may have been more aware of these items, or at least reminded of them at a more frequent rate, than those in the country were. From a sensory perspective, urban soundscapes were important in spreading information about what was new and desirable to own.[41] There would have also been more non-necessities available to paupers on the urban second-hand market and through informal means such as street sellers.[42]

Notes

1 McKendrick, 'The Consumer Revolution', pp. 9–33; Neil McKendrick, 'Home Demand and Economic Growth: A new view of the role of women and children in the industrial revolution', in Neil McKendrick (ed.), *Historical Perspectives: Studies in English thought and society in honour of J. H. Plumb* (London: Europa Publications, 1974), pp. 152–210.

2 Mandeville, *Fable of the Bees*, p. 132.

3 See for instance: John Brewer, 'The Error of Our Ways: Historians and the birth of consumer society', Lecture to the Cultures of Consumption Programme, The Royal Society (2003) (from: https://view.officeapps.live.com/op/view.aspx?src=http%3A%2F%2Fwww.consume.bbk.ac.uk%2Fworking_papers%2FBrewer%2520talk.doc&wdOrigin=BROWSELINK, accessed 16/12/2022).

4 Weatherill, 'A Possession of One's Own', pp. 131–56; Berg, 'Women's Consumption', pp. 415–34; Kowaleski-Wallace, *Consuming Subjects*; Finn, 'Men's Things', pp. 133–55; Finn, 'Women, Consumption and Coverture', pp. 703–22; Victoria de Grazia and Ellen Furlough (eds), *The Sex of Things: Gender and consumption in historical perspective* (Berkeley: University of California Press, 1996); Vickery, *Gentleman's Daughter*; Vickery, *Behind Closed Doors*; Amanda Vickery, 'His and Hers: Gender, consumption and household accounting in eighteenth-century England' *Past and Present*, 1: supplement (2006), pp. 12–38; David Hussey, 'Guns, Horses and Stylish Waistcoats? Male consumer activity and domestic shipping in late-eighteenth- and early nineteenth-century England', in David Hussey and Margaret Ponsonby (eds), *Buying for the Home: Shopping for the domestic from the seventeenth century to the present* (Aldershot: Ashgate, 2008), pp. 47–69; Lemire, *Business*, pp. 187–226; Harvey, *Little Republic*, esp. pp. 82–6, 99–133; Cohen, *Household Gods*, pp. 89–121; Whittle and Griffiths, *Consumption and Gender*; Jon Stobart, 'Status, Gender and Life Cycle in the Consumption Practices of the English Elite: The case of Mary Leigh, 1736–1806', *Social History*, 40:1 (2015), pp. 82–103.

5 Lemire, *Fashion's Favourite*; Lemire, *Dress, Culture*, pp. 43–74, 95–146; Lemire, *Business*; Styles, *Dress*; Toplis, *Clothing Trade*; Penelope Byrde, *The Male Image: Men's fashion in Britain 1300–1970* (London: B. T. Batsford, 1979); Jennie Batchelor, *Dress, Distress and Desire: Clothing and the female body in eighteenth-century literature* (Basingstoke: Palgrave, 2005).

6 Lemire, 'Men of the World', pp. 288–319.

7 Griffin, *Bread Winner*, pp. 31–2, 75–6, 84–5.

8 More precisely, for 1670–1769 46 and 54 per cent of the inventories were male- and female-headed respectively, while for 1770–1835 the percentages are 63 and 37 per cent.

9 Lorna Weatherill, 'A Possession of One's Own', pp. 131–56; Berg, 'Women's Consumption', pp. 415–34.

10 This has proven to be a fruitful method of analysis for the middling sort and has revealed that women often had a greater emotional connection to their possessions. See for example: Berg, 'Women's Consumption', pp. 415–34; Vickery, 'Women and the World of Goods', pp. 274–301; Vickery, *Gentleman's Daughter*; Finn, 'Men's Things', pp. 133–55.

11 On these concepts, see, among others: Leonore Davidoff and Catherine Hall, *Family Fortunes: Men and women of the English middle class 1780–1850* (London: Routledge, 2nd edn, 2002); Robert B. Shoemaker, *Gender in English Society 1650–1850: The emergence of separate spheres?* (Harlow: Longman, 1998); Amanda Vickery, 'Golden Age to Separate Spheres? A review of the categories and chronologies of English women's history', *Historical Journal*, 36:2 (1993), pp. 383–414; Vickery, *Gentleman's Daughter*; Harvey, *Little Republic*; Smith, *Making of Respectability*.

12 Smith, *Making of Respectability*, esp. pp. 121–31, 171–81; Smith, 'From Coffeehouse', pp. 148–64; Kowaleski-Wallace, *Consuming Subjects*, pp. 19–36; Berg, *Luxury and*

Pleasure, pp. 229–32; Emmerson, *British Teapots*, pp. 13–27; Stobart, *Sugar and Spice*, pp. 242–57; Vickery, *Behind Closed Doors*, pp. 271–6.

13 Kowaleski-Wallace, *Consuming Subjects*, pp. 19–36.

14 There are exceptions to these views, such as John Scott, who argued that tea helped labouring people to rest from work and was a good alternative to alcohol and other vices. John Scott, *Observations on the Present State of the Parochial and Vagrant Poor* (London: Edward and Charles Dilly, 1773), pp. 56–7.

15 Simon Mason, *The Good and Bad Effects of Tea Consider'd* (London: M. Cooper, 1745), pp. 41–2.

16 Jonas Hanway, 'An Essay on Tea', in Jonas Hanway, *A Journal of Eight Days Journey* (London: H. Woodfall, 1756), pp. 203–361.

17 Kowaleski-Wallace, *Consuming Subjects*, pp. 19–36; Mason, *Tea Consider'd*; Hanway, 'Essay on Tea'.

18 Weatherill, 'A Possession of One's Own', pp. 138–40.

19 Similar arguments have been made elsewhere, such as: Hussey and Ponsonby, *Single Homemaker*, pp. 125–7; Stobart, *Sugar and Spice*, pp. 196–8.

20 John Styles and Amanda Vickery, 'Introduction', in Styles and Vickery, *Gender, Taste*, pp. 2–14; Kowaleski-Wallace, *Consuming Subjects*.

21 Finn, 'Men's Things', pp. 133–55; Hussey, 'Guns, Horses', pp. 47–69.

22 Berg, 'Women's Consumption', pp. 415–34.

23 Hussey and Ponsonby, *Single Homemaker*, pp. 44–51.

24 As summarised in: Alannah Tomkins, 'Women and Poverty', in Hannah Barker and Elaine Chalus (eds), *Women's History: Britain 1700–1850: An introduction* (London: Routledge, 2005), pp. 152–73. This is not to say that being a woman was as easy as being a man over the industrial revolution. In fact, the gains of industrialisation were usually uneven and weighted towards men: Emma Griffin, 'Writing about Life Writing: Women, autobiography and the British industrial revolution', *Transactions of the Royal Historical Society*, 32 (2022), pp. 5–23.

25 Styles, *Dress*, pp. 96–107; Moira Donald, 'The Greatest Necessity of Every Rank of Men: Gender, clocks and watches', in Moira Donald and Linda Hurcombe (eds), *Gender and Material Culture in Historical Perspective* (Basingstoke: Palgrave, 2000), pp. 54–75; Helmreich, Hitchcock and Turkel, 'Rethinking Inventories', p. 15.

26 Doolittle, 'Time, Space', p. 258.

27 John Langton, 'Urban Growth and Economic Change: From the late seventeenth century to 1841', in Clark, *Cambridge Urban History*, Vol. 2, pp. 462–8.

28 Such as: Mui and Mui, *Shops and Shopkeeping*; Peter Borsay, *The English Urban Renaissance: Culture and society in the provincial town 1660–1770* (Oxford: Clarendon Press, 1989); Dyer, 'Small Market Towns', pp. 425–50; Jon Stobart (ed.), *A Cultural History of Shopping*, Vols. 1–6 (London: Bloomsbury, 2022).

29 Estabrook, *Urbane and Rustic*, pp. 128–91; Overton et al., *Production and Consumption*, pp. 153–65; Weatherill, *Consumer Behaviour*, pp. 70–90.

30 Styles, 'Lodging at the Old Bailey', pp. 61–80; Helmreich, Hitchcock and Turkel, 'Rethinking Inventories', pp. 1–25; Horrell, Humphries and Sneath, 'Conundrums', pp. 830–57.

31 Rosemary Sweet, *The English Town: Government, society and culture* (Harlow: Routledge, 1999), pp. 7–10; John Patten, *English Towns 1500–1700* (Folkestone: Wm Dawson & Sons, 1978), pp. 21–8; P. J. Corfield, *The Impact of English Towns 1700–1800* (Oxford: Oxford University Press, 1982), pp. 4–6; Borsay, *Urban Renaissance*, pp. 3–5; Peter Clark and Paul Slack, *English Towns in Transition 1500–1700* (Oxford: Oxford University Press, 1976), pp. 2–7; C. M. Law, 'Some Notes on the Urban Population of England and Wales in the Eighteenth Century', *Local Historian*, 10:1 (1972), p. 16.

32 Sweet, *English Town*, p. 7.

33 Corfield, *Impact of English Towns*, pp. 7–9; Joyce M. Ellis, *The Georgian Town 1680–1840* (Basingstoke: Palgrave, 2001), pp. 11–12, 14; Weatherill, *Consumer Behaviour*, pp. 73–4; Sneath, 'Consumption, Wealth', pp. 58–61.
34 Corfield, *Impact of English Towns*, pp. 4–7; Law, 'Some Notes', p. 16.
35 E. A. Wrigley, 'Urban Growth and Agricultural Change: England and the continent in the early modern period', *Journal of Interdisciplinary History*, 15:4 (1985), p. 684; Jan de Vries, *European Urbanization 1500–1800* (London: Routledge, 1984), pp. 18–19.
36 For further information on this definition of urban and rural spaces, see: Harley, *Norfolk Pauper Inventories*, pp. 38–42; Harley, 'Material Lives of the English Poor: A regional perspective', pp. 232–5.
37 Such as local and national censuses, hearth and tax records, trade directories, parish registers, and estimates made by historians and geographers.
38 Overton et al., for example, found that chests of drawers were more common in the towns. Overton et al., *Production and Consumption*, p. 157.
39 Glennie and Thrift, *Shaping*; Overton et al., *Production and Consumption*, p. 169; Estabrook, *Urbane and Rustic*, pp. 140–1.
40 For example: Peter Borsay, 'Nature, the Past and the English Town: A countercultural history', *Urban History*, 44:1 (2017), pp. 27–43; Paul A. Elliott, *British Urban Trees: A social and cultural history c.1800–1914* (Winwick: White Horse Press, 2016).
41 David Garrioch, 'Sounds of the City: The soundscape of early modern European towns', *Urban History*, 30:1 (2003), pp. 5–25.
42 YALH Accession 38; Tomkins, *Urban Poverty*, pp. 204–34; Lemire, *Business*; Margaret Spufford, *The Great Reclothing of Rural England: Petty chapmen and their wares in the seventeenth century* (London: Hambledon Press, 1983); Charlie Taverner, *Street Food: Hawkers and the History of London* (Oxford: Oxford University Press, 2023).

Conclusion

It was once usual for historians to argue that the poor had limited scope to engage in new forms of consumption and to emphasise what the poor *did not* own or what they had lost from industrialisation. The classic example of this is E. P. Thompson, who, in perhaps the most significant history book of the twentieth century, *The Making of the English Working Class*, argued that 'The "average" working man remained very close to subsistence level … His own share in the "benefits of economic progress" consisted of more potatoes, a few articles of cotton clothing for his family, soap and candles, some tea and sugar.'[1] These views have been diluted in recent decades following the work of Peter King, Craig Muldrew, John Styles and others, but unfortunately they continue to be rehearsed even by leading experts in the field. In a 2022 textbook on the 'consumer revolution', for example, Michael Kwass argued that 'whole swathes of the working classes … were barred from participating in the new consumer culture' and that 'all but the wealthiest peasants were excluded from the acquisition of new furnishings'.[2] Using the most diverse and largest sample of sources ever assembled to study the poor's material culture, this book shows once and for all that the poor were *not* barred from consumer markets but were *actively* engaged in consumption. Whether this was purchasing chairs over stools, acquiring more efficient fire irons, or purchasing non-necessities such as clocks and looking glasses, this change was significant and shows that indigent priorities had shifted. The poor were not content with a bare home and worked hard to create the best possible domestic environment that they could manage.

In no way does this book deny the existence of squalor. A significant proportion of the paupers who had their goods inventoried were no doubt destitute and owned little of utilitarian or financial value. Periods of being pauperised could be unceasing and draining for families who gradually pawned and sold off their possessions until the workhouse was their only option. Even the most detailed and extensive pauper inventories might be viewed as desolate compared with the probate inventories of the lower middling sort.[3] However, just because people were poor, that does not mean that they lived their whole lives in degradation and were satisfied with limited engagement in the consumer market. Even those who could not spare a penny could source goods creatively, such as through credit, the parish and neighbours. People made the best of what they owned, such as the pauper who used a stool as a table trestle or the individual who used a table leaf as a fire screen. As well as prolonged periods of hardship, most enjoyed phases in their lives when they had some disposable income and proactively amassed goods. Many people ended their days with only a few additional items of furniture, fire irons and tea goods, but these changes built on what their parents had owned and transformed their daily lives.

Despite taking a social and cultural approach to the home, this book has important implications for two touchstones of economic history: the importance of the wage in the standard of living debate, and the industrial revolution. First, the standard of living debate seeks to uncover whether living standards improved or declined over the eighteenth and nineteenth centuries. Today, most economic historians take a pessimistic stance and argue that consumption was low among the poor, because data shows that wages were stagnating and costs of living were high.[4] The results here show that indigent populations were clearly engaged in new forms of consumption, despite being financially poor and economically disadvantaged. People were very creative and used a wide variety of methods to make do, such as credit, theft, inheritance, gifts, charity, common rights, the second-hand market and welfare.[5] Studies need to move away from relying on wages and statistics on the cost of living to form conclusions and look at the bigger picture, which includes informal economies and the life-cycle of poverty.[6] People were not continually poor throughout their lifetimes and would go through periods when they had a decent disposable income and other times when they had to sell things to make ends meet.

Second, these results have important implications for our understanding of why the industrial revolution happened. At its most basic level, the industrial revolution can be conceived of as a production- or demand-led change in society. That is, there have been questions as to whether the industrial revolution stemmed from changes in production (such as supply and manufacture) which then spurred the consumer to acquire more, or demand from the consumer which then inspired industrialists to change the nature of production to meet need. Most economic historians suggest that the former was most important,[7] and, of course, there is no doubt that the poor benefited from many goods becoming more widely available, as well as improvements in production which helped to drive down prices. In fact, the better supply of goods in the home counties was an important reason why the poor there engaged in new forms of consumption before their counterparts elsewhere. However, this change in supply could not have been brought about without demand from the most numerically significant proportion of the English population: the poor. Their voices and the data presented in the book testify to this demand. It is no accident that industrialisation became more marked in Britain when the poor started to demand more goods during the second half of the eighteenth century.[8]

The reasons for people's changing demands are too numerous to name. There was no single motive which underpinned all consumption but a multitude of interwoven reasons which differed from one person to another. Nevertheless, the desire for adornment, comfort, convenience, respectability and identity appear to have been particularly important. The abodes of the poor have commonly been portrayed by contemporaries and historians as small and generally worn out – and in many respects these ideas were corroborated in Chapter 1. Yet despite this, the poor were able to enhance and personalise their spaces using various colours, materials and non-necessities such as looking glasses, clocks and pictures. Everyday life became a little easier when people had a comfortable bed to get into after a hard day's work or owned a chest of drawers for conveniently organising their clothes into. Aged and sub-standard items such as stained bedsheets and worn furniture were present in dwellings not only because people could not afford better ones. These items could be held on to because they were familiar and evoked feelings of safety, comfort and joy in their owners. Even pots with broken handles and cracked mirrors continued to be used by householders, as they still had some use and were viewed as dependable despite being damaged. Respectability was a key precursor to the actions and decisions of many people, and in this spirit the poor might consume what they needed or wanted in accordance with what they viewed as most aligned to this idea. While the poor never had the means to be as selective in the possessions they owned as those with larger incomes did, they nonetheless often exercised an element of choice, led by motivations which varied and depended upon the items in question.

Going forward, the poor need to be taken much more seriously by scholars of material culture and consumer behaviour. It is far too common – no matter the period, country or item(s) that are considered – to open up any book and see the poor conspicuously absent. Although difficult to find and often very tricky to use, in contrast to what others have said, there are enough sources to study indigent populations.[9] Moreover, these sources have been shown to be representative of the millions of others who did not leave any records behind.[10] As happened with early work on probate inventories,[11] it is hoped that this book will inspire readers to build on these findings and expand the analysis, through looking at the items covered here in more detail, focusing on different sub-groups of the poor, and considering further why and how the poor were interested in consumption. Much more is needed on the many informal economies that the poor used to engage in consumer markets. We need to know which informal economies were most important to the poor and when in their lifetimes they tended to turn to them, as well as whether particular networks were used for specific goods and how the poor felt about them. This is crucial to further unlocking the role of demand and understanding how people could be simultaneously poor and active consumers. Moreover, there are many more items and factors which await their historian. We know little, for example, about the poor's consumption and use of religious objects or the ways in which they might have shopped for pleasure. The potential for future work is vast, and this research has only begun to scratch the surface.

Notes

1 Thompson, *Making*, p. 351. Similarly, also see: Malcolmson, *Life and Labour*, p. 149; G. E. Fussell, *The English Rural Labourer: His home, furniture, clothing and food from Tudor to Victorian times* (London: Batchworth Press, 1949), pp. 68–81; Fernand Braudel, *Civilization and Capitalism 15th–18th century*, Vol. 1: *The Structures of Everyday Life: The limits of the possible*, trans. Sian Reynolds (London: William Collins Sons & Co., 1985), p. 283; Stearns, *Consumerism*, pp. 1–14.

2 Michael Kwass, *The Consumer Revolution, 1650–1800* (Cambridge: Cambridge University Press, 2022), pp. 35, 216.

3 Harley, 'Consumption and Poverty', pp. 81–104.

4 Horrell and Humphries, 'Old Questions', pp. 849–80; Sara Horrell, 'Home Demand', pp. 561–604; Charles H. Feinstein, 'Pessimism Perpetuated', pp. 625–58.

5 King and Tomkins, *Poor in England*.

6 In a similar vein, see: John Hatcher and Judy Z. Stephenson (eds), *Seven Centuries of Unreal Wages: The unreliable data, sources and methods that have been used for measuring standards of living in the past* (London: Palgrave, 2018).

7 Mokyr, 'Demand vs. Supply', pp. 981–1008; Horrell, 'Consumption, 1700–1870', p. 247.

8 This is not to say that the industrial revolution was sudden or akin to a 'take-off' as writers such as W. W. Rostow have argued. Rather, as decades of research have shown, change was much more gradual and prolonged, even if the second half of the eighteenth century remained a vital turning point.

9 Weatherill, *Consumer Behaviour*, p. 194; Pounds, *Hearth and Home*, p. 184; Overton et al., *Production and Consumption*, p. 170.

10 Discussed further in: Harley, *Norfolk Pauper Inventories*, pp. 47–53, 63–5; Harley, 'Consumption and Poverty', pp. 81–104; Harley, 'Pauper Inventories, Social Relations', pp. 375–98.

11 Weatherill, *Consumer Behaviour*; Shammas, *Pre-Industrial Consumer*.

Select bibliography

Archival sources[1]

Bolton Archives and Local Studies Service, Bolton

PGB/7/1

Canterbury Cathedral Archives and Library, Canterbury

U3/76/18/B/3	U3/221/12/2–3	U3/100/16/24	U3/100/11A/2*
U3/100/12/B/30	U3/154/18/1	U3/154/11/21	U3/191/18/4
U3/138/11/3*	U3/146/18/1	U3/117/12/1	U3/235/8/1
U3/235/18/2	U3/245/16/92–93	U3/269/16/1	U3/174/8/A/18

Dorset History Centre, Dorchester

PE-ABB/OV/1/3/1	PE-BE/OV/1/3–7	PE-BE/OV/7/1–2	PE-BE/OV/7/4–5
PE-BE/OV/9/1	PE-BE/OV/7/5	PE-BE/OV/7/10	PE-BER/OV/11/2*
PE-BER/OV/1/9–10*	PE-BCD/OV/1/3	PE-BF/OV/4/2	PE-BF/OV/9/2
MICRO/R/1419	PE-BDW/OV/6/3/3	PE-BRY/OV/1	PE-BCN/OV/4/2*
PE-BCN/OV/3/2*	PE-BBK/OV/1/1–2*	PE-CAM/OV/7/1–8*	PE-CAN/OV/1/2
PE-CAS/OV/1/2	PE-CDM/OV/1/1*	PE-CEA/OV/1/4	PE-CHH/OV/1/1
PE-COC/OV/2/1*	PE-COC/OV/2/4	NG-PR/1/D/2/1–2	NG-PR/1/D/1/3
PE-EST/OV/1/1*	PE-FOL/OV/1/1	PE-FOM/OV/10/2	PE-HAM/OV/1/1*
PE-HAZ/VE/1/1	PE-HIL/OV/2/7	PE-LOB/OV/1/2	PE-LYD/OV/1/1–3

Select bibliography   **225**

PE-LR/OV/1/1	PE-LR/VE/1/1	PE-MOT/OV/3/2	PE-OBN/OV/1/1*
PE-PDH/OV/1/1*	PE-PL/OV/1/3/4–5	PE-POW/OV/1/2*	PE-PUD/OV/1/1
PE-PUD/OV/1/4	PE-SHG/OV/7/1	PE-SPV/OV/1/2*	PE-SPV/OV/1/4
PE-SML/OV/11/1	PE-SW/OV/1/3*	PE-SW/OV/1/5*	PE-SW/VE/1/1
PE-TTG/OV/1/1*	PE-WA/OV/1/2*	PE-WOR/VE/1/1*	PE-WCC/OV/8/1
PE-WSG/OV/1/2	PE-WMN/OV/1/1	PE-WWH/OV/1/1	

Essex Record Office, Chelmsford

D/P 204/5/1	D/P 204/12/1*	D/P 221/18/1	D/P 336/12/2–3*
D/P 263/12/7–8	D/P 263/18/8	D/P 18/12/1	D/P 18/12/4
D/P 18/12/6–7*	D/P 157/12/2	D/P 157/18/9	D/P 157/12/7
D/P 157/18/10*	D/P 157/8/3*	D/P 63/12/4*	D/P 153/12*
D/P 146/8	D/P 215/18/1–2	D/P 215/18/6	D/P 173/12/2
D/P 51/18/2	D/P 264/18/14–15*	D/P 264/18/35	D/P 264/18/9
D/P 264/8/10	D/P 248/18/1–2*	D/P 19/18/1	D/P 239/8
D/P 162/12/1–2	D/P 219/12/29*	D/P 48/12/1*	D/P 94/12/6
D/P 94/8/1	D/P 94/8/12	D/P 94/18/54*	D/P 94/18/45
D/P 94/18/55	D/P 36/28/3	D/P 94/18/38	D/P 355/8/2*
D/P 36/18/1	D/P 36/36/12/14	D/P 36/36/11/6A	D/P 36/36/12/6
D/P 200/12/3–6	D/P 200/18/8*	D/P 246/18/1	D/P 246/18/5
D/P 246/18/14–15	D/P 246/12/4	D/P 203/18/1*	D/P 203/18/14
D/P 138/18/6	D/P 138/12/1	D/P 138/8/7	D/P 245/18/4–5*
D/P 176/12/1	T/R 300/1	D/P 178/1/15	D/P 178/18/8
D/P 177/12/8*	D/P 193/12/2	D/P 186/12/1*	D/P 186/12/4
D/P 186/12/6	D/P 118/8/6	D/P 26/12/11	D/P 26/18/7*
D/P 26/12/8–9	D/P 26/18/2	D/P 209/12/4	D/P 209/18/4
D/P 168/12/6	D/P 231/12/1*	D/P 14/18/11*	D/P 14/18/1
D/P 369/18/1	D/P 369/12/2*	D/P 249/8/2	D/P 57/18/1*
D/P 171/8/2	D/P 171/18/1	D/P 171/8/3–4	D/P 139/8/1
D/P 139/8/16	D/P 139/18/10	D/P 103/12/1–2	D/P 210/18/4*
D/P 210/12/6	D/P 210/8	D/P 179/18/1	D/P 11/18/3–5
D/P 11/18/17	D/P 11/28/12	D/P 232/18/7*	D/P 27/8/2
D/P 137/18/2	D/P 184/18/2	D/P 289/8/1	D/P 195/12/3
D/P 195/18	D/P 96/18/2	D/CR 164	D/P 4/18/8*
D/P 4/18/14	D/P 4/18/17	D/P 4/12/8	D/P 4/12/11
D/P 4/12/13	D/P 4/18/25–26*	D/P 4/18/5	D/P 4/18/30

226 Select bibliography

D/P 4/18/44* D/P 4/18/52 D/P 4/8/7* D/P 4/18/38
D/P 4/18/75 D/P 42/12/1 D/P 64/18/7 D/P 64/18/8*
D/P 64/18/5 D/P 56/8/2 D/P 143/12/1 D/P 31/8/3–4
D/P 169/18/2 D/P 169/12/1 D/P 234/12/1 D/P 35/8/1*
D/P 100/12/1* D/P 95/12/2* D/P 307/12/1–2 D/P 388/18/1–2*
D/P 297/8/2 D/P 194/18/2 D/P 194/18/4* D/P 220/28/1
D/P 220/12/1 D/P 220/18/6–7* D/P 220/12/3 D/P 220/12/4*
D/P 66/12/2 D/P 201/12/2 D/P 235/12/2–3* D/P 305/12*
D/P 138/12/3 D/P 82/8/1C D/P 287/8/1 D/P 287/5/3*
D/P 197/18/4* D/P 197/12/6* D/P 197/18/2 D/P 202/18/5–6*
D/P 55/12/1* D/P 7/8/1* D/P 40/8/1–2* D/P 40/18/3*
D/P 332/18/10 D/P 129/18/3 D/P 129/18/5 D/P 129/11/2
D/P 60/8/4* D/B 2/PAR10/5 D/B 2/PAR10/9 D/B 2/PAR9/33
D/P 253/18/3* D/P 259/12/11 D/P 51/18/1 D/P 259/8/4*
D/P 259/18 D/P 300/12/3* D/P 128/18/18–19 D/P 128/18/1–2
D/P 128/28/58 D/P 211/8/2 D/P 322/18/31* D/P 322/12/2
D/P 140/18/3–4 D/P 141/12/2 D/P 86/8/1* D/P 86/12
D/P 384/12/4–5* D/P 384/8/1* D/P 21/18/10–11 D/P 21/18/33
D/P 98/12/3 D/P 299/12/0 D/P 299/12/1C* D/P 299/8/1
D/P 152/12/2 D/P 152/18/9* D/P 152/18/4 D/P 8/18/4
D/P 357/12/1* D/P 357/12/3 D/P 357/8/2 D/P 164/18/6
D/P 327/12/2 D/P 105/18/5–6* D/P 105/12/1–2 D/P 105/8/1–2*
D/P 105/1/19 D/P 240/12/3* D/P 240/18/1* D/P 117/12/7
D/P 117/8/6–8* D/P 117/18/2F D/P 88/12/1 D/P 88/18/7*
D/P 91/8 D/P 119/12/1* D/P 119/8/3 D/P 119/8/5
D/P 39/18/2 D/P 236/18/1* D/P 337/12/1* D/P 30/18/4
D/P 30/18/1 D/P 167/8/1 D/P 167/12/30 D/P 185/12/1–2
D/P 185/18/3–4* D/P 50/8/3 D/P 50/18/3 D/P 50/18/6
D/P 275/18/4

Kent History Library Centre, Maidstone

PRC11 PRC27 DRb/Pi P10/18/3
P26/12/7 U908/E36 P36/11/1 P41/5/1*
P42/18/1 P45/18/4 P222B/12/1* P222B/16/1*
P78/12/1 P78/12/10 P89/12/3 U908/Q5
P89/12/17* EK/U1496/E1 EK/U1496/E4 U908/E15/1
P99/18/2* P99/12/2 P99/12/4–5 P99/8/1

Select bibliography

P100/18/3	De/JQs1	P125/18/1	P145/8/1
P145/28/7	P145/21/1	P145/8/2	U120/E2
U120/T97	EK/U270/E14	P152/12/3–4*	P157/8/1
P163/11/2	P173/12/1	P173/18/3	P173/28/1
P178/18/19B	P178/12/8	P178/18/14*	P178/18/19A-20
P178/18/30	P178/18/8	P181/18/18/1–8*	P181/28/3/3
P181/8/3/1	P181/18/10	P164/18/2	P164/8/1
P192/12/2	P192/18/8	P192/18/10	P202/12/2*
P202/18/5*	P202/8/1–2*	P202/18/7	P202/12/9
P206/12/3	P206/18/5	P206/12/4–5	P206/28/6–7*
P207/11/2	P207/11/5*	P212/12/1*	P216/12/1
P216/8/1	P216/12/2	P222/12/1*	P222/28/5*
P222/12/2	P222/12/10*	P222/12/4	P222/10/1
P222/18/10	U908/E16/1	P224/18/12	P224/18/18
P224/12/2	P224/18/7–9	P224/18/19–20	P224/18/21–22
P224/18/10–11	P224/8/1*	P224/18/24	P224/8/3
P224/12/14	P242/28/1	P82/12/1*	P168/12/7
P168/18/1	P241/19/10	U24/E26	P244/16/5
P247/18/3	P247/21/1	P250/12/2	P253/16/1
P309/11/4	P309/18/27	P279/8/2–3*	P287/18/5*
P289/7/1	P289/8/2*	P289/18/1–2*	P295/8/3
Qb/ZB/91	P308/12/1–2	P308/12/8	P312/11/1*
P321/12/3*	P321/18/3	P339/11/4	P339/28/39–40
P339/28/32	P339/11/7	P339/8/1*	U442/O22/3–4
P344/18/18	P344/18/20*	P344/18/8	P344/18/9
P344/18/5	P317/12/B/2	P317/16/1	P347/12/4*
P347/18/10*	P347/18/1	P347/12/10	P347/12/12
P347/18/3	P364/18/2–4A	P364/18/19	P364/18/16
P364/18/7	P364/18/9	U442/E8/6	P243/18/164
P285/18/3–4*	P285/12/2	P389/6/E/2	P389/16/4
P390/12/93	P390/12/14	P390/18/9	P390/12/15
P390/18/2*	P406/28/2	P406/12/6	P406/18/17

Lancashire Record Office, Preston

DDSC 2/10	QSP/838/4	FRL 2/1/33/95	DDSC 2/9
PR 3053/14/26	QSP/1556/33	PR 1349	PR 3440/7/18
PR 2392/1	PR 2392/5–6	PR 3073/7/1	QSP/2477/39

228 Select bibliography

PR 3431/7/1	PR 2851/12/6–7	PR 1288	DDX 188/24
RCCL/2/2–3	RCCL/2/24	UDCL/12/2*	UDCL/9/7*
MBC/637*	DDX 8/3	QSP/2453/7	QSP/2453/8–9
MBRA/acc9017/11	PR 627	PR 2853/1/5*	QSP/1629/15*
PR 2956/3/13	PR 2956/3/4	PR 2956/3/15	PR 2995/11/2
QSP/2348/3	PR 2942/4/5	RCHY 2/1/45	QSP/1824/9
PR 2725/17	PR 2725/19	DDHE 62/154	QSP/1564/5
DDPR 16/9	QSP/1740/6	QSP/374/14	QSP/391/6
DDX/8/66–67	DDHE 108/16	QSP/1374/6–7	DDHE 111/38
PR 2765/1	DDHE 116/21a		

Liverpool Record Office and Local History Library, Liverpool

354 EVE/5/123

Manchester Archives and Local History, Manchester

M10/4/2/1a	L82/2/1	L21/3/4/1	L21/7/2/1–2
M10/16/5/23			

Medway Archives and Local Studies Centre, Rochester

P52/18/6*	P110/18/52	P193/12/3	P193/12/5
P193/12/15	P193/18/1	P306/18/17	P336/12/12
P336/12/14	P343/18/1–3		

Norfolk Record Office, Norwich

PD 548/71	PC 88/1–2*	PD 326/58	PD 187/58
PD 309/51–53*	PD 276/35	PD 434/42	PD 111/170*
PD 111/114–115*	PD 477/43*	PD 712/49*	MC 2941/2, 1025X2*
PD 254/92	PD 193/93*	HIL 3/61–2, 879X4	PD 603/128
PC 15/42	PD 100/335	PD 100/139–140	PD 100/105
PD 100/155	PD 219/94	PD 219/114*	PD 447/57–58
PD 144/67	PD 421/133*	PD 50/47	PD 50/44*
PD 50/68	PD 50/71*	PD 50/45–46*	PD 34/39
PD 489/29–31*	PD 489/51*	PD 5/22	PD 236/51*

PD 437/91	PD 435/27	PD 382/40	PD 382/45*
PD 382/78	PD 678/36	PD 575/128*	PD 629/50*
PD 2/97	PD 2/106	PD 2/167	PD 2/134
PD 563/49*	PD 642/38	PD 642/35*	PD 713/64
PD 713/55	PD 691/74	PD 521/26*	PD 521/34
PD 521/37	PD 439/67	PD 108/84	MC 76/50, 534X10*
PD 595/22*	PD 672/6	PD 653/98	PD 404/54
PD 710/68*	PD 313/41	PD 93/31	PD 83/15
PD 209/211	PD 338/13	PD 654/48	PD 711 box 47
PD 499/79*	PD 53/46	PD 295/93–94*	PD 295/3
PD 295/102*	PD 295/103	PD 295/113	PD 295/116–117*
PD 295/133	PD 295/106*	PD 465/59	PD 335/9
PD 80/46	PD 358/33	PD 358/41–42*	PD 358/61*
PD 102/32*	PD 102/36	PD 337/158*	PD 147/31
PD 122/50	PD 122/54*	PD 122/38–39*	PD 611/37–38*
PD 52/404	PD 52/206–207	PD 44/32	PD 199/54
PD 708/84*	PD 228/104	PD 515/73	PC 35/13
PD 216/90*	PD 496/64	PD 496/79	PD 218/3
PD 27/21*	PD 553/79*	PD 78/91	PD 78/66*
PD 259/6	PD 259/46	PD 388/74	PD 316/46*

Oldham Local Studies and Archives, Oldham

B-UDR 2/4/5/10/14

Record Office for Leicestershire, Leicester and Rutland, Wigston

DE 199/24*	DE 199/2–3*	DE 437/11*	DE 432/15
DE 432/13/1–3	DE 5199/6*	17D64/F/7	DE 2492/21
DE 3352/239–241	DE 2249/80	DE 765/6	DE 3367/242
DE 3367/255	DE 2774/72	DE 2774/281	DE 3066/2*
DE 1617/9*	DE 5242/2	DE 659/18*	DE 2753/11*
DE 2575/71	DE 729/95	DE 1166/8–9	DE 2209/63*
45D31/8	DE 2299/141*	DE 390/42–43	DE 801/19
DE 801/38*	DE 539/4	7D59/4*	23 D 52/8
DE 1425/106	DE 1369/40–42*	DE 1369/46	DE 2559/38
DE 2559/127	DE 2559/131	DE 1881/44	DE 1938/18

DE 1212/7	DE 2132/3	DE 1212/6	DE 1010/1*
DE 287/8	DE 2694/281	DE 1668/86*	DE 1266/9
DE 2461/60*	DE 491/14*	DE 640/6	DE 2401/19
DE 812/18	DE 394/49*	DE 1437/11	DE 1416/142
DE 157/40	DE 400/1–3*	DE 1784/25	DE 1784/36*
DE 625/1	DE 1831/18*	DE 384/41	DE 4492/106
DE 308/14	DE 260/2–3*		

Rochdale Local Studies and Archive, Rochdale

F/8/4/MATT/4

Salford City Archive, Salford

P12/AZ7/1–5   P12/024/1–27

St Helens Local History and Archives Library, St Helens

PAR/2/6/1–79*   PAR/10/15

Suffolk Archives, Ipswich

HD 1025/1–2	HA 42/1–2	HD 1888/1	HD 368/1
HA 11/A13/10			

Tameside Local Studies and Archives Centre, Ashton-under-Lyne

PCA/DEN/11/1*

Wigan Archives Service, Leigh

TR/Ab/1–3	TR/Ab/5–7	TR/Ath/C/2/37–58	TR/Ath/F/13*
TR/Ath/F/17	TR/Ath/C/7/17	TR/Hi/C/7/2	DP 17/12/23/1–40
DP 17/12/3	DP 17/12/11	DP 17/8/3	DP 17/12/7
DP 17/17/21	DP 17/17/15	DDHE 87/68a	DDX 188/36

York Archives and Local History, York

Accession 38

Select bibliography   231

Published primary materials

Autobiographies and diaries of the poor/working people

Ablett, William, *Reminiscences of an Old Draper* (London: Sampson Low, Marston, Searle & Rivington, 1876).

An old potter, 'When I Was a Child', in John Burnett (ed.), *Useful Toil: Autobiographies of working people from the 1820s to 1920s* (London: Penguin, 1976), pp. 297–304.

Anderson, Robert, *The Poetical Works of Robert Anderson … to Which Is Prefixed the Life of the Author, Written by Himself* (Carlisle: B Scott, 1820).

Anonymous, 'Autobiography of a Navvy', in John Burnett (ed.), *Useful Toil: Autobiographies of working people from the 1820s to 1920s* (London: Penguin, 1976), pp. 55–63.

Anonymous, *Memoirs of a Printer's Devil; Interspersed with Pleasing Recollections, Local Descriptions and Anecdotes* (Gainsborough: J. M. Mozley, 1793).

Ashley, James, 'Account of Life', in the Burnett Archive of Working Class Autobiographies, Brunel University, London (from: http://bura.brunel.ac.uk/handle/2438/9356, accessed 12/6/2020).

Bamford, Samuel, *Early Days* (London: Simpkin, Marshall, & Co., 1849).

Bangs, Benjamin, *Memoirs of the Life and Convincement of that Worthy Friend Benjamin Bangs* (London: Luke Hinde, 1757).

Barker, Joseph, *The Life of Joseph Barker, Written by Himself*, ed. John Thomas Barker (London: Hodder and Stoughton, 1880).

Barker, Robert, *The Unfortunate Shipwright; or, Cruel Captain* (London: self-published, 1758).

Barker, Robert, *The Second Part of the Unfortunate Shipwright; or the Blind Man's Travels* (London: self-published, 1771).

Barlow, Edward, *Barlow's Journal of His Life at Sea in the King's Ships*, ed. Basil Lubbock (London: Hurst & Blackett, 1934).

Basset, Josiah, *The Life of a Vagrant or the Testimony of an Outcast* (London: Charles Gilpin, 1850).

Bent, Charles, *Autobiography of Charles Bent, a Reclaimed Drunkard* (Sheffield: D. T. Ingham, 1866).

Bethune, Alexander, *Memoirs of Alexander Bethune, embracing Selections from His Correspondence*, ed. William McCombie (Aberdeen: George and Robert King, 1845).

Bethune, John, *Poems by the Late John Bethune; with a Sketch of the Author's Life, by His Brother* (Edinburgh: Adam and Charles Black, 1840).

Bewley, George, *A Narrative of the Christian Experiences of George Bewley, Late of the City of Corke* (Dublin: I. Jackson, 1750).

Bezer, John James, 'The Autobiography of One of the Chartist Rebels of 1848', in David Vincent (ed.), *Testaments of Radicalism: Memoirs of working class politicians 1790–1885* (London: Europa Publications Limited, 1997), pp. 147–87.

Black, James, 'Local Autobiography: Glasgow in the past century', *Glasgow Herald*, 5 May 1851, p. 6.

Blacket, Joseph, *Specimens of the Poetry of Joseph Blacket, with an Account of His Life*, ed. Mr Pratt (London: self-published, 1809).

Blincoe, Robert, *A Memoir of Robert Blincoe, by John Broad* (Manchester: J. Doherty, 1832).

Bownas, Samuel, *The Life, Travels, and Christian Experiences of Samuel Bownas* (Lindfield: self-published, 1836).

Brown, John, *Sixty Years' Gleanings from Life's Harvests: A Genuine Autobiography* (Cambridge: J. Palmer, 1858).

Brown, William, *A Narrative of the Life and Adventures of William Brown* (York: T. Weightman, 1829).

Brunskill, Stephen, *The Life of Stephen Brunskill of Orton, Sixty Years a Wesleyan Methodist Local Preacher* (London: Whittaker and Co., 1837).

Burgess, John, *No Continuing City: The diary and letters of John Burgess, a craftsman from Sussex, from 1785 to 1819*, ed. Donald F. Burgess (Redhill: self-published, 1989).

Butler, Robert, *Narrative of the Life and Travels of Serjeant B – Written by Himself* (Edinburgh: David Brown, 1823).

Buxton, Richard, *A Botanical Guide to the Flowering Plants ... together with a Sketch of the Author's Life* (London: Longman and Co., 1849).

Calladine, George, *The Diary of Colour-Serjeant George Calladine, 19th Foot, 1793–1837*, ed. M. L. Ferrar (London: Eden Fisher & Co., 1922).

Campbell, Charles, *Memoirs of Charles Campbell, at Present Prisoner in the Jail of Glasgow* (Glasgow: James Duncan & Co., 1828).

Candler, Ann, *Poetical Attempts, by Ann Candler, a Suffolk Cottager; with a Short Narrative of her Life* (Ipswich: John Raw, 1803).

Carter, Henry, *The Autobiography of a Cornish Smuggler (Captain Harry Carter, of Prussia Cove) 1749–1809*, ed. John B. Cornish (Truro: Gibbings & Co., 1894).

Carter, Thomas, *Memoirs of a Working Man* (London: Charles Knight & Co., 1845).

Carter, Thomas, *A Continuation of the Memoirs of a Working Man* (London: Charles Cox, 1850).

Carvosso, William, *The Efficacy of Faith in the Atonement of Christ: Exemplified in a memoir of Mr William Carvosso*, ed. Benjamin Carvosso (London: J. Mason, 2nd edn, 1836).

Castle, John, 'The Diary of John Castle', in the Burnett Archive of Working Class Autobiographies, Brunel University, London (from: http://bura.brunel.ac.uk/handle/2438/9430, accessed 12/6/2020).

Chubb, Thomas, *The Posthumous Works of Mr Thomas Chubb*, Vol. 1 (London: R. Baldwin, 1748).

Clare, John, *John Clare's Autobiographical Writings*, ed. Eric Robinson (Oxford: Oxford University Press, 1983).

Claxton, Timothy, *Hints to Mechanics, on Self-Education and Mutual Instruction* (London: Taylor and Walton, 1839).

Cooper, George, *The Story of George Cooper, Stockport's Last Town Crier, 1824–1895*, ed. Anne Swift (no place or publisher, 1974).

Crocker, Charles, *The Vale of Obscurity, the Lavant, and Other Poems* (Chichester: W. Mason, 1830).

Davenport, Allen, *The Life and Literary Pursuits of Allen Davenport*, ed. Malcolm Chase (Aldershot: Scolar Press, 1994).

Davidson, Margaret, *The Extraordinary Life and Christian Experience of Margaret Davidson (as Dictated by Herself)*, by Edward Smyth (Dublin: Bennett Dugdale, 1782).

Donaldson, Joseph, *Recollections of an Eventful Life Chiefly Passed in the Army* (Glasgow: W. R. McPhun, 1824).

Select bibliography · **233**

Downing, James, *A Narrative of the Life of James Downing (a Blind Man), Late* (London: J. Haddon, 5th edn, 1817).

Dunhill, Snowden, *The Life of Snowden Dunhill of Spaldington, East Riding (1766–1838)*, ed. David Neave (Howden: Mr Pye Books, 1987).

Dunning, Thomas, 'Reminiscences of Thomas Dunning', in David Vincent (ed.), *Testaments of Radicalism: Memoirs of working class politicians 1790–1885* (London: Europa Publications Limited, 1997), pp. 115–46.

Errington, Anthony, *Coals on Rails or the Reason of My Wrighting: The autobiography of Anthony Errington*, ed. P. E. H. Hair (Liverpool: Liverpool University Press, 1988).

Farish, William, *The Autobiography of William Farish: The struggles of a handloom weaver*, ed. Owen R. Ashton and Stephen Roberts (London: Caliban Books, 1996).

G. J., *The Prisoner Set Free: The narrative of a convict in the Preston house of correction, with a few remarks from the Rev. John Clay* (Preston: L. Clarke, 1846).

Gibbs, John, *The Life and Experience of … John Gibbs* (Lewes: self-published, 1827).

Gifford, William, *Memoir of William Gifford, written by Himself* (London: Hunt and Clarke, 1827).

Gooch, Richard, *Memoirs, Remarkable Vicissitudes … of Cassiel, The Norfolk Astrologer* (Norwich: Benjamin Norman, 1852).

Green, John, *The Vicissitudes of a Soldier's Life, or a Series of Occurrences from 1806 to 1815* (Louth: J. and J. Jackson, 1827).

Haggart, David, *The Life of David Haggart … Written by Himself, while under Sentence of Death* (Edinburgh: W. and C. Tait, 2nd edn, 1821).

Hardy, Thomas, *Memoir of Thomas Hardy, Founder of, and Secretary to, the London Corresponding Society* (London: James Ridgway, 1832).

Hart, William, 'The Autobiography of William Hart, Cooper, 1776–1857: A respectable artisan in the industrial revolution', Parts I–II, ed. Pat Hudson and Lynette Hunter, *London Journal*, 7:2 (1981), pp. 144–60, and 8:1 (1982), pp. 63–75.

Heaton, William, 'A Sketch of the Author's Life', in William Heaton, *The Old Soldier; the Wandering Lover, and Other Poems* (London: Simpkin, Marshall, & Co., 1857), pp. xv–xxiv.

Hick, Samuel, *The Village Blacksmith; or, Piety and Usefulness Exemplified* (London: Hamilton, Adams and Co., 5th edn, 1834).

Hogg, James, *Memoirs of the Author's Life and Familiar Anecdotes of Sir Walter Scott*, ed. Douglas S. Mack (Edinburgh: Scottish Academic Press, 1972).

Holcroft, Thomas, *Memoirs of the Late Thomas Holcroft, Written by Himself* (London: Longman Brown, 1852).

Holloway, John William, *An Authentic and Faithful History of the Atrocious Murder of Celia Holloway* (Brighton: W. Nute, 1832).

Hopkinson, James, *Victorian Cabinet Maker: The memoirs of James Hopkinson 1819–1894*, ed. Jocelyne Baty Goodman (London: Routledge & Kegan Paul, 1968).

Hopwood, D. Caroline, *An Account of the Life and Religious Experiences of D. Caroline Hopwood of Leeds, Deceased* (Leeds: E. Baines, 1801).

Hutton, William, *The Life of William Hutton* (London: Baldwin, Cradock and Joy, 1816).

Jekyll, Gertrude, *Old West Surrey: Some notes and memories* (London: Longmans, Green and Co., 1904).

Jewell, Joseph, 'Autobiographical Memoir of Joseph Jewell 1763–1846', ed. Arthur Walter Slater, *Camden Miscellany*, 22 (1964), pp. 113–61.

234   Select bibliography

Lackington, James, *Memoirs of the First Forty-Five Years of the Life of James Lackington* (London: self-published, 1792).

Lomas, John, 'The Autobiography of a Pedlar: John Lomas of Hollinsclough, Staffordshire (1747–1823), ed. David Brown, *Midland History*, 21:1 (1996), pp. 156–66.

Longden, Henry, *The Life of Mr Henry Longden (Late of Sheffield)* (Baltimore: Armstrong & Plaskitt, 1824).

Love, David, *The Life, Adventures, and Experience, of David Love. Written by himself* (Nottingham: Sutton and Son, 3rd edn, 1823).

Lovekin, Emanuel, 'Autobiography', in John Burnett (ed.), *Useful Toil: Autobiographies of working people from the 1820s to 1920s* (London: Penguin, 1976), pp. 289–96.

Lowe, Roger, *The Diary of Roger Lowe of Ashton-in-Makerfield, Lancashire 1663–74*, ed. William L. Sachse (New Haven: Yale University Press, 1938).

MacDonald, John, *Travels in Various Parts of Europe, Asia, and Africa, during a Series of Thirty Years and Upwards* (London: self-published, 1790).

Marsden, Joshua, *Sketches of the Early Life of a Sailor* (Hull: William Ross, 3rd edn, 1821).

Martin, Jonathan, *The Life of Jonathan Martin, of Darlington, Tanner, Written by Himself* (Barnard Castle: self-published, 1826).

Mayett, Joseph, *The Autobiography of Joseph Mayett of Quainton (1783–1839)*, ed. Ann Kussmaul (Chesham: Buckingham Record Society, 1986).

McAdam, John, *Autobiography of John McAdam (1806–1883) with Selected Letters*, ed. Janet Fyfe (Edinburgh: Scottish History Society, 1980).

Melhuish, Thomas, *An Account of the Early Part of the Life and Convincement of Thomas Melhuish, Late of Taunton* (London: Phillips and Fardon, 1805).

Metford, Joseph, 'The Life of Joseph Metford 1776–1863', *Journal of the Friends of Historical Society*, 25 (1928), pp. 33–50.

Millhouse, Robert, *The Songs of the Patriot, Sonnets, and Songs* (London: self-published, 1826).

Mitchell, George, 'Autobiography and Recollections of "One from the Plough"', in Stephen Price (ed.), *The Skeleton at the Plough, or the Poor Farm Labourers of the West* (London: G. Potter, 1874), pp. 95–120.

M'Kaen, James, *The Life of James M'Kaen, Shoemaker in Glasgow* (Glasgow: Brash and Reid, 2nd edn, 1797).

Mockford, George, *Wilderness Journeyings and Gracious Deliverances: The autobiography of George Mockford* (Oxford: J. C. Pembrey, 1901).

Place, Francis, *The Autobiography of Francis Place (1771–1854)*, ed. Mary Thale (Cambridge: Cambridge University Press, 1972).

Preston, Thomas, *The Life and Opinions of Thomas Preston, Patriot and Shoemaker* (London: self-published, 1817).

Rattenbury, John, *Memoirs of a Smuggler, Compiled from His Diary and Journal* (London: J. Harvey, 1837).

Rymer, Edward Allen, 'The Martyrdom of the Mine', ed. Robert G. Neville, *History Workshop Journal*, 1:1 (1976), pp. 220–44.

Saville, Jonathan, *Memoir of Jonathan Saville of Halifax, Eng. including His Autobiography*, ed. Francis A. West (New York: G. Lane & B. Tippet, 1845).

Saxby, Mary, *Memoirs of a Female Vagrant* (London: J. W. Morris, 1806).

Shaw, Benjamin, *The Family Records of Benjamin Shaw Mechanic of Dent, Dolphinholme and Preston, 1772–1841*, ed. Alan G. Crosby (Stroud: Alan Sutton Publishing, 1991).

Select bibliography   235

Shaw, John, *A Narrative of the Life and Travels of John Robert Shaw, the Well-Digger* (Lexington: Daniel Bradford, 1807).

Shinn, John, 'A Sketch of my Life and Times', in John Burnett (ed.), *Destiny Obscure: Autobiographies of childhood, education and family from the 1820s to the 1920s* (London: Penguin Books, 1982), pp. 186–92.

Sholl, Samuel, *A Short Historical Account of the Silk Manufacture in England* (London: M. Jones, 1811).

Smith, Thomas W., *A Narrative of the Life, Travels and Sufferings of Thomas W. Smith* (Boston: Wm C. Hill, 1844).

Smith, William, 'The Memoir of William Smith', ed. B. S. Trinder, *Transactions of the Shropshire Archaeological Society*, 58 (1966), pp. 178–85.

Starkey, Benjamin, *Memoirs of the Life of Benj. Starkey, Late of London* (Newcastle: William Hall, 1818).

Story, Robert, *Love and Literature; Being the Reminiscences* (London: Longman, Brown, Green and Longmans, 1842).

Taylor, Dan, *Memoirs of the Rev. Dan Taylor, Late Pastor of the General Baptist Church, Whitechapel, London*, by Adam Taylor (London: Self-published, 1820).

Terry, Joseph, 'Recollections of My Life', in John Burnett (ed.), *Destiny Obscure: Autobiographies of childhood, education and family from the 1820s to the 1920s* (London: Penguin Books, 1982), pp. 66–71.

Thelwall, Cecil, *The Life of John Thelwall, By His Widow*, Vols 1–2 (London: John Macrone, 1837).

Thom, William, *Rhymes and Recollections of a Hand-Loom Weaver* (London: Smith, Elder & Co., 1844).

Thomson, Christopher, *The Autobiography of an Artisan* (London: J. Chapman, 1847).

Tough, John, *A Short Narrative of the Life, and Some Incidents in the Recollection, of an Aberdonian* (Aberdeen: self-published, 1848).

Tyron, Thomas, *Some Memoirs of the Life of Mr Tho. Tyron, Late of London, Merchant* (London: T. Sowle, 1705).

Varley, William, 'Diary of William Varley of Hingham', in W. Bennett (ed.), *The History of Burnley 1650 to 1850* (Burnley: Burnley Corporation, 1948), pp. 379–89.

Watson, James, 'Reminiscences of James Watson', in David Vincent (ed.), *Testaments of Radicalism: Memoirs of working class politicians 1790–1885* (London: Europa Publications Limited, 1997), pp. 103–14.

Wheatcroft, Leonard, *The Autobiography of Leonard Wheatcroft of Ashover 1627–1706*, ed. Dorothy Riden (Chesterfield: Derbyshire Record Society, 1993).

Whetstone, Charles, *Truths. No. I or the Memoirs of Charles Whetstone* (no place or publisher, 1807).

Whitehead, David, *The Autobiography of David Whitehead of Rawtenstall (1790–1865): Cotton spinner and merchant*, ed. Stanley Chapman (Helmshore: Helmshore Local History Society, 2001).

Wilson, Benjamin, 'The Struggles of an Old Chartist', in David Vincent (ed.), *Testaments of Radicalism: Memoirs of working class politicians 1790–1885* (London: Europa Publications Limited, 1997), pp. 189–242.

Wood, Thomas, 'The Autobiography of Thomas Wood, 1822–1880', in John Burnett (ed.), *Useful Toil: Autobiographies of working people from the 1820s to 1920s* (London: Penguin, 1976), pp. 304–12.

Other published sources

Burn, Richard, *The Justice of the Peace and Parish Officer*, Vols 1–4 (London: H. Woodfall and W. Strahan, 12th edn, 1772).

Clare, John, *The Village Minstrel, and Other Poems*, Vol. 2 (London: Taylor and Hessey, 1821).

Clark, Ann (ed.), *Sherborne Almshouse Register* (Dorchester: Dorset Record Society, 2013).

Cobbett, William, *Cottage Economy* (London: self-published, 3rd edn, 1826).

Cobbett, William, *Rural Rides* (London: self-published, 1830).

Cobbett, William, *Two-Penny Trash: Politics for the poor* (London: self-published, 1831).

Davies, David, *The Case of Labourers in Husbandry* (London: G. G. and J. Robinson, 1795).

Davis, Thomas, 'Address to the Landholders of this Kingdom', in *Letters and Papers on Agricultural Planting*, Vol. 7 (London: R. Cruttwell, 1795), pp. 294–7.

De Tocqueville, Alexis, *Memoir on Pauperism*, trans. Seymour Drescher, ed. Gertrude Himmelfarb (London: Civitas, 1997).

Dymond, David (ed.), *Parson and People in a Suffolk Village: Richard Cobbold's Wortham, 1824–77* (Ipswich: Wortham Research Group/Suffolk Family History Society, 2007).

Eden, Frederic Morton, *The State of the Poor*, Vols 1–3 (London: J. Davis, 1797).

Emmison, F. G. (ed.), *Jacobean Household Inventories* (Aspley Guise: Bedfordshire Historical Record Society, 1938).

Engels, Friedrich, *The Condition of the Working Class in England*, ed. Victor Kiernan and Tristram Hunt (London: Penguin, reprint of 1845 edn, 2009).

Fletcher, Ronald (ed.), *The Biography of a Victorian Village: Richard Cobbold's account of Wortham, Suffolk* (London: B. T. Batsford Ltd, 1977).

Hanway, Jonas, 'An Essay on Tea', in Jonas Hanway, *A Journal of Eight Days Journey* (London: H. Woodfall, 1756), pp. 203–361.

Harley, Joseph (ed.), *Norfolk Pauper Inventories, c.1690–1834* (Oxford: British Academy/Oxford University Press, 2020).

Holme, Randle, *The Academy of Armory*, Vol. 2, ed. I. H. Jeayes (London: Rorburghe Club, reprint of 1688 edn, 1905).

Howitt, William, *The Rural Life of England*, Part II (London: Manning and Smithson, 1838).

Jacob, Giles, *The Compleat Parish-Officer* (London: Henry Lintot, 10th edn, 1744).

Jones, Peter, and Steven King, *Navigating the Old English Poor Law: The Kirkby Lonsdale letters, 1809–1836* (Oxford: British Academy/Oxford University Press, 2020).

Kent, Nathaniel, *Hints to Gentlemen of Landed Property* (London: J. Dodsley, 1775).

King, Steven, Thomas Nutt and Alannah Tomkins (eds), *Narratives of the Poor in Eighteenth-Century Britain*. Vol. 1: *Voices of the Poor: Poor law depositions and letters* (London: Pickering & Chatto, 2006).

Malthus, Thomas Robert, *An Essay on the Principle of Population as It Affects the Future Improvement of Society* (London: J. Johnson, 1798).

Mandeville, Bernard, *The Fable of the Bees or Private Vices, Publick Benefits*, Vols 1–2, ed. F. B. Kaye (Oxford: Clarendon Press, reprint of 1732 edn, 1988).

Mason, Simon, *The Good and Bad Effects of Tea Consider'd* (London: M. Cooper, 1745).

Mayhew, Henry, *London Labour and the London Poor*, Vols 1–3 (London: George Woodfall and Son, 1851).

Robinson's Commercial Directory of the Six Counties forming the Norfolk Circuit: Beds, Cambridgeshire, Hunts, Norfolk, and Suffolk, with Oxfordshire (London: William Robson & Co., 1839).

Rowntree, B. Seebohm, *Poverty: A study of town life* (London: Macmillan and Co., 3rd edn, 1902).

Scott, John, *Observations on the Present State of the Parochial and Vagrant Poor* (London: Edward and Charles Dilly, 1773).

Silliman, Benjamin, *A Journey of Travels in England, Holland and Scotland* (New Haven: S. Converse, 3rd edn, 1820).

Smith, Adam, *The Theory of Moral Sentiments*, ed. D. D. Raphael and A. L. Macfie (Indianapolis: Liberty Fund, reprint of 1759 edn, 1984).

Smith, Adam, *An Inquiry into the Nature and Causes of the Wealth of Nations*, Vols 1–2, ed. R. H. Campbell and A. S. Skinner (Indianapolis: Liberty Classics, reprint of 1776 edn, 1981).

Sokoll, Thomas (ed.), *Essex Pauper Letters, 1731–1837* (Oxford: Oxford University Press/British Academy, 2001).

Steer, Francis W. (ed.), *Farm and Cottage Inventories of Mid-Essex, 1635–1749* (Chichester: Phillimore & Co., 2nd edn, 1969).

Trinder, Barrie, and Jeff Cox (eds), *Yeoman and Colliers in Telford: Probate inventories for Dawley, Lilleshall, Wellington and Wrockwardine, 1660–1750* (London: Phillimore & Co., 1980).

Tuke, John, *General View of the Agriculture of the North Riding of Yorkshire* (London: B. McMillan, 1800).

Vaisey, David (ed.), *The Diary of Thomas Turner, 1754–1765* (Oxford: Oxford University Press, 1984).

Walker, George, *The Costume of Yorkshire* (London: T. Bensley, 1814).

Wight, John, *Mornings at Bow Street: A selection of the most humourous and entertaining reports which have appeared in the Morning Herald* (London: Charles Baldwin, 1824).

Williams, Thomas Walter, *The Whole Law relative to the Duty and Office of a Justice of the Peace*, Vols 1–4 (London, 3rd edn, 1812).

Wood, John, *A Series of Plans for Cottages or Habitations of the Labourer* (London: I. and J. Taylor, 2nd edn, 1792).

Selected secondary materials

Published

Allen, Robert C., *The British Industrial Revolution in Global Perspective* (Cambridge: Cambridge University Press, 2009).

Arkell, Tom, Nesta Evans and Nigel Goose (eds), *When Death Do Us Part: Understanding and interpreting the probate records of early modern England* (Oxford: Leopard's Head Press, 2000).

Backhouse, Alison, *The Worm-Eaten Waistcoat* (York: self-published, 2003).

Bailey, C. T. P., *Knives and Forks: Selected and described with an introduction* (London: Medici Society, 1927).

Barclay, Katie, Sharon Crozier-De Rosa and Peter N. Stearns (eds), *Sources for the History of Emotions: A guide* (London: Routledge, 2020).

Barker, Hannah, and Jane Hamlett, 'Living above the Shop: Home, business, and family in the English "industrial revolution"', *Journal of Family History*, 35:4 (2010), pp. 311–28.

Barrell, John, *The Dark Side of the Landscape: The rural poor in English painting 1730–1840* (Cambridge: Cambridge University Press, 1992).

Beaudry, Mary C., 'Words for Things: Linguistic analysis of probate inventories', in Mary C. Beaudry (ed.), *Documentary Archaeology in the New World* (Cambridge: Cambridge University Press, 1988), pp. 43–50.

Begiato, Joanne, 'Selfhood and "Nostalgia": Sensory and material memories of the childhood home in late Georgian Britain', *Journal for Eighteenth-Century Studies*, 42:2 (2019), pp. 229–46.

Berg, Maxine, 'Women's Consumption and the Industrial Classes of Eighteenth-Century England', *Journal of Social History*, 30:2 (1996), pp. 415–34.

Berg, Maxine, *Luxury and Pleasure in Eighteenth-Century Britain* (Oxford: Oxford University Press, 2005).

Boddice, Rob, *The History of Emotions* (Manchester: Manchester University Press, 2018).

Boddice, Rob, and Mark Smith, *Emotion, Sense, Experience* (Cambridge: Cambridge University Press, 2020).

Borsay, Peter, *The English Urban Renaissance: Culture and society in the provincial town 1660–1770* (Oxford: Clarendon Press, 1989).

Brett, Gerard, *Dinner Is Served: A history of dining in England 1400–1900* (London: Rupert Hart-Davis, 1968).

Brewer, John, and Roy Porter (eds), *Consumption and the World of Goods* (London: Routledge, 1993).

Burnett, John, David Vincent and David Mayall, *The Autobiography of the Working Class: An annotated critical bibliography*. Vol. 1: *1790–1900* (Brighton: Harvester, 1984).

Cohen, Deborah, *Household Gods: The British and their possessions* (New Haven: Yale University Press, 2006).

Cornford, Barbara, 'Inventories of the Poor', *Norfolk Archaeology*, 35 (1970–73), pp. 118–25.

Cowan, Brian, *The Social Life of Coffee: The emergence of the British coffeehouse* (New Haven: Yale University Press, 2005).

Cox, Nancy, *Retailing and the Language of Goods, 1550–1850* (Farnham: Ashgate, 2015).

Cressy, David, *Literacy and the Social Order: Reading and writing in Tudor and Stuart England* (Cambridge: Cambridge University Press, 1980).

Crewe, V. A., and D. M. Hadley, '"Uncle Tom was there, in crockery": Material culture and a Victorian working-class childhood', *Childhood in the Past*, 6:2 (2013), pp. 89–105.

Crowley, John E., *The Invention of Comfort: Sensibilities and design in early modern Britain and early America* (Baltimore: Johns Hopkins University Press, 2001).

Davidson, Caroline, *A Woman's Work Is Never Done: A history of housework in the British Isles 1650–1950* (London: Chatto & Windus, 1982).

De Vries, Jan, *The Industrious Revolution: Consumer behaviour and the household economy 1650 to present* (Cambridge: Cambridge University Press, 2008).

Doolittle, Megan, 'Time, Space, and Memories', *Home Cultures*, 8:3 (2011), pp. 245–64.

Downes, Stephanie, Sally Holloway and Sarah Randles (eds), *Feeling Things: Objects and emotions through history* (Oxford: Oxford University Press, 2018).

Emmerson, Robin, *British Teapots and Tea Drinking 1700–1850* (London: The Stationery Office, 1992).

Estabrook, Carl B., *Urbane and Rustic England: Cultural ties and social spheres in the provinces 1660–1780* (Manchester: Manchester University Press, 1998).

Fastnedge, Ralph, *English Furniture Styles from 1500–1830* (Harmondsworth: Penguin, reprint of 1955 edn, 1961).

Feinstein, Charles H., 'Pessimism Perpetuated: Real wages and the standard of living in Britain during and after the industrial revolution', *Journal of Economic History*, 58:3 (1998), pp. 625–58.

Findlen, Paula, *Early Modern Things: Objects and their histories, 1500–1800* (London: Routledge, 2013).

Finn, Margot, 'Men's Things: Masculine possession in the consumer revolution', *Social History*, 25:2 (2000), pp. 133–55.

Finn, Margot, 'Women, Consumption and Coverture in England, c.1760–1860', *Historical Journal*, 39:3 (1996), pp. 703–22.

Flinn, Michael W., *The History of the British Coal Industry*. Vol. 2: *1700–1830: The industrial revolution* (Oxford: Oxford University Press, 1984).

Floud, Roderick, Robert W. Fogel, Bernard Harris and Sok Chul Hong, *The Changing Body: Health, nutrition, and human development in the Western world since 1700* (Cambridge: Cambridge University Press, 2011).

Fogel, Robert, 'New Sources and Techniques for the Study of Secular Trends in Nutritional Status, Health, Mortality, and the Process of Aging', *Historical Methods*, 26:1 (1993), pp. 5–43.

Forrest, Denys, *Tea for the British: The social and economic history of a famous trade* (London: Chatto & Windus, 1973).

French, Henry, *The Middle Sort of People in Provincial England 1600–1750* (Oxford: Oxford University Press, 2007).

Fussell, G. E., *The English Rural Labourer: His home, furniture, clothing and food from Tudor to Victorian times* (London: Batchworth Press, 1949).

Gerritsen, Anne, and Giorgio Riello (eds), *Writing Material Culture History* (London: Bloomsbury, 2015).

Gestrich, Andreas, Steven King and Lutz Raphael (eds), *Being Poor in Modern Europe: Historical perspectives 1800–1940* (Bern: Peter Lang, 2006).

Gilboy, Elizabeth W., 'Demand as a Factor in the Industrial Revolution' (originally published in 1932), in R. M. Hartwell (ed.), *The Causes of the Industrial Revolution* (London: Routledge, 1967), pp. 121–38.

Glennie, Paul, and Nigel Thrift, *Shaping the Day: A history of timekeeping in England and Wales 1300–1800* (Oxford: Oxford University Press, 2009).

Goffman, Erving, *The Presentation of Self in Everyday Life* (London: Penguin, reprint of 1959 edn, 1990).

Gowing, Laura, 'The Twinkling of a Bedstaff: Recovering the social life of English beds 1500–1700', *Home Cultures*, 11:3 (2014), pp. 275–304.

Green, Adrian, 'Heartless and Unhomely? Dwellings of the poor in East Anglia and north-east England', in Joanne McEwan and Pamela Sharpe (eds), *Accommodating Poverty: The housing and living arrangements of the English poor, c.1600–1850* (Basingstoke: Palgrave, 2011), pp. 69–101.

Griffin, Carl, *Politics of Hunger: Protest, poverty and policy in England, c.1750–c.1840* (Manchester: Manchester University Press, 2020).

Griffin, Emma, *Liberty's Dawn: A people's history of the industrial revolution* (New Haven: Yale University Press, 2013).

Griffin, Emma, 'Diets, Hunger and Living Standards during the British Industrial Revolution', *Past and Present*, 239 (2018), pp. 71–111.

Griffin, Emma, *Bread Winner: An intimate history of the Victorian economy* (New Haven: Yale University Press, 2020).

Griffin, Emma, 'Writing about Life Writing: Women, autobiography and the British industrial revolution', *Transactions of the Royal Historical Society*, 32 (2022), pp. 5–23.

Hailwood, Mark, 'Rethinking Literacy in Rural England, 1500–1700', *Past and Present*, 260:1 (2023), pp. 38–70.

Hamlett, Jane, *Material Relations: Domestic interiors and middle-class families* (Manchester: Manchester University Press, 2010).

Hamling, Tara, and Catherine Richardson (eds), *Everyday Objects: Medieval and early modern material culture and its meanings* (London: Routledge, 2010).

Hamling, Tara, and Catherine Richardson, *A Day at Home in Early Modern England: Material culture and domestic life, 1500–1700* (New Haven: Yale University Press, 2017).

Hammond, J. L., and Barbara Hammond, *The Village Labourer*, ed. G. E. Mingay (London: Longman Group, reprint of 1911 edn, 1978).

Handley, Sasha, *Sleep in Early Modern England* (New Haven: Yale University Press, 2016).

Hannan, Leonie, and Sarah Longair, *History through Material Culture* (Manchester: Manchester University Press, 2017).

Harley, Joseph, 'Material Lives of the Poor and their Strategic Use of the Workhouse during the Final Decades of the English Old Poor Law', *Continuity and Change*, 30:1 (2015), pp. 71–103.

Harley, Joseph, 'Consumption and Poverty in the Homes of the English Poor, c.1670–1834', *Social History*, 43:1 (2018), pp. 81–104.

Harley, Joseph, 'Pauper Inventories, Social Relations, and the Nature of Poor Relief under the Old Poor Law, England, c.1601–1834', *Historical Journal*, 62:2 (2019), pp. 375–98.

Harley, Joseph, 'Domestic Production and Consumption in English Pauper Households, 1670–1840', *Agricultural History Review*, 69:1 (2021), pp. 25–49.

Harley, Joseph, '"I can barely provide the common necessaries of life": Material wealth over the life-cycle of the English poor, 1790–1834', in Harley, Holmes and Nevalainen, *Working Class at Home* (Cham: Palgrave, 2022), pp. 25–45.

Harley, Joseph, and Vicky Holmes (eds), *Objects of Poverty: Material Culture in Britain from 1700* (London: Bloomsbury, forthcoming).

Harley, Joseph, Vicky Holmes and Laika Nevalainen (eds), *The Working Class at Home, 1790–1940* (Cham: Palgrave, 2022).

Harvey, Karen (ed.), *History and Material Culture: A student's guide to approaching alternative sources* (London: Routledge, 2009).

Harvey, Karen, *The Little Republic: Masculinity and domestic authority in eighteenth-century Britain* (Oxford: Oxford University Press, 2012).

Hatcher, John, *The History of the British Coal Industry*. Vol. 1: *Before 1700: Towards the age of coal* (Oxford: Oxford University Press, 1993).

Hatcher, John, and T. C. Barker, *A History of British Pewter* (London: Longman, 1974).

Helmreich, Anne, Tim Hitchcock and William J. Turkel, 'Rethinking Inventories in the Digital Age: The case of the Old Bailey', *Journal of Art Historiography*, 11 (2014), pp. 1–25.

Hitchcock, David, and Julia McClure (eds), *The Routledge History of Poverty, c.1450–1800* (London: Routledge, 2021).

Hitchcock, Tim, *Down and Out in Eighteenth-Century London* (London: Hambledon & London, 2004).

Hitchcock, Tim, Peter King and Pamela Sharpe (eds), *Chronicling Poverty: The voices and strategies of the English poor, 1640–1840* (Basingstoke: Palgrave, 1997).

Holmes, Vicky, *In Bed with the Victorians: The life-cycle of working-class marriage* (Basingstoke: Palgrave, 2017).

Horrell, Sara, 'Home Demand and British Industrialization', *Journal of Economic History*, 56:3 (1996), pp. 561–604.

Horrell, Sara, and Jane Humphries, 'Old Questions, New Data, and Alternative Perspectives: Families' living standards in the industrial revolution', *Journal of Economic History*, 52:4 (1992), pp. 849–80.

Horrell, Sara, Jane Humphries and Ken Sneath, 'Cupidity and Crime: Consumption as revealed by insights from the Old Bailey records of thefts in the eighteenth and nineteenth centuries', in Mark Casson and Nigar Hashimzade (eds), *Large Databases in Economic History: Research methods and case studies* (London: Routledge, 2013), pp. 246–67.

Horrell, Sara, Jane Humphries and Ken Sneath, 'Consumption Conundrums Unravelled', *Economic History Review*, 68:3 (2015), pp. 830–57.

Hoskins, W. G., 'The Rebuilding of Rural England, 1570–1640', *Past and Present*, 4 (1953), pp. 44–59.

Hurdley, Rachel, *Home, Materiality, Memory and Belonging: Keeping culture* (Basingstoke: Palgrave, 2013).

Hussey, David, and Margaret Ponsonby (eds), *Buying for the Home: Shopping for the domestic from the seventeenth century to the present* (Aldershot: Ashgate, 2008).

Hussey, David, and Margaret Ponsonby, *The Single Homemaker and Material Culture in the Long Eighteenth Century* (Abingdon: Ashgate, 2012).

Jekyll, Gertrude, and Sydney R. Jones, *Old English Household Life* (London: B. T. Batsford, 2nd edn, 1945).

King, Peter, 'Pauper Inventories and the Material Lives of the Poor in the Eighteenth and Early Nineteenth Centuries', in Tim Hitchcock, Peter King and Pamela Sharpe (eds), *Chronicling Poverty: The voices and strategies of the English poor, 1640–1840* (Basingstoke: Palgrave, 1997), pp. 155–91.

King, Steven, *Poverty and Welfare in England 1700–1850: A regional perspective* (Manchester: Manchester University Press, 2000).

King, Steven, *Writing the Lives of the English Poor, 1750s–1830s* (London: McGill-Queen's University Press, 2019).

Select bibliography

King, Steven, and Alannah Tomkins, *The Poor in England 1700–1850: An economy of makeshifts* (Manchester: Manchester University Press, 2003).

Korsmeyer, Carolyn (ed.), *The Taste Culture Reader: Experiencing food and drink* (Oxford: Berg, 2005).

Kowaleski-Wallace, Elizabeth, *Consuming Subjects: Women, shopping, and business in the eighteenth century* (New York: Columbia University Press, 1997).

Kwass, Michael, *The Consumer Revolution, 1650–1800* (Cambridge: Cambridge University Press, 2022).

Lemire, Beverly, *Fashion's Favourite: The cotton trade and the consumer in Britain, 1660–1800* (Oxford: Oxford University Press, 1991).

Lemire, Beverly, *Dress, Culture and Commerce: The English clothing trade before the factory, 1660–1800* (Basingstoke: Palgrave, 1997).

Lemire, Beverly, *The Business of Everyday Life: Gender, practice and social politics in England, c.1600–1900* (Manchester: Manchester University Press, 2005).

Lemire, Beverly, '"Men of the world": British mariners, consumer practice, and material culture in an era of global trade, c.1660–1800', *Journal of British Studies*, 54:2 (2015), pp. 288–319.

MacKay, Lynn, *Respectability and the London Poor, 1780–1870* (London: Pickering & Chatto, 2013).

Mather, Ruth, 'Remembering Protest in the Late-Georgian Working-Class Home', in Carl Griffin and Briony McDonagh (eds), *Remembering Protest in Britain since 1500: Memory, materiality and the landscape* (Basingstoke: Palgrave, 2018), pp. 135–58.

McEwan, Joanne, and Pamela Sharpe (eds), *Accommodating Poverty: The housing and living arrangements of the English poor, c.1600–1850* (Basingstoke: Palgrave, 2011).

McKendrick, Neil, John Brewer and J. H. Plumb, *The Birth of a Consumer Society: The commercialization of eighteenth-century England* (London: Hutchinson, 1982).

Mintz, Sidney W., *Sweetness and Power: The place of sugar in modern history* (New York: Penguin Books, 1985).

Mui, H. C., and L. H. Mui, *Shops and Shopkeeping in Eighteenth-Century England* (London: Routledge, 1989).

Muldrew, Craig, *Food, Energy and the Creation of Industriousness: Work and material culture in agrarian England, 1550–1780* (Cambridge: Cambridge University Press, 2011).

Neeson, J. M., *Commoners: Common right, enclosure and social change in England, 1700–1820* (Cambridge: Cambridge University Press, 1993).

Nichols, Tom, 'Motives of Control/Motifs of Creativity: The visual imagery of poverty in early modern Europe', in Hitchcock and McClure, *Routledge History*, pp. 138–63.

North, Susan, *Sweet and Clean? Bodies and clothes in early modern England* (Oxford: Oxford University Press, 2020).

Orlin, Lena Cowen (ed.), *Material London, ca. 1600* (Philadelphia: University of Pennsylvania Press, 2000).

Overton, Mark, Jane Whittle, Darron Dean and Andrew Hann, *Production and Consumption in English Households, 1600–1750* (London: Routledge, 2004).

Owens, Alastair, Nigel Jeffries, Karen Wehner and Rupert Featherby, 'Fragments of the Modern City: Material culture and the rhythms of everyday life in Victorian London', *Journal of Victorian Culture*, 15:2 (2010), pp. 212–25.

Payne, Christiana, 'Rural Virtues for Urban Consumption: Cottage scenes in early Victorian painting', *Journal of Victorian Culture*, 3:1 (1998), pp. 45–68.

Pennell, Sara, '"Pots and Pans History": The material culture of the kitchen in early modern England, *Journal of Design History*, 11:3 (1998), pp. 201–16.

Pennell, Sara, *The Birth of the English Kitchen, 1600–1850* (London: Bloomsbury, 2016).

Pounds, Norman J. G., *Hearth and Home: A history of material culture* (Bloomington: Indiana University Press, 1989).

Priestly, Ursula, and P. J. Corfield, 'Rooms and Room Use in Norwich Housing, 1580–1730', *Post-Medieval Archaeology*, 16 (1982), pp. 93–123.

Richards, Sarah, *Eighteenth-Century Ceramics: Products for a civilised society* (Manchester: Manchester University Press, 1999).

Richardson, Catherine, Tara Hamling and David Gaimster (eds), *The Routledge Handbook of Material Culture in Early Modern Europe* (London: Routledge, 2017).

Richmond, Vivienne, *Clothing the Poor in Nineteenth-Century England* (Cambridge: Cambridge University Press, 2013).

Roe, F. Gordon, *English Cottage Furniture* (London: Phoenix House, 3rd edn, 1961).

Saberi, Helen, *Tea: A global history* (London: Reaktion Books, 2010).

Sear, Joanne, and Ken Sneath, *The Origins of the Consumer Revolution in England: From brass pots to clocks* (London: Routledge, 2020).

Shammas, Carole, *The Pre-Industrial Consumer in England and America* (Oxford: Oxford University Press, 1990).

Shave, Samantha, *Pauper Policies: Poor law practice in England, 1780–1850* (Manchester: Manchester University Press, 2017).

Shepard, Alexandra, *Accounting for Oneself: Worth, status, and the social order* (Oxford: Oxford University Press, 2015).

Smith, Mark M., *Sensory History* (Oxford: Berg, 2007).

Smith, Woodruff D., *Consumption and the Making of Respectability, 1600–1800* (London: Routledge, 2002).

Snell, K. D. M., *Annals of the Labouring Poor: Social change and agrarian England, 1660–1900* (Cambridge: Cambridge University Press, 1985).

Stobart, Jon, *Sugar and Spice: Grocers and groceries in provincial England, 1650–1830* (Oxford: Oxford University Press, 2013).

Styles, John, 'Product Innovation in Early Modern London', *Past and Present*, 168 (2000), pp. 124–69.

Styles, John, 'Lodging at the Old Bailey: Lodgings and their furnishings in eighteenth-century London', in John Styles and Amanda Vickery (eds), *Gender, Taste, and Material Culture in Britain and North America 1700–1830* (New Haven: Yale University Press, 2006), pp. 61–80.

Styles, John, *The Dress of the People: Everyday fashion in eighteenth-century England* (New Haven: Yale University Press, 2007).

Styles, John, *Threads of Feeling: The London foundling hospital's textile tokens, 1740–1770* (London: The Foundling Museum, 2010).

Styles, John, and Amanda Vickery (eds), *Gender, Taste, and Material Culture in Britain and North America 1700–1830* (New Haven: Yale University Press, 2006).

Tankard, Danae, *Clothing in 17th-Century Provincial England* (London: Bloomsbury, 2020).

Thompson, E. P., *The Making of the English Working Class* (London: Penguin, reprint of 1963 edn, 1991).

Thompson, E. P., 'Time, Work-Discipline and Industrial Capitalism', *Past and Present*, 38 (1967), pp. 56–97.

Tilley, Chris, Webb Keane, Susan Kuechler, Mike Rowlands and Patricia Spyer (eds), *Handbook of Material Culture* (London: Sage, 2006).

Tomkins, Alannah, *The Experience of Urban Poverty, 1723–82* (Manchester: Manchester University Press, 2006).

Toplis, Alison, *The Clothing Trade in Provincial England, 1800–1850* (London: Pickering & Chatto, 2011).

Trentmann, Frank (ed.), *The Oxford Handbook of the History of Consumption* (Oxford: Oxford University Press, 2012).

Vickery, Amanda, *The Gentleman's Daughter: Women's lives in Georgian England* (New Haven: Yale University Press, 1998).

Vickery, Amanda, 'An Englishman's Home is his Castle? Thresholds, boundaries and privacies in the eighteenth-century London house', *Past and Present*, 199 (2008), pp. 147–73.

Vickery, Amanda, *Behind Closed Doors: At home in Georgian England* (New Haven: Yale University Press, 2009).

Visser, Margaret, *The Rituals of Dinner: The origins, evolution, eccentricities, and meaning of table manners* (London: Viking, 1992).

Voth, Hans-Joachim, *Time and Work in England 1750–1830* (Oxford: Oxford University Press, 2000).

Wahrman, Dror, *The Making of the Modern Self: Identity and culture in eighteenth century England* (New Haven: Yale University Press, 2004).

Wales, Tim, 'Poverty, Poor Relief and Life-Cycle: Some evidence from seventeenth century Norfolk', in Richard M. Smith (ed.), *Land, Kinship and Life-Cycle* (Cambridge: Cambridge University Press, 1984), pp. 351–404.

Warde, Paul, *Energy Consumption in England and Wales 1560–2000* (Naples: CNR, 2007).

Weatherill, Lorna, 'A Possession of One's Own: Women and consumer behaviour in England, 1660–1740', *Journal of British Studies*, 25:2 (1986), pp. 131–56.

Weatherill, Lorna, *Consumer Behaviour and Material Culture in Britain 1660–1760* (London: Routledge, 2nd edn, 1996).

Whittle, Jane, 'A Critique of Approaches to "Domestic Work": Women, work and the pre-industrial economy', *Past and Present*, 243:1 (2019), pp. 35–70.

Whittle, Jane, and Elizabeth Griffiths, *Consumption and Gender in the Early Seventeenth-Century Household: The world of Alice Le Strange* (Oxford: Oxford University Press, 2012).

Wilcox, H. A., *The Woodlands and Marshlands of England* (London: University Press of Liverpool, 1933).

Williams, Samantha, *Poverty, Gender and Life-Cycle under the English Poor Law 1760–1834* (Woodbridge: Boydell and Brewer, 2011).

Wilson, Bee, *Consider the Fork: A history of invention in the kitchen* (London: Particular Books, 2012).

Unpublished

Harley, Joseph, 'Material Lives of the English Poor: A regional perspective, c.1670–1834', PhD thesis (University of Leicester, 2016).

Sneath, Ken, 'Consumption, Wealth, Indebtedness and Social Structure in Early Modern England', PhD thesis (University of Cambridge, 2008).

White, Jonathan, 'Luxury and Labour: Ideas of labouring-class consumption in eighteenth-century England', PhD thesis (University of Warwick, 2001).

Note

1 In addition to other manuscript sources, the following section includes references to every inventory used in this book. Records which contain pauper inventories are marked with an asterisk. The following list does not include the archival sources used to cross-reference and categorise each inventory, unless they are referenced in the text. Due to the volume of sources, only reference numbers are given here.

Index

agency 4, 26
 see also economy of makeshifts
agriculture *see* food production
almshouses 9, 13, 60, 86, 91
animals
  asses 155
  bees 155
  birds 196, 198
  cats 129
  chickens 155
  cows 155, 170
  dogs 187–8
  geese 155
  horses 155, 156
  pigs 155
  sheep 155
Ashwellthorpe, Norfolk 86
 see also Norfolk
autobiographies, as sources 10, 17–18,
  64, 182

Beaminster, Dorset 77, 78, 195
 see also Dorset
Beauchamp Roding, Essex 93
 see also Essex
bed hangings 11, 12, 21, 85,
  89–90, 97
beds 11, 36, 39, 43, 60, 71, 74, 85–9,
  90, 102
  bedsteads 85, 87–8
  children's 88
  cradles 36, 38, 39, 40–1, 88

feather 21, 74, 84, 86–7, 88, 97
flock 84, 86–7
makeshift 85–6, 88, 93, 129
selling of 69, 70, 77
sharing 88–9
straw/chaff 84, 86–7
trundle 88
 see also bed hangings; linen; sleep;
  warming pan; window curtains
bedwarmers 96–7
 see also warming pans
Bere Regis, Dorset 162
 see also Dorset
Berg, Maxine 208, 211
biographies, as sources 17–18
Blandford Forum, Dorset 170
 see also Dorset
bolsters 90–5, 114
 see also pillows
books *see* print
boxes (any type) 11, 74, 97–9, 101,
  102, 115
Braintree, Essex 93, 195
 see also Essex
Buckinghamshire 69
buildings 44–51
  perceptions of 43–4, 222

Canewdon, Essex 148
 see also Essex
Canterbury, Kent 127, 163, 188, 190
 see also Kent

Index   **247**

Chelmsford, Essex 10, 64, 67, 151, 192, 195
  see also Essex
chests of drawers 11, 21, 74, 77, 84, 97, 98, 99–100, 115, 180, 212, 214, 215
Chiddingstone, Kent 100, 162
  see also Kent
Clare, John (poet)
  cottage 47–9, 155
  reading 184, 185, 186
class distinction 7–9
Clayton-le-Moors, Lancashire 153
  see also Lancashire
cleanliness 49–50, 117, 124–8, 132
  lack of 43, 71, 106, 125, 127, 132–3
  see also laundry and washing
clocks *see* timepieces
clothing 15, 20, 43, 55, 72, 92, 95, 106, 132, 134, 138, 193, 207
  bibs 133
  coats 63
  frocks 133
  giving of 9, 77
  gowns 11, 71, 72, 206
  lack of 6, 17, 56, 65, 66, 68, 70, 71, 72, 132, 134, 171, 197, 209
  literature 2, 6, 12, 22, 55, 220
  nightwear 71, 95, 132
  petticoats 72, 133, 206
  ready-made 181
  school clothes 63
  selling of 11, 12, 67, 68, 69, 70, 71, 72–3, 79, 92, 112, 195
  shifts 60
  shirts 180
  shoes 71, 77, 197
  stays 72
  stockings 71, 125
  storage of 11, 97, 99, 222
  trousers 73
  undergarments 124
  see also laundry and washing; linen; textile production
Cobbett, William (radical) 125, 132, 136, 151
Cobbold, Richard (clergyman)
  background 18–19, 29, 44

paintings 18–19, 44–6, 47, 48, 49–51, 85–6, 87, 90, 92, 93–4, 101, 130–1, 156, 187–8, 193
Cohen, Deborah 18
Colchester, Essex 69, 88, 132
  see also Essex
colour 9, 222
  dinnerware 100, 144, 159, 162, 168, 172
  japanned (lacquered) 109
  painted 22, 97, 99, 100, 101, 105, 106, 107, 109, 193
  textiles 1, 4, 43, 86, 90, 93–4, 97
comfort 3, 9, 12, 21, 36, 47, 63, 68, 85, 86–9, 90, 97, 112, 117, 139, 169, 172, 180, 212, 222
  discomfort 43, 86, 91, 96, 105–6, 117, 131–5, 139, 152
  meaning of 10–11
  physical 2, 36, 39, 84, 86–9, 90, 96, 97, 101, 104, 105, 106, 110, 117, 139, 169, 222
  psychological 22, 86–9, 90, 94, 97, 99, 112, 117, 128–30, 135, 137, 139, 166, 169, 215, 222
consumption
  conspicuous consumption 7–9, 41, 101–2, 166–9, 180, 209
  economic historians on 3, 6–7, 143, 221–2
  involuntary consumption 6, 9, 14, 56, 65, 67, 84, 85, 91, 114, 122, 130, 166, 195, 198, 221
  for savings 12, 55, 62, 64, 167, 168, 192
  trickle-down consumption 7–9
convenience 2, 21, 36, 39, 43, 84, 85, 97, 99–100, 101, 107, 110, 112, 130, 131, 139, 180, 190, 192, 222
  meaning of 11
cooking 21, 117, 120, 138, 143, 144–52, 181
  boilers 144, 145, 146
  cauldrons 144, 145
  cooking pots 144, 145, 146, 147, 173
  crocks 144, 145, 146
  dripping pans 148, 149, 151
  frying pans 74, 149, 151, 174
  gridirons 149, 150, 151, 174
  jacks 149, 151, 152, 180

248 Index

cooking (*continued*)
  kettles 144, 145, 146
  location of 31, 34–41, 51, 119
  porridge pots 144, 145, 146
  posnets 144, 145, 146, 147
  pot hooks 146, 147, 173
  pottage pots 144, 145, 146
  ranges 148, 149, 151
  saucepans 74, 144, 145, 146, 148,
    151, 152, 172, 180, 214, 215
  skillets 144, 145, 146–8
  spits 149, 151, 152, 174, 214, 215
  trivets 148
  value of cooking items 148
Corfield, Penelope 213
Cornwall 3, 33
Cressy, David 181
Crossick, Geoffrey 11
Crowley, John 11
Cumbria 3
cupboards 74, 84, 97, 98, 99, 100–1,
  214, 215
cushions 106

Davies, David (social investigator) 151,
  164, 170
Davis, Jennifer 11
Davis, Ralph 164–5
decoration 2, 18, 21, 41, 43, 51, 62,
  84, 85, 90, 93–4, 97, 99, 100, 101,
  105, 106, 107, 108–9, 110, 130–1,
  138–9, 162, 168, 172, 180, 181,
  187–8, 189, 190, 193, 194, 211,
  212, 215, 222
  see also colour; woods
demand 4, 7, 20, 55, 63–4, 72, 195,
  200, 221–2, 223
de Tocqueville, Alexis
  (philosopher) 181
de Vries, Jan 7, 26, 27, 157, 191, 213
diaries, as sources 17–18
dining 21, 110, 120, 138, 144,
  158–64
  china 159, 160, 161, 162–3, 166,
    167, 168, 176
  delftware 159, 160, 161, 162–3
  dinnerware 72, 100, 130, 160, 161
  earthenware 62, 110, 144, 158,
    159–62, 167, 168, 172, 214–15
  glassware 159, 160, 161, 162, 215

knives and forks 21, 100, 110, 144,
  158, 163–4, 172, 214, 215
location of 34–41, 42, 51, 119
pewterware 21, 62, 144, 159–62
spoons 161, 163–4, 167
stoneware 159, 160, 161, 162
tinware 159, 160, 161, 162
woodenware 21, 62, 144, 158,
  159–62
see also cooking; food and drink;
  linen; tables; tea
distraint of goods 10, 14–15, 71, 194
Dorset 3, 13–14, 16–17, 19–20, 21, 32,
  33, 57, 59, 60, 61, 62, 73–4, 77,
  78, 84, 86, 88, 90, 91, 93, 96, 98,
  100, 103, 105, 110, 111, 119, 121,
  122, 123, 137, 146, 150, 151, 157,
  158, 161, 162, 165, 167, 170, 189,
  191, 195, 207, 209, 210, 211, 214
dressers 84, 97, 98, 99, 100, 215
drink *see* food and drink
durability 62, 160–2

Earsham, Norfolk 105
  see also Norfolk
East Harling, Norfolk 93, 105, 195
  see also Norfolk
economy of makeshifts 5, 6, 64, 200,
  216, 221, 222–3
  begging 72
  black market 166
  borrowing 65, 186, 187, 197
  charity 6, 49, 186, 221
  credit 6, 11, 71, 187, 221
  customary rights 6, 19, 221
  foraging 19, 65, 66, 72, 123, 152,
    154, 171
  friends and kin 6, 65, 66, 67, 69, 85,
    183, 221
  inheritance 221
  making items 64–5, 190
  outdoor relief 6, 11, 49, 64, 65, 66,
    67, 68, 69, 71, 75, 78, 85, 91, 221
  pawning 11, 12, 20, 56, 62, 63, 67,
    68, 69–70, 71, 72–9, 91–3, 99, 112,
    126–7, 163, 168, 186, 187, 190,
    192, 195, 196, 203, 220
  selling of goods 6, 12, 20, 49, 56, 62,
    63, 66, 67, 69–70, 72–9, 91–3, 106,
    168, 192, 195, 196, 220

Index   **249**

theft 6, 71, 221
workhouse 66, 77–9, 85
see also consumption: involuntary
   consumption *and* for
   savings
Eden, Frederic Morton (social
   investigator) 110, 151, 164,
   170, 174
emotions 17, 18, 60, 208, 212
  anxiety 107, 117
  attachments to objects 60, 85, 93,
    95, 97, 102, 106, 112–13, 148,
    184, 190, 193–4, 195, 196, 198,
    211, 217, 222
  happiness 21, 37, 85, 102, 117,
    128–30, 135, 169, 181, 184,
    187–8, 196, 197–8, 222
  meaning of 9–10
  sadness 67–8, 94–5, 132, 135,
    194, 196
emulation 7–9, 144, 168–9, 180,
   206, 209
Essex 1–2, 4, 10, 11, 13–14, 16–17,
   19–20, 21, 32, 33, 38, 57, 59, 61,
   62, 64, 65, 67, 68, 69, 71, 73–4,
   76, 77, 84, 88, 89, 90, 91, 93, 95,
   96, 98, 99, 100, 101, 102, 103,
   105, 111, 118, 119, 121, 122,
   123–4, 126, 132, 137, 145, 146,
   148, 151, 157, 158, 159, 161,
   162, 165, 167, 168, 187, 189, 190,
   191, 192, 194, 195, 207, 209, 210,
   211, 214
  see also home counties
Estabrook, Carl 213

fashion 18, 19, 20, 62, 63–4, 100, 106,
   107, 109, 162–3, 188, 192–3, 206,
   207, 209, 211, 213, 214, 216
Fettes, George (pawnbroker) 99, 112,
   126–7, 163, 168, 186, 187, 190,
   192, 195, 203
fire irons 10, 11, 21, 41, 74, 118,
   120–2, 134–5, 139
  andirons 118, 121
  bellows 74, 118, 134, 135
  fenders 121, 134
  fire pans 118
  fire screens 134–5
  fire shovels 134, 135

grates 118, 120, 121
pokers 121, 134, 140
selling of 76, 77
tongs 74, 118, 134, 135
see also cooking; fuel; hearths
Fogel, Robert 172
food and drink 12, 20, 55, 72, 100, 127,
   153, 166, 181, 192
  alcohol (unspec) 172
  apples 155, 171
  barley 155
  beans 155
  beef 63
  beer 143, 153, 157
  berries 155
  biscuits 154
  bread 21, 56, 63, 65, 66, 68, 69, 70,
    72, 101, 151, 152, 153–4, 159,
    163, 166, 171, 181
  broths 144, 149, 161
  butter 38, 66, 143, 151, 152, 153,
    156, 157
  cakes 154
  cheese 38, 101, 143, 153, 156, 157
  chocolate 144, 172
  cider 157
  coffee 144, 164, 170–2, 178
  currants 153
  dumplings 152
  eggs 150, 172
  fish 152, 157
  flour 65, 69, 77, 170
  fruits 72, 155, 157
  gin 181
  giving of 9
  hay 155
  herbs and spices (unspec) 72, 143,
    152–3, 172
  honey 155
  jam 157
  lack of 6, 13, 17, 20, 56, 62, 63,
    65–6, 67, 68, 69–70, 71, 72, 143,
    151, 170, 171, 195, 197, 209
  literature 6, 13, 55, 143, 172, 207, 220
  meat 66, 143, 144, 149, 150, 151,
    153, 155, 157, 161
  milk 152, 155, 156, 170, 172
  mint 152
  molasses 170
  mustard 153

250 Index

food and drink (*continued*)
  nutmeg 153
  oatcakes 154, 161
  olive oil 152
  pastries 154, 171
  peas 155
  pepper 153
  plums 63
  pork 157
  porridge 144, 149, 153, 161, 172
  potatoes 71, 151, 152, 155, 161, 220
  puddings 63, 149
  rosemary 152
  salt 151, 152–3
  sauces 148, 153
  soups 144, 148, 149, 172
  southernwood 152
  spirits (unspec) 162
  stews 144, 148, 149, 150, 164, 172
  sugar 66, 153, 165, 170, 171, 220
  thyme 152
  treacle 170, 171
  vegetables 144, 155, 157
  vinegar 153
  water 157, 170, 171, 181
  wheat 155, 171
  wine 162
  see also cooking; dining; food
    and drink production; rooms:
    kitchen; tea
food and drink production 101, 120,
    138, 153–8
  baking 38, 40, 119, 143, 153–4,
    157, 158
  brewing 40, 117, 157
  cider making 154, 157
  dairying 38, 154, 156–7, 158, 170
  distillation 154, 157
  farming 34, 37, 38–9, 40, 143, 152,
    153, 154–5, 158
  food preservation 40, 154, 157, 158
  honey 155
  livestock 154, 155, 158
  location of 31, 34–41, 119
Forncett, Norfolk 137
  see also Norfolk
French, Henry 60
fuel 20, 21, 55, 67, 96, 117, 120–4, 182
  coal 21, 65, 77, 117, 120–4, 140

  lack of 20, 56, 65, 66, 72, 95, 132,
    139, 149, 163, 197
  literature 55
  peat 21, 65, 117, 120–4, 155
  wood 21, 84, 117, 120–4, 149, 155

gardens 12, 34, 38–9, 49, 152, 154–5
  see also farming; food and drink
    production
gender 18
  influence on consumption 3, 22, 64,
    206–12
  sources 15, 18
Goffman, Erving 41
gold 194–5, 203, 212
Gray, Robert 11
Griffin, Emma 6, 25, 64, 207

Hanway, Joseph (philanthropist) 210
Hatfield Broad Oak, Essex 80, 93, 101,
    137, 162, 168, 193
  see also Essex
Havering-atte-Bower, Essex 99
  see also Essex
hearths 21, 117–35, 137, 138, 139
  blocked 132–3
  danger 117, 131, 133–5, 139
  location of 34–41, 118–19
  mantelpieces 130–1, 162
  number of 36, 37, 38, 40, 117,
    118–19
  stoves 118
  see also cooking; fire irons; fuel;
    lighting
heating *see* hearths
home counties 3, 19, 21, 57, 86, 100,
    102, 126, 145, 157, 165, 167, 181,
    191, 192, 214, 221
  see also Essex; Kent
Hussey, David 211

identity 4, 9, 10, 18, 22, 26, 51, 97,
    112, 188–9, 190, 192–3, 196,
    199, 222
industrious revolution 7, 26, 143,
    157–8, 191
informal economies *see* economy of
    makeshifts
inheritance 3, 6, 44, 63, 70, 95, 221
inventories, other

results from 32–3, 37, 56, 57,
74, 108–9, 115, 122, 182,
187, 192
as sources 13–15
transcriptions of 76, 77, 78

jewellery 194–5
see also gold; silver

Kenninghall, Norfolk 60, 86
see also Norfolk
Kent 13–14, 16–17, 19–20, 21, 33, 41,
57, 59, 61, 62, 84, 88, 89, 90, 91,
93, 95, 96, 98, 99, 100, 101, 102,
103, 105, 110, 111, 119, 121, 122,
123, 127, 137, 146, 148, 151, 152,
153, 157, 158, 159, 161, 162, 163,
165, 167, 181, 187, 188, 189, 190,
191, 192, 194, 197, 207, 209, 210,
211, 214
see also home counties
King, Gregory (statistician) 213
King, Peter 220
King, Steven 181
Kirkby Lonsdale, Lancashire 64,
66, 151
see also Lancashire
Kwass, Michael 220

Lancashire 13–14, 16, 21, 64, 66,
70, 86, 95, 117, 122, 123, 127,
128, 145, 151, 153, 174,
192, 196
laundry and washing 21, 93, 95, 101,
105, 117, 124–8
basins 125, 126
brushes 127
clothes baskets 125, 126
clothes horses 125, 126
clothes irons 100, 125, 126–7
mops 127
soap 180, 220
tubs 125
see also cleanliness; clothing;
linen
Law, C. M. 213
Leeds, Kent 99
see also Kent
Leicester, Leicestershire 195
see also Leicestershire

Leicestershire 3, 13–14, 16–17, 19–20,
21, 32, 33, 38, 57, 59, 62, 84, 86,
88, 89, 90, 91, 93, 96, 98, 100,
102, 103, 111, 117, 119, 121, 122,
123, 137, 146, 151, 157, 158, 161,
165, 166, 167, 187, 189, 191, 195,
207, 209, 210, 211, 214
Lemire, Beverley 55, 207
Lenham, Kent 194
see also Kent
Levine, David 118
lighting 21, 117, 120, 135–9, 189
candles 6, 135–6, 180, 189, 220
candlesticks 34–6, 77, 136, 137,
138–9
lamps/lanterns 34–6, 136, 137,
138–9, 180
location of 34–41
makeshift holders 136
rushlights 6, 135–6, 189
see also hearths
linen 92, 100, 101
bedding 90–5, 97, 112, 114, 181
handkerchiefs 63, 71
napkins 84, 107, 110–12
selling of 72, 77, 112
storage of 99, 100
tablecloths 22, 84, 107, 110–12
see also clothing; laundry and
washing; textile production
linguistic analysis 20, 34, 60–2, 93,
97, 148
literacy 17, 181–2, 183, 185, 186
Little Wakering, Essex 168
see also Essex
Little Waltham, Essex 76, 190
see also Essex
location
definition of urban and rural 213
influence on consumption 3–4,
19–20, 21, 56–60, 62, 74, 84, 86,
88, 89–90, 91, 93, 95, 96, 98,
100–1, 102, 103, 105, 106, 110,
111, 115, 117, 118, 119, 121,
122–4, 137, 145, 146, 150–1,
157–8, 161, 165, 167, 181, 189,
191–2, 209, 210–11, 214
influence on lexicons 31–2, 144
urban–rural differences 3, 15, 21, 22,
33, 42, 206, 212–16

Index

locks 12, 97, 99, 101
London 3, 11, 19, 20, 21, 63, 100,
    106, 112, 170, 186, 187, 188, 191,
    192, 213
    see also Essex; Kent
Long, Jason 6
looking glasses 21–2, 42, 43, 74, 76,
    110, 138–9, 180, 188–90, 198,
    215, 216, 222
Lower Halstow, Kent 110
    see also Kent
luxury, meaning of 180–1

MacKay, Lynn 11
Maidstone, Kent 41
    see also Kent
Malthus, Thomas Robert
    (demographer) 143
Manchester, Lancashire 67
    see also Lancashire
Mandeville, Bernard (philosopher)
    180, 206
Market Harborough, Leicestershire 187
    see also Leicestershire
Martham, Norfolk 110, 135, 162
    see also Norfolk
McKendrick, Neil 206, 207
medicine 17, 21, 56, 67, 68,
    153, 166
metals
    brass 95, 146
    copper 95, 146, 151, 172
    iron 146
    pewter 168
    tin 146, 168
Middleton, Lancashire 128
    see also Lancashire
Morland, George (painter) 18, 104
Muldrew, Craig 57, 58, 220
Mundon, Essex 71
    see also Essex
musical instruments 196–7
    clarinets 197
    fiddles 129, 196
    flutes 196–7
    organs 197
    pianos 197
    singing 129, 196
    violins 196–7

Norfolk 4, 12, 13–14, 16–17, 19–20,
    33, 39, 56, 57, 59, 60, 62, 75–6,
    86, 88, 89, 90, 91, 93, 96, 98, 100,
    103, 105, 109, 110, 111, 115, 119,
    121, 122, 123–4, 135, 137, 146,
    151, 158, 161, 162, 165, 167, 168,
    173, 183, 189, 191, 195, 207, 209,
    210, 211, 214
Northamptonshire 47, 155
Norwich, Norfolk 12, 33, 100
    see also Norfolk
Nottinghamshire 63, 192
number of pauper goods 55, 188,
    189–90, 208–9, 213–14

objects, as sources 18, 144
occupations and status
    apprentice 64, 106, 129, 163,
        186, 190
    artisan 5
    beggar 4, 95
    bellhanger 68
    bird scarer 132
    blacksmith 5
    bricklayer 44, 45, 171
    builder 5
    cabinet maker 89
    cook 129
    dairymaid 65
    dockyard worker 64
    elite 2, 3, 7–9, 10, 18, 19, 31, 37, 84,
        101–2, 106, 112, 118, 124, 157,
        158, 162, 164, 165, 166, 169, 172,
        180, 194, 206, 209
    fellmonger 67
    housemaid 129
    industrial worker 5
    knitter 63
    labourer 2, 3–4, 5, 16, 19, 25, 43,
        45, 46, 49, 56–7, 68, 69, 85,
        101, 136, 155, 163, 172, 193,
        196, 206
    labouring sort 2, 5, 6, 7, 16, 17, 19,
        21, 43–50, 69, 72, 110, 118, 125,
        127, 137, 144, 151, 154, 163,
        170, 180, 181, 184, 188, 194, 197,
        198, 218
    mantua maker 78
    mechanic 64, 163

middling sort 2, 3, 5, 9, 10, 11, 16, 18, 20, 31, 33, 36, 39, 56, 60, 84, 85, 89, 95, 106, 107, 110, 112, 124, 144, 151–2, 155, 157, 158, 162, 164, 165, 166, 167, 169, 191, 194, 206, 209, 211, 221
miner 5, 125, 171
navvy 67
nurse 49
porter 5
sailor 207
servant 5, 45, 183
shoemaker 63, 65, 125, 152, 166, 185, 188
soldier 5, 131, 152, 163, 171, 183, 194, 195, 196, 198
tailoress 46
thatcher 155
turner 64, 163
vagrant 4, 95
weaver 5, 16, 70, 73, 77, 129, 186, 196
wheelwright 5
Oldham, Lancashire 86
    see also Lancashire
Osgathorpe, Leicestershire 157
    see also Leicestershire
Otford, Kent 194
    see also Kent
Overton, Mark 213, 219

pails 102
pauper inventories
    as sources 10, 13–14, 15–17, 31–2, 56, 59, 60, 74, 91, 95, 120–2, 153, 159, 195, 196, 207–8, 217, 222
    transcriptions of 75, 76, 77
pauper letters, as sources 17–18
Peak District 43
Penshurst, Kent 99
    see also Kent
pictures 21, 42, 130, 181, 187–8, 212, 215, 216, 222
pillows 90–5, 106, 114
    see also bolsters
Pluckley, Kent 101, 187
    see also Kent

Ponsonby, Margaret 211
poorhouse *see* workhouse
poor rates 67
poverty life-cycle *see* poverty, reasons for: life-cycle of poverty
poverty, meaning of 2–3, 4–6, 11, 14, 22, 68, 220–1
poverty, reasons for
    alcohol 5, 12, 63, 68, 70, 171, 195
    burglary 21, 56, 70
    character 5, 71, 77–9
    children 63, 64–6, 67, 75, 79
    customary rights 123
    death 1, 15, 65, 67–8, 75
    desertion 14, 21, 56, 71–2, 79, 170
    disability 45, 66, 73
    economic problems 12, 19, 63, 66, 69–70
    financial mismanagement 12, 21, 56, 63, 71, 79
    fire 21, 56, 63, 70, 93
    flood 21, 56, 70
    gambling 70
    harvest failure 69
    imprisonment 21, *56*, 70, 71, 78, 79, 195
    inheritance 70
    lack of friends and family 73
    life-cycle of poverty 4, 5, 6, 7, 8, 12, 15, 17, 20–1, 44, 55–79, 180, 220–1, 222–3
    marriage 64–5
    old age 7, 15, 20, 56, 63, 68–9, 73, 79
    sickness 7, 12, 15, 20, 46, 56, 63, 66–7, 68–9, 71, 75, 78
    single parent 4, 14, 71
    under-employment 19, 66, 69, 78
    unemployment 17, 19, 21, 56, 64, 65, 69
    see also economy of makeshifts; wages
print 17, 129, 138, 181–7, 198, 212, 216
    bibles 12, 182, 183–4, 186
    books 9, 17, 21, 74, 100, 130, 181–7, 198, 212, 216
    ephemeral 4, 22, 129, 182, 183, 196

Index

print (*continued*)
 novels 184–5, 186
 prayer books 12, 183, 186
 second-hand 73, 185–6
 see also literacy; pictures
privacy 2, 3, 9, 11–12, 21, 46, 85, 89,
  90, 97, 99
probate inventories 3–4, 16, 33, 52,
  56–7, 58, 110, 112, 194, 208, 210,
  211, 221, 222
 as sources 31, 56, 182

quantities of pauper goods 16, 20,
  59–60, 61, 62, 87, 90, 91, 97,
  98, 102, 103, 104–5, 108, 111,
  118, 137, 145, 150, 155, 159,
  160, 161

Rainham, Essex 68
 see also Essex
Randles, Sarah 60
Rawtenstall, Lancashire 196
 see also Lancashire
Rayleigh, Essex 11, 132
 see also Essex
recycling 166, 182, 197, 222
Redenhall with Harleston and
  Wortwell, Norfolk 75–6, 162, 173
 see also Norfolk
rent 10, 15, 17, 48, 49, 65, 67, 77, 155
repair 84, 148, 173
respectability 2, 3, 9, 41, 42, 89, 101,
  107, 124, 127–8, 135, 161, 162,
  166–7, 168, 192–3, 209, 222
 meaning of 11
Ribchester, Lancashire 70
 see also Lancashire
Romford, Essex 71
 see also Essex
rooms
 brewhouse 34, 35
 buttery 34, 35, 38, 40–1
 chamber 20, 34, 35, 36–7, 42, 43,
  51, 119
 dwelling room/house 34, 35, 38,
  52, 119
 hall 20, 34, 35, 37–8, 44, 51, 119
 kitchen 20, 34, 35, 38–9, 42, 43, 44,
  51, 52, 53, 100, 119

 number of 32–3, 35
 pantry 34, 35, 38, 40–1, 45, 51
 parlour 34, 35, 39, 40, 42, 51, 119
 upstairs 34, 36, 45
 washhouse 34, 35
 see also room use
room use 12, 20, 31, 34–41, 42, 44–50,
  51, 89
 frontstage and backstage 20,
  41–3, 51
 see also rooms
Rowntree, B. Seebohm (social
  investigator) 7, 8
 see also poverty, reasons for:
  life-cycle of poverty
Rule, John 165
Rutland 3, 13–14, 16–17, 19–20, 21,
  32, 33, 38, 57, 59, 62, 84, 86, 88,
  89, 90, 91, 93, 96, 98, 100, 102,
  103, 111, 117, 119, 121, 122,
  123, 137, 146, 151, 158, 161, 165,
  166, 167, 189, 191, 207, 209, 210,
  211, 214

Sandhurst, Kent 153
 see also Kent
Sear, Joanne 58
seating 11, 101–6, 120, 128–9, 138
 alternatives to 102
 benches/forms 84, 102, 103, 105,
  106, 107, 109
 chairs 74, 84, 103, 104–5, 106, 107,
  214, 215
 location of 34–41, 42, 119
 selling of 77
 settles 103, 105, 107, 109
 stools 84, 102, 103, 104, 105, 106
 upholstered 84, 103, 106
second-hand goods 6, 9, 12, 73, 85,
  86, 95, 163, 185–6, 187, 190, 194,
  200, 216, 221
senses
 meaning of 9–10
Shammas, Carole 172
Shelton, Norfolk 183
 see also Norfolk
Shepard, Alexandra 55
Sherborne, Dorset 91
 see also Dorset

Index

shopping 19, 112, 157, 185, 186, 206, 212–13, 216, 221–2, 223
  fairs 73, 185, 186
  markets 20, 152
  street sellers 185, 186, 216
silver 12, 167, 194–5, 203, 212
  selling of 167, 195, 203
sleep 10, 12, 85, 89, 95, 106, 120, 137–8
  location of 20, 31, 36, 37, 38, 40, 41, 42, 51, 53
  see also beds
Smarden, Kent 190
  see also Kent
Smith, Adam (economist) 63, 180
Smith, Woodruff 11, 165
Sneath, Ken 57, 58, 213
Somerset 12
Speldhurst, Kent 146
  see also Kent
Springfield, Essex 65
  see also Essex
Staffordshire 93, 151, 158
standard of living debate 6, 143, 221
Staplehurst, Kent 153, 162, 197
  see also Kent
Styles, John 220
Suffolk 19, 29, 44–6, 49–51, 86, 94, 130, 155, 187

tables 74, 102, 106–12, 167, 168, 209, 214, 215
  alternatives to 108, 112
  boards/trestles 108, 110, 111
  long 106, 107, 108, 109
  round/oval 107, 108–10, 111
  selling of 77
  square 107, 108–10, 111
  see also linen
tea 21, 74, 144, 164–70, 171, 172, 180, 181, 210, 214, 215, 218, 220
  comfort 166
  cost 165–6, 171, 180
  drinking rituals 41, 110, 166–9, 171–2
  gendered differences 166, 209–11
  leaves 169–70
  location of 42, 43
  milk 170

paraphernalia 12, 41, 107, 109, 144, 162, 166–9, 178, 210–11
  selling of 72, 79
  sugar 165, 170, 220
  see also food and drink: chocolate *and* coffee
textile production 101, 120, 138
  location of 31, 34–41, 119
  sewing 167
  spinning wheels 37, 38, 105
Thompson, E. P. 191, 192, 220
Thompson, F. M. L. 11
Thundersley, Essex 101, 194
  see also Essex
timepieces 21, 74, 180, 191–4, 198, 212, 215–16
  clocks 12, 42, 43, 212, 215–16, 222
  desire to own 22, 63, 192–3
  hourglasses 192
  selling of 71, 72, 192
  sundials 192
  watches 12, 191–4, 212, 215–16
tobacco 129–30, 131
Tolleshunt D'Arcy, Essex 1–2, 77
  see also Essex
toys and games 110, 138, 155, 183, 197–8

Upminster, Essex 10, 67, 69
  see also Essex

valuations of pauper goods 16, 20, 56–9, 79, 86, 95, 99, 148, 163, 187, 190, 193, 198
Vickery, Amanda 12
visual sources 10, 18–19, 44, 102, 108, 128, 182–3, 197
Voth, Hans-Joachim 191

wages 6, 7, 19, 25, 63–4, 65, 66, 67, 68, 72, 78, 221
  see also economy of makeshifts
Wahrman, Dror 9
Walker, George (illustrator) 108, 109
warming pans 74, 95–7
  see also bedwarmers
watches *see* timepieces
Weatherill, Lorna 52, 56, 58, 112, 208, 210, 213

Index

West Harling, Norfolk 60
   see also Norfolk
Wethersfield, Essex 146, 187
   see also Essex
window curtains 11, 12, 42, 43, 90,
   91, 216
window shutters 90
woods
   ash 99, 101, 105, 109
   deal 99, 100, 110, 193
   elm 99, 101, 105
   mahogany 84, 99, 105, 212, 215, 216
   oak 88, 105, 106, 110
   rush 105
   wainscot 109, 193
   walnut 84, 99, 105, 109

workhouse 13, 14, 15, 56, 63,
   66, 73–5, 76, 77–9, 80, 85,
   88, 106, 146, 152, 155, 166,
   170, 171, 187, 190, 192, 195,
   197, 220
Wortham, Suffolk 19, 29, 44–6, 49–51,
   86, 93, 130, 155, 187
   see also Suffolk
Wrightston, Keith 118
Wrigley, E. A. 213
Wrotham, Kent 194
   see also Kent

Yorkshire 43, 72, 92, 112, 126,
   158, 163, 168, 186, 187, 190,
   192, 195

www.ingramcontent.com/pod-product-compliance
Ingram Content Group UK Ltd.
Pitfield, Milton Keynes, MK11 3LW, UK
UKHW052142050225
454721UK00009B/74